Hands-On Machine Learning with C++

Build, train, and deploy end-to-end machine learning and deep learning pipelines

Kirill Kolodiazhnyi

BIRMINGHAM - MUMBAI

Hands-On Machine Learning with C++

Commissioning Editor: Sunith Shetty
Acquisition Editor: Yogesh Deokar
Content Development Editor: Sean Lobo
Senior Editor: Roshan Kumar
Technical Editor: Manikandan Kurup
Copy Editor: Safis Editing
Language Support Editors: Jack Cummings and Martin Whittemore
Project Coordinator: Aishwarya Mohan
Proofreader: Safis Editing
Indexer: Priyanka Dhadke
Production Designer: Aparna Bhagat

First published: May 2020

Production reference: 1140520

Published by Packt Publishing Ltd.
Livery Place
35 Livery Street
Birmingham
B3 2PB, UK.

ISBN 978-1-78995-533-0

www.packt.com

Subscribe to our online digital library for full access to over 7,000 books and videos, as well as industry leading tools to help you plan your personal development and advance your career. For more information, please visit our website.

Why subscribe?

- Spend less time learning and more time coding with practical eBooks and Videos from over 4,000 industry professionals

- Improve your learning with Skill Plans built especially for you

- Get a free eBook or video every month

- Fully searchable for easy access to vital information

- Copy and paste, print, and bookmark content

Did you know that Packt offers eBook versions of every book published, with PDF and ePub files available? You can upgrade to the eBook version at www.packt.com and as a print book customer, you are entitled to a discount on the eBook copy. Get in touch with us at customercare@packtpub.com for more details.

At www.packt.com, you can also read a collection of free technical articles, sign up for a range of free newsletters, and receive exclusive discounts and offers on Packt books and eBooks.

Contributors

About the author

Kirill Kolodiazhnyi is a seasoned software engineer with expertise in custom software development. He has several years of experience in building machine learning models and data products using C++. He holds a bachelor's degree in computer science from Kharkiv National University of Radio Electronics. He currently works in Kharkiv, Ukraine, where he lives with his wife and daughter.

About the reviewers

Davor Lozić is a university lecturer living in Croatia. He likes working on algorithmic/mathematical problems, and reviewing books for Packt makes him read new IT books. He has also worked on *Data Analysis with R – Second Edition*; *Mastering Predictive Analytics with R, Second Edition*; *R Data Analysis Cookbook, Second Edition*; *R Deep Learning Projects*; *Mastering Linux Network Administration*; *R Machine Learning Projects*; *Learning Ext JS, Fourth Edition*; and *R Statistics Cookbook*. Davor is a meme master and an Uno master, and he likes cats.

Dr. Ashwin Nanjappa works at NVIDIA on deep learning inference acceleration on GPUs. He has a Ph.D. from the National University of Singapore, where he invented the fastest 3D Delaunay computational geometry algorithms for GPUs. He was a postdoctoral research fellow at the BioInformatics Institute (Singapore), inventing machine learning algorithms for hand and rodent pose estimation using depth cameras. He also worked at Visenze (Singapore) developing computer vision deep learning models for the largest e-commerce portals in the world. He is a published author of two books: *Caffe2 Quick Start Guide* and *Instant GLEW*.

Ryan Riley has been involved in the futures and derivatives industry for almost 20 years. He received a bachelor's degree and a master's degree from DePaul University in applied statistics. Doing his coursework in math meant that he had to teach himself how to program, forcing him to read more technical books on programming than he would otherwise have done. Ryan has worked with numerous AI libraries in various languages and is currently using the Caffe2 C++ library to develop and implement futures and derivatives trading strategies at PNT Financial.

Packt is searching for authors like you

If you're interested in becoming an author for Packt, please visit authors.packtpub.com and apply today. We have worked with thousands of developers and tech professionals, just like you, to help them share their insight with the global tech community. You can make a general application, apply for a specific hot topic that we are recruiting an author for, or submit your own idea.

Table of Contents

Preface

Machine learning (**ML**) is a popular approach to solve different kinds of problems. ML allows you to deal with various tasks without knowing a direct algorithm to solve them. The key feature of ML algorithms is their ability to learn solutions by using a set of training samples, or even without them. Nowadays, ML is a widespread approach used in various areas of industry. Examples of areas where ML outperforms classical direct algorithms include computer vision, natural language processing, and recommender systems.

This book is a handy guide to help you learn the fundamentals of ML, showing you how to use C++ libraries to get the most out of data. C++ can make your ML models run faster and more efficiently compared to other approaches that use interpreted languages, such as Python. Also, C++ allows you to significantly reduce the negative performance impact of data conversion between different languages used in the ML model because you have direct access to core algorithms and raw data.

Who this book is for

You will find this book useful if you want to get started with ML algorithms and techniques using the widespread C++ language. This book also appeals to data analysts, data scientists, and ML developers who are looking to implement different ML models in production using native development toolsets such as the GCC or Clang ecosystems. Working knowledge of the C++ programming language is mandatory to get started with this book.

What this book covers

Hands-On Machine Learning with C++'s example-based approach will show you how to implement supervised and unsupervised ML algorithms with the help of real-world examples. The book also gives you hands-on experience of tuning and optimizing a model for different use cases, helping you to measure performance and model selection. You'll then cover techniques such as object classification and clusterization, product recommendations, ensemble learning, and anomaly detection using modern C++ libraries such as the PyTorch C++ API, Caffe2, Shogun, Shark-ML, mlpack, and dlib. Moving ahead, the chapters will take you through neural networks and deep learning using examples such as image classification and sentiment analysis, which will help you solve a wide range of problems.

Later, you'll learn how to handle production and deployment challenges on mobile and cloud platforms, before discovering how to export and import models using the ONNX format. By the end of this book, you'll have learned how to leverage C++ to build powerful ML systems.

Chapter 1, *Introduction to Machine Learning with C++*, will guide you through the necessary fundamentals of ML, including linear algebra concepts, ML algorithm types, and their building blocks.

Chapter 2, *Data Processing*, will show you how to load data from different file formats for ML model training and how to initialize dataset objects in various C++ libraries.

Chapter 3, *Measuring Performance and Selecting Models*, will show you how to measure the performance of various types of ML models, how to select the best set of hyperparameters to achieve better model performance, and how to use the grid search method in various C++ libraries for model selection.

Chapter 4, *Clustering*, will discuss algorithms for grouping objects by their essential characteristics, show why we usually use unsupervised algorithms for solving such types of tasks, and lastly, will outline the various types of clustering algorithms, along with their implementations and usage in different C++ libraries.

Chapter 5, *Anomaly Detection*, will discuss the basics of anomaly and novelty detection tasks and guide you through the different types of anomaly detection algorithms, their implementation, and their usage in various C++ libraries.

Chapter 6, *Dimensionality Reduction*, will discuss various algorithms for dimensionality reduction that preserve the essential characteristics of data, along with their implementation and usage in various C++ libraries.

Chapter 7, *Classification*, will show you what a classification task is and how it differs from a clustering task. You will be guided through various classification algorithms, their implementation, and their usage in various C++ libraries.

Chapter 8, *Recommender Systems*, will give you familiarity with recommender system concepts. You will be shown the different approaches to deal with recommendation tasks, and you will see how to solve such types of tasks using the C++ language.

Chapter 9, *Ensemble Learning*, will discuss various methods of combining several ML models to get better accuracy and to deal with learning problems. You will encounter ensemble implementations with the usage of different C++ libraries.

Chapter 10, *Neural Networks for Image Classification*, will give you familiarity with the fundamentals of artificial neural networks. You will encounter the essential building blocks, the required math concepts, and learning algorithms. You will be guided through different C++ libraries that provide functionality for neural network implementations. Also, this chapter will show you the implementation of a deep convolutional network for image classification with the PyTorch library.

Chapter 11, *Sentiment Analysis with Recurrent Neural Networks*, will guide you through the fundamentals of recurrent neural networks. You will learn about the different types of network cells, the required math concepts, and the differences of this learning algorithm compared to feedforward networks. Also, in this chapter, we will develop a recurrent neural network for sentiment analysis with the PyTorch library.

Chapter 12, *Exporting and Importing Models*, will show you how to save and load model parameters and architectures using various C++ libraries. Also, you will see how to use the ONNX format to load and use a pre-trained model with the C++ API of the Caffe2 library.

Chapter 13, *Deploying Models on Mobile and Cloud Platforms*, will guide you through the development of applications for image classification using neural networks for the Android and Google Compute Engine platforms.

To get the most out of this book

To be able to compile and run the examples included in this book, you will need to configure a particular development environment. All code examples have been tested with the Arch and Ubuntu 18.04 Linux distributions. The following list outlines the packages you'll need to install on the Ubuntu platform:

- build-essential
- unzip
- git
- cmake
- cmake-curses-gui
- python
- python-pip
- libblas-dev
- libopenblas-dev
- libatlas-base-dev
- liblapack-dev

- `libboost-all-dev`
- `libopencv-core3.2`
- `libopencv-imgproc3.2`
- `libopencv-dev`
- `libopencv-highgui3.2`
- `libopencv-highgui-dev`
- `protobuf-compiler`
- `libprotobuf-dev`
- `libhdf5-dev`
- `libjson-c-dev`
- `libx11-dev`
- `openjdk-8-jdk`
- `wget`
- `ninja-build`

Also, you need to install the following additional packages for Python:

- `pyyaml`
- `typing`

Besides the development environment, you'll have to check out requisite third-party libraries' source code samples and build them. Most of these libraries are actively developed and don't have strict releases, so it's easier to check out a particular commit from the development tree and build it than downloading the latest official release. The following table shows you the libraries you have to check out, their repository URLs, and the hash number of the commit to check out:

Library repository	Branch name	Commit
`https://github.com/ shogun-toolbox/shogun`	`master`	`f7255cf2cc6b5116e50840816d70d21e7cc039bb`
`https://github.com/ Shark-ML/Shark`	`master`	`221c1f2e8abfffadbf3c5ef7cf324bc6dc9b4315`
`https://gitlab.com/ conradsnicta/armadillo-code`	`9.500.x`	`442d52ba052115b32035a6e7dc6587bb6a462dec`
`https://github.com/ davisking/dlib`	`v19.15`	`929c630b381d444bbf5d7aa622e3decc7785ddb2`

https://github.com/eigenteam/eigen-git-mirror	3.3.7	cf794d3b741a6278df169e58461f8529f43bce5d
https://github.com/mlpack/mlpack	master	e2f696cfd5b7ccda2d3af1c7c728483ea6591718
https://github.com/Kolkir/plotcpp	master	c86bd4f5d9029986f0d5f368450d79f0dd32c7e4
https://github.com/pytorch/pytorch	v1.2.0	8554416a199c4cec01c60c7015d8301d2bb39b64
https://github.com/xtensor-stack/xtensor	master	02d8039a58828db1ffdd2c60fb9b378131c295a2
https://github.com/xtensor-stack/xtensor-blas	master	89d9df93ff7306c32997e8bb8b1ff02534d7df2e
https://github.com/xtensor-stack/xtl	master	03a6827c9e402736506f3ded754e890b3ea28a98
https://github.com/opencv/opencv_contrib/releases/tag/3.3.0	3.3.0	
https://github.com/ben-strasser/fast-cpp-csv-parser	master	3b439a664090681931c6ace78dcedac6d3a3907e
https://github.com/Tencent/rapidjson	master	73063f5002612c6bf64fe24f851cd5cc0d83eef9

Also, for the last chapter, you'll have to install the Android Studio IDE. You can download it from the official site at `https://developer.android.com/studio`. Besides the IDE, you'll also need to install and configure the Android SDK. The respective example in this book was developed and tested with this SDK, which can be downloaded from `https://dl.google.com/android/repository/sdk-tools-linux-4333796.zip`. To configure this SDK, you have to unzip it and install particular packages. The following script shows how to do it:

```
mkdir /android
cd /android

wget https://dl.google.com/android/repository/sdk-tools-linux-4333796.zip
unzip sdk-tools-linux-4333796.zip

yes | ./tools/bin/sdkmanager --licenses
yes | ./tools/bin/sdkmanager "platform-tools"
yes | ./tools/bin/sdkmanager "platforms;android-25"
yes | ./tools/bin/sdkmanager "build-tools;25.0.2"
yes | ./tools/bin/sdkmanager "system-images;android-25;google_apis;armeabi-
```

```
v7a"
yes | ./tools/bin/sdkmanager --install "ndk;20.0.5594570"

export ANDROID_NDK=/android/ndk/20.0.5594570
export ANDROID_ABI='armeabi-v7a'
```

Another way to configure the development environment is through the use of Docker. Docker allows you to configure a lightweight virtual machine with particular components. You can install Docker from the official Ubuntu package repository. Then, use the scripts provided with this book to automatically configure the environment. You will find the docker folder in the examples package. The following steps show how to use Docker configuration scripts:

1. Run the following commands to create the image, run it, and configure the environment:

```
cd docker
docker build -t buildenv:1.0 .
docker run -it buildenv:1.0 bash
cd /development
./install_env.sh
./install_android.sh
exit
```

2. Use the following command to save our Docker container with the configured libraries and packages into a new Docker image:

```
docker commit [container id]
```

3. Use the following command to rename the updated Docker image:

```
docker tag [image id] [new name]
```

4. Use the following command to start a new Docker container and share the book examples sources to it:

```
docker run -it -v [host_examples_path]:[container_examples_path]
[tag name] bash
```

After running the preceding command, you will be in the command-line environment with the necessary configured packages, compiled third-party libraries, and with access to the programming examples package. You can use this environment to compile and run the code examples in this book. Each programming example is configured to use the CMake build system so you will be able to build them all in the same way. The following script shows a possible scenario of building a code example:

```
cd [example folder name]
mkdir build
cd build
cmake ..
cmake --build . --target all
```

Also, you can configure your local machine environment to share X Server with a Docker container to be able to run graphical UI applications from this container. It will allow you to use, for example, the Android Studio IDE or a C++ IDE (such as Qt Creator) from the Docker container, without local installation. The following script shows how to do this:

```
xhost +local:root
docker run --net=host -e DISPLAY=$DISPLAY -v /tmp/.X11-unix:/tmp/.X11-unix
-it -v [host_examples_path]:[container_examples_path] [tag name] bash
```

If you are using the digital version of this book, we advise you to type the code yourself or access the code via the GitHub repository (link available in the following section). Doing so will help you avoid any potential errors related to the copying and pasting of code.

To be more comfortable with understanding and building the code examples, we recommend you carefully read the documentation for each third-party library, and take some time to learn the basics of the Docker system and of development for the Android platform. Also, we assume that you have sufficient working knowledge of the C++ language and compilers, and that you are familiar with the CMake build system.

Download the example code files

You can download the example code files for this book from your account at www.packt.com. If you purchased this book elsewhere, you can visit www.packtpub.com/support and register to have the files emailed directly to you.

You can download the code files by following these steps:

1. Log in or register at `www.packt.com`.
2. Select the **Support** tab.
3. Click on **Code Downloads**.
4. Enter the name of the book in the **Search** box and follow the onscreen instructions.

Once the file is downloaded, please make sure that you unzip or extract the folder using the latest version of:

- WinRAR/7-Zip for Windows
- Zipeg/iZip/UnRarX for Mac
- 7-Zip/PeaZip for Linux

The code bundle for the book is also hosted on GitHub at `https://github.com/PacktPublishing/Hands-On-Machine-Learning-with-CPP`. In case there's an update to the code, it will be updated on the existing GitHub repository.

We also have other code bundles from our rich catalog of books and videos available at `https://github.com/PacktPublishing/`. Check them out!

Download the color images

We also provide a PDF file that has color images of the screenshots/diagrams used in this book. You can download it here: `http://www.packtpub.com/sites/default/files/downloads/9781789955330_ColorImages.pdf`.

Conventions used

There are a number of text conventions used throughout this book.

`CodeInText`: Indicates code words in text, database table names, folder names, filenames, file extensions, pathnames, dummy URLs, user input, and Twitter handles. Here is an example: "We downloaded a pre-trained model with the `torch.hub.load()` function."

A block of code is set as follows:

```
class Network {
    public:
        Network(const std::string& snapshot_path,
                const std::string& synset_path,
                torch::DeviceType device_type);
        std::string Classify(const at::Tensor& image);
    private:
        torch::DeviceType device_type_;
        Classes classes_;
        torch::jit::script::Module model_;
};
```

Any command-line input or output is written as follows:

```
cd ~/[DEST_PATH]/server
mkdir build
cd build
cmake .. -DCMAKE_PREFIX_PATH=~/dev/server/third-party/libtorch
cmake --build . --target all
```

Bold: Indicates a new term, an important word, or words that you see onscreen. For example, words in menus or dialog boxes appear in the text like this. Here is an example: " Start it by clicking the **Start** button at the top of the page. "

Warnings or important notes appear like this.

Tips and tricks appear like this.

Get in touch

Feedback from our readers is always welcome.

General feedback: If you have questions about any aspect of this book, mention the book title in the subject of your message and email us at customercare@packtpub.com.

Errata: Although we have taken every care to ensure the accuracy of our content, mistakes do happen. If you have found a mistake in this book, we would be grateful if you would report this to us. Please visit www.packtpub.com/support/errata, selecting your book, clicking on the Errata Submission Form link, and entering the details.

Piracy: If you come across any illegal copies of our works in any form on the Internet, we would be grateful if you would provide us with the location address or website name. Please contact us at copyright@packt.com with a link to the material.

If you are interested in becoming an author: If there is a topic that you have expertise in and you are interested in either writing or contributing to a book, please visit authors.packtpub.com.

Reviews

Please leave a review. Once you have read and used this book, why not leave a review on the site that you purchased it from? Potential readers can then see and use your unbiased opinion to make purchase decisions, we at Packt can understand what you think about our products, and our authors can see your feedback on their book. Thank you!

For more information about Packt, please visit packt.com.

Section 1: Overview of Machine Learning

In this section, we will delve into the basics of machine learning with the help of examples in C++ and various machine learning frameworks. We'll demonstrate how to load data from various file formats and describe model performance measuring techniques and the best model selection approaches.

This section comprises the following chapters:

- Chapter 1, *Introduction to Machine Learning with C++*
- Chapter 2, *Data Processing*
- Chapter 3, *Measuring Performance and Selecting Models*

1
Introduction to Machine Learning with C++

There are different approaches to make computers solve tasks. One of them is to define an explicit algorithm, and another one is to use implicit strategies based on mathematical and statistical methods. **Machine Learning (ML)** is one of the implicit methods that uses mathematical and statistical approaches to solve tasks. It is an actively growing discipline, and a lot of scientists and researchers find it to be one of the best ways to move forward toward systems acting as human-level **artificial intelligence (AI)**.

In general, ML approaches have the idea of searching patterns in a given dataset as their basis. Consider a recommendation system for a news feed, which provides the user with a personalized feed based on their previous activity or preferences. The software gathers information about the type of news article the user reads and calculates some statistics. For example, it could be the frequency of some topics appearing in a set of news articles. Then, it performs some predictive analytics, identifies general patterns, and uses them to populate the user's news feed. Such systems periodically track a user's activity, and update the dataset and calculate new trends for recommendations.

There are many areas where ML has started to play an important role. It is used for solving enterprise business tasks as well as for scientific researches. In **customer relationship management (CRM)** systems, ML models are used to analyze sales team activity, to help them to process the most important requests first. ML models are used in **business intelligence (BI)** and analytics to find essential data points. **Human resource (HR)** departments use ML models to analyze their employees' characteristics in order to identify the most effective ones and use this information when searching applicants for open positions.

A fast-growing direction of research is self-driving cars, and deep learning neural networks are used extensively in this area. They are used in computer vision systems for object identification as well as for navigation and steering systems, which are necessary for car driving.

Another popular use of ML systems is electronic personal assistants, such as Siri from Apple or Alexa from Amazon. Such products also use deep learning models to analyze natural speech or written text to process users' requests and make a natural response in a relevant context. Such requests can activate music players with preferred songs, as well as update a user's personal schedule or book flight tickets.

This chapter describes what ML is and which tasks can be solved with ML, and discusses different approaches used in ML. It aims to show the minimally required math to start implementing ML algorithms. It also covers how to perform basic linear algebra operations in libraries such as `Eigen`, `xtensor`, `Shark-ML`, `Shogun`, and `Dlib`, and also explains the linear regression task as an example.

The following topics will be covered in this chapter:

- Understanding the fundamentals of ML
- An overview of linear algebra
- An overview of a linear regression example

Understanding the fundamentals of ML

There are different approaches to create and train ML models. In this section, we show what these approaches are and how they differ. Apart from the approach we use to create a ML model, there are also parameters that manage how this model behaves in the training and evaluation processes. Model parameters can be divided into two distinct groups, which should be configured in different ways. The last crucial part of the ML process is a technique that we use to train a model. Usually, the training technique uses some numerical optimization algorithm that finds the minimal value of a target function. In ML, the target function is usually called a loss function and is used for penalizing the training algorithm when it makes errors. We discuss these concepts more precisely in the following sections.

Venturing into the techniques of ML

We can divide ML approaches into two techniques, as follows:

- Supervised learning is an approach based on the use of labeled data. Labeled data is a set of known data samples with corresponding known target outputs. Such a kind of data is used to build a model that can predict future outputs.
- Unsupervised learning is an approach that does not require labeled data and can search hidden patterns and structures in an arbitrary kind of data.

Let's have a look at each of the techniques in detail.

Supervised learning

Supervised ML algorithms usually take a limited set of labeled data and build models that can make reasonable predictions for new data. We can split supervised learning algorithms into two main parts, classification and regression techniques, described as follows:

- Classification models predict some finite and distinct types of categories—this could be a label that identifies if an email is spam or not, or whether an image contains a human face or not. Classification models are applied in speech and text recognition, object identification on images, credit scoring, and others. Typical algorithms for creating classification models are **Support Vector Machine (SVM)**, decision tree approaches, **k-nearest neighbors (KNN)**, logistic regression, Naive Bayes, and neural networks. The following chapters describe the details of some of these algorithms.
- Regression models predict continuous responses such as changes in temperature or values of currency exchange rates. Regression models are applied in algorithmic trading, forecasting of electricity load, revenue prediction, and others. Creating a regression model usually makes sense if the output of the given labeled data is real numbers. Typical algorithms for creating regression models are linear and multivariate regressions, polynomial regression models, and stepwise regressions. We can use decision tree techniques and neural networks to create regression models too. The following chapters describe the details of some of these algorithms.

Unsupervised learning

Unsupervised learning algorithms do not use labeled datasets. They create models that use intrinsic relations in data to find hidden patterns that they can use for making predictions. The most well-known unsupervised learning technique is **clustering**. Clustering involves dividing a given set of data in a limited number of groups according to some intrinsic properties of data items. Clustering is applied in market researches, different types of exploratory analysis, **deoxyribonucleic acid** (**DNA**) analysis, image segmentation, and object detection. Typical algorithms for creating models for performing clustering are k-means, k-medoids, Gaussian mixture models, hierarchical clustering, and hidden Markov models. Some of these algorithms are explained in the following chapters of this book.

Dealing with ML models

We can interpret ML models as functions that take different types of parameters. Such functions provide outputs for given inputs based on the values of these parameters. Developers can configure the behavior of ML models for solving problems by adjusting model parameters. Training a ML model can usually be treated as a process of searching the best combination of its parameters. We can split the ML model's parameters into two types. The first type consists of parameters internal to the model, and we can estimate their values from the training (input) data. The second type consists of parameters external to the model, and we cannot estimate their values from training data. Parameters that are external to the model are usually called **hyperparameters**.

Internal parameters have the following characteristics:

- They are necessary for making predictions.
- They define the quality of the model on the given problem.
- We can learn them from training data.
- Usually, they are a part of the model.

If the model contains a fixed number of internal parameters, it is called **parametric**. Otherwise, we can classify it as **non-parametric**.

Examples of internal parameters are as follows:

- Weights of **artificial neural networks** (**ANNs**)
- Support vector values for SVM models
- Polynomial coefficients for linear regression or logistic regression

On the other hand, hyperparameters have the following characteristics:

- They are used to configure algorithms that estimate model parameters.
- The practitioner usually specifies them.
- Their estimation is often based on using heuristics.
- They are specific to a concrete modeling problem.

It is hard to know the best values for a model's hyperparameters for a specific problem. Also, practitioners usually need to perform additional research on how to tune required hyperparameters so that a model or a training algorithm behaves in the best way. Practitioners use rules of thumb, copying values from similar projects, as well as special techniques such as grid search for hyperparameter estimation.

Examples of hyperparameters are as follows:

- C and sigma parameters used in the SVM algorithm for a classification quality configuration
- The learning rate parameter that is used in the neural network training process to configure algorithm convergence
- The k value that is used in the KNN algorithm to configure the number of neighbors

Model parameter estimation

Model parameter estimation usually uses some optimization algorithm. The speed and quality of the resulting model can significantly depend on the optimization algorithm chosen. Research on optimization algorithms is a popular topic in industry, as well as in academia. ML often uses optimization techniques and algorithms based on the optimization of a loss function. A function that evaluates how well a model predicts on the data is called a **loss function**. If predictions are very different from the target outputs, the loss function will return a value that can be interpreted as a bad one, usually a large number. In such a way, the loss function penalizes an optimization algorithm when it moves in the wrong direction. So, the general idea is to minimize the value of the loss function to reduce penalties. There is no one universal loss function for optimization algorithms. Different factors determine how to choose a loss function. Examples of such factors are as follows:

- Specifics of the given problem—for example, if it is a regression or a classification model

- Ease of calculating derivatives
- Percentage of outliers in the dataset

In ML, the term **optimizer** is used to define an algorithm that connects a loss function and a technique for updating model parameters in response to the values of the loss function. So, optimizers tune ML models to predict target values for new data in the most accurate way by fitting model parameters. There are many optimizers: Gradient Descent, Adagrad, RMSProp, Adam, and others. Moreover, developing new optimizers is an active area of research. For example, there is the *ML and Optimization* research group at Microsoft (located in Redmond) whose research areas include combinatorial optimization, convex and non-convex optimization, and their application in ML and AI. Other companies in the industry also have similar research groups; there are many publications from Facebook Research, Amazon Research, and OpenAI groups.

An overview of linear algebra

The concepts of linear algebra are essential for understanding the theory behind ML because they help us understand how ML algorithms work under the hood. Also, most ML algorithm definitions use linear algebra terms.

Linear algebra is not only a handy mathematical instrument, but also the concepts of linear algebra can be very efficiently implemented with modern computer architectures. The rise of ML, and especially deep learning, began after significant performance improvement of the modern **Graphics Processing Unit** (**GPU**). GPUs were initially designed to work with linear algebra concepts and massive parallel computations used in computer games. After that, special libraries were created to work with general linear algebra concepts. Examples of libraries that implement basic linear algebra routines are `Cuda` and `OpenCL`, and one example of a specialized linear algebra library is `cuBLAS`. Moreover, it became more common to use **general-purpose graphics processing units** (**GPGPUs**) because these turn the computational power of a modern GPU into a powerful general-purpose computing resource.

Also, **Central Processing Units** (**CPUs**) have instruction sets specially designed for simultaneous numerical computations. Such computations are called **vectorized**, and common vectorized instruction sets are `AVx`, `SSE`, and `MMx`. There is also a term **Single Instruction Multiple Data** (**SIMD**) for these instruction sets. Many numeric linear algebra libraries, such as `Eigen`, `xtensor`, `VienaCL`, and others, use them to improve computational performance.

Learning the concepts of linear algebra

Linear algebra is a big area. It is the section of algebra that studies objects of a linear nature: vector (or linear) spaces, linear representations, and systems of linear equations. The main tools used in linear algebra are determinants, matrices, conjugation, and tensor calculus.

To understand ML algorithms, we only need a small set of linear algebra concepts. However, to do researches on new ML algorithms, a practitioner should have a deep understanding of linear algebra and calculus.

The following list contains the most valuable linear algebra concepts for understanding ML algorithms:

- **Scalar:** This is a single number.
- **Vector:** This is an array of ordered numbers. Each element has a distinct index. Notation for vectors is a bold lowercase typeface for names and an italic typeface with a subscript for elements, as shown in the following example:

$$\vec{x} = \begin{bmatrix} x_1 \\ x_2 \\ \cdot \\ \cdot \\ \cdot \\ x_n \end{bmatrix}$$

- **Matrix:** This is a two-dimensional array of numbers. Each element has a distinct pair of indices. Notation for matrices is a bold uppercase typeface for names and an italic but not bold typeface with a comma-separated list of indices in subscript for elements, as shown in the following example:

$$A = \begin{bmatrix} A_{1,1} & A_{1,2} \\ A_{2,1} & A_{2,2} \\ A_{3,1} & A_{3,2} \end{bmatrix}$$

- **Tensor:** This is an array of numbers arranged in a multidimensional regular grid, and represents generalizations of matrices. It is like a multidimensional matrix. For example, tensor **A** with dimensions 2 x 2 x 2 can look like this:

$$A = \begin{bmatrix} \begin{bmatrix} 1 & 2 \\ 3 & 4 \end{bmatrix} \\ \begin{bmatrix} 5 & 6 \\ 7 & 8 \end{bmatrix} \end{bmatrix}$$

Linear algebra libraries and ML frameworks usually use the concept of a tensor instead of a matrix because they implement general algorithms, and a matrix is just a special case of a tensor with two dimensions. Also, we can consider a vector as a matrix of size n x 1.

Basic linear algebra operations

The most common operations used for programming linear algebra algorithms are the following ones:

- **Element-wise operations**: These are performed in an element-wise manner on vectors, matrices, or tensors of the same size. The resulting elements will be the result of operations on corresponding input elements, as shown here:

$$A + B = C, C_{i,j} = A_{i,j} + B_{i,j}$$

$$A - B = C, C_{i,j} = A_{i,j} - B_{i,j}$$

$$A * B = C, C_{i,j} = A_{i,j} * B_{i,j}$$

$$A/B = C, C_{i,j} = A_{i,j}/B_{i,j}$$

The following example shows the element-wise summation:

$$\begin{bmatrix} 1 & 2 \\ 3 & 4 \end{bmatrix} + \begin{bmatrix} 5 & 6 \\ 7 & 8 \end{bmatrix} = \begin{bmatrix} 1+5 & 2+6 \\ 3+7 & 4+8 \end{bmatrix}$$

- **Dot product**: There are two types of multiplications for tensor and matrices in linear algebra—one is just element-wise, and the second is the dot product. The dot product deals with two equal-length series of numbers and returns a single number. This operation applied on matrices or tensors requires that the matrix or tensor A has the same number of columns as the number of rows in the matrix or tensor B. The following example shows the dot-product operation in the case when **A** is an *n* x *m* matrix and **B** is an *m* x *p* matrix:

$$\boldsymbol{A} \cdot \boldsymbol{B} = \boldsymbol{C}, C_{i,j} = \sum_{k=1}^{m} A_{i,k} B_{k,j}, i = 1, \ldots, n, j = 1, \ldots, p$$

- **Transposing**: The transposing of a matrix is an operation that flips the matrix over its diagonal, which leads to the flipping of the column and row indices of the matrix, resulting in the creation of a new matrix. In general, it is swapping matrix rows with columns. The following example shows how transposing works:

$$(\boldsymbol{A})^{T}_{i,j} = \boldsymbol{A}_{j,i} \begin{bmatrix} 1 & 3 & 5 \\ 2 & 4 & 6 \end{bmatrix}^{T} = \begin{bmatrix} 1 & 2 \\ 3 & 4 \\ 5 & 6 \end{bmatrix}$$

- **Norm**: This operation calculates the size of the vector; the result of this is a non-negative real number. The norm formula is as follows:

$$\|x\|_{p} = \left(\sum_{i} |x_i|^p \right)^{\frac{1}{p}}$$

The generic name of this type of norm is L^P *norm* for $p \in R, p \geq 1$. Usually, we use more concrete norms such as an L^2 *norm* with $p = 2$, which is known as the Euclidean norm, and we can interpret it as the Euclidean distance between points. Another widely used *norm* is the *squared* L^2 *norm*, whose calculation formula is $x^T x$. The squared L^2 norm is more suitable for mathematical and computational operations than the L^2 norm. Each partial derivative of the squared L^2 norm depends only on the corresponding element of x, in comparison to the partial derivatives of the L^2 norm which depends on the entire vector; this property plays a vital role in optimization algorithms. Another widely used *norm* operation is the L^1 *norm* with $p=1$, which is commonly used in ML when we care about the difference between zero and nonzero elements.

- **Inverting**: The inverse matrix is such a matrix that $A^{-1}A = I$, where I is an identity matrix. The identity matrix is a matrix that does not change any vector when we multiply that vector by that matrix.

We considered the main linear algebra concepts as well as operations on them. Using this math apparatus, we can define and program many ML algorithms. For example, we can use tensors and matrices to define training datasets for training, and scalars can be used as different types of coefficients. We can use element-wise operations to perform arithmetic operations with a whole dataset (a matrix or a tensor). For example, we can use element-wise multiplication to scale a dataset. We usually use transposing to change a view of a vector or matrix to make them suitable for the dot-product operation. The dot product is usually used to apply a linear function with weights expressed as matrix coefficients to a vector; for example, this vector can be a training sample. Also, dot-product operations are used to update model parameters expressed as matrix or tensor coefficients according to an algorithm.

The norm operation is often used in formulas for loss functions because it naturally expresses the distance concept and can measure the difference between target and predicted values. The inverse matrix is a crucial concept for the analytical solving of linear equations systems. Such systems often appear in different optimization problems. However, calculating the inverse matrix is very computationally expensive.

Tensor representation in computing

We can represent tensor objects in computer memory in different ways. The most obvious method is a simple linear array in computer memory (**random-access memory**, or **RAM**). However, the linear array is also the most computationally effective data structure for modern CPUs. There are two standard practices to organize tensors with a linear array in memory: row-major ordering and column-major ordering. In row-major ordering, we place consecutive elements of a row in linear order one after the other, and each row is also placed after the end of the previous one. In column-major ordering, we do the same but with the column elements. Data layouts have a significant impact on computational performance because the speed of traversing an array relies on modern CPU architectures that work with sequential data more efficiently than with non-sequential data. CPU caching effects are the reasons for such behavior. Also, a contiguous data layout makes it possible to use SIMD vectorized instructions that work with sequential data more efficiently, and we can use them as a type of parallel processing.

Different libraries, even in the same programming language, can use different ordering. For example, `Eigen` uses column-major ordering, but `PyTorch` uses row-major ordering. So, developers should be aware of internal tensor representation in libraries they use, and also take care of this when performing data loading or implementing algorithms from scratch.

Consider the following matrix:

$$A = \begin{bmatrix} a_{1,1} & a_{1,2} & a_{1,3} \\ a_{2,1} & a_{2,2} & a_{2,3} \end{bmatrix}$$

Then, in the row-major data layout, members of the matrix will have the following layout in memory:

0	1	2	3	4	5
a11	a12	a13	a21	a22	a23

In the case of the column-major data layout, order layout will be the next, as shown here:

0	1	2	3	4	5
a11	a21	a12	a22	a13	a23

Linear algebra API samples

Consider some C++ linear algebra APIs (short for **Application Program Interface**), and look at how we can use them for creating linear algebra primitives and perform algebra operations with them.

Using Eigen

`Eigen` is a general-purpose linear algebra C++ library. In `Eigen`, all matrices and vectors are objects of the `Matrix` template class, and the vector is a specialization of the matrix type, with either one row or one column. Tensor objects are not presented in official APIs but exist as submodules.

We can define the type for a matrix with known dimensions and floating-point data type like this:

```
typedef Eigen::Matrix<float, 3, 3> MyMatrix33f;
```

We can define a vector in the following way:

```
typedef Eigen::Matrix<float, 3, 1> MyVector3f;
```

`Eigen` already has a lot of predefined types for vector and matrix objects—for example, `Eigen::Matrix3f` (floating-point 3x3 matrix type) or `Eigen::RowVector2f` (floating-point 1 x 2 vector type). Also, `Eigen` is not limited to matrices whose dimensions we know at compile time. We can define matrix types that will take the number of rows or columns at initialization during runtime. To define such types, we can use a special type variable for the `Matrix` class template argument named `Eigen::Dynamic`. For example, to define a matrix of doubles with dynamic dimensions, we can use the following definition:

```
typedef Eigen::Matrix<double, Eigen::Dynamic, Eigen::Dynamic> MyMatrix;
```

Objects initialized from the types we defined will look like this:

```
MyMatrix33f a;
MyVector3f v;
MyMatrix m(10,15);
```

To put some values into these objects, we can use several approaches. We can use special predefined initialization functions, as follows:

```
a = MyMatrix33f::Zero(); // fill matrix elements with zeros
a = MyMatrix33f::Identity(); // fill matrix as Identity matrix
v = MyVector3f::Random(); // fill matrix elements with random values
```

We can use the *comma-initializer* syntax, as follows:

```
a << 1,2,3,
     4,5,6,
     7,8,9;
```

This code construction initializes the matrix values in the following way:

$$\begin{bmatrix} 1 & 2 & 3 \\ 4 & 5 & 6 \\ 7 & 8 & 9 \end{bmatrix}$$

We can use direct element access to set or change matrix coefficients. The following code sample shows how to use the `()` operator for such an operation:

```
a(0,0) = 3;
```

We can use the object of the `Map` type to wrap an existent C++ array or vector in the `Matrix` type object. This kind of mapping object will use memory and values from the underlying object, and will not allocate the additional memory and copy the values. The following snippet shows how to use the `Map` type:

```
int data[] = {1,2,3,4};
Eigen::Map<Eigen::RowVectorxi> v(data,4);
std::vector<float> data = {1,2,3,4,5,6,7,8,9};
Eigen::Map<MyMatrix33f> a(data.data());
```

We can use initialized matrix objects in mathematical operations. Matrix and vector arithmetic operations in the `Eigen` library are offered either through overloads of standard C++ arithmetic operators such as `+`, `-`, `*`, or through methods such as `dot()` and `cross()`. The following code sample shows how to express general math operations in `Eigen`:

```
using namespace Eigen;
auto a = Matrix2d::Random();
auto b = Matrix2d::Random();
auto result = a + b;
result = a.array() * b.array(); // element wise multiplication
result = a.array() / b.array();
a += b;
result = a * b; // matrix multiplication
//Also it's possible to use scalars:
a = b.array() * 4;
```

Notice that in `Eigen`, arithmetic operators such as `operator+` do not perform any computation by themselves. These operators return an *expression object*, which describes what computation to perform. The actual computation happens later when the whole expression is evaluated, typically in the `operator=` arithmetic operator. It can lead to some strange behaviors, primarily if a developer uses the `auto` keyword too frequently.

Sometimes, we need to perform operations only on a part of the matrix. For this purpose, `Eigen` provides the `block` method, which takes four parameters: `i,j,p,q`. These parameters are the block size `p,q` and the starting point `i,j`. The following code shows how to use this method:

```
Eigen::Matrixxf m(4,4);
Eigen::Matrix2f b = m.block(1,1,2,2); // copying the middle part of matrix
m.block(1,1,2,2) *= 4; // change values in original matrix
```

There are two more methods to access rows and columns by index, which are also a type of block operation. The following snippet shows how to use the `col` and the `row` methods:

```
m.row(1).array() += 3;
m.col(2).array() /= 4;
```

Another important feature of linear algebra libraries is broadcasting, and `Eigen` supports this with the `colwise` and `rowwise` methods. Broadcasting can be interpreted as a matrix by replicating it in one direction. Take a look at the following example of how to add a vector to each column of the matrix:

```
Eigen::Matrixxf mat(2,4);
Eigen::Vectorxf v(2); // column vector
mat.colwise() += v;
```

This operation has the following result: $\begin{bmatrix} 1 & 2 & 3 \\ 4 & 5 & 6 \end{bmatrix}.colwise() + \begin{bmatrix} 0 \\ 1 \end{bmatrix} = \begin{bmatrix} 1 & 2 & 3 \\ 5 & 6 & 7 \end{bmatrix}$.

Using xtensor

The `xtensor` library is a C++ library for numerical analysis with multidimensional array expressions. Containers of `xtensor` are inspired by NumPy, the Python array programming library. ML algorithms are mainly described using Python and NumPy, so this library can make it easier to move them to C++. The following container classes implement multidimensional arrays in the `xtensor` library.

The `xarray` type is a dynamically sized multidimensional array, as shown in the following code snippet:

```
std::vector<size_t> shape = { 3, 2, 4 };
xt::xarray<double, xt::layout_type::row_major> a(shape);
```

The `xtensor` type is a multidimensional array whose dimensions are fixed at compilation time. Exact dimension values can be configured in the initialization step, as shown in the following code snippet:

```
std::array<size_t, 3> shape = { 3, 2, 4 };
xt::xtensor<double, 3> a(shape);
```

The `xtensor_fixed` type is a multidimensional array with a dimension shape fixed at compile time, as shown in the following code snippet:

```
xt::xtensor_fixed<double, xt::xshape<3, 2, 4>> a;
```

The `xtensor` library also implements arithmetic operators with expression template techniques such as `Eigen` (this is a common approach for math libraries implemented in C++). So, the computation happens lazily, and the actual result is calculated when the whole expression is evaluated. The container definitions are also expressions. There is also a function to force an expression evaluation named `xt::eval` in the `xtensor` library.

There are different kinds of container initialization in the `xtensor` library. Initialization of `xtensor` arrays can be done with C++ initializer lists, as follows:

```
xt::xarray<double> arr1{{1.0, 2.0, 3.0},
                        {2.0, 5.0, 7.0},
                        {2.0, 5.0, 7.0}}; // initialize a 3x3 array
```

The `xtensor` library also has builder functions for special tensor types. The following snippet shows some of them:

```
std::vector<uint64_t> shape = {2, 2};
xt::ones(shape);
xt::zero(shape);
xt::eye(shape); //matrix with ones on the diagonal
```

Also, we can map existing C++ arrays into the `xtensor` container with the `xt::adapt` function. This function returns the object that uses the memory and values from the underlying object, as shown in the following code snippet:

```
std::vector<float> data{1,2,3,4};
std::vector<size_t> shape{2,2};
auto data_x = xt::adapt(data, shape);
```

We can use direct access to container elements, with the `()` operator, to set or change tensor values, as shown in the following code snippet:

```
std::vector<size_t> shape = {3, 2, 4};
xt::xarray<float> a = xt::ones<float>(shape);
a(2,1,3) = 3.14f;
```

The `xtensor` library implements linear algebra arithmetic operations through overloads of standard C++ arithmetic operators such as +, – and *. To use other operations such as dot-product operations, we have to link an application with the library named `xtensor-blas`. These operators are declared in the `xt::linalg` namespace.

The following code shows the use of arithmetic operations with the `xtensor` library:

```
auto a = xt::random::rand<double>({2,2});
auto b = xt::random::rand<double>({2,2});
auto c = a + b;
```

```
a -= b;
c = xt::linalg::dot(a,b);
c = a + 5;
```

To get partial access to the `xtensor` containers, we can use the `xt::view` function. The following sample shows how this function works:

```
xt::xarray<int> a{{1,  2,  3,  4},
                  {5,  6,  7,  8}
                  {9,  10, 11, 12}
                  {13, 14, 15, 16}};
auto b = xt::view(a, xt::range(1, 3), xt::range(1, 3));
```

This operation takes a rectangular block from the tensor, which looks like this:

$$\begin{bmatrix} 1 & 2 & 3 & 4 \\ 5 & 6 & 7 & 8 \\ 9 & 10 & 11 & 12 \\ 13 & 14 & 15 & 16 \end{bmatrix} \rightarrow \begin{bmatrix} 6 & 7 \\ 10 & 11 \end{bmatrix}$$

The `xtensor` library implements automatic broadcasting in most cases. When the operation involves two arrays of different dimensions, it transmits the array with the smaller dimension across the leading dimension of the other array, so we can directly add a vector to a matrix. The following code sample shows how easy it is:

```
auto m = xt::random::rand<double>({2,2});
auto v = xt::random::rand<double>({2,1});
auto c = m + v;
```

Using Shark-ML

`Shark-ML` is a C++ ML library with rich functionality. It also provides an API for linear algebra routines.

There are four container classes for representing matrices and vectors in the `Shark-ML` library. Notice that the linear algebra functionality is declared in the `remora` namespace instead of the `shark` namespace, which is used for other routines.

The following code sample shows container classes that exist in the `Shark-ML` library, wherein the `vector` type is a dynamically sized array:

```
remora::vector<double> b(100, 1.0); // vector of size 100 and filled
with 1.0
```

The `compressed_vector` type is a sparse array storing values in a compressed format.

The `matrix` type is a dynamically sized dense matrix, as shown in the following code snippet:

```
remora::matrix<double> C(2, 2); // 2x2 matrix
```

The `compressed_matrix` type is a sparse matrix storing values in a compressed format.

There are two main types of container initialization in the `Shark-ML` library.

We can initialize a container object with the constructor that takes the initializer list. The following code sample shows this:

```
remora::matrix<float> m_ones{{1, 1}, {1, 1}}; // 2x2 matrix
```

The second option is to wrap the existing C++ array into the container object and reuse its memory and values. The following code sample shows how to use the same array for the initialization of matrix and vector objects:

```
float data[]= {1,2,3,4};
remora::matrix<float> m(data, 2, 2);
remora::vector<float> v(data, 4);
```

Also, we can initialize values with direct access to the container elements, with the `()` operator. The following code sample shows how to set a value for matrix and vector objects:

```
remora::matrix<float> m(data, 2, 2);
m(0,0) = 3.14f;
remora::vector<float> v(data, 4);
v(0) = 3.14f;
```

The `Shark-ML` library implements linear algebra arithmetic operations through overloads of standard C++ arithmetic operators such as +, – and *. Some other operations such as the dot product are implemented as standalone functions.

The following code sample shows how to use arithmetic operations in the `Shark-ML` library:

```
remora::matrix<float> a(data, 2, 2);
remora::matrix<float> b(data, 2, 2);
auto c = a + b;
a -= b;
c = remora::prod(a,b);
c = a%b; // also dot product operation
c = a + 5;
```

We can use the following functions for partial access to the Shark ML containers:

- `subrange (x,i,j)`: This function returns a sub-vector of x with the elements $xi,..., xj-1$.
- `subrange (A,i,j,k,l)`: This function returns a sub-matrix of A with elements indicated by $i,...,j-1$ and $k, ..., l-1$.
- `row (A,k)`: This function returns the kth row of A as a vector proxy.
- `column (A,k)`: This function returns the kth column of A as a vector proxy.
- `rows (A,k,l)`: This function returns the rows $k,...,l-1$ of A as a matrix proxy.
- `columns (A,k,l)`: This function returns the columns $k,..., l-1$ of A as a matrix proxy.

There is no broadcasting implementation in the `Shark-ML` library. Limited support of broadcasting exists only in the form of reduction functions (the set of functions that calculate one numeric value for a whole matrix or vector). There are two functions—the `as_rows()` and `as_columns()` function—that allow reduction operations to be performed independently on matrix rows or columns respectively. We can pass the result of these functions to any of the reduction functions. The following code sample shows how to perform summation reduction:

```
remora::matrix<float> m{{1, 2, 3, 4}, {5, 6, 7, 8}};
auto cols = remora::as_columns(m);
remora::sum(cols)
```

A different way to work with columns and rows independently is the use of partial access functions. The following code sample shows how to add the same vector to each of the matrix columns:

```
remora::vector<float> v{10, 10};
// Update matrix rows
for (size_t i = 0; i < m.size2(); ++i) {
    remora::column(m, i) += v;
}
```

Using Dlib

Dlib is a modern C++ toolkit containing ML algorithms and tools for creating computer vision software in C++. Most of the linear algebra tools in Dlib deal with dense matrices. However, there is also limited support for working with sparse matrices and vectors. In particular, the Dlib tools represent sparse vectors using the containers from the C++ **standard template library (STL)**.

There are two main container types in Dlib to work with linear algebra: the matrix and the vector classes. Matrix operations in Dlib are implemented using the expression templates technique, which allows them to eliminate the temporary matrix objects that would usually be returned from expressions such as M = A+B+C+D.

We can create a matrix sized at compile time in the following way, by specifying dimensions as template arguments:

```
Dlib::matrix<double,3,1> y;
```

Alternatively, we can create dynamically sized matrix objects. In such a case, we pass the matrix dimensions to the constructor, as shown in the following code snippet:

```
Dlib::matrix<double> m(3,3);
```

Later, we can change the size of this matrix, with the following method:

```
m.set_size(6,6);
```

We can initialize matrix values with a comma operator, as shown in the following code snippet:

```
m = 54.2,  7.4, 12.1,
    1,     2,    3,
    5.9,   0.05, 1;
```

As in the previous libraries, we can wrap an existing C++ array to the matrix object, as shown in the following code snippet:

```
double data[] = {1,2,3,4,5,6};
auto a = Dlib::mat(data, 2,3); // create matrix with size 2x3
```

Also, we can access matrix elements with the () operator to modify or get a particular value, as shown in the following code snippet:

```
m(1,2) = 3;
```

The Dlib library has a set of predefined functions to initialize a matrix with values such as identity matrix, 1s, or random values, as illustrated in the following code snippet:

```
auto a = Dlib::identity_matrix<double>(3);
auto b = Dlib::ones_matrix<double>(3,4);
auto c = Dlib::randm(3,4); // matrix with random values with size 3x3
```

Most linear algebra arithmetic operations in the Dlib library are implemented through overloads of standard C++ arithmetic operators such as +, -, *. Other complex operations are provided by the library as standalone functions.

The following example shows the use of arithmetic operations in the Dlib library:

```
auto c = a + b;
auto e = a * b; // real matrix multiplication
auto d  = Dlib::pointwise_multiply(a, b); // element wise multiplication
a += 5;
auto t = Dlib::trans(a); // transpose matrix
```

To work with partial access to matrices, Dlib provides a set of special functions. The following code sample shows how to use some of them:

```
a = Dlib::rowm(b,0); // takes first row of matrix
a = Dlib::rowm(b,Dlib::range(0,1));//takes first two rows
a = Dlib::colm(b,0); // takes first column
a = Dlib::subm(b, range(1,2), range(1,2)); // takes a rectangular part from
center
Dlib::set_subm(b,range(0,1), range(0,1)) = 7; // initialize part of the
matrix
Dlib::set_subm(b,range(0,1), range(0,1)) += 7; // add a value to the part
of the matrix
```

Broadcasting in the Dlib library can be modeled with set_rowm(), set_colm(), and set_subm() functions that give modifier objects for a particular matrix row, column, or a rectangular part of the original matrix. Objects returned from these functions support all set or arithmetic operations. The following code snippet shows how to add a vector to the columns:

```
Dlib::matrix<float, 2,1> x;
Dlib::matrix<float, 2,3> m;
Dlib::set_colm(b,Dlib::range(0,1)) += x;
```

An overview of linear regression

Consider an example of the real-world supervised ML algorithm called linear regression. In general, **linear regression** is an approach for modeling a target value (dependent value) based on an explanatory value (independent value). This method is used for forecasting and finding relationships between values. We can classify regression methods by the number of inputs (independent variables) and the type of relationship between the inputs and outputs (dependent variables).

Simple linear regression is the case where the number of independent variables is 1, and there is a linear relationship between the independent (x) and dependent (y) variable.

Linear regression is widely used in different areas, such as scientific research, where it can describe relationships between variables, as well as in applications within industry, such as a revenue prediction. For example, it can estimate a trend line that represents the long-term movement in the stock price time-series data. It tells whether the interest value of in a specific dataset has increased or decreased over the given period, as illustrated in the following screenshot:

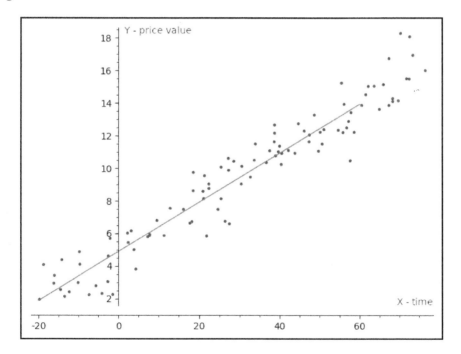

If we have one input variable (independent variable) and one output variable (dependent variable) the regression is called simple, and we use the term **simple linear regression** for it. With multiple independent variables, we call this **multiple linear regression** or **multivariable linear regression**. Usually, when we are dealing with real-world problems, we have a lot of independent variables, so we model such problems with multiple regression models. Multiple regression models have a universal definition that covers other types, so even simple linear regression is often defined using the multiple regression definition.

Solving linear regression tasks with different libraries

Assume that we have a dataset, $\{y_i, x_{i1}, \ldots, x_{ip}\}_{i=1}^{n}$, so that we can express the linear relation between y and x with mathematical formula in the following way:

$$y_i = \beta_0 1 + \beta_1 * x_{i1} + \ldots + \beta_{p+1} x_{ip} + \epsilon_i = x_i^T \beta + \epsilon_i, i = 1, \ldots, n$$

Here, p is the dimension of the independent variable, and T denotes the transpose, so that $x_i^T \beta$ is the inner product between vectors x_i and β. Also, we can rewrite the previous expression in matrix notation, as follows:

$$y = X\beta + \epsilon$$

$$y = \begin{pmatrix} y_1 \\ y_2 \\ \vdots \\ y_n \end{pmatrix}, \quad X = \begin{pmatrix} x_1^T \\ x_2^T \\ \vdots \\ x_n^T \end{pmatrix} = \begin{pmatrix} 1 & x_{11} & \cdots & x_{1p} \\ 1 & x_{21} & \cdots & x_{2p} \\ \vdots & \vdots & \ddots & \vdots \\ 1 & x_{n1} & \cdots & x_{np} \end{pmatrix}, \quad \beta = \begin{pmatrix} \beta_0 \\ \beta_1 \\ \vdots \\ \beta_p \end{pmatrix}, \quad \epsilon = \begin{pmatrix} \epsilon_1 \\ \epsilon_2 \\ \vdots \\ \epsilon_n \end{pmatrix}$$

The preceding matrix notation can be explained as follows:

- y: This is a vector of observed target values.
- x: This is a matrix of row-vectors, x_i, which are known as explanatory or independent values.
- ß: This is a (*p+1*) dimensional parameters vector.
- ε: This is called an error term or noise. This variable captures all other factors that influence the y dependent variable other than the regressors.

When we are considering simple linear regression, p is equal to 1, and the equation will look like this:

$$y_i = \beta_0 1 + \beta_1 x_i + \epsilon_i$$

The goal of the linear regression task is to find parameter vectors that satisfy the previous equation. Usually, there is no exact solution to such a system of linear equations, so the task is to estimate parameters that satisfy these equations with some assumptions. One of the most popular estimation approaches is one based on the principle of least squares: minimizing the sum of the squares of the differences between the observed dependent variable in the given dataset and those predicted by the linear function. This is called the **ordinary least squares (OLS)** estimator. So, the task can be formulated with the following formula:

$$\hat{\beta} = argmin_\beta S(\beta)$$

In the preceding formula, the objective function S is given by the following matrix notation:

$$S(\beta) = \sum_{i=1}^{n} \left| y_i - \sum_{j=1}^{p} X_{ij}\beta_j^2 \right| = \left\| y - X\beta^2 \right\|$$

This minimization problem has a unique solution, in the case that the p columns of the x matrix are linearly independent. We can get this solution by solving the *normal equation*, as follows:

$$\beta = (X^T X)^{-1} X^T y$$

Linear algebra libraries can solve such equations directly with an analytical approach, but it has one significant disadvantage—computational cost. In the case of large dimensions of y and x, requirements for computer memory amount and computational time are too big to solve real-world tasks.

So, usually, this minimization task is solved with iterative approaches. **Gradient descent (GD)** is an example of such an algorithm. GD is a technique based on the observation that if the function $S(\beta)$ is defined and is differentiable in a neighborhood of a point β, then $S(\beta)$ decreases fastest when it goes in the direction of the negative gradient of S at the point β.

We can change our $S(\beta)$ objective function to a form more suitable for an iterative approach. We can use the **mean squared error** (**MSE**) function, which measures the difference between the estimator and the estimated value, as illustrated here:

$$S(\beta) = \frac{1}{n} \sum_{i=1}^{n} (y_i - X_i \beta)^2$$

In the case of the multiple regression, we take partial derivatives for this function for each of x components, as follows:

$$\frac{\partial S}{\partial \beta_j}$$

So, in the case of the linear regression, we take the following derivatives:

$$\frac{\partial S}{\partial \beta_0} = \frac{2}{n} \sum_{i=1}^{n} (X_i \beta - y_i)$$

$$\frac{\partial S}{\partial \beta_1} = \frac{2}{n} \sum_{i=1}^{n} (X_i \beta - y_i) X_i$$

The whole algorithm has the following description:

1. Initialize β with zeros.
2. Define a value for the learning rate parameter that controls how much we are adjusting parameters during the learning procedure.
3. Calculate the following values of β:

$$\beta_0 = \beta_0 - \gamma \frac{2}{n} \sum_{i=1}^{n} (X_i \beta - y_i)$$

$$\beta_1 = \beta_1 - \gamma \frac{2}{n} \sum_{i=1}^{n} (X_i \beta - y_i) X_i$$

4. Repeat steps 1-3 for a number of times or until the MSE value reaches a reasonable amount.

The previously described algorithm is one of the simplest supervised ML algorithms. We described it with the linear algebra concepts we introduced earlier in the chapter. Later, it became more evident that almost all ML algorithms use linear algebra under the hood. The following samples show the higher-level API in different linear algebra libraries for solving the *linear regression* task, and we provide them to show how libraries can simplify the complicated math used underneath. We will give the details of the APIs used in these samples in the following chapters.

Solving linear regression tasks with Eigen

There are several iterative methods for solving problems of the $Ax = b$ form in the `Eigen` library. The `LeastSquaresConjugateGradient` class is one of them, which allows us to solve linear regression problems with the conjugate gradient algorithm. The `ConjugateGradient` algorithm can converge more quickly to the function's minimum than regular GD but requires that matrix A is positively defined to guarantee numerical stability. The `LeastSquaresConjugateGradient` class has two main settings: the maximum number of iterations and a tolerance threshold value that is used as a stopping criteria as an upper bound to the relative residual error, as illustrated in the following code block:

```
typedef float DType;
using Matrix = Eigen::Matrix<DType, Eigen::Dynamic, Eigen::Dynamic>;
int n = 10000;
Matrix x(n,1);
Matrix y(n,1);
Eigen::LeastSquaresConjugateGradient<Matrix> gd;
gd.setMaxIterations(1000);
gd.setTolerance(0.001) ;
gd.compute(x);
auto b = dg.solve(y);
```

For new *x* inputs, we can predict new *y* values with matrices operations, as follows:

```
Eigen::Matrixxf new_x(5, 2);
new_x << 1, 1, 1, 2, 1, 3, 1, 4, 1, 5;
auto new_y = new_x.array().rowwise() * b.transpose().array();
```

Also, we can calculate parameter's *b* vector (the linear regression task solution) by solving the *normal equation* directly, as follows:

```
auto b = (x.transpose() * x).ldlt().solve(x.transpose() * y);
```

Solving linear regression tasks with Shogun

`Shogun` is an open source ML library that provides a wide range of unified ML algorithms. The `Shogun` library has the `CLinearRidgeRegression` class for solving simple linear regression problems. This class solves problems with standard Cholesky matrix decomposition in a noniterative way, as illustrated in the following code block:

```
auto x = some<CDenseFeatures<float64_t>>(x_values);
auto y= some<CRegressionLabels>(y_values); // real-valued labels
float64_t tau_regularization = 0.0001;
auto lr = some<CLinearRidgeRegression>(tau_regularization, nullptr,
nullptr); // regression model with regularization
lr->set_labels(y);
r->train(x)
```

For new *x* inputs, we can predict new *y* values in the following way:

```
auto new_x = some<CDenseFeatures<float64_t>>(new_x_values);
auto y_predict = lr->apply_regression(new_x);
```

Also, we can get the calculated parameters (the linear regression task solution) vector, as follows:

```
auto weights = lr->get_w();
```

Moreover, we can calculate the value of MSE, as follows:

```
auto y_predict = lr->apply_regression(x);
auto eval = some<CMeanSquaredError>();
auto mse = eval->evaluate(y_predict , y);
```

Solving linear regression tasks with Shark-ML

The `Shark-ML` library provides the `LinearModel` class for representing linear regression problems. There are two trainer classes for this kind of model: the `LinearRegression` class, which provides analytical solutions, and the `LinearSAGTrainer` class, which provides a stochastic average gradient iterative method, as illustrated in the following code block:

```
using namespace shark;
using namespace std;
Data<RealVector> x;
Data<RealVector> y;
RegressionDataset data(x, y);
LinearModel<> model;
```

```
LinearRegression trainer;
trainer.train(model, data);
```

We can get the calculated parameters (the linear regression task solution) vector by running the following code:

```
auto b = model.parameterVector();
```

For new *x* inputs, we can predict new *y* values in the following way:

```
Data<RealVector> new_x;
Data<RealVector> prediction = model(new_x);
```

Also, we can calculate the value of squared error, as follows:

```
SquaredLoss<> loss;
auto se = loss(y, prediction)
```

Linear regression with Dlib

The `Dlib` library provides the `krr_trainer` class, which can get the template argument of the `linear_kernel` type to solve linear regression tasks. This class implements direct analytical solving for this type of problem with the kernel ridge regression algorithm, as illustrated in the following code block:

```
std::vector<matrix<double>> x;
std::vector<float> y;
krr_trainer<KernelType> trainer;
trainer.set_kernel(KernelType());
decision_function<KernelType> df = trainer.train(x, y);
```

For new *x* inputs, we can predict new *y* values in the following way:

```
std::vector<matrix<double>> new_x;
for (auto& v : x) {
    auto prediction = df(v);
    std::cout << prediction << std::endl;
}
```

Summary

In this chapter, we learned what ML is, how it differs from other computer algorithms, and how it became so popular. We also became familiar with the necessary mathematical background required to begin to work with ML algorithms. We looked at software libraries that provide APIs for linear algebra, and also implemented our first ML algorithm—linear regression.

There are other linear algebra libraries for C++. Moreover, the popular deep learning frameworks use their own implementations of linear algebra libraries. For example, the MXNet framework is based on the `mshadow` library, and the PyTorch framework is based on the `ATen` library. Some of these libraries can use GPU or special CPU instructions for speeding up calculations. Such features do not usually change the API but require some additional library initialization settings or explicit object conversion to different backends such as CPUs or GPUs.

In the next two chapters, we will learn more about available software tools that are necessary to implement more complicated algorithms, and we will also learn more theoretical background on how to manage ML algorithms.

Further reading

- Basic Linear Algebra for Deep Learning: `https://towardsdatascience.com/linear-algebra-for-deep-learning-f21d7e7d7f23`
- Deep Learning - An MIT Press book: `https://www.deeplearningbook.org/contents/linear_algebra.html`
- What is Machine Learning?: `https://www.mathworks.com/discovery/machine-learning.html`
- The `Eigen` library documentation: `http://eigen.tuxfamily.org`
- The `xtensor` library documentation: `https://xtensor.readthedocs.io/en/latest/`
- The `Dlib` library documentation: `http://dlib.net/`
- The `Shark-ML` library documentation: `http://image.diku.dk/shark/`
- The `Shogun` library documentation: `http://www.shogun-toolbox.org/`

2
Data Processing

One of the essential things in machine learning is the data that we use for training. We can gather training data from the processes we work with, or we can take already prepared training data from third-party sources. In any case, we have to store training data in a file format that should satisfy our development requirements. These requirements depend on the task we solve, as well as the data-gathering process. Sometimes, we need to transform data stored in one format to another to satisfy our needs. Examples of such needs are as follows:

- Increasing human readability to ease communication with engineers
- The existence of compression possibility to allow data to occupy less space on secondary storage
- The use of data in the binary form to speed up the parsing process
- Supporting the complex relations between different parts of data to make precise mirroring of a specific domain
- Platform independence to be able to use the dataset in different development and production environments

Today, there exists a variety of file formats that is used for storing different kinds of information. Some of these are very specific, and some of them are general-purpose. There are software libraries that allow us to manipulate these file formats. There is rarely a need to develop a new format and parser from scratch. Using existing software for reading a format can significantly reduce development and testing time, which allows us to focus on particular tasks.

This chapter discusses how to process popular file formats that we use for storing data. It shows what libraries exist for working with **JavaScript Object Notation (JSON)**, **Comma-Separated Values (CSV)**, and **Hierarchical Data Format v5 (HDF5)** formats. This chapter also introduces the basic operations required to load and process image data with the OpenCV and Dlib libraries, and how to convert the data format used in these libraries to data types used in linear algebra libraries. It also describes data normalization techniques such as feature scaling and standardization procedures to deal with heterogeneous data.

This chapter will cover the following topics:

- Parsing data formats to C++data structures
- Initializing matrix and tensor objects from C++ data structures
- Manipulating images with the `OpenCV` and `Dlib` libraries
- Transforming images into matrix and tensor objects of various libraries
- Normalizing data

Technical requirements

The required technologies and installations for this chapter are as follows:

- Modern C++ compiler with C++17 support
- CMake build system version >= 3.8
- `Dlib` library installation
- `Shogun` toolbox library installation
- `Shark-ML` library installation
- `Eigen` library installation
- `hdf5lib` library installation
- `HighFive` library installation
- `RapidJSON` library installation
- `Fast-CPP-CSV-Parser` library installation

The code for this chapter can be found at the following GitHub
repo: https://github.com/PacktPublishing/Hands-On-Machine-Learning-with-CPP/tree/master/Chapter02

Parsing data formats to C++ data structures

The most popular format for representing structured data is called CSV. This format is just a text file with a two-dimensional table in it whereby values in a row are separated with commas, and rows are placed on every new line. It looks like this:

```
1, 2, 3, 4
5, 6, 7, 8
9, 10, 11, 12
```

The advantages of this file format are that it has a straightforward structure, there are many software tools that can process it, it is human-readable, and it is supported on a variety of computer platforms. Disadvantages are a lack of support of multidimensional data and data with complex structuring, as well as slow parsing speed in comparison with binary formats.

Another widely used format is JSON. Although the format contains JavaScript in its abbreviation, we can use it with almost all programming languages. This is a file format with name-value pairs and arrays of such pairs. It has rules on how to group such pairs to distinct objects and array declarations, and there are rules on how to define values of different types. The following code sample shows a file in JSON format:

```
{
    name:"Bill",
    age: 25,
    phones:[
        {
            type:"home"
            number:43534590
        },
        {
            type:"work"
            number:56985468
        }
    ]
}
```

The advantages of this format are human readability, software support on many computer platforms, and the possibility to store hierarchical and nested data structures. Disadvantages are its slow parsing speed in comparison with binary formats, and the fact it is not very useful for representing numerical matrices.

Often, we use a combination of file formats to represent a complex dataset. For example, we can describe object relations with JSON, and data/numerical data in the binary form can be stored in a folder structure on the filesystem with references to them in JSON files.

HDF5 is a specialized file format for storing scientific data. This file format was developed to store heterogeneous multidimensional data with a complex structure. It provides fast access to single elements because it has optimized data structures for using secondary storage. Furthermore, HDF5 supports data compression. In general, this file format consists of named groups that contain multidimensional arrays of multitype data. Each element of this file format can contain metadata, as illustrated in the following diagram:

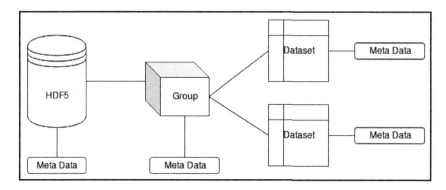

HDF5 format structure

The advantages of this format are its high read-and-write speed, fast access to distinct elements, and its ability to support data with a complex structure and various types of data. Disadvantages are the requirement of specialized tools for editing and viewing by users, the limited support of type conversions among different platforms, and using a single file for the whole dataset. The last issue makes data restoration almost impossible in the event of file corruption.

There are a lot of other formats for representing datasets for machine learning, but we found the ones mentioned to be the most useful.

Reading CSV files with the Fast-CPP-CSV-Parser library

Consider how to deal with CSV format in C++. There are many different libraries for parsing CSV format with C++. They have different sets of functions and different ways to integrate into applications. The easiest way to use C++ libraries is to use headers-only libraries because this eliminates the need to build and link them. We propose to use the `Fast-CPP-CSV-Parser` library because it is a small single-file header-only library with the minimal required functionality, which can be easily integrated into a development code base.

As an example of a CSV file format, we use the Iris dataset, which describes three different types of iris plants and was conceived by R.A. Fisher. Each row in the file contains the following fields: sepal length, sepal width, petal length, petal width, and a string with a class name.

 The reference to the Iris dataset is the following: Dua, D. and Graff, C. (2019). UCI Machine Learning Repository [http://archive.ics.uci.edu/ml]. Irvine, CA: University of California, School of Information and Computer Science.

To read this dataset with the `Fast-CPP-CSV-Parser` library, we need to include a single header file, as follows:

```
#include <csv.h>
```

Then, we define an object of the type `io::CSVReader`. We must define the number of columns as a template parameter. This parameter is one of the library limitations because we need to be aware of the CSV file structure. The code for this is illustrated in the following snippet:

```
const uint32_t columns_num = 5;
io::CSVReader<columns_num> csv_reader(file_path);
```

Next, we define containers for storing the values we read, as follows:

```
std::vector<std::string> categorical_column;
std::vector<double> values;
```

Then, to make our code more generic and gather all information about column types in one place, we introduce the following helper types and functions. We define a tuple object that describes values for a row, like this:

```
using RowType = std::tuple<double, double, double, double, std::string>;
RowType row;
```

The reason for using a tuple is that we can easily iterate it with metaprogramming techniques. Then, we define two helper functions. One is for reading a row from a file, and it uses the `read_row()` method of the `io::CSVReader` class. The `read_row()` method takes a variable number of parameters of different types. Our `RowType` type describes these values. We do automatic parameter filling by using the `std::index_sequence` type with the `std::get` function, as illustrated in the following code snippet:

```
template <std::size_t... Idx, typename T, typename R>
bool read_row_help(std::index_sequence<Idx...>, T& row, R& r) {
  return r.read_row(std::get<Idx>(row)...);
```

```
    }
```

The second helper function uses a similar technique for transforming a row tuple object to our value vectors, as follows:

```
template <std::size_t... Idx, typename T>
void fill_values(std::index_sequence<Idx...>,
 T& row,
 std::vector<double>& data) {
 data.insert(data.end(), {std::get<Idx>(row)...});
}
```

Now, we can put all the parts together. We define a loop where we continuously read row values and move them to our containers. After we read a row, we check the return value of the `read_row()` method, which tells us if the read was successful or not. A `false` return value means that we have reached the end of the file. In the case of a parsing error, we catch an exception from the `io::error` namespace. There are exception types for different parsing fails. In the following example, we handle number parsing errors:

```
try {
  bool done = false;
  while (!done) {
    done = !read_row_help(
    std::make_index_sequence<std::tuple_size<RowType>::value>{}, row,
        csv_reader);
    if (!done) {
        categorical_column.push_back(std::get<4>(row));
        fill_values(std::make_index_sequence<columns_num - 1>{}, row,
            values);
    }
  }
} catch (const io::error::no_digit& err) {
  // ignore badly formatted samples
  std::cerr << err.what() << std::endl;
}
```

Also, notice that we moved only four values to our vector of doubles because the last column contains string objects that we put to another vector of categorical values.

Preprocessing CSV files

Sometimes, the data we have comes in a format that's incompatible with libraries we want to use. For example, the Iris dataset file contains a column that contains strings. Many machine learning libraries cannot read such values, because they assume that CSV files contain only numerical values that can be directly loaded to internal matrix representation.

So, before using such datasets, we need to preprocess them. In the case of the Iris dataset, we need to replace the categorical column containing string labels with numeric encoding. In the following code sample, we replace strings with distinct numbers, but in general, such an approach is a bad idea, especially for classification tasks. Machine learning algorithms usually learn only numerical relations, so a more suitable approach would be to use specialized encoding—for example, one-hot encoding. The code can be seen in the following block:

```
#include <fstream>
#include <regex>
...
std::ifstream data_stream("iris.data");
std::string data_string((std::istreambuf_iterator<char>(data_stream)),
                        std::istreambuf_iterator<char>());
data_string =
    std::regex_replace(data_string, std::regex("Iris-setosa"), "1");
data_string =
    std::regex_replace(data_string, std::regex("Iris-versicolor"), "2");
data_string =
    std::regex_replace(data_string, std::regex("Iris-virginica"), "3");
std::ofstream out_stream("iris_fix.csv");
out_stream << data_string;
```

We read the CSV file content to the `std::string` object with the `std::ifstream` object. Also, we use `std::regex` routines to replace string class names with numbers. Using the `regex` functions allows us to reduce code size and make it more expressive in comparison with the loop approach, which typically uses the `std::string::find()` and `std::string::replace()` methods. After replacing all categorical class names in the file, we create a new file with the `std::ofstream` object.

Reading CSV files with the Shark-ML library

Many machine learning frameworks already have routines for reading the CSV file format to their internal representations. In the following code sample, we show how to load a CSV file with the `Shark-ML` library to the `ClassificationDataset` object. The CSV parser in this library assumes that all values in a file have a numerical type only, so it is unable to read the original file with the Iris dataset we used in the previous example. However, in the previous section, we already fixed this problem by replacing string values with numeric ones, and we can use our new file named `iris_fix.csv`.

To read a CSV file with the `Shark-ML` library, we have to include corresponding headers, as follows:

```
#include <shark/Data/Csv.h>
#include <shark/Data/Dataset.h>
using namespace shark;
```

We can use the `importCSV()` method of the `ClassificationDataset` object to load the CSV data from a file. Notice that the last function's argument specifies which column in the dataset contains labels, as illustrated in the following code snippet:

```
ClassificationDataset dataset;
importCSV(dataset, "iris_fix.csv", LAST_COLUMN);
```

Then, we can use this object in machine learning algorithms provided by the `Shark-ML` library. Also, we can also print some statistics about the imported dataset, as follows:

```
std::size_t classes = numberOfClasses(dataset);
std::cout << "Number of classes " << classes << std::endl;
std::vector<std::size_t> sizes = classSizes(dataset);
std::cout << "Class size: " << std::endl;
for (auto cs : sizes) {
  std::cout << cs << std::endl;
}
std::size_t dim = inputDimension(dataset);
std::cout << "Input dimension " << dim << std::endl;
```

Reading CSV files with the Shogun library

The `Shogun` library also has functionality for reading CSV files, and it also interprets them as numerical matrices only. So, to load a CSV file as a dataset with the `Shogun` library, we need to preprocess it and replace string values with numeric ones, as we did in an earlier section. We can load the CSV file with the Iris dataset to the matrix object, and then use this matrix to initialize the `Shogun` library dataset objects for use in machine learning algorithms. First of all, we need to include the required headers and make definitions for the helper types, as follows:

```
#include <shogun/base/init.h>
#include <shogun/base/some.h>
#include <shogun/io/File.h>

using namespace shogun;
using DataType = float64_t;
using Matrix = shogun::SGMatrix<DataType>
```

Then, we define the `shogun::CCSVFile` object to parse the dataset file. The initialized `shogun::CCSVFile` object is used for loading values into a matrix object, as illustrated in the following code snippet:

```
auto csv_file = shogun::some<shogun::CCSVFile>("iris_fix.csv");
Matrix data;
data.load(csv_file);
```

To be able to use this data for machine learning algorithms, we need to split this matrix object into two parts: one will contain training samples, and the second one will contain labels. The Shogun CSV parser loads matrices in the column-major order. So, to make the matrix look like the original file, we need to transpose, as illustrated in the following code snippet:

```
Matrix::transpose_matrix(data.matrix, data.num_rows, data.num_cols);
Matrix inputs = data.submatrix(0, data.num_cols - 1); // make a view
inputs = inputs.clone(); // copy exact data
Matrix outputs = data.submatrix(data.num_cols - 1, data.num_cols);
        // make a view
outputs = outputs.clone(); // copy exact data
```

Now, we have our training data in the `inputs` matrix object and labels in the `outputs` matrix object. To be able to use the `inputs` object in the Shogun algorithms, we need to transpose it back, because Shogun algorithms expect that training samples are placed in matrix columns. To do this, we run the following code:

```
Matrix::transpose_matrix(inputs.matrix, inputs.num_rows, inputs.num_cols);
```

We can use these matrices for initializing the `shogun::CDenseFeatures` and the `shogun::CMulticlassLabels` objects, which we can eventually use for the training of machine learning algorithms. To do this, we run the following code:

```
auto features = shogun::some<shogun::CDenseFeatures<DataType>>(inputs);
auto labels =
shogun::wrap(new shogun::CMulticlassLabels(outputs.get_column(0)));
```

After initialization of these objects, we can print some statistics about training data, as follows:

```
std::cout << "samples num = " << features->get_num_vectors() << "\n"
 << "features num = " << features->get_num_features() << std::endl;
auto features_matrix = features->get_feature_matrix();
// Show first 5 samples
for (int i = 0; i < 5; ++i) {
    std::cout << "Sample idx " << i << " ";
    features_matrix.get_column(i).display_vector();
```

```
    }
    std::cout << "labels num = " << labels->get_num_labels() << std::endl;
```

Reading CSV files with the Dlib library

The `Dlib` library can load CSV files directly to its matrix type as the `Shogun` library does, but it does not require them to create a parser object. For this operation, we can use a simple C++ streaming operator and a standard `std::ifstream` object.

As a first step, we make the necessary includes, as follows:

```
include <Dlib/matrix.h>
using namespace Dlib;
```

Then, we define the `matrix` object and load data from the file, like this:

```
matrix<double> data;
std::ifstream file("iris_fix.csv");
file >> data;
std::cout << data << std::endl;
```

In the `Dlib` library, `matrix` objects are used for training machine learning algorithms directly, without the need to transform them into intermediate dataset types.

Reading JSON files with the RapidJSON library

Some datasets come with structured annotations and can contain multiple files and folders. An example of such a complex dataset is the **Common Objects in Context (COCO)** dataset. This dataset contains a text file with annotations for describing relations between objects and their structural parts. This widely-known dataset is used to train models for segmentation, object detection, and classification tasks. Annotations in this dataset are defined in the JSON file format. JSON is a widely used file format for objects' (entities') representations. It is just a text file with special notations for describing relations between objects and their parts. In the following code samples, we show how to work with this file format using the `RapidJSON` C++ library. However, we are going to use a more straightforward dataset that defines paper reviews. The authors of this dataset are Keith, B., Fuentes, E., & Meneses, C. (2017), and they made this dataset for their work titled *A Hybrid Approach for Sentiment Analysis Applied to Paper Reviews*. The following code sample shows a reduced part of this dataset:

```
{
    "paper": [
```

```
{
    "id": 1,
    "preliminary_decision": "accept",
    "review": [
        {
            "confidence": "4",
            "evaluation": "1",
            "id": 1,
            "lan": "es",
            "orientation": "0",
            "remarks": "",
            "text": "- El artículo aborda un problema contingente
                y muy relevante, e incluye tanto un diagnóstico
                nacional de uso de buenas prácticas como una solución
                (buenas prácticas concretas)...",
            "timespan": "2010-07-05"
        },
        {
            "confidence": "4",
            "evaluation": "1",
            "id": 2,
            "lan": "es",
            "orientation": "1",
            "remarks": "",
            "text": "El artículo presenta recomendaciones
                prácticas para el desarrollo de software seguro...",
            "timespan": "2010-07-05"
        },
        {
            "confidence": "5",
            "evaluation": "1",
            "id": 3,
            "lan": "es",
            "orientation": "1",
            "remarks": "",
            "text": "- El tema es muy interesante y puede ser de
                mucha ayuda una guía para incorporar prácticas de
                seguridad...",
            "timespan": "2010-07-05"
        }
    ]
},
...
]
}
```

There are two main approaches to parse and process JSON files, which is listed as follows:

- The first approach assumes the parsing of whole files at once and creating a **Document Object Model (DOM)**. The DOM is a hierarchical structure of objects that represents entities stored in files. It is usually stored in computer memory, and, in the case of large files, it can occupy a significant amount of memory.
- Another approach is to parse the file continuously and provide an **application program interface (API)** for a user to handle and process each event related to the file-parsing process. This second approach is usually called **Simple API for XML (SAX)**. Despite its name, it's a general approach that is used with non-XML data too.

Using a DOM for working with training datasets usually requires a lot of memory for structures that are useless for machine learning algorithms. So, in many cases, it is preferable to use the SAX interface. It allows us to filter irrelevant data and initialize structures that we can use directly in our algorithms. In the following code sample, we use this approach.

As a preliminary step, we define types for `paper/review` entities, as follows:

```
...
struct Paper {
  uint32_t id{0};
  std::string preliminary_decision;
  std::vector<Review> reviews;
};

using Papers = std::vector<Paper>;
...
struct Review {
  std::string confidence;
  std::string evaluation;
  uint32_t id{0};
  std::string language;
  std::string orientation;
  std::string remarks;
  std::string text;
  std::string timespan;
};
...
```

Then, we declare a type for the object, which will be used by the parser to handle parsing events. This type should be inherited from the `rapidjson::BaseReaderHandler` base class, and we need to override virtual handler functions that the parser will call when a particular parsing event occurs, as illustrated in the following code block:

```
#include <rapidjson/error/en.h>
#include <rapidjson/filereadstream.h>
#include <rapidjson/reader.h>
...
struct ReviewsHandler
 : public rapidjson::BaseReaderHandler<rapidjson::UTF8<>, ReviewsHandler> {
 ReviewsHandler(Papers* papers) : papers_(papers) {}
 bool Uint(unsigned u) ;
 bool String(const char* str, rapidjson::SizeType length, bool /*copy*/);
 bool Key(const char* str, rapidjson::SizeType length, bool /*copy*/);
 bool StartObject();
 bool EndObject(rapidjson::SizeType /*memberCount*/);
 bool StartArray();
 bool EndArray(rapidjson::SizeType /*elementCount*/);

 Paper paper_;
 Review review_;
 std::string key_;
 Papers* papers_{nullptr};
 HandlerState state_{HandlerState::None};
};
```

Notice that we made handlers only for objects and arrays parsing events, and events for parsing unsigned `int`/`string` values. Now, we can create the `rapidjson::FileReadStream` object and initialize it with a handler to the opened file and with a buffer object that the parser will use for intermediate storage. We use the `rapidjson::FileReadStream` object as the argument to the `Parse()` method of the `rapidjson::Reader` type object. The second argument is the object of the type we derived from `rapidjson::BaseReaderHandler`, as illustrated in the following code block:

```
auto file = std::unique_ptr<FILE, void (*)(FILE*)>(
     fopen(filename.c_str(), "r"), [](FILE* f) {
       if (f)
         ::fclose(f);
     });
  if (file) {
    char readBuffer[65536];
    rapidjson::FileReadStream is(file.get(), readBuffer,
        sizeof(readBuffer));
    rapidjson::Reader reader;
    Papers papers;
```

```
    ReviewsHandler handler(&papers);
    auto res = reader.Parse(is, handler);
    if (!res) {
      throw std::runtime_error(rapidjson::GetParseError_En(res.Code()));
    }
    return papers;
  } else {
    throw std::invalid_argument("File can't be opened " + filename);
  }
```

When there are no parsing errors, we will have an initialized array of `Paper` type objects. Consider, more precisely, the event handler's implementation details. Our event handler works as a state machine. In one state, we populate it with the `Review` objects, and in another one, with the `Papers` objects, and there are states for other events, as shown in the following code snippet:

```
enum class HandlerState {
  None,
  Global,
  PapersArray,
  Paper,
  ReviewArray,
  Review
};
```

We parse the unsigned `unit` values only for the `Id` attributes of the `Paper` and the `Review` objects, and we update these values according to the current state and the previously parsed key, as follows:

```
bool Uint(unsigned u) {
    bool res{true};
    try {
      if (state_ == HandlerState::Paper && key_ == "id") {
        paper_.id = u;
      } else if (state_ == HandlerState::Review && key_ == "id") {
        review_.id = u;
      } else {
        res = false;
      }
    } catch (...) {
      res = false;
    }
    key_.clear();
    return res;
}
```

String values also exist in both types of objects, so we do the same checks to update corresponding values, as follows:

```cpp
bool String(const char* str, rapidjson::SizeType length, bool /*copy*/) {
    bool res{true};
    try {
      if (state_ == HandlerState::Paper && key_ == "preliminary_decision")
{
        paper_.preliminary_decision = std::string(str, length);
      } else if (state_ == HandlerState::Review && key_ == "confidence") {
        review_.confidence = std::string(str, length);
      } else if (state_ == HandlerState::Review && key_ == "evaluation") {
        review_.evaluation = std::string(str, length);
      } else if (state_ == HandlerState::Review && key_ == "lan") {
        review_.language = std::string(str, length);
      } else if (state_ == HandlerState::Review && key_ == "orientation") {
        review_.orientation = std::string(str, length);
      } else if (state_ == HandlerState::Review && key_ == "remarks") {
        review_.remarks = std::string(str, length);
      } else if (state_ == HandlerState::Review && key_ == "text") {
        review_.text = std::string(str, length);
      } else if (state_ == HandlerState::Review && key_ == "timespan") {
        review_.timespan = std::string(str, length);
      } else {
        res = false;
      }
    } catch (...) {
      res = false;
    }
    key_.clear();
    return res;
}
```

The event handler for the JSON `key` attribute stores the `key` value to the appropriate variable, which we use to identify a current object in the parsing process, as follows:

```cpp
bool Key(const char* str, rapidjson::SizeType length, bool /*copy*/) {
    key_ = std::string(str, length);
    return true;
}
```

The `StartObject` event handler switches states according to the `current key` values and the previous state value. We base the current implementation on the knowledge of the structure of the current JSON file: there is no array of `Paper` objects, and each `Paper` object includes an array of reviews. It is one of the limitations of the SAX interface—we need to know the structure of the document to implement all event handlers correctly. The code can be seen in the following block:

```
bool StartObject() {
    if (state_ == HandlerState::None && key_.empty()) {
      state_ = HandlerState::Global;
    } else if (state_ == HandlerState::PapersArray && key_.empty()) {
      state_ = HandlerState::Paper;
    } else if (state_ == HandlerState::ReviewArray && key_.empty()) {
      state_ = HandlerState::Review;
    } else {
      return false;
    }
    return true;
}
```

In the `EndObject` event handler, we populate arrays of `Paper` and `Review` objects according to the current state. Also, we switch the current state back to the previous one by running the following code:

```
bool EndObject(rapidjson::SizeType /*memberCount*/) {
    if (state_ == HandlerState::Global) {
      state_ = HandlerState::None;
    } else if (state_ == HandlerState::Paper) {
      state_ = HandlerState::PapersArray;
      papers_->push_back(paper_);
      paper_ = Paper();
    } else if (state_ == HandlerState::Review) {
      state_ = HandlerState::ReviewArray;
      paper_.reviews.push_back(review_);
    } else {
      return false;
    }
    return true;
}
```

In the `StartArray` event handler, we switch the current state to a new one according to the current state value by running the following code:

```
bool StartArray() {
    if (state_ == HandlerState::Global && key_ == "paper") {
      state_ = HandlerState::PapersArray;
      key_.clear();
```

```
    } else if (state_ == HandlerState::Paper && key_ == "review") {
      state_ = HandlerState::ReviewArray;
      key_.clear();
    } else {
      return false;
    }
    return true;
  }
```

In the `EndArray` event handler, we switch the current state to the previous one based on our knowledge of the document structure by running the following code:

```
  bool EndArray(rapidjson::SizeType /*elementCount*/) {
    if (state_ == HandlerState::ReviewArray) {
      state_ = HandlerState::Paper;
    } else if (state_ == HandlerState::PapersArray) {
      state_ = HandlerState::Global;
    } else {
      return false;
    }
    return true;
  }
```

The vital thing in this approach is to clear the `current key` value after object processing. This helps us to debug parsing errors, and we always have actual information about the currently processed entity.

For small files, using the DOM approach can be preferable because it leads to less code and cleaner algorithms.

Writing and reading HDF5 files with the HighFive library

HDF5 is a highly efficient file format for storing datasets and scientific values. The `HighFive` library provides a higher-level C++ interface for the C library provided by the HDF Group. In this example, we propose to look at its interface by transforming the dataset used in the previous section to HDF5 format.

The main concepts of HDF5 format are groups and datasets. Each group can contain other groups and have attributes of different types. Also, each group can contain a set of dataset entries. Each dataset is a multidimensional array of values of the same type, which also can have attributes of different types.

Let's start with including required headers, as follows:

```
#include <highfive/H5DataSet.hpp>
#include <highfive/H5DataSpace.hpp>
#include <highfive/H5File.hpp>
```

Then, we have to create a file object where we will write our dataset, as follows:

```
HighFive::File file(file_name, HighFive::File::ReadWrite |
                              HighFive::File::Create |
                              HighFive::File::Truncate);
```

After we have a file object, we can start creating groups. We define a group of papers that should hold all paper objects, as follows:

```
auto papers_group = file.createGroup("papers");
```

Then, we iterate through an array of papers (as shown in the previous section) and create a group for each paper object with two attributes: the numerical `id` attribute and the `preliminary_decision` attribute of the string type, as illustrated in the following code block:

```
for (const auto& paper : papers) {
  auto paper_group =
      papers_group.createGroup("paper_" + std::to_string(paper.id));
  std::vector<uint32_t> id = {paper.id};
  auto id_attr = paper_group.createAttribute<uint32_t>(
      "id", HighFive::DataSpace::From(id));

  id_attr.write(id);
  auto dec_attr = paper_group.createAttribute<std::string>(
      "preliminary_decision",
      HighFive::DataSpace::From(paper.preliminary_decision));
  dec_attr.write(paper.preliminary_decision);
```

After we have created an attribute, we have to put in its value with the `write()` method. Notice that the `HighFive::DataSpace::From` function automatically detects the size of the attribute value. The size is the amount of memory required to hold the attribute's value. Then, for each `paper_group`, we create a corresponding group of reviews, as follows:

```
auto reviews_group = paper_group.createGroup("reviews");
```

We insert into each `reviews_group` a dataset of numerical values of `confidence`, `evaluation`, and `orientation` fields. For the dataset, we define the `DataSpace` (the number of elements in the dataset) of size 3 and define a storage type as a 32-bit integer, as follows:

```
std::vector<size_t> dims = {3};
 std::vector<int32_t> values(3);
 for (const auto& r : paper.reviews) {
     auto dataset = reviews_group.createDataSet<int32_t>(
     std::to_string(r.id), HighFive::DataSpace(dims));
     values[0] = std::stoi(r.confidence);
     values[1] = std::stoi(r.evaluation);
     values[2] = std::stoi(r.orientation);
     dataset.write(values);
 }
 }
```

After we have created and initialized all objects, the Papers/Reviews dataset in HDF5 format is ready. When the `file` object leaves the scope, its destructor saves everything to the secondary storage.

Having the file in the HDF5 format, we can consider the `HighFive` library interface for file reading. As the first step, we again create the `HighFive::File` object, but with attributes for reading, as follows:

```
HighFive::File file(file_name, HighFive::File::ReadOnly);
```

Then, we use the `getGroup()` method to get the top-level `papers_group` object, as follows:

```
auto papers_group = file.getGroup("papers");
```

We need to get a list of all nested objects in this group because we can access objects only by their names. We can do this by running the following code:

```
auto papers_names = papers_group.listObjectNames();
```

Using a loop, we iterate over all `papers_group` objects in the `papers_group` container, like this:

```
for (const auto& pname : papers_names) {
   auto paper_group = papers_group.getGroup(pname);
   ...
 }
```

For each `paper` object, we read its attributes, and the memory space required for the attribute value. Also, because each attribute can be multidimensional, we should take care of it and allocate an appropriate container, as follows:

```
std::vector<uint32_t> id;
paper_group.getAttribute("id").read(id);
std::cout << id[0];

std::string decision;
paper_group.getAttribute("preliminary_decision").read(decision);
std::cout << " " << decision << std::endl;
```

For reading datasets, we can use the same approach: get the `reviews` group, then get a list of dataset names, and, finally, read each dataset in a loop, as follows:

```
auto reviews_group = paper_group.getGroup("reviews");
auto reviews_names = reviews_group.listObjectNames();
std::vector<int32_t> values(2);
for (const auto& rname : reviews_names) {
  std::cout << "\t review: " << rname << std::endl;
  auto dataset = reviews_group.getDataSet(rname);
  auto selection = dataset.select(
      {1}, {2});  // or use just dataset.read method to get whole data
  selection.read(values);
  std::cout << "\t\t evaluation: " << values[0] << std::endl;
  std::cout << "\t\t orientation: " << values[1] << std::endl;
}
```

Notice that we use the `select()` method for the dataset, which allows us to read only a part of the dataset. We define this part with ranges given as arguments. There is the `read()` method in the dataset type to read a whole dataset at once.

Using these techniques, we can read and transform any HDF5 datasets. This file format allows us to work only with part of the required data and not to load the whole file to the memory. Also, because this is a binary format, its reading is more efficient than reading large text files.

Initializing matrix and tensor objects from C++ data structures

There are a variety of file formats used for datasets, and not all of them might be supported by libraries. For using data from unsupported formats, we might need to write custom parsers. After we read values to regular C++ containers, we usually need to convert them into object types used in the machine learning framework we use. As an example, let's consider the case of reading matrix data from files into C++ objects.

Eigen

Using the `Eigen` library, we can wrap a C++ array into the `Eigen::Matrix` object with the `Eigen::Map` type. The wrapped object will behave as a standard `Eigen` matrix. We have to parametrize the `Eigen::Map` type with the type of matrix that has the required behavior. Also, when we create the `Eigen::Map` object, it takes as arguments a pointer to the C++ array and matrix dimensions, as illustrated in the following code snippet:

```
std::vector<double> values;
...
auto x_data = Eigen::Map<Eigen::Matrix<double, Eigen::Dynamic,
                         Eigen::Dynamic, Eigen::RowMajor>>(values.data(),
                                                           rows_num,
                                                           columns_num );
```

Shark-ML

The `Shark-ML` framework has special adaptor functions that create wrappers for C++ arrays. These functions create objects that behave as regular `Shark-ML` matrices. To wrap a C++ container with adaptor functions, we have to pass a pointer to the data and corresponding dimensions as arguments, as illustrated in the following code snippet:

```
std::vector<float> data{1, 2, 3, 4};
auto m = remora::dense_matrix_adaptor<float>(data.data(), 2, 2);
auto v = remora::dense_vector_adaptor<float>(data.data(), 4);
```

Dlib

The `Dlib` library has the `Dlib::mat()` function for wrapping C++ containers into the `Dlib` matrix object. It also takes a pointer to the data and matrix dimensions as arguments, as illustrated in the following code snippet:

```
double data[] = {1, 2, 3, 4, 5, 6};
auto m2 = Dlib::mat(data, 2, 3);  // create matrix with size 2x3
```

Shogun

Using the `Shogun` library, we can use a particular constructor of the `SGMatrix` type to initialize it with the C++ array. It takes a pointer to the data and matrix dimensions, as illustrated in the following code snippet:

```
std::vector<double> values;
...
SGMatrix<float64_t> matrix(values.data(), num_rows, numcols);
```

Notice that all of these functions only make a wrapper for the original C++ array where the data is stored, and don't copy the values into a new location. If we want to copy values from a C++ array to a `matrix` object, we usually need to call a `clone()` method or an analog of it for the wrapper object.

After we have a matrix object for a machine learning framework we use, we can initialize other specialized objects for training machine learning algorithms. Examples of such objects are the `CDenseFeatures` noun for the `Shogun` library or the `CClassificationDataset` noun for the `Shark-ML` library.

Manipulating images with the OpenCV and Dlib libraries

Many machine learning algorithms are related to computer vision problems. Such tasks are object detection in images, segmentation, image classification, and others. To be able to deal with such tasks, we need instruments for working with images. We usually need routines to load images to computer memory, as well as routines for image processing. For example, the standard operation is image scaling, because many machine learning algorithms are trained only on images of a specific size. This limitation follows from the algorithm structure or is a hardware requirement. For example, we cannot load large images to the **graphics processing unit (GPU)** memory because of its limited size.

Also, hardware requirements can lead to a limited range of numeric types our hardware supports, so we will need to change initial image representation to one that our hardware can efficiently process. Also, machine learning algorithms usually assume a predefined layout of image channels, which can be different from the layout in the original image file.

Another type of image processing task is the creation of training datasets. In many cases, we have a limited number of available images for a specific task. However, to make a machine algorithm train well, we usually need more training images. So, the typical approach is to augment existing images. Augmentation can be done with operations such as random scaling, cropping parts of images, rotations, and other operations that can be used to make different images from the existing set.

In this section, we show how to use two of the most popular libraries for image processing for C++. OpenCV is a framework for solving computer vision problem that includes many ready-to-use implementations of computer vision algorithms. Also, it has many functions for image processing. Dlib is a computer vision and machine learning framework with a large number of implemented algorithms, as well as a rich set of image processing routines.

Using OpenCV

In the OpenCV library, an image is treated as a multidimensional matrix of values. There is a special cv::Mat type for this purpose. There are two base functions: the cv::imread() function loads the image, and the cv::imwrite() function writes the image to a file, as illustrated in the following code snippet:

```
#include <opencv2/opencv.hpp>
..
cv::Mat img = cv::imread(file_name);
cv::imwrite(new_file_name, img);
```

Also, there are functions to manage images located in a memory buffer. The cv::imdecode() function loads an image from the memory buffer, and the cv::imencode() function writes an image to the memory buffer.

Scaling operations in the OpenCV library can be done with the cv::resize() function. This function takes an input image, an output image, the output image size or scale factors, and an interpolation type as arguments. The interpolation type governs how the output image will look after the scaling. General recommendations are as follows:

- Use cv::INTER_AREA for shrinking.
- Use cv::INTER_CUBIC (slow) or cv::INTER_LINEAR for zooming.

- Use cv::INTER_LINEAR for all resizing purposes because it is fast.

The following code sample shows how to scale an image:

```
cv::resize(img, img, {img.cols / 2, img.rows / 2}, 0, 0, cv::INTER_AREA);
cv::resize(img, img, {}, 1.5, 1.5, cv::INTER_CUBIC);
```

There is no special function for image cropping in the OpenCV library, but the cv::Mat type overrides the operator() method, which takes a cropping rectangle as an argument and returns a new cv::Mat object with part of the image surrounded by the specified rectangle. Also, note that this object will share the same memory with the original image, so its modification will change the original image too. To make a deep copy of the cv::Mat object, we need to use the clone() method, as follows:

```
img = img(cv::Rect(0, 0, img.cols / 2, img.rows / 2));
```

Sometimes, we need to move or rotate an image. The OpenCV library supports translation and rotation operations for images through affine transformations. We have to manually—or with helper functions—create a matrix of 2D affine transformations and then apply it to our image. For the move (the translation), we can create such a matrix manually, and then apply it to an image with the cv::wrapAffine() function, as follows:

```
cv::Mat trm = (cv::Mat_<double>(2, 3) << 1, 0, -50, 0, 1, -50);
cv::wrapAffine(img, img, trm, {img.cols, img.rows});
```

We can create a rotation matrix with the cv::getRotationMatrix2D() function. This takes a point of origin and the rotation angle in degrees, as illustrated in the following code snippet:

```
auto rotm = cv::getRotationMatrix2D({img.cols / 2, img.rows / 2}, 45, 1);
cv::wrapAffine(img, img, rotm, {img.cols, img.rows});
```

Another useful operation is extending an image size without scaling but with added borders. There is the cv::copyMakeBorder() function in the OpenCV library for this purpose. This function has different options on how to create borders. It takes an input image, an output image, border sizes for the top, the bottom, the left and the right sides, type of the border, and border color. Border types can be one of the following:

- BORDER_CONSTANT—Make function fill borders with a single color.
- BORDER_REPLICATE—Make function fill borders with copies of last pixel values on each side (for example, *aaaaaa | abcdefgh | hhhhhhh*).

- `BORDER_REFLECT`—Make function fill borders with copies of opposite pixel values on each side (for example, *fedcba | abcdefgh | hgfedcb*).
- `BORDER_WRAP`—Make function fill borders by simulating the image duplication (for example, *cdefgh | abcdefgh | abcdefg*).

The following example shows how to use this function:

```
int top = 50;       // px
int bottom = 20;    // px
int left = 150;     // px
int right = 5;      // px
cv::copyMakeBorder(img, img, top, bottom, left, right,
                   cv::BORDER_CONSTANT | cv::BORDER_ISOLATED,
                   cv::Scalar(255, 0, 0));
```

When we are using this function, we should take care of the origin of the source image. The `OpenCV` documentation says: *If the source image is a part of a bigger image, the function will try to use the pixels outside of the ROI (short for region of interest) to form a border. To disable this feature and always do extrapolation, as if the source image was not a part of another image, use border type* `BORDER_ISOLATED`.

The function described previously is very helpful when we need to adapt training images of different sizes to the one standard image size used in some machine learning algorithms because, with this function, we do not distort target image content.

There is the `cv::cvtColor()` function to convert different color spaces in the `OpenCV` library. The function takes an input image, an output image, and a conversion scheme type. For example, in the following code sample, we convert the **red, green, and blue (RGB)** color space to a grayscaled one:

```
cv::cvtColor(img, img,
             cv::COLOR_RGB2GRAY);   // now pixels values are in range 0-1
```

Using Dlib

`Dlib` is another popular library for image processing. This library has different types used for math routines and image processing. The library documentation recommends using the `Dlib::array2d` type for images. The `Dlib::array2d` type is a template type that has to be parametrized with a pixel type. Pixel types in the `Dlib` library are defined with pixel-type traits. There are the following predefined pixel types: `rgb_pixel`, `bgr_pixel`, `rgb_alpha_pixel`, `hsi_pixel`, `lab_pixel`, and any scalar type can be used for the grayscaled pixels' representation.

We can use the `load_image()` function to load an image from disk, as follows:

```
#include <Dlib/image_io.h>
#include <Dlib/image_transforms.h>
using namespace Dlib;
...
array2d<rgb_pixel> img;
load_image(img, file_path);
```

For a scaling operation, there is the `Dlib::resize_image()` function. This function has two different overloads. One takes a single scale factor and a reference to an image object. The second one takes an input image, an output image, the desired size, and an interpolation type. To specify the interpolation type in the `Dlib` library, we should call special functions: the `interpolate_nearest_neighbor()`, the `interpolate_quadratic()`, and the `interpolate_bilinear()` functions. The criteria for choosing one of them is the same as ones that we discussed in the *Using OpenCV* section. Notice that the output image for the `resize_image()` function should be already preallocated, as illustrated in the following code snippet:

```
array2d<rgb_pixel> img2(img.nr() / 2, img.nc() / 2);
resize_image(img, img2, interpolate_nearest_neighbor());
resize_image(1.5, img);   // default interpolate_bilinear
```

To crop an image with `Dlib`, we can use the `Dlib::extract_image_chips()` function. This function takes an original image, rectangle-defined bounds, and an output image. Also, there are overloads of this function that take an array of rectangle bounds and an array of output images, as follows:

```
extract_image_chip(img, rectangle(0, 0, img.nc() / 2, img.nr() / 2), img2);
```

The `Dlib` library supports image transformation operations through affine transformations. There is the `Dlib::transform_image()` function, which takes an input image, an output image, and an affine transformation object. An example of the transformation object could be an instance of the `Dlib::point_transform_affine` class, which defines the affine transformation with a rotation matrix and a translation vector. Also, the `Dlib::transform_image()` function can take an interpolation type as the last parameter, as illustrated in the following code snippet:

```
transform_image(img, img2, interpolate_bilinear(),
                point_transform_affine(identity_matrix<double>(2),
                                       Dlib::vector<double, 2>(-50, -50)));
```

In case we only need to do a rotation, `Dlib` has the `Dlib::rotate_image()` function. The `Dlib::rotate_image()` function takes an input image, an output image, a rotation angle in degrees, and an interpolation type, as follows:

```
rotate_image(img, img2, -45, interpolate_bilinear());
```

There is no complete analog of a function for adding borders to images in the `Dlib` library. There are two functions: the `Dlib::assign_border_pixels()` and the `Dlib::zero_border_pixels()` for filling image borders with specified values. Before using these routines, we should resize the image and place the content in the right position. The new image size should include borders' widths. We can use the `Dlib::transform_image()` function to move the image content into the right place. The following code sample shows how to add borders to an image:

```
int top = 50;      // px
int bottom = 20;   // px
int left = 150;    // px
int right = 5;     // px
img2.set_size(img.nr() + top + bottom, img.nc() + left + right);
    transform_image(
        img, img2, interpolate_bilinear(),
        point_transform_affine(identity_matrix<double>(2),
                            Dlib::vector<double, 2>(-left/2, -top/2)));
```

For color space conversions, there exists the `Dlib::assign_image()` function in the `Dlib` library. This function uses color-type information from pixel-type traits we used for the image definition. So, to convert an image to another color space, we should define a new image with the desired type of pixels and pass it to this function. The following example shows how to convert the RGB image to a **blue, green, red (BGR)** one:

```
array2d<bgr_pixel> img_bgr;
assign_image(img_bgr, img);
```

To make a grayscale image, we can define an image with the `unsigned char` pixel type, as follows:

```
array2d<unsigned char> img_gray;
assign_image(img_gray, img);
```

Transforming images into matrix or tensor objects of various libraries

In most cases, images are represented in computer memory in an interleaved format, which means that pixel values are placed one by one in linear order. Each pixel value consists of several numbers representing a color. For example, for the RGB format, it will be three values placed together. So, in the memory, we will see the following layout for a 4 x 4 image:

```
rgb rgb rgb rgb
rgb rgb rgb rgb
rgb rgb rgb rgb
rgb rgb rgb rgb
```

For image processing libraries, such a value layout is not a problem, but many machine learning algorithms require different ordering. For example, it's a common approach for neural networks to take image channels separately ordered, one by one. The following example shows how such a layout is usually placed in memory:

```
r r r r    g g g g    b b b b
r r r r    g g g g    b b b b
r r r r    g g g g    b b b b
r r r r ,  g g g g ,  b b b b
```

So, often, we need to deinterleave image representation before passing it to some machine learning algorithm.

Moreover, we usually need to convert a color's value data type too. For example, OpenCV library users often use floating-point formats, which allows them to preserve more color information in image transformations and processing routines. The opposite case is when we use a 256-bit type for color channel information, but then we need to convert it to a floating-point type. So, in many cases, we need to convert the underlying data type to another one more suitable for our needs.

Deinterleaving in OpenCV

By default, when we load an image with the OpenCV library, it loads the image in the BGR format and with char as the underlying data type. So, we need to convert it to the RGB format, like this:

```
cv::cvtColor(img, img, cv::COLOR_BGR2RGB);
```

Then, we can convert the underlying data type to the `float` type, like this:

```
img.convertTo(img, CV_32FC3, 1/255.0);
```

Next, to deinterleave channels, we need to split them with the `cv::split()` function, like this:

```
cv::Mat bgr[3];
cv::split(img, bgr);
```

Then, we can place channels back to the `cv::Mat` object in the order we need with the `cv::vconcat()` function, which concatenates matrices vertically, as follows:

```
cv::Mat ordered_channels;
cv::vconcat(bgr[2], bgr[1], ordered_channels);
cv::vconcat(ordered_channels, bgr[0], ordered_channels);
```

There is a useful method in the `cv::Mat` type named `isContinuous` that allows us to check if the matrix's data is placed in memory with a single contiguous block. If that is true, we can copy this block of memory or pass it to the routines that work with plain C arrays.

Deinterleaving in Dlib

The `Dlib` library uses the `unsigned char` type for pixel color representation, and we can use floating-point types only for grayscaled images. The `Dlib` library stores pixels in the row-major order with interleaved channels and data is placed in memory continuously with a single block. There are no special functions in the `Dlib` library to manage image channels, so we cannot deinterleave them or mix them. However, we can use raw pixel data to manage color values manually. There are two functions in the `Dlib` library that can help us: the `image_data()` function to access raw pixel data, and the `width_step()` function to get the padding value.

The most straightforward approach to deinterleave the `Dlib` image object is using a loop over all pixels. In such a loop, we can split each pixel value into separate colors.

As a first step, we define containers for each of the channels, as follows:

```
auto channel_size = static_cast<size_t>(img.nc() * img.nr());
std::vector<unsigned char> ch1(channel_size);
std::vector<unsigned char> ch2(channel_size);
std::vector<unsigned char> ch3(channel_size);
```

Then, we read color values for each pixel with two nested loops over image rows and columns, like this:

```
size_t i{0};
for (long r = 0; r < img.nr(); ++r) {
  for (long c = 0; c < img.nc(); ++c) {
    ch1[i] = img[r][c].red;
    ch2[i] = img[r][c].green;
    ch3[i] = img[r][c].blue;
    ++i;
  }
}
```

The result is three containers with color channel values, which we can use separately. They are suitable to initialize grayscaled images for use in the image processing routines. Alternatively, we can use them to initialize a matrix-type object that we can process with linear algebra routines.

Normalizing data

Data normalization is a crucial preprocessing step in machine learning. In general, data normalization is a process that transforms multiscaled data to the same scale. Feature values in a dataset can have very different scales—for example, the height can be given in centimeters with small values, but the income can have large-value amounts. This fact has a significant impact on many machine learning algorithms. For example, if some feature values differ from values of other features several times, then this feature will dominate over others in classification algorithms based on the Euclidean distance. Some algorithms have a strong requirement for normalization of input data; an example of such an algorithm is the **Support Vector Machine** (**SVM**) algorithm. Neural networks also usually require normalized input data. Also, data normalization has an impact on optimization algorithms. For example, optimizers based on the **gradient descent** (**GD**) approach can converge much quicker if data has the same scale.

There are several methods of normalization, but from our point of view, the most popular are the standardization, the min-max, and the mean normalization methods.

Standardization is a process of making data to have a zero mean and a standard deviation equal to 1. The formula for standardized vector is $x' = \dfrac{x - \bar{x}}{\sigma}$, where x is an original vector, $\bar{x}$ is an average value of x calculated with the formula $\bar{x} = \dfrac{1}{n}\sum_{i=1}^{n} x_i$, and σ isthe standard deviation of x calculated with the formula $\sigma = \sqrt{\dfrac{\sum_{i=1}^{n}(x_i - \bar{x})^2}{n-1}}$.

Min-max normalization or **rescaling** is a process of making data fit the range of $[0,\ 1]$. We can do rescaling with the following formula:

$$x' = \frac{x - \min(x)}{\max(x) - \min(x)}$$

Mean normalization is used to fit data into the range $[-1,\ 1]$, so its mean becomes zero. We can use the following formula to do mean normalization:

$$x' = \frac{x - \bar{x}}{\max(x) - \min(x)}$$

Consider how we can implement these normalization techniques and which machine learning framework functions can be used to calculate them.

We assume that each row of this matrix $x = \begin{bmatrix} x_{1,1} & x_{1,2} & x_{1,3} \\ x_{2,1} & x_{2,1} & x_{2,3} \\ x_{3,1} & x_{3,2} & x_{3,3} \end{bmatrix}$ is one training sample, and the value in each column is the value of one feature of the current sample.

Normalizing with Eigen

There are no functions for data normalization in the `Eigen` library. However, we can implement them according to the provided formulas.

For the standardization, we first have to calculate the standard deviation, as follows:

```
Eigen::Array<double, 1, Eigen::Dynamic> std_dev =
  ((x.rowwise() - x.colwise().mean())
      .array()
      .square()
      .colwise()
      .sum() /
```

```
     (x_data.rows() - 1))
        .sqrt();
```

Notice that some reduction functions in the `Eigen` library work only with array representation; examples are the `sum()` and the `sqrt()` functions. We have also calculated the mean for each feature—we used the `x.colwise().mean()` function combination that returns a vector of `mean`. We can use the same approach for other feature statistics' calculations.

Having the standard deviation value, the rest of the formula for standardization will look like this:

```
Eigen::Matrix<double, Eigen::Dynamic, Eigen::Dynamic> x_std =
  (x.rowwise() - x.colwise().mean()).array().rowwise() /
  std_dev;
```

Implementation of `min_max` normalization is very straightforward and does not require intermediate values, as illustrated in the following code snippet:

```
Eigen::Matrix<double, Eigen::Dynamic, Eigen::Dynamic> x_min_max =
  (x.rowwise() - x.colwise().minCoeff()).array().rowwise() /
  (x.colwise().maxCoeff() - x.colwise().minCoeff()).array();
```

We implement the `mean` normalization in the same way, like this:

```
Eigen::Matrix<double, Eigen::Dynamic, Eigen::Dynamic> x_avg =
  (x.rowwise() - x.colwise().mean()).array().rowwise() /
  (x.colwise().maxCoeff() - x.colwise().minCoeff()).array();
```

Notice that we implement formulas in a vectorized way without loops; this approach is more computationally efficient because it can be compiled for execution on a GPU or the **central processing unit's (CPU's) Single Instruction Multiple Data (SIMD)** instructions.

Normalizing with Shogun

The `shogun::CRescaleFeatures` class in the `Shogun` library implements min-max normalization (or rescaling). We can reuse objects of this class for scaling different data with the same learned statistics. It can be useful in cases when we train a machine learning algorithm on one data format with applied rescaling, and then we use the algorithm for predictions on new data. To make this algorithm work as we want, we have to rescale new data in the same way as we did in the training process, as follows:

```
include <shogun/preprocessor/RescaleFeatures.h>
...
```

```
auto features = shogun::some<shogun::CDenseFeatures<DataType>>(inputs);
...
auto scaler = shogun::wrap(new shogun::CRescaleFeatures());
scaler->fit(features); // learn statistics - min and max values
scaler->transform(features); // apply scaling
```

To learn statistics values, we use the `fit()` method, and for features modification, we use the `transform()` method of the `CRescaleFeatures` class.

We can print updated features with the `display_vector()` method of the `SGVector` class, as follows:

```
auto features_matrix = features->get_feature_matrix();
for (int i = 0; i < n; ++i) {
  std::cout << "Sample idx " << i << " ";
  features_matrix.get_column(i).display_vector();
}
```

Some algorithms in the `Shogun` library can perform normalization of input data as an internal step of their implementation, so we should read the documentation to determine if manual normalization is required.

Normalizing with Dlib

The `Dlib` library provides functionality for feature standardization with the `Dlib::vector_normalizer` class. There is one limitation for using this class—we cannot use it with one big matrix containing all training samples. Alternatively, we should represent each sample with a separate vector object and put them into the C++ `std::vector` container, as follows:

```
std::vector<matrix<double>> samples;
...
vector_normalizer<matrix<double>> normalizer;
samples normalizer.train(samples);
samples = normalizer(samples);
```

We see that the object of this class can be reused, but it should be trained at first. The train method implementation can look like this:

```
matrix<double> m(mean(mat(samples)));
matrix<double> sd(reciprocal(stddev(mat(samples))));
for (size_t i = 0; i < samples.size(); ++i)
    samples[i] = pointwise_multiply(samples[i] - m, sd);
```

Notice that the `Dlib::mat()` function has different overloads for matrix creation from different sources. Also, we use the `reciprocal()` function that makes the $m' = \dfrac{1}{m}$ matrix if the *m* is the input matrix.

Printing matrices for debugging purpose in the `Dlib` library can be done with the simple streaming operator, as illustrated in the following code snippet:

```
std::cout << mat(samples) << std::endl;
```

Normalizing with Shark-ML

The `Shark-ML` library implements several normalization approaches. They are implemented as trainer classes for the `Normalizer` model type. We can reuse the `Normalizer` type after training on different data. There are the following normalization trainer classes:

- `NormalizeComponentsUnitInterval`—This class trains a normalization model that transforms data to fit a unit interval.
- `NormalizeComponentsUnitVariance`—This class trains a normalization model that transforms data to have unit variance and, optionally, a zero mean.
- `NormalizeComponentsWhitening`—This class trains a normalization model that transforms data to have zero mean and unit variance by default, but we can specify the target variance value.

The following code sample shows how to use a normalization model with a trainer:

```
#include <shark/Algorithms/Trainers/NormalizeComponentsUnitVariance.h>
#include <shark/Models/Normalizer.h>
...
Normalizer<RealVector> normalizer;
NormalizeComponentsUnitVariance<RealVector> normalizingTrainer(
    /*removeMean*/ true);
normalizingTrainer.train(normalizer, dataset.inputs());
dataset = transformInputs(dataset, normalizer);
```

After defining the model and the trainer objects, we have to call the `train()` method to learn statistics from the input dataset, and then we use the `transformInputs()` function to update the target dataset. We can print a `Shark-ML` dataset with the standard C++ streaming operator, as follows:

```
std::cout << dataset << std::endl;
```

Summary

In this chapter, we considered how to load data from CSV, JSON, and HDF5 formats. We saw how to convert the loaded data in the objects suitable to use in different machine learning frameworks. We used the libraries' APIs to convert raw C++ arrays into matrices and higher-level datasets' objects for machine learning algorithms. We looked at how to load and process images with the OpenCV and Dlib libraries. We became familiar with the data normalization process, which is very important for many machine learning algorithms. Also, we saw which normalization techniques are available in machine learning libraries, and we implemented some normalization approaches with linear algebra functions from the Eigen library.

In the following chapter, we will see how to measure a model's performance on different types of data. We will look at special techniques that help us to understand how the model describes the training dataset well and how it performs on new data. Also, we will learn different types of parameters machine learning models depend on, and see how to select the best combination of them to improve the model's performance.

Further reading

- THE HDF5® LIBRARY & FILE FORMAT: https://www.hdfgroup.org/solutions/hdf5/
- GitHub link for Fast C++ CSV Parser: https://github.com/ben-strasser/Fast-CPP-CSV-Parser
- OpenCV: https://opencv.org/
- Dlib C++ Library: http://Dlib.net/
- RapidJSON Documentation: http://rapidjson.org/
- The official page of the Iris dataset: https://archive.ics.uci.edu/ml/datasets/iris

3
Measuring Performance and Selecting Models

This chapter describes the bias and variance effects and their pathological cases, which usually appear when training **machine learning** (**ML**) models. For example, the high variance effect, also known as overfitting, is a phenomenon in ML where the constructed model explains the examples from the training set but works relatively poorly on the examples that did not participate in the training process. This occurs because while training a model, random patterns will start appearing that are normally absent from the general population. The opposite of overfitting is known as underfitting. This happens when the trained model becomes unable to predict patterns in new data or even in the training data. Such an effect can be the result of a limited training dataset or weak model design.

In this chapter, we will learn how to deal with overfitting by using regularization and discuss the different techniques we can use. We shall also consider the different model performance estimation metrics and how they can be used to detect training problems. Toward the end of this chapter, we shall look at how to find the best hyperparameters for a model by introducing the grid search technique and its implementation in C++.

The following topics will be covered in this chapter:

- Performance metrics for ML models
- Understanding the bias and variance characteristics
- Model selection with the grid search technique

Technical requirements

For this chapter, you will need the following:

- A modern C++ compiler with C++17 support
- CMake build system version >= 3.8
- `Dlib` library
- `Shogun-toolbox` library
- `Shark-ML` library
- `Plotcpp` library

The code files for this chapter can be found at the following GitHub repo: `https://github.com/PacktPublishing/Hands-On-Machine-Learning-with-CPP/tree/master/Chapter03`

Performance metrics for ML models

When we develop or implement a particular ML algorithm, we need to estimate how well it works. In other words, we need to estimate how well it solves our task. Usually, we use some numeric metrics for algorithm performance estimation. An example of such a metric could be a value of mean squared error that's been calculated for target and predicted values. We can use this value to estimate how distant our predictions are from the target values we used for training. Another use case for performance metrics is their use as objective functions in optimization processes. Some performance metrics are used for manual observations, though others can be used for optimization purposes too.

Performance metrics are different for each of the ML algorithms types. In `Chapter 1`, *Introduction to Machine Learning with C++*, we discussed that two main categories of ML algorithms exist: regression algorithms and classification algorithms. There are other types of algorithms in the ML discipline, but these two are the most common ones. This section will go over the most popular performance metrics for regression and classification algorithms.

Regression metrics

Regression task metrics are used to measure how close the predicted values are to the ground truth ones. Such measurements can help us estimate the prediction quality of the algorithm. Under regression metrics, there are four main metrics.

Mean squared error and root mean squared error

Mean squared error (**MSE**) is a widely used metric for regression algorithms to estimate their quality. It is an average squared difference between the predictions and ground truth values. This is given by the following equation:

$$MSE = \frac{1}{n}\sum_{i=1}^{n}(y_i - \hat{y}_i)^2$$

Here, n is the number of predictions and ground truth items, y_i is the ground truth value for the ith item, and $\hat{y}_i$ is the prediction value for the ith item.

MSE is often used as a target loss function for optimization algorithms because it is smoothly differentiable and is a convex function.

The **root mean squared error** (**RMSE**) metric is usually used to estimate performance, such as when we need to give bigger weights to higher errors (to penalize them). We can interpret this as the standard deviation of the differences between predictions and ground truth values. This is given by the following equation:

$$RMSE = \sqrt{\frac{1}{n}\sum_{i=1}^{n}(y_i - \hat{y}_i)^2}$$

The following sample shows an MSE calculation being performed with the `Shark-ML` library:

```
SquaredLoss<> mse_loss;
auto mse = mse_loss(train_data.labels(), predictions);
auto rmse = std::sqrt(mse);
```

In this example, we calculated the MSE value by using the `SquaredLoss` type object. Objects of the `SquaredLoss` type can be used functional objects, and they take the training labels (ground truth values) values and prediction values as arguments. The calculation result is a floating-point value. Notice that to get the RMSE value, we just take the square root of the result value.

The following example shows an MSE calculation being performed with the `Shogun` library:

```
auto mse_error = some<CMeanSquaredError>();
auto mse = mse_error->evaluate(predictions, train_labels);
```

In this example, we calculated the MSE value using the `CMeanSquareError` type object. The `evaluate` method takes the prediction values and training labels (ground truth values) as arguments and returns the floating-point value as the result.

Mean absolute error

Mean absolute error (**MAE**) is another popular metric that's used for quality estimation for regression algorithms. The MAE metric is a linear function with equally weighted prediction errors. This metric is more robust for outliers than RMSE. It is given by the following equation:

$$MAE = \frac{1}{n} \sum_{i=1}^{n} |y_i - \hat{y}_i|$$

The following example shows how to calculate MSE with the `Shark-ML` library:

```
AbsoluteLoss<> abs_loss;
auto mae = abs_loss(train_data.labels(), prediction);
```

The following example shows how to calculate MSE with the `Shogun` library:

```
auto mae_error = some<CMeanAbsoluteError>();
auto mae = mae_error->evaluate(predictions, train_labels);
```

R squared

The R squared metric is also known as a coefficient of determination. It is used to measure how good our independent variables (features from the training set) describe the problem and explain the variability of dependent variables (prediction values). The higher values tell us that the model explains our data well enough, while lower values tell us that the model makes many errors. This is given by the following equations:

$$SS_{\text{tot}} = \sum_i (y_i - \bar{y})^2$$

$$SS_{\text{res}} = \sum_i (y_i - \hat{y}_i)^2$$

$$R^2 = 1 - \frac{SS_{\text{res}}}{SS_{\text{tot}}} = 1 - \frac{\frac{1}{n} \sum_{i-1}^{n} (y_i - \hat{y}_i)^2}{\frac{1}{n} \sum_{i-1}^{n} (y_i - \bar{y}_i)^2}$$

Here, n is the number of predictions and ground truth items, y_i is the ground truth value for the ith item, and $\hat{y}_i$ is the prediction value for the ith item.

The only problem with this metric is that the value will always increase as we add new independent variables to the model. It may seem that the model begins to explain data better, but this isn't true – this value only increases if there are more training items. There are no out of the box functions for calculating this metric in the libraries we use. However, it is simple to implement it with linear algebra functions.

The following example shows how to calculate MSE with the `Shark-ML` library:

```
auto var = shark::variance(train_data.labels());
auto r_squared = 1 - mse / var(0);
```

Adjusted R squared

The adjusted R squared metric was designed to solve the previously described problem of the R squared metric. It is the same as the R squared metric but with a penalty for a large number of independent variables. The main idea is that if new independent variables improve the model's quality, the values of this metric increase; otherwise, they decrease. This can be given by the following equation:

$$R^2_{adj} = 1 - \frac{SS_{res}/(n-k)}{SS_{tot}/(n-1)} = 1 - (1 - R^2)\frac{k-1}{k-n-1}$$

Here, k is the number of parameters and n is the number of samples.

Classification metrics

Before we start discussing classification metrics, we have to introduce an important concept called the **confusion matrix**. Let's assume that we have two classes and an algorithm that assigns them to an object. Here, the confusion matrix will look like this:

	$y = 1$	$y = 0$
$\hat{y} = 1$	**True positive** (TP)	**False positive** (FP)
$\hat{y} = 0$	**False negative** (FN)	**True negative** (TN)

Here, $\hat{y}$ is the predicted class of the object and y is the ground truth label. The confusion matrix is an abstraction that we use to calculate different classification metrics. It gives us the number of items that were classified correctly and misclassified. It also provides us with information about the misclassification type. The false negatives are items that our algorithm incorrectly classified as negative ones, while the false positives are items that our algorithm incorrectly classified as positive ones. In this section, we'll learn how to use this matrix and calculate different classification performance metrics.

Accuracy

One of the most obvious classification metrics is accuracy:

$$accuracy = \frac{TP + TN}{TP + TN + FP + FN}$$

This provides us with a ratio of all positives predictions to all others. In general, this metric is not very useful because it doesn't show us the real picture in terms of cases with an odd number of classes. Let's consider a spam classification task and assume we have 10 spam letters and 100 non-spam letters. Our algorithm predicted 90 of them correctly as non-spam and classified only 5 spam letters correctly. In this case, accuracy will have the following value:

$$accuracy = \frac{5 + 90}{5 + 90 + 10 + 5} = 86.4$$

However, if the algorithm predicts all letters as non-spam, then its accuracy should be as follows:

$$accuracy = \frac{0 + 100}{0 + 100 + 0 + 10} = 90.9$$

This example shows that our model still doesn't work because it is unable to predict all the spam letters, but the accuracy value is good enough.

There is a class called `ZeroOneLoss` in the `Shark-ML` library that can be used to calculate the accuracy value for classification tasks. We can also use the objects of this class as a target loss function for learning purposes.

In the `Shogun` library, there's a class called `CAccuracyMeasure` that can be used to calculate the value of the accuracy.

Precision and recall

To estimate algorithm quality for each classification class, we shall introduce two metrics: *precision* and *recall*. The following diagram shows all the objects that are used in classification and how they have been marked according to the algorithm's results:

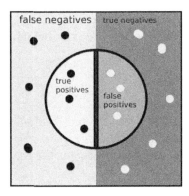

The circle in the center contains *selected elements* – the elements our algorithm predicted as positive ones.

Precision is proportional to the number of correctly classified items within selected ones. Another name for precision is *specificity*:

$$precision = \frac{TP}{TP + FP}$$

Recall is proportional to the number of correctly classified items within all ground truth positive items. Another name for the recall is *sensitivity*:

$$recall = \frac{TP}{TP + FN}$$

Let's assume that we are interested in the detection of positive items – let's call them relevant ones. So, we use the recall value as a measure of an algorithm's ability to detect relevant items and the precision value as a measure of an algorithm's ability to see the differences between classes. These measures do not depend on the number of objects in each of the classes, and we can use them for imbalanced dataset classification.

There are two classes in the Shogun library called CRecallMeasure and CPrecisionMeasure that we can use to calculate these measures. The Shark-ML and Dlib libraries do not contain functions to calculate these measures.

F-score

In many cases, it is useful to have only one metric that shows the classification's quality. For example, it makes sense to use some algorithms to search for the best hyperparameters, such as the GridSearch algorithm, which will be discussed later in this chapter. Such algorithms usually use one metric to compare different classification results after applying various parameter values during the search process. One of the most popular metrics for this case is the F-measure (or the F-score), which can be given as follows:

$$F_\beta = (1 + \beta^2) \cdot \frac{precision \cdot recall}{(\beta^2 \cdot precision) + recall}$$

Here, β is the precision metric weight. Usually, the β value is equal to one. In such a case, we have the multiplier value equal to 2, which gives us $F_1 = 1$ if the *precision = 1* and the *recall = 1*. In other cases, when the precision value or the recall value tends to be zero, the F-measure value will also decrease.

There's a class called CF1Measure in the Shogun library that we can use to calculate this metric. The Shark-ML and Dlib libraries do not have classes or functions to calculate the F-measure.

AUC–ROC

Usually, a classification algorithm will not return a concrete class identifier but a probability of an object belonging to some class. So, we usually use a threshold to decide whether an object belongs to a class or not. The most apparent threshold is 0.5, but it can work incorrectly in the case of imbalanced data (when we have a lot of values for one class and significantly fewer for other class).

One of the methods we can use to estimate a model without the actual threshold is the value of the **Area Under Receiver Operating Characteristic curve (AUC-ROC)**. This curve is a line from (0,0) to (1,1) in coordinates of the **True Positive Rate (TPR)** and the **False Positive Rate (FPR)**:

$$TPR = \frac{TP}{TP + FN}$$

$$FPR = \frac{FP}{FP + TN}$$

The TPR is equal to the recall, while the FPR value is proportional to the number of objects of negative class that were classified incorrectly (they should be positive). In an ideal case, when there are no classification errors, we have FPR = 0, TPR =1, and the area under the ROC curve will be equal to 1. In the case of random predictions, the area under the ROC curve will be equal to 0.5 because we will have an equal number of TP and FP classifications:

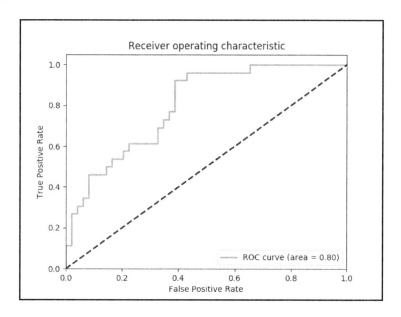

Each point on the curve corresponds to some threshold value. Notice that the curve's steepness is an essential characteristic because we want to minimize FPR, so we usually want this curve to tend to point (0,1). We can also successfully use the AUC-ROC metric with imbalanced datasets. There is a class called NegativeAUC in the Shark-ML library that can be used to calculate AUC-ROC. The Shogun library has a class called CROCEvaluation for the same purpose.

Log-Loss

The logistic loss function value (the Log-Loss) is used as a target loss function for optimization purposes. It is given by the following equation:

$$logloss = -\frac{1}{n} \cdot \sum_{i=1}^{l}(y_i \cdot log(\hat{y}_i) + (1 - y_i) \cdot log(1 - \hat{y}_i))$$

We can understand the Log-Loss value as the accuracy being corrected, but with penalties for incorrect predictions. This function gives significant penalties, even for single miss-classified objects, so all outlier objects in the data should be processed separately or removed from the dataset.

There is a class called `CrossEntropy` in the `Shark-ML` library that can be used to calculate this metric and use it as the loss function. The `Shogun` library has a class called `CLogLoss` for the same purpose.

Understanding the bias and variance characteristics

The bias and variance characteristics are used to predict model behavior. They are universal keywords. Before we go any further and describe what they mean, we should consider validation. Validation is a technique that's used to test model performance. It estimates how well the model makes predictions on new data. New data is data that we did not use for the training process. To perform validation, we usually divide our initial dataset in two or three parts. One part should contain most of the data and will be used for training, while other ones will be used to validate and test the model. Usually, validation is performed for iterative algorithms after one training cycle (often called an epoch). Alternatively, we perform testing after the overall training process.

The validation and testing operations evaluate the model on the data we have excluded from the training process, which results in the values of the performance metrics that we chose for this particular model. The values of these validation metrics can be used to estimate models, prediction error trends. The most crucial issue for validation and testing is that the data for them should always be from the same distribution as the training data.

Throughout the rest of this chapter, we will use the polynomial regression model to show different prediction behaviors. The polynomial degree will be used as a hyperparameter.

Bias

The bias is a prediction characteristic that tells us about the distance between model predictions and ground truth values. Usually, we use the term high bias or underfitting to say that model prediction is too far from the ground truth values, which means that the model generalization ability is weak. Consider the following graph:

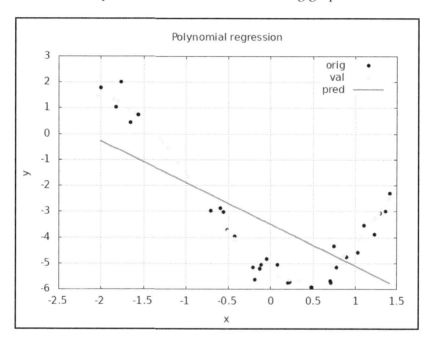

This graph shows the original values with black dots, the values used for validation with green dots, and a line that represents the polynomial regression model output. In this case, the polynomial degree is equal to one. We can see that the predicted values do not describe the original data at all, so we can say that this model has a high bias. Also, we can plot validation metrics for each training cycle to get more information about the training process and the model's behavior.

The following graph shows the MAE metric values for the training process of the polynomial regression model, where the polynomial degree is equal to one:

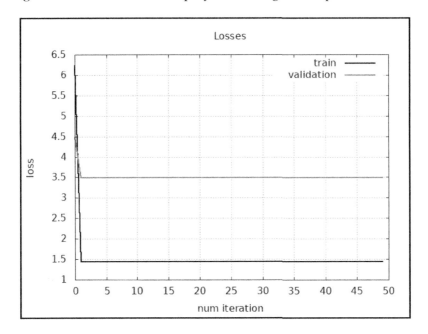

We can see that the lines for the metric values for the train and validation data are parallel and distant enough. Moreover, these lines do not change their direction after numerous training iterations. These facts also tell us that the model has a high bias because, for a regular training process, validation metric values should be close to the training values.

To deal with high bias, we can add more features to the training samples. For example, increasing the polynomial degree for the polynomial regression model adds more features; these all-new features describe the original training sample because each additional polynomial term is based on the original sample value.

Variance

Variance is a prediction characteristic that tells us about the variability of model predictions; in other words, how big the range of output values can be. Usually, we use the term high variance or overfitting in the case when a model tries to incorporate many training samples very precisely. In such a case, the model cannot provide a good approximation for new data but has excellent performance on the training data.

The following graph shows the behavior of the polynomial regression model, with the polynomial degree equal to 15:

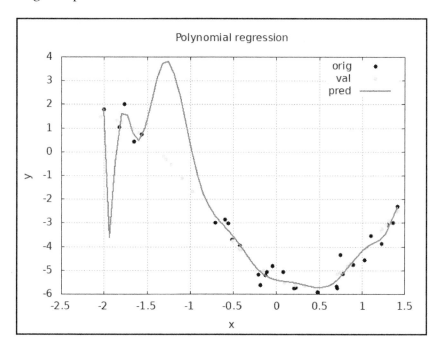

We can see that the model incorporates almost all the training data. Notice that the training data is indicated with black dots, while the data used for validation is indicated with green dots. We can see that these two sets of data are somehow distant from each other and that our model misses the validation data because of a lack of approximation. The following graph shows the MAE values for the learning process:

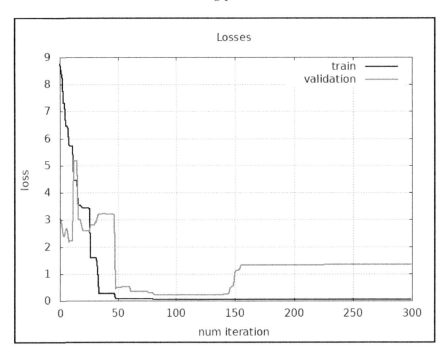

We can see that after approximately 75 learning iterations, the model began to predict training data much better, and the error value became lower. However, for the validation data, the MAE values began to increase. To deal with high variance, we can use special regularization techniques, which we will discuss in the following sections. We can also increase the number of training samples and decrease the number of features in one sample to reduce high variance.

The performance metrics plots we discussed in the preceding paragraphs can be drawn at the runtime of the training process. We can use them to monitor the training process to see high bias or high variance problems. Notice that for the polynomial regression model, MAE is a better performance characteristic than MSE or RMSE because squared functions average errors too much. Moreover, even a straight-line model can have low MSE values for such data because errors from both sides of the line compensate for each other.

Normal training

Consider the case of a training process where the model has balanced bias and variance:

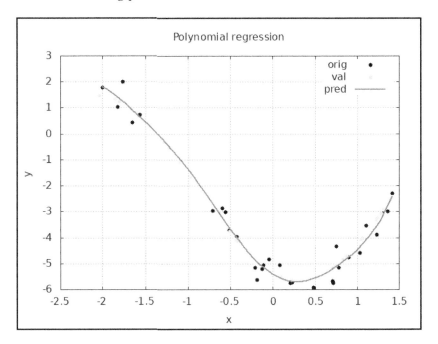

In this graph, we can see that the polynomial regression model's output for the polynomial degree is equal to eight. The output values are close to both the training data and validation data. The following graph shows the MAE values during the training process:

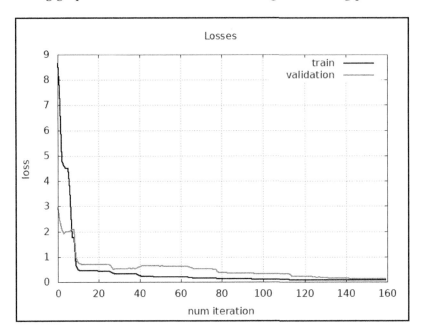

We can see that the MAE value decreases consistently and that the predicted values for the training and validation data become close to the ground truth values. This means that the model's hyperparameters were good enough to balance bias and variance.

Regularization

Regularization is a technique that's used to reduce model overfitting. There are two main approaches to regularization. The first one is known as training data preprocessing. The second one is loss function modification. The main idea of the loss function modification techniques is to add terms to the loss function that penalize algorithm results, thereby leading to significant variance. The idea of training data preprocessing techniques is to add more distinct training samples. Usually, in such an approach, new training samples are generated by augmenting existing ones. In general, both approaches add some prior knowledge about the task domain to the model. This additional information helps us with variance regularization. Therefore, we can conclude that regularization is any technique that leads to minimizing the generalization error.

L1 regularization – Lasso

L1 regularization is an additional term to the loss function:

$$loss + \lambda \sum_{j=1}^{p} |\beta_j|$$

This additional term adds the absolute value of the magnitude of parameters as a penalty. Here, λ is a regularization coefficient. Higher values of this coefficient lead to stronger regularization and can lead to underfitting. Sometimes, this type of regularization is called the **Least Absolute Shrinkage and Selection Operator** (**Lasso**) regularization. The general idea behind L1 regularization is to penalize less important features. We can think about it as a feature selection process.

There is a class called `shark::OneNormRegularizer` in the `Shark-ML` library whose instances can be added to trainers to perform L1 regularization. In the `Shogun` library, regularization is usually incorporated into the model (algorithm) classes and cannot be changed.

L2 regularization – Ridge

L2 regularization is also an additional term to the loss function:

$$loss + \lambda \sum_{j=1}^{p} \beta_j^2$$

This additional term adds a squared value of magnitude of parameters as a penalty. λ is also a coefficient of regularization. Its higher values lead to stronger regularization and can lead to underfitting. Another name for this regularization type is Ridge regularization. Unlike L1 regularization, this type does not have a feature selection characteristic. Instead, we can interpret it as a model smoothness configurator. In addition, L2 regularization is computationally more efficient for gradient descent-based optimizers because its differentiation has an analytical solution.

There is a class called `shark::TwoNormRegularizer` in the `Shark-ML` library whose instances can be added to trainers to perform L2 regularization. In the `Shogun` library, regularization is usually incorporated into the model (algorithm) classes and cannot be changed. An example of such an algorithm is the `CKernelRidgeRegression` class, which implements a linear regression model with L2 regularization.

Data augmentation

The data augmentation process can be treated as regularization because it adds some prior knowledge about the problem to the model. This approach is common in computer vision tasks such as image classification or object detection. In such cases, when we can see that the model begins to overfit and does not have enough training data, we can augment the images we already have to increase the size of our dataset and provide more distinct training samples. Image augmentations are random image rotations, cropping and translations, mirroring flips, scaling, and proportion changes.

Early stopping

Stopping the training process early can also be interpreted as a form of regularization. This means that if we detected that the model started to overfit, we can stop the training process. In this case, the model will have parameters once the training has stopped.

Regularization for neural networks

L1 and L2 regularizations are widely used to train neural networks and are usually called weight decay. Data augmentation also plays an essential role in the training processes for neural networks. There are other regularization methods that can be used neural networks. For example, Dropout is a particular type of regularization that was developed especially for neural networks. This algorithm randomly drops some neural network nodes; it makes other nodes more insensitive to the weights of other nodes, which means the model becomes more robust and stops overfitting.

Model selection with the grid search technique

It is necessary to have a set of proper hyperparameter values to create a good ML model. The reason for this is that having random values leads to controversial results and behaviors that are not expected by the practitioner. There are several approaches we can follow to choose the best set of hyperparameter values. We can try to use hyperparameters from the algorithms we have already trained that are similar to our task. We can also try to find some heuristics and tune them manually. However, this task can be automated. The grid search technique is the automated approach for searching for the best hyperparameter values. It uses the cross-validation technique for model performance estimation.

Cross-validation

We have already discussed what the validation process is. It is used to estimate the model's performance data that we haven't used for training. If we have a limited or small training dataset, randomly sampling the validation data from the original dataset leads to the following problems:

- The size of the original dataset is reduced.
- There is the probability of leaving data that's important for validation in the training part.

To solve these problems, we can use the cross-validation approach. The main idea behind it is to split the original dataset in such a way that all the data will be used for training and validation. Then, the training and validation processes are performed for all partitions, and the resulting values are averaged.

K-fold cross-validation

The most well-known method of cross-validation is K-fold cross-validation. The idea is to divide the dataset into K blocks of the same size. Then, we use one of the blocks for validation and the others for training. We repeat this process K times, each time choosing a different block for validation, and in the end, we average all the results. The data splitting scheme during the whole cross-validation cycle looks like this:

1. Divide the dataset into K blocks of the same size.
2. Select one of the blocks for validation and the remaining ones for training.
3. Repeat this process, making sure that each block is used for validation and the rest are used for training.
4. Average the results of the performance metrics that were calculated for the validation sets on each iteration.

The following diagram shows the cross-validation cycle:

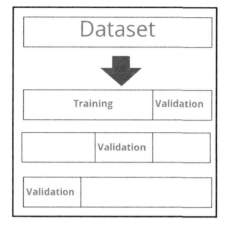

Grid search

The main idea behind the grid search approach is to create a grid of the most reasonable hyperparameter values. The grid is used to generate a reasonable number of distinct parameter sets quickly. We should have some prior knowledge about the task domain to initialize the minimum and maximum values for grid generation, or we can initialize the grid with some reasonable broad ranges. However, if the chosen ranges are too broad, the process of searching for parameters can take a long time and will require a significant amount of computational resources.

At each step, the grid search algorithm chooses a set of hyperparameter values and trains a model. After that, the training step algorithm uses the K-fold cross-validation technique to estimate model performance. We should also define a single model performance estimation metric for model comparison that the algorithm will calculate at each training step for every model. After completing the model training process with each set of parameters from every grid cell, the algorithm chooses the best set of hyperparameter values by comparing the metric's values and selecting the best one. Usually, the set with the smallest value is the best one.

Consider an implementation of this algorithm in different libraries. Our task is to select the best set of hyperparameters for the polynomial regression model, which gives us the best curve that fits the given data. The data in this example is some cosine function values with some random noise.

Shogun example

The Shogun library contains all the necessary classes for the grid search approach. We start by defining the base model. In the Shogun library, we can use the CKernelRidgeRegression class for this purpose. This class implements the polynomial regression model based on the SVM algorithm, and it uses kernels for precise model specialization. Therefore, we can use the polynomial kernel to simulate the polynomial regression model. Also, this kernel type has a configurable hyperparameter called the polynomial degree. The following code sample shows how to create the kernel object:

```
auto kernel = some<CPolyKernel>(/*cache size*/ 256, /*degree*/ 15);
kernel->init(x, x);
```

Notice that the kernel object requires our training data for initialization. Despite the fact that data normalization routines are usually incorporated into the algorithm pipelines in the Shogun library, the kernel object requires additional configuration, so we add the normalization object to the kernel object:

```
auto kernel_normaiizer = some<CSqrtDiagKernelNormalizer>();
kernel->set_normalizer(kernel_normaiizer);
```

The CKernelRidgeRegression class already has an implementation of L2 (Ridge) regularization. The following code sample shows us how to configure the initial values for the regularization coefficient:

```
float64_t tau_regularization = 0.00000001;
float64_t tau_regularization_max = 0.000001;
auto model = some<CKernelRidgeRegression>(tau_regularization, kernel, y);
```

Next, we define the cross-validation object for the grid search. There are several data splitting strategies in the Shogun library that we can use. We have selected the CStratifiedCrossValidationSplitting class here, which implements the same size folds (the data blocks) for splitting. In the following code snippet, we're dividing our dataset into five folds:

```
auto splitting_strategy = some<CStratifiedCrossValidationSplitting>(y, 5);
```

We chose MSE as a performance metric. The CMeanSquaredError class implements it:

```
auto evaluation_criterium = some<CMeanSquaredError>();
```

Then, we create the `CCrossValidation` object and initialize it with the instances of the splitting strategy object and the performance metric object:

```
auto cross_validation = some<CCrossValidation>(
    model, x, y, splitting_strategy, evaluation_criterium);
cross_validation->set_autolock(false);
cross_validation->set_num_runs(1);
```

We disabled `autolock` for the `CCrossValidation` object because this class does not support this option. This option can speed up the training process in cases where the model supports it. We also only configured one number of runs for the cross-validation process. We did this for demonstration purposes, but for real-life projects, it makes sense to run cross-validation several times.

To define a parameter grid, we use the `CModelSelectionParameters` class. An object of this class implements a node of a tree that contains a predefined range of values for one hyperparameter. The following code shows how to make a tree of such nodes, which will be an analog for the parameter grid:

```
auto params_root = some<CModelSelectionParameters>();
auto param_tau = some<CModelSelectionParameters>("tau");
params_root->append_child(param_tau);
param_tau->build_values(tau_regularization, tau_regularization_max,
                        ERangeType::R_LINEAR, tau_regularization_max);
auto param_kernel = some<CModelSelectionParameters>("kernel", kernel);
auto param_kernel_degree = some<CModelSelectionParameters>("degree");
param_kernel_degree->build_values(5, 15, ERangeType::R_LINEAR, 1);
param_kernel->append_child(param_kernel_degree);
params_root->append_child(param_kernel);
```

Notice that we used the `build_values()` method to generate a range of values. This method takes the minimum and the maximum values as arguments. After we've configured the cross-validation and the parameter grid (the tree, in our case) objects, we can initialize and run the grid search algorithm. The `CGridSearchModelSelection` class implements the grid search algorithm:

```
auto model_selection =
    some<CGridSearchModelSelection>(cross_validation, params_root);
auto best_parameters = model_selection->select_model(/*print_state*/
                                                      true);
best_parameters->apply_to_machine(model);
```

After instantiating the `CGridSearchModelSelection` object, we used the `select_model()` method to search for the best parameter values. Then, we applied them to the model with the `apply_to_machine()` method. The `Shogun` library does not guarantee that the model will be in a trained state with the best parameters after model selection. It will in a trained state with the last ones. Therefore, we need to retrain the model with the whole dataset to get better performance:

```
if (!model->train(x)) {
  std::cerr << "training failed\n";
}
```

After the final training process, the model is ready to be evaluated.

Shark-ML example

The `Shark-ML` library also contains classes for the grid search algorithm. However, it does not have an implementation of the polynomial regression model, so we implemented this model and the code in this example. First, we define the partitions of our dataset, which are five chunks of the same size. The following example shows how to use the `createCVSameSize` function for this purpose:

```
const unsigned int num_folds = 5;
CVFolds<RegressionDataset> folds =
    createCVSameSize<RealVector, RealVector>(train_data, num_folds);
```

As a result, we have the `CVFolds<RegressionDataset>` object, which contains our partition. Then, we initialize and configure our model. In the Shark-ML library, the model parameters are usually configured with trainer objects, which pass them to the model objects:

```
double regularization_factor = 0.0;
double polynomial_degree = 8;
int num_epochs = 300;
PolynomialModel<> model;
PolynomialRegression trainer(regularization_factor, polynomial_degree,
                             num_epochs);
```

Now that we have the trainer, model, and folds objects, we initialize the `CrossValidationError` object. As a performance metric, we used the `AbsoluteLoss` object, which implements the MAE metric:

```
AbsoluteLoss<> loss;
CrossValidationError<PolynomialModel<>, RealVector> cv_error(
                    folds, &trainer, &model, &trainer, &loss);
```

There is a class called `GridSearch` in the `Shark-ML` library that we can use to perform the grid search algorithm. We should configure the object of this class with the parameter ranges. There is the `configure()` method, which takes three containers as arguments. The first one specifies the minimum values for each parameter range, the second specifies the maximum values for each parameter range, and the third specifies the number of values in each parameter range. Notice that the order of the parameters in the range containers should be the same as how they were defined in the trainer class. Information about parameter order can be found in the appropriate documentation or source code:

```
GridSearch grid;
std::vector<double> min(2);
std::vector<double> max(2);
std::vector<size_t> sections(2);
// regularization factor
min[0] = 0.0;
max[0] = 0.00001;
sections[0] = 6;
// polynomial degree
min[1] = 4;
max[1] = 10.0;
sections[1] = 6;
grid.configure(min, max, sections);
```

After initializing the grid, we can use the `step()` method to perform the grid search for the best hyperparameter values; this method should be called only once. As in the previous example for the `Shogun` library, we have to retrain our model with the parameters we found:

```
grid.step(cv_error);

trainer.setParameterVector(grid.solution().point);
trainer.train(model, train_data)
```

Dlib example

The `Dlib` library also contains all the necessary functionality for the grid search algorithm. However, we should use functions instead of classes. The following code snippet shows the `CrossValidationScore` function's definition. This function performs cross-validation and returns the value of the performance metric:

```
auto CrossValidationScore = [&](const double gamma, const double c,
                                const double degree_in) {
  auto degree = std::floor(degree_in);
  using KernelType = Dlib::polynomial_kernel<SampleType>;
```

```
    Dlib::svr_trainer<KernelType> trainer;
    trainer.set_kernel(KernelType(gamma, c, degree));
    Dlib::matrix<double> result = Dlib::cross_validate_regression_trainer(
        trainer, samples, raw_labels, 10);
    return result(0, 0);
};
```

The `CrossValidationScore` function takes the hyperparameters that were set as arguments. Inside this function, we defined a trainer for a model with the `svr_trainer` class, which implements kernel ridge regression based on the SVM algorithm. We used the polynomial kernel, just like we did for the `Shogun` library example. After we defined the model, we used the `cross_validate_regression_trainer()` function to train the model with the cross-validation approach. This function splits our data into folds automatically, with its last argument being the number of folds. The `cross_validate_regression_trainer()` function returns the matrix, along with the values of different performance metrics. Notice that we do not need to define them because they are predefined in the library's implementation.

The first value in this matrix is the average MSE value. We used this value as a function result. However, there is no strong requirement for what value this function should return; the requirement is that the return value should be numeric and comparable. Also, notice that we defined the `CrossValidationScore` function as a lambda to simplify access to the training data container defined in the outer scope.

Next, we can search for the best parameters that were set with the `find_min_global` function:

```
auto result = find_min_global(
CrossValidationScore,
{0.01, 1e-8, 5}, // minimum values for gamma, c, and degree
{0.1, 1, 15}, // maximum values for gamma, c, and degree
max_function_calls(50));
```

This function takes the cross-validation function, the container with minimum values for parameter ranges, the container with maximum values for parameter ranges, and the number of cross-validation repeats. Notice that the initialization values for parameter ranges should go in the same order as the arguments that were defined in the `CrossValidationScore` function. Then, we can extract the best hyperparameters and train our model with them:

```
double gamma = result.x(0);
double c = result.x(1);
double degree = result.x(2);
using KernelType = Dlib::polynomial_kernel<SampleType>;
Dlib::svr_trainer<KernelType> trainer;
```

```
trainer.set_kernel(KernelType(gamma, c, degree));
auto descision_func = trainer.train(samples, raw_labels)
```

We used the same model definition as in the `CrossValidationScore` function. For the training process, we used all of our training data. The `train` method of the trainer object was used to complete the training process. The training result is a function that takes a single sample as an argument and returns a prediction value.

Summary

In this chapter, we discussed how to estimate the ML model's performance and what metrics can be used for such estimation. We considered different metrics for regression and classification tasks and what characteristics they have. We have also seen how performance metrics can be used to determine the model's behavior, and also looked at the bias and variance characteristics. We looked at some high bias (underfitting) and high variance (overfitting) problems and considered how to solve them. We also learned about the regularization approaches, which are often used to deal with overfitting. We then studied what validation is and how it is used in the cross-validation technique. We saw that the cross-validation technique allows us to estimate model performance while training limited data. In the last section, we combined an evaluation metric and cross-validation in the grid search algorithm, which we can use to select the best set of hyperparameters for our model.

In the next chapter, we'll learn about the ML algorithms we can use to solve concrete problems. The next topic we will discuss in depth is clustering – the procedure of splitting the original set of objects into groups classified by properties. We will look at different clustering approaches and their characteristics.

Further reading

- Choosing the Right Metric for Evaluating Machine Learning Models—Part 1: `https://medium.com/usf-msds/choosing-the-right-metric-for-machine-learning-models-part-1-a99d7d7414e4`
- Understand Regression Performance Metrics: `https://becominghuman.ai/understand-regression-performance-metrics-bdb0e7fcc1b3`
- Classification Performance Metrics: `https://nlpforhackers.io/classification-performance-metrics/`

- REGULARIZATION: An important concept in Machine Learning: `https://towardsdatascience.com/regularization-an-important-concept-in-machine-learning-5891628907ea`

- An Overview of Regularization Techniques in Deep Learning (with Python code): `https://www.analyticsvidhya.com/blog/2018/04/fundamentals-deep-learning-regularization-techniques`

- Understanding the Bias-Variance Tradeoff: `https://towardsdatascience.com/understanding-the-bias-variance-tradeoff-165e6942b229`

- Deep Learning: Overfitting: `https://towardsdatascience.com/deep-learning-overfitting-846bf5b35e24`

- A Gentle Introduction to k-fold Cross-Validation: `https://machinelearningmastery.com/k-fold-cross-validation/`

Section 2: Machine Learning Algorithms

In this section, we'll show you how to implement different well-known machine learning models (algorithms) using a variety of C++ frameworks.

This section comprises the following chapters:

- Chapter 4, *Clustering*
- Chapter 5, *Anomaly Detection*
- Chapter 6, *Dimensionality Reduction*
- Chapter 7, *Classification*
- Chapter 8, *Recommender Systems*
- Chapter 9, *Ensemble Learning*

4
Clustering

Clustering is an unsupervised machine learning method that is used for splitting the original dataset of objects into groups classified by properties. An object in machine learning is usually treated as a point in the multidimensional metric space. Every space dimension corresponds to an object property (feature), and the metric is a function of the values of these properties. Depending on the types of dimensions in this space, which can be both numerical and categorical, we choose the type of clustering algorithm and specific metric function. This choice depends on the nature of different object properties' types.

The main difference between clustering and classification is an undefined set of target groups, which is determined by the clustering algorithm. The set of target groups (clusters) is the algorithm's result.

We can split cluster analysis into the following phases:

- Selecting objects for clustering
- Determining the set of object properties that we will use for the metric
- Normalizing property values
- Calculating the metric
- Identifying distinct groups of objects based on metric values

After the analysis of clustering results, some correction may be required for the selected metric of the chosen algorithm.

We can use clustering for various real-world tasks, including the following:

- Splitting news into several categories for advertisers
- Identifying customer groups by their preferences for market analysis
- Identifying plant and animal groups for biological studies
- Identifying and categorizing properties for city planning and management
- Detecting earthquake epicenter clusters to identify danger zones
- Categorizing groups of insurance policyholders for risk management

- Categorizing books in libraries
- Searching for hidden structural similarities in the data

The following topics will be covered in this chapter:

- Measuring distance in clustering
- Types of clustering algorithms
- Examples of using the `Shogun` library for dealing with the clustering task samples
- Examples of using the `Shark-ML` library for dealing with the clustering task samples
- Examples of using the `Dlib` library for dealing with the clustering task samples
- Plotting data with C++

Technical requirements

The required technologies and installations for this chapter include the following:

- Modern C++ compiler with C++17 support
- CMake build system version >= 3.8
- `Dlib` library installation
- `Shogun-toolbox` library installation
- `Shark-ML` library installation
- `plotcpp` library installation

The code files for this chapter can be found at the following GitHub repo: `https://github.com/PacktPublishing/Hands-On-Machine-Learning-with-CPP/tree/master/Chapter04`

Measuring distance in clustering

A metric or a distance measure is an essential concept in clustering because it is used to determine the similarity between objects. However, before applying a distance measure to objects, we have to make a vector of object characteristics; usually, this is a set of numerical values such as human height or weight. Also, some algorithms can work with categorical object features (or characteristics). The standard practice is to normalize feature values. Normalization ensures that each feature gives the same impact in a distance measure calculation. There are many distance measure functions that can be used in the scope of the clustering task. The most popular ones used for numerical properties are Euclidean distance, Squared Euclidean distance, Manhattan distance, and Chebyshev distance. The following subsections describe them in detail.

Euclidean distance

Euclidean distance is the most widely used distance measure. In general, this is a geometric distance in the multidimensional space. Here is the formula for Euclidean distance:

$$\delta(x, \bar{x}) = \sqrt{\sum_i^n (x_i - \bar{x}_i)^2}$$

Squared Euclidean distance

Squared Euclidean distance has the same properties as Euclidean distance, but it also adds more significance (weight) to the distant values than to closer ones. Here is the formula for Squared Euclidean distance:

$$\delta(x, \bar{x}) = \sum_i^n (x_i - \bar{x}_i)^2$$

Manhattan distance

Manhattan distance is an average difference by coordinates. In most cases, its value gives the same clustering results as Euclidean distance. However, it reduces the significance (weight) of the distant values (outliers). Here is the formula for Manhattan distance:

$$\delta(x, \bar{x}) = \sum_i^n |x_i - \bar{x}_i|$$

Chebyshev distance

Chebyshev distance can be useful when we need to classify two objects as different when they differ only by one of the coordinates. Here is the formula for Chebyshev distance:

$$\delta(x, \bar{x}) = \max(|x_i - \bar{x}_i|)$$

The following diagram displays the differences between the various distances:

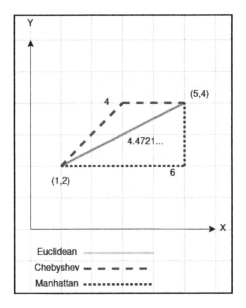

We can see that *Manhattan* distance is the sum of the distances in both dimensions, like walking along city blocks. *Euclidean* distance is just the length of a straight line. *Chebyshev* distance is a more flexible alternative to *Manhattan* distance because diagonal moves are also taken into account.

In the current section, we became familiar with the main clustering concept, which is a distance measure. In the following section, we will discuss various types of clustering algorithms.

Types of clustering algorithms

There are different types of clustering, which we can classify into the following groups: partition-based, spectral, hierarchical, density-based, and model-based. The partition-based group of clustering algorithms can be logically divided into distance-based methods and ones based on graph theory.

Partition-based clustering algorithms

The partition-based methods use a similarity measure to combine objects into groups. A practitioner usually selects the similarity measure for such kinds of algorithms by themself, using prior knowledge about a problem or heuristics to select the measure properly. Sometimes, several measures need to be tried with the same algorithm to choose the best one. Also, partition-based methods usually require either the number of desired clusters or a threshold that regulates the number of output clusters to be explicitly specified.

Distance-based clustering algorithms

The most known representatives of this family of methods are the k-means and k-medoids algorithms. They take the *k* input parameter and divide the data space into *k* clusters, such that the similarity between objects in one cluster is maximal. Also, they minimize the similarity between objects of different clusters. The similarity value is calculated as the distance from the object to the cluster center. The main difference between these methods lies in the way the cluster center is defined.

With the k-means algorithm, the similarity is proportional to the distance to the cluster center of mass. The cluster center of mass is the average value of cluster objects' coordinates in the data space. The k-means algorithm can be briefly described with the following steps. At first, we select *k* random objects and define each of them as a cluster prototype that represents the cluster's center of mass. Then, remaining objects are attached to the cluster with greater similarity. After that, the center of mass of each cluster is recalculated. For each obtained partition, a particular evaluation function is calculated, the values of which at each step form a converging series. The process continues until the specified series converges to its limit value.

In other words, moving objects from one cluster to another cluster ends when the clusters remain unchanged. Minimizing the evaluation function allows the resulting clusters to be as compact and separate as possible. The k-means method works well when clusters are compact *clouds* that are significantly separated from each other. It is useful for processing large amounts of data but is not applicable for detecting clusters of non-convex shapes or clusters with very different sizes. Moreover, the method is susceptible to noise and isolated points, since even a small number of such points can significantly affect the calculation of the center mass of the cluster.

To reduce the influence of noise and isolated points on the clustering result, the k-medoids algorithm, in contrast to the k-means algorithm, uses one of the cluster objects (named representative object) as the center of the cluster. As in the k-means method, k representative objects are selected at random. Each of the remaining objects is combined into a cluster with the nearest representative object. Then, each representative object is iteratively replaced with an arbitrary unrepresentative object from the data space. The replacement process continues until the quality of the resulting clusters improves. The clustering quality is determined by the sum of deviations between objects and the representative object of the corresponding cluster, which the method tries to minimize. Thus, the iterations continue until the representative object in each of clusters becomes the medoid. A medoid is the object closest to the center of the cluster. The algorithm is poorly scalable for processing large amounts of data, but this problem is solved by the **CLARANS (Clustering Large Applications based on RANdomized Search)** algorithm, which complements the k-medoids method. For multidimensional clustering, the **PROCLUS (Projected Clustering)** algorithm is constructed.

Graph theory-based clustering algorithms

The essence of algorithms based on the graph theory is to represent target objects in graph form. Graph vertices correspond to objects, and the edge weights are equal to the distance between vertices. The advantages of graph clustering algorithms are their excellent visibility, relative ease of implementation, and their ability to make various improvements based on geometrical considerations. The main algorithms based on graph theory are the algorithm for selecting connected components, the algorithm for constructing the minimum spanning tree, and the multilayer clustering algorithm.

The algorithm for selecting connected components is based on the R input parameter, and the algorithm removes all edges in the graph with distances greater than R. Only the closest pairs of objects remain connected. The algorithm's goal is to find the R value at which the graph collapses into several connected components. The resulting components are clusters. For the selection of the R parameter, a histogram of the distribution of pairwise distances is usually constructed. For problems with a well-defined cluster data structure, there will be two peaks in the histogram—one corresponds to in-cluster distances and the second to inter-cluster distances. The R parameter is selected from the minimum zone between these peaks. Managing the number of clusters using the distance threshold can be difficult.

The minimum spanning tree algorithm first builds a minimal spanning tree on the graph, and then successively removes the edges with the highest weight. The following diagram shows the minimum spanning tree obtained for nine objects:

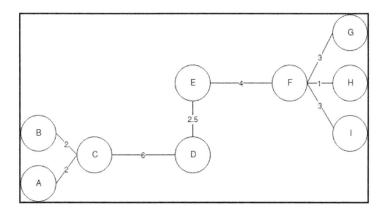

By removing the link between C and D, with a length of 6 units (the edge with the maximum distance), we obtain two clusters: {A, B, C} and {D, E, F, G, H, I}. We can divide the second cluster into two more clusters by removing the edge *EF*, which has a length of 4 units.

The multilayer clustering algorithm is based on identifying connected components of a graph at some level of distance between objects (vertices). The threshold *C* defines the distance level—for example, if the distance between objects is $0 \leq \delta(x, \bar{x}) \leq 1$, then $0 \leq c \leq 1$.

The layer clustering algorithm generates a sequence of sub-graphs of the graph *G* that reflect the hierarchical relationships between clusters $G^0 \subseteq G^1 \subseteq \ldots \subseteq G^m$, where the following applies:

- $G^t = (V, E^t)$: A sub-graph on the c^t level
- $E^t = e_{ij} \in E : \delta_{ij} \leq c^t$
- c^t: The tth threshold of distance
- *m*: The number of hierarchy levels
- $G^0 = (V, o)$, o: An empty set of graph edges, when $t^0 = 1$
- $G^m = G$: A graph of objects without thresholds on distance, when $t^m = 1$

By changing the $c^0, \ldots, c^m$ distance thresholds, where $0 = c^0 < c^1 < \ldots < c^m = 1$, it is possible to control the hierarchy depth of the resulting clusters. Thus, a multilayer clustering algorithm can create both flat and hierarchical data partitioning.

Spectral clustering algorithms

Spectral clustering refers to all methods that divide a set of data into clusters using the eigenvectors of the adjacency matrix of a graph or other matrices derived from it. An adjacency matrix describes a complete graph with vertices in objects and edges between each pair of objects with a weight corresponding to the degree of similarity between these vertices. Spectral clustering is a transformation of the initial set of objects into a set of points in space whose coordinates are elements of eigenvectors. The formal name of such a task is the **normalized cuts problem**. The resulting set of points is then clustered using standard methods—for example, with the k-means algorithm. Changing the representation created by eigenvectors allows us to set the properties of the original set of clusters more clearly. Thus, spectral clustering can separate points that cannot be separated by applying k-means—for example, when the k-means method gets a convex set of points. The main disadvantage of spectral clustering is its cubic computational complexity and quadratic memory requirements.

Hierarchical clustering algorithms

Among the algorithms of hierarchical clustering, there are two main types: bottom-up- and top-down-based algorithms. Top-down algorithms work on the next principle: at the beginning, all objects are placed in one cluster, which is then divided into smaller and smaller clusters. Bottom-up algorithms are more common than top-down ones. They place each object in a separate cluster at the beginning of the work, and then merge clusters into larger ones until all the objects in the dataset are contained in the one cluster, building a system of nested partitions. The results of such algorithms are usually presented in tree form, called a dendrogram. A classic example of such a tree is the tree of life, which describes the classification of animals and plants.

The main problem of hierarchical methods is the difficulty of determining the stop condition in such a way as to isolate natural clusters and, at the same time, prevent their excessive splitting. Another problem with hierarchical clustering methods is choosing the point of separation or merging of clusters. This choice is critical because after splitting or merging clusters at each subsequent step, the method will operate only on newly formed clusters. Therefore, the wrong choice of a merge or split point at any step can lead to poor-quality clustering. Also, hierarchical methods cannot be applied to large datasets, because deciding whether to divide or merge clusters requires a large number of objects and clusters to be analyzed, which leads to a significant computational complexity of the method.

There are several metrics or linkage criteria for cluster union used in hierarchical clustering methods, listed as follows:

- **Single linkage** (nearest neighbor distance): In this method, the distance between the two clusters is determined by the distance between the two closest objects (nearest neighbors) in different clusters. The resulting clusters tend to chain together.

- **Complete linkage** (distance between the most distant neighbors): In this method, the distances between clusters are determined by the largest distance between any two objects in different clusters (that is, the most distant neighbors). This method usually works very well when objects come from separate groups. If the clusters are elongated or their natural type is *chained*, then this method is unsuitable.

- **Unweighted pairwise mean linkage**: In this method, the distance between two different clusters is calculated as an average distance between all pairs of objects in them. This method is useful when objects form different groups, but it works equally well in the case of elongated (chained-type) clusters.

- **Weighted pairwise mean linkage**: This method is identical to the unweighted pairwise mean method, except that the size of the corresponding clusters (the number of objects contained in them) is used as a weighting factor in the calculations. Therefore, this method should be used when we assume unequal cluster sizes.

- **Weighted centroid linkage**: In this method, the distance between two clusters is defined as the distance between their centers of mass.

- **Weighted centroid linkage (median)**: This method is identical to the previous one, except that the calculations use weights for the distance measured between cluster sizes. Therefore, if there are significant differences in cluster sizes, this method is preferable to the previous one.

The following diagram displays a hierarchical clustering dendrogram:

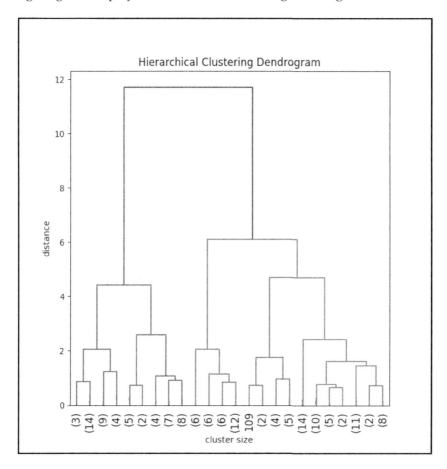

The preceding diagram shows an example of a dendrogram for hierarchical clustering, and you can see how the number of clusters depends on the distance between objects. Larger distances lead to a smaller number of clusters.

Density-based clustering algorithms

In density-based methods, clusters are considered as regions where the multiple objects' density is high, which are separated by regions with a low density of objects.

The **DBSCAN (Density-Based Spatial Clustering of Applications with Noise)** algorithm is one of the first density clustering algorithms. The basis of this algorithm is several statements, detailed as follows:

- The ϵ- neighborhood of an object is a neighborhood of the ϵ radius of an object.
- The root object is an object whose ϵ- neighborhood contains a minimum non-zero number of objects. Assume that this minimum number equals to a predefined value named *MinPts*.
- The p object is directly densely accessible from the q object if p is in the ϵ- neighborhood of q and q is the root object.
- The p object is densely accessible from the q object for the given ϵ and *MinPts* if there is a sequence of $p_1, \cdots, p_n$ objects, where $p_1 = q$ and $p_n = p$, such that $p_i + 1$ is directly densely accessible from p_i, $1 \leq i \leq n$.
- The p object is densely connected to the q object for the given ϵ and *MinPts* if there is an o object such that p and q are densely accessible from o.

The DBSCAN algorithm checks the neighborhood of each object to search for clusters. If the ϵ- neighborood of the p object contains more points than *MinPts*, then a new cluster is created with the p object as a root object. DBSCAN then iteratively collects objects directly densely accessible from root objects, which can lead to the union of several densely accessible clusters. The process ends when no new objects can be added to any cluster.

Unlike the partition-based methods, DBSCAN does not require the number of clusters to be specified in advance; it only requires the values of the ϵ and *MinPts* parameters, which directly affect the result of clustering. The optimal values of these parameters are difficult to determine, especially for multidimensional data spaces. Also, the distribution of data in such spaces is often asymmetrical, which makes it impossible to use global density parameters for their clustering. For clustering multidimensional data spaces, there is the **SUBCLU (Subspace Clustering)** algorithm, which is based on the DBSCAN algorithm.

Model-based clustering algorithms

Model-based algorithms assume that there is a particular mathematical model of the cluster in the data space and try to maximize the likelihood of this model and the available data. Often, this uses the apparatus of mathematical statistics.

The **EM (Expectation–Maximization)** algorithm assumes that the dataset can be modeled using a linear combination of multidimensional normal distributions. Its purpose is to estimate distribution parameters that maximize the likelihood function used as a measure of model quality. In other words, it assumes that the data in each cluster obeys a particular distribution law—namely, the normal distribution. With this assumption, it is possible to determine the optimal parameters of the distribution law—the mean and variance at which the likelihood function is maximal. Thus, we assume that any object belongs to all clusters, but with a different probability. Then, the task will be to fit the set of distributions to the data and then to determine the probabilities of the object belonging to each cluster. The object should be assigned to the cluster for which this probability is higher than the others.

The EM algorithm is simple and easy to implement. It is not sensitive to isolated objects and quickly converges in the case of successful initialization. However, it requires us to specify the k number of clusters, which implies a *priori* knowledge about the data. Also, if the initialization failed, the convergence of the algorithm may be slow, or we might obtain a poor-quality result. Such algorithms do not apply to high dimensionality spaces since, in this case, it is complicated to assume a mathematical model for the distribution of data in this space.

In this section, we discussed various clustering algorithms, and in the following sections, we will see how to use them in real examples with various C++ libraries.

Examples of using the Shogun library for dealing with the clustering task samples

The Shogun library contains implementations of the model-based, hierarchical, and partition-based clustering approaches. The model-based algorithm is called **GMM (Gaussian Mixture Models)**, the partition one is the k-means algorithm, and hierarchical clustering is based on the bottom-up method.

GMM with Shogun

The GMM algorithm assumes that clusters can be fit to some Gaussian (normal) distributions; it uses the EM approach for training. There is a CGMM class in the Shogun library that implements this algorithm, as illustrated in the following code snippet:

```
Some<CDenseFeatures<DataType>> features;
int num_clusters = 2;
...
auto gmm = some<CGMM>(num_clusters);
gmm->set_features(features);
gmm->train_em();
```

Notice that the constructor of the CGMM class takes the desired number of clusters as an argument. After CGMM object initialization, we pass training features and use the EM method for training. The following piece of code shows these steps and also plots the results of clustering:

```
Clusters clusters;
auto feature_matrix = features->get_feature_matrix();
for (index_t i = 0; i < features->get_num_vectors(); ++i) {
    auto vector = feature_matrix.get_column(i);
    auto log_likelihoods = gmm->cluster(vector);
    auto max_el = std::max_element(log_likelihoods.begin(),
    std::prev(log_likelihoods.end()));
    auto label_idx = std::distance(log_likelihoods.begin(), max_el);
    clusters[label_idx].first.push_back(vector[0]);
    clusters[label_idx].second.push_back(vector[1]);
}
PlotClusters(clusters, "GMM", name + "-gmm.png");
```

We used the CGMM::cluster() method to identify which cluster our objects belong to. This method returns a vector of probabilities. Then, we searched for the vector's element with the maximum probability value and took its index as the number of the cluster.

The resulting cluster indices were used as an argument for the `PlotClusters()` function, which visualized the clustering result, as illustrated in the following screenshot:

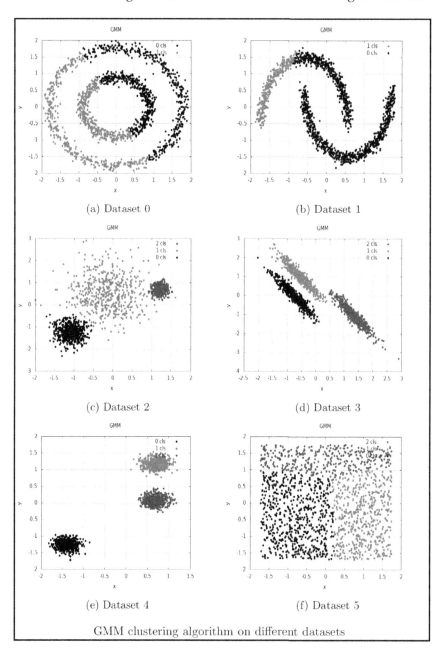

(a) Dataset 0

(b) Dataset 1

(c) Dataset 2

(d) Dataset 3

(e) Dataset 4

(f) Dataset 5

GMM clustering algorithm on different datasets

In the preceding screenshot, we can see how the GMM algorithm works on different artificial datasets.

K-means clustering with Shogun

The k-means algorithm in the Shogun library is implemented in the CKMeans class. The constructor of this class takes two parameters: the number of clusters and the object for distance measure calculation. In the following example, we will use the distance object defined with the CEuclideanDistance class. After we construct the object of the CKMeans type, we use the CKMeans::train() method to train our model on our training set, as follows:

```
Some<CDenseFeatures<DataType>> features;
int num_clusters = 2;
...
CEuclideanDistance* distance = new CEuclideanDistance(features, features);
CKMeans* clustering = new CKMeans(num_clusters, distance);
clustering->train(features);
```

When we have trained the k-means object, we can use the CKMeans::apply() method to classify the input dataset. If we use this method without arguments, the training dataset is used for classification. The result of applying classification is a container object with labels. We can cast it to the CMulticlassLabels type for more natural use. The following code sample shows how to classify the input data and also plots the results of clustering:

```
Clusters clusters;
auto feature_matrix = features->get_feature_matrix();
CMulticlassLabels* result = clustering->apply()->as<CMulticlassLabels>();
for (index_t i = 0; i < result->get_num_labels(); ++i) {
   auto label_idx = result->get_label(i);
    auto vector = feature_matrix.get_column(i);
    clusters[label_idx].first.push_back(vector[0]);
    clusters[label_idx].second.push_back(vector[1]);
}
PlotClusters(clusters, "K-Means", name + "-kmeans.png");
```

We used the CMulticlassLabels::get_label() method for getting the index of a cluster for a particular sample in our dataset. The CMulticlassLabels::get_label() method takes the sample's index as an argument.

We used resulting cluster indices to visualize the clustering result with the `PlotClusters()` function, as illustrated in the following screenshot:

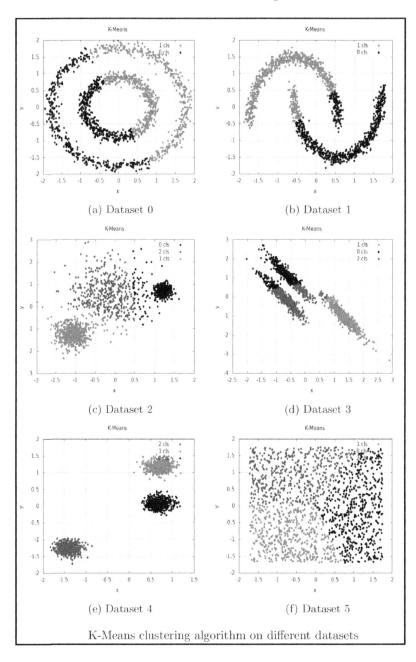

(a) Dataset 0

(b) Dataset 1

(c) Dataset 2

(d) Dataset 3

(e) Dataset 4

(f) Dataset 5

K-Means clustering algorithm on different datasets

In the preceding screenshot, we can see how the k-means algorithm works on different artificial datasets.

Hierarchical clustering with Shogun

There is no feature-complete implementation of the hierarchical clustering algorithm in the Shogun library. There is the CHierarachical class, which implements the hierarchical clustering of the distance values. The distances can represent distances between actual objects for clustering. However, the CHierarachical object returns the new distance values it got after clustering. So, such an object cannot be directly used for object clustering; instead, we can use it as a building block for a custom clustering algorithm.

Examples of using the Shark-ML library for dealing with the clustering task samples

The Shark-ML library implements two clustering algorithms: hierarchical clustering and the k-means algorithm.

Hierarchical clustering with Shark-ML

The Shark-ML library implements the hierarchical clustering approach in the following way: first, we need to put our data into a space-partitioning tree. For example, we can use the object of the LCTree class, which implements binary space partitioning. Also, there is the KHCTree class, which implements kernel-induced feature space partitioning. The constructor of this class takes the data for partitioning and an object that implements some stopping criteria for the tree construction. We use the TreeConstruction object, which we configure with the maximal depth of the tree and the maximum number of objects in the tree node. The LCTree class assumes the existence of a Euclidean distance function for the feature type used in the dataset. The code can be seen in the following block:

```
UnlabeledData<RealVector>& features;
int num_clusters = 2;
  ...
LCTree<RealVector> tree(features,
                        TreeConstruction(0,
features.numberOfElements() / num_clusters));
```

Having constructed the partitioning tree, we initialize an object of the
HierarchicalClustering class with the tree object as an argument.
The HierarchicalClustering class implements the actual clustering algorithm. There
are two strategies to get clustering results—namely, hard and soft. In the hard clustering
strategy, each object is assigned to one cluster. However, in the soft strategy, each object is
assigned to all clusters, but with a specific probability or likelihood value. In the following
example, we use the object of the HardClusteringModel class to assign objects to distinct
clusters. Objects of the HardClusteringModel class override the function operator, so you
can use them as functors for evaluation. The code can be seen in the following snippet:

```
HierarchicalClustering<RealVector> clustering(&tree);
HardClusteringModel<RealVector> model(&clustering);
Data<unsigned> clusters = model(features);
```

The clustering result is a container with cluster indices for each element in the dataset, as
shown in the following code snippet:

```
for (std::size_t i = 0; i != features.numberOfElements(); i++) {
    auto cluster_idx = clusters.element(i);
    auto element = features.element(i);
    ...
}
```

We iterated over all items in the features container and got a cluster index for each item
to visualize our clustering result. This index was used to assign a distinct color for every
item, as illustrated in the following screenshot:

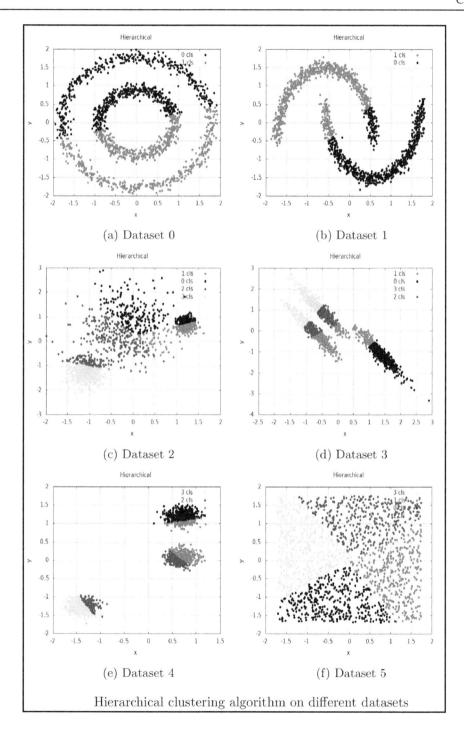

(a) Dataset 0

(b) Dataset 1

(c) Dataset 2

(d) Dataset 3

(e) Dataset 4

(f) Dataset 5

Hierarchical clustering algorithm on different datasets

In the preceding screenshot, we can see how the hierarchical clustering algorithm implemented in the Shark-ML library works on different artificial datasets.

K-means clustering with Shark-ML

The Shark-ML library implements the k-means algorithm in the kMeans() function, which takes three parameters: the training dataset, the desired number of clusters, and the output parameter for cluster centroids. The following code sample shows how to use this function:

```
UnlabeledData<RealVector> features;
int num_clusters = 2;
...
Centroids centroids;
kMeans(features, num_clusters, centroids);
```

After we get the centroids, we can initialize an object of the HardClusteringModel class. As in the previous example, we can use this object for the evaluation of the trained model on new data or the training data, as follows:

```
HardClusteringModel<RealVector> model(&centroids);
Data<unsigned> clusters = model(features);

for (std::size_t i = 0; i != features.numberOfElements(); i++) {
    auto cluster_idx = clusters.element(i);
    auto element = features.element(i);
    ...
}
```

After, we used the model object as a functor to perform clustering. The result was a container with cluster indices for each element of the input dataset. Then, we used these cluster indices to visualize the final result, as illustrated in the following screenshot:

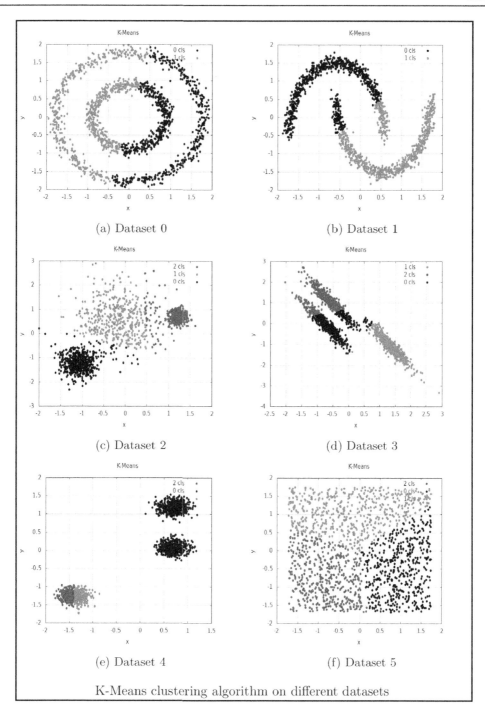

(a) Dataset 0

(b) Dataset 1

(c) Dataset 2

(d) Dataset 3

(e) Dataset 4

(f) Dataset 5

K-Means clustering algorithm on different datasets

In the preceding screenshot, we can see how the k-means clustering algorithm implemented in the `Shark-ML` library works on different artificial datasets.

Examples of using the Dlib library for dealing with the clustering task samples

The `Dlib` library provides the following clustering methods: k-means, spectral, hierarchical, and two more graph clustering algorithms: Newman and Chinese Whispers.

K-means clustering with Dlib

The `Dlib` library uses kernel functions as the distance functions for the k-means algorithm. An example of such a function is the radial basis function. As an initial step, we define the required types, as follows:

```
typedef matrix<double, 2, 1> sample_type;
typedef radial_basis_kernel<sample_type> kernel_type;
```

Then, we initialize an object of the `kkmeans` type. Its constructor takes an object that will define cluster centroids as input parameters. We can use an object of the `kcentroid` type for this purpose. Its constructor takes three parameters: the first one is the object that defines the kernel (distance function), the second is the numerical accuracy for the centroid estimation, and the third one is the upper limit on the runtime complexity (actually, the maximum number of dictionary vectors the `kcentroid` object is allowed to use), as illustrated in the following code snippet:

```
kcentroid<kernel_type> kc(kernel_type(0.1), 0.01, 8);
kkmeans<kernel_type> kmeans(kc);
```

As a next step, we initialize cluster centers with the `pick_initial_centers()` function. This function takes the number of clusters, the output container for center objects, the training data, and the distance function object as parameters, as follows:

```
std::vector<sample_type> samples; //training data-set
...
size_t num_clusters = 2;
std::vector<sample_type> initial_centers;
pick_initial_centers(num_clusters, initial_centers, samples,
kmeans.get_kernel());
```

When initial centers are selected, we can use them for the `kkmeans::train()` method to determine exact clusters, as follows:

```
kmeans.set_number_of_centers(num_clusters);
kmeans.train(samples, initial_centers);

for (size_t i = 0; i != samples.size(); i++) {
    auto cluster_idx = kmeans(samples[i]);
    ...
}
```

We used the `kmeans` object as a functor to perform clustering on a single data item. The clustering result will be the cluster's index for the item. Then, we used cluster indices to visualize the final clustering result, as illustrated in the following screenshot:

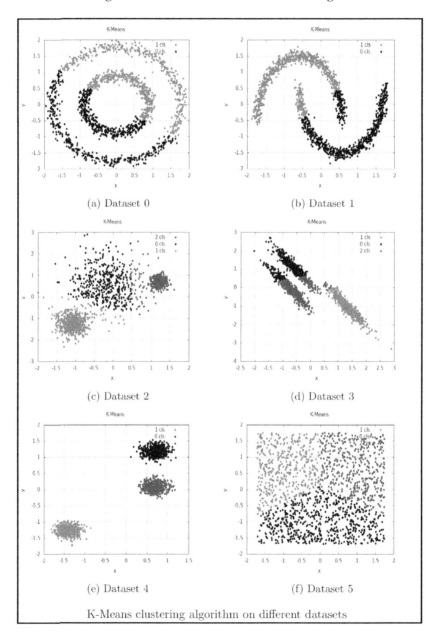

(a) Dataset 0

(b) Dataset 1

(c) Dataset 2

(d) Dataset 3

(e) Dataset 4

(f) Dataset 5

K-Means clustering algorithm on different datasets

In the preceding screenshot, we can see how the k-means clustering algorithm implemented in the `Dlib` library works on different artificial datasets.

Spectral clustering with Dlib

The spectral clustering algorithm in the `Dlib` library is implemented in the `spectral_cluster` function. It takes the distance function object, the training dataset, and the number of clusters as parameters. As a result, it returns a container with cluster indices, which have the same ordering as the input data. In the following sample, the object of the `knn_kernel` type is used as a distance function. You will find its implementation in the samples provided with the book. This `knn_kernel` distance function object estimates the first **k-nearest neighbor** (**KNN**) objects to the given one. These objects are determined with the KNN algorithm, which uses the Euclidean distance for the distance measure, as follows:

```
typedef matrix<double, 2, 1> sample_type;
typedef knn_kernel<sample_type> kernel_type;
...
std::vector<sample_type> samples;
...
std::vector<unsigned long> clusters =
spectral_cluster(kernel_type(samples, 15), samples, num_clusters);
```

The `spectral_cluster()` function call filled the `clusters` object with cluster index values, which we can use to visualize the clustering result, as illustrated in the following screenshot:

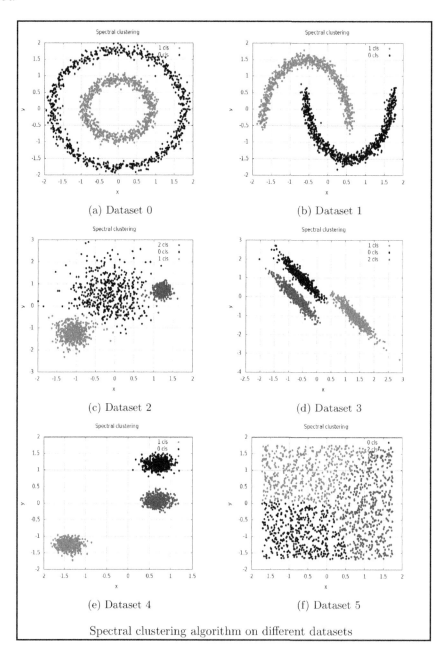

(a) Dataset 0

(b) Dataset 1

(c) Dataset 2

(d) Dataset 3

(e) Dataset 4

(f) Dataset 5

Spectral clustering algorithm on different datasets

In the preceding screenshot, we can see how the spectral clustering algorithm implemented in the Dlib library works on different artificial datasets.

Hierarchical clustering with Dlib

The Dlib library implements the agglomerative hierarchical (bottom-up) clustering algorithm. The bottom_up_cluster() function implements this algorithm. This function takes the matrix of distances between dataset objects, the cluster indices container (as the output parameter), and the number of clusters as input parameters. Notice that it returns the container with cluster indices in the order of distances provided in the matrix.

In the following code sample, we fill the distance matrix with pairwise Euclidean distances between each pair of elements in the input dataset:

```
matrix<double> dists(inputs.nr(), inputs.nr());
for (long r = 0; r < dists.nr(); ++r) {
    for (long c = 0; c < dists.nc(); ++c) {
        dists(r, c) = length(subm(inputs, r, 0, 1, 2) - subm(inputs, c, 0,
        1, 2));
    }
}
std::vector<unsigned long> clusters;
bottom_up_cluster(dists, clusters, num_clusters);
```

The `bottom_up_cluster()` function call filled the `clusters` object with cluster index values, which we can use to visualize the clustering result, as illustrated in the following screenshot:

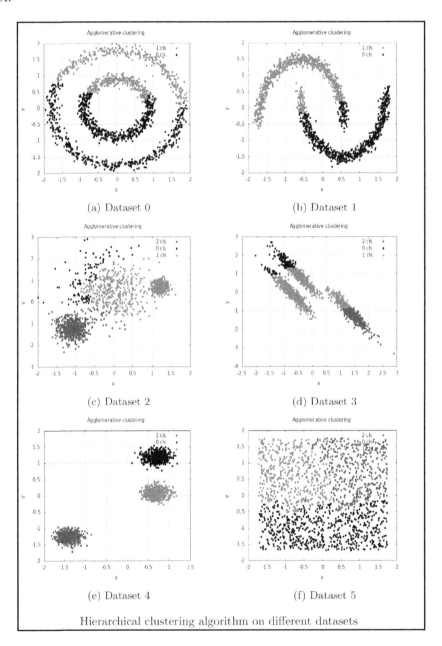

(a) Dataset 0   (b) Dataset 1

(c) Dataset 2   (d) Dataset 3

(e) Dataset 4   (f) Dataset 5

Hierarchical clustering algorithm on different datasets

In the preceding screenshot, we can see how the hierarchical clustering algorithm implemented in the `Dlib` library works on different artificial datasets.

Newman modularity-based graph clustering algorithm with Dlib

Implementation of this algorithm is based on the work *Modularity and community structure in networks* by M. E. J. Newman. This algorithm is based on the modularity matrix for a network or a graph and it is not based on particular graph theory, but it has instead some similarities with spectral clustering because it also uses eigenvectors.

The `Dlib` library implements this algorithm in the `newman_cluster()` function, which takes a vector of weighted graph edges and outputs the container with cluster indices for each vertex. The initial step for using this algorithm is the definition of graph edges. In the following code sample, we make edges between almost every pair of dataset objects. Notice that we use pairs only with a distance greater than a threshold (this was done for performance considerations).

Also, this algorithm does not require prior knowledge of the number of clusters. It can determine the number of clusters by itself. The code can be seen in the following block:

```
std::vector<sample_pair> edges;
for (long i = 0; i < inputs.nr(); ++i) {
    for (long j = 0; j < inputs.nr(); ++j) {
        auto dist = length(subm(inputs, i, 0, 1, 2) - subm(inputs, j, 0,
        1, 2));
        if (dist < 0.5)
            edges.push_back(sample_pair(i, j, dist));
    }
}
remove_duplicate_edges(edges);
std::vector<unsigned long> clusters;
const auto num_clusters = newman_cluster(edges, clusters);
```

The `newman_cluster()` function call filled the `clusters` object with cluster index values, which we can use to visualize the clustering result. Notice that another approach for edge weight calculation can lead to another clustering result. Also, edge weight values should be initialized according to a certain task. The edge length was chosen only for demonstration purposes.

The result can be seen in the following screenshot:

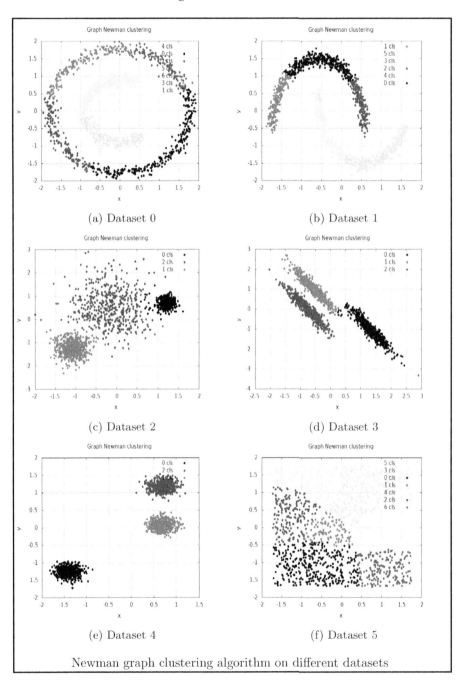

(a) Dataset 0

(b) Dataset 1

(c) Dataset 2

(d) Dataset 3

(e) Dataset 4

(f) Dataset 5

Newman graph clustering algorithm on different datasets

In the preceding screenshot, we can see how the Newman clustering algorithm implemented in the Dlib library works on different artificial datasets.

Chinese Whispers – graph clustering algorithm with Dlib

The Chinese Whispers algorithm is an algorithm to partition the nodes of weighted, undirected graphs. It was described in the paper *Chinese Whispers—an Efficient Graph Clustering Algorithm and its Application to Natural Language Processing Problems* by Chris Biemann. This algorithm also does not use any unique graph theory methods but it uses the idea of using local contexts for clustering, so it can be classified as a density-based method.

In the Dlib library, this algorithm is implemented in the chinese_whispers() function, which takes the vector of weighted graph edges and outputs the container with cluster indices for each of the vertices. For the performance consideration, we limit the number of edges between dataset objects with a threshold on distance. Moreover, as with the Newman algorithm, this one also determines the number of resulting clusters by itself. The code can be seen in the following snippet:

```
std::vector<sample_pair> edges;
    for (long i = 0; i < inputs.nr(); ++i) {
        for (long j = 0; j < inputs.nr(); ++j) {
            auto dist = length(subm(inputs, i, 0, 1, 2) - subm(inputs, j,
            0, 1, 2));
            if (dist < 1)
              edges.push_back(sample_pair(i, j, dist));
        }
}
std::vector<unsigned long> clusters;
const auto num_clusters = chinese_whispers(edges, clusters);
```

The chinese_whispers() function call filled the clusters object with cluster index values, which we can use to visualize the clustering result. Notice that we used 1 as the threshold for edge weights, and another threshold value can lead to another clustering result. Also, edge weight values should be initialized according to a certain task. The edge length was chosen only for demonstration purposes.

The result can be seen in the following screenshot:

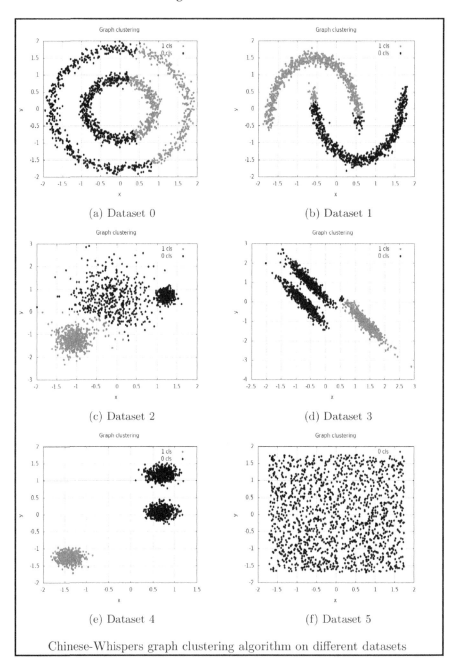

(a) Dataset 0   (b) Dataset 1

(c) Dataset 2   (d) Dataset 3

(e) Dataset 4   (f) Dataset 5

Chinese-Whispers graph clustering algorithm on different datasets

In the preceding screenshot, we can see how the Chinese Whispers clustering algorithm implemented in the Dlib library works on different artificial datasets.

In the current and previous sections, we saw a lot of examples of images that show clustering results. The following section will show details of using the plotcpp library, which we used to plot these images.

Plotting data with C++

We plot with the plotcpp library, which is a thin wrapper around the gnuplot command-line utility. With this library, we can draw points on a scatter plot or draw lines. The initial step to start plotting with this library is creating an object of the Plot class. Then, we have to specify the output destination of the drawing. We can set the destination with the Plot::SetTerminal() method and this method takes a string with a destination point abbreviation. It can be the qt string value to show the **operating system (OS)** window with our drawing, or it can be a string with a picture file extension to save a drawing to a file, as in the code sample that follows. Also, we can configure a title of the drawing, the axis labels, and some other parameters with the Plot class methods. However, it does not cover all possible configurations available for gnuplot. In a case where we need some unique options, we can use the Plot::gnuplotCommand() method to make direct gnuplot configuration.

There are two drawing modes to draw a set of different graphics on one plot. We can use the Draw2D() method with objects of the Points or Lines classes, but in this case, we should specify all graphics configurations before compilation. The second option is to use the Plot::StartDraw2D() method to get an intermediate drawing state object. Then, we can use the Plot::AddDrawing() method to add different drawings to the one plot. The Plot::EndDraw2D() method should be called after we drew the last graphics.

We can use the Points type for drawing points. An object of this type should be initialized with start and end forward iterators to the integral numeric data types, which represent coordinates. We should specify three iterators to points coordinates, two iterators for the x coordinates where they start and end, and one iterator to the y coordinates' start. The number of coordinates in the containers should be the same. The last parameter is the gnuplot visual style configuration. Objects of the Lines class can be configured in the same way.

When we have completed all drawing operations, we should call the `Plot::Flush()` method to render all commands to the window or the file, as shown in the following code block:

```
...
using Coords = std::vector<DataType>;
using PointCoords = std::pair<Coords, Coords>;
using Clusters = std::unordered_map<index_t, PointCoords>;

const std::vector<std::string> colors{"black", "red",   "blue",
                                       "green", "cyan", "yellow",
                                       "brown", "magenta"};
...
void PlotClusters(const Clusters& clusters,
    const std::string& name,
    const std::string& file_name) {
    plotcpp::Plot plt;
    plt.SetTerminal("png");
    plt.SetOutput(file_name);
    plt.SetTitle(name);
    plt.SetXLabel("x");
    plt.SetYLabel("y");
    plt.SetAutoscale();
    plt.gnuplotCommand("set grid");

    auto draw_state = plt.StartDraw2D<Coords::const_iterator>();
    for (auto& cluster : clusters) {
        std::stringstream params;
        params << "lc rgb '" << colors[cluster.first] << "' pt 7";
        plt.AddDrawing(draw_state,
        plotcpp::Points(
        cluster.second.first.begin(), cluster.second.first.end(),
        cluster.second.second.begin(),
        std::to_string(cluster.first) + " cls", params.str()));
    }

    plt.EndDraw2D(draw_state);
    plt.Flush();
}
```

Summary

In this chapter, we considered what clustering is and how it differs from classification. We saw different types of clustering methods, such as the partition-based, the spectral, the hierarchical, the density-based, and the model-based methods. Also, we observed that partition-based methods could be divided into more categories, such as the distance-based methods and the ones based on graph theory. We used implementations of these algorithms, including the k-means algorithm (the distance-based method), the GMM algorithm (the model-based method), the Newman modularity-based algorithm, and the Chinese Whispers algorithm for graph clustering. We also saw how to use the hierarchical and spectral clustering algorithm implementations in programs. We saw that the crucial issues for successful clustering are as follows:

- The choice of the distance measure function
- The initialization step
- The splitting or merging strategy
- Prior knowledge about cluster numbers

The combination of these issues is unique for each specific algorithm. Also, we saw that a clustering algorithm's results depend a lot on dataset characteristics and that we should choose the algorithm according to these.

The list of application areas where clustering is applied is comprehensive: image segmentation, marketing, anti-fraud, forecasting, and text analysis, among many others. At the present stage, clustering is often used as the first step in data analysis. The task of clustering was formulated in such scientific areas as statistics, pattern recognition, optimization, and machine learning. At the moment, the number of methods for partitioning groups of objects into clusters is quite large—several dozen algorithms, and even more when you take into account their various modifications.

At the end of the chapter, we studied how we can visualize clustering results with the `plotcpp` library.

In the following chapter, we will learn what a data anomaly is and what machine learning algorithms exist for anomaly detection. Also, we will see how anomaly detection algorithms can be used for solving real-life problems, and which properties of such algorithms play a more significant role in different tasks.

Further reading

- The 5 Clustering Algorithms Data Scientists Need to Know: `https://towardsdatascience.com/the-5-clustering-algorithms-data-scientists-need-to-know-a36d136ef68`
- Clustering: `https://scikit-learn.org/stable/modules/clustering.html`
- Different Types of Clustering Algorithm: `https://www.geeksforgeeks.org/different-types-clustering-algorithm/`
- An Introduction to Clustering and different methods of clustering: `https://www.analyticsvidhya.com/blog/2016/11/an-introduction-to-clustering-and-different-methods-of-clustering/`
- Graph theory introductory book: *Graph Theory* (*Graduate Texts in Mathematics*) by Adrian Bondy and U.S.R. Murty.
- This book covers a lot of aspects of ML theory and algorithms: *The Elements of Statistical Learning: Data Mining, Inference, and Prediction* by Trevor Hastie, Robert Tibshirani, and Jerome Friedman

Anomaly Detection 5

Anomaly detection is where we search for unexpected values in a given dataset. An anomaly is a system behavior deviation or data value deviation from the standard value. There are other names for anomalies, such as outliers, errors, deviations, and exceptions. They can occur in data that's of diverse nature and structure as a result of technical failures, accidents, deliberate hacks, and more.

There are many methods and algorithms we can use to search for anomalies in various types of data. These methods use different approaches to solve the same problem. There are unsupervised, supervised, and semi-supervised algorithms. However, in practice, unsupervised methods are the most popular. The unsupervised anomaly detection technique detects anomalies in unlabeled test datasets, under the assumption that most of the dataset is normal. It does this by searching for data points that are unlikely to fit the rest of the dataset. Unsupervised algorithms are more popular because of the nature of anomaly events, which are significantly rare compared to the normal or expected data, so it is usually very difficult to get a suitably labeled dataset for anomaly detection.

Broadly speaking, anomaly detection applies to a wide range of areas, such as intrusion detection, fraud detection, fault detection, health monitoring, event detection (in sensor networks), and the detection of environmental disruptions. Often, anomaly detection is used as the preprocessing step for data preparation, before the data is passed on to other algorithms.

So, in this chapter, we'll discuss the most popular unsupervised algorithms for anomaly detection and its applications.

The following topics will be covered in this chapter:

- Exploring the applications of anomaly detection
- Learning approaches for anomaly detection
- Examples of using different C++ libraries for anomaly detection

Technical requirements

The list of software that you'll need to complete the examples in this chapter is as follows:

- `Shogun-toolbox` library
- `Shark-ML` library
- `Dlib` library
- `PlotCpp` library
- Modern C++ compiler with C++17 support
- CMake build system version >= 3.8

The code files for this chapter can be found at the following GitHub repo: `https://github.com/PacktPublishing/Hands-On-Machine-Learning-with-CPP/tree/master/Chapter05`

Exploring the applications of anomaly detection

There are two areas in data analysis that look for anomalies: outlier detection and novelty detection.

A *new object* or novelty is an object that differs in its properties from the objects in the training dataset. Unlike an outlier, the new object is not in the dataset itself, but it can appear at any point after a system has started working. Its task is to detect when it appears. For example, if we were to analyze existing temperature measurements and identify abnormally high or low values, then we would be detecting outliers. On the other hand, if we were to create an algorithm that, for every new measurement, evaluates the temperature's similarity to past values and identifies significantly unusual ones, then we are detecting novelties.

The reasons for outliers appearing include data errors, the presence of noise, misclassified objects, and foreign objects from other datasets or distributions. Let's explain two of the most obscure types of outliers: data errors and data from different distributions. Data errors can broadly refer to inaccuracies in measurements, rounding errors, and incorrect entries. An example of an object belonging to a different distribution is measurements that have come from a broken sensor. This is because these values will belong to a range that may be different from what was expected.

Novelties usually appear as a result of fundamentally new object behavior. For example, if our objects are computer system behavior descriptions, then after a virus has penetrated the computer and deleted some information from these descriptions, they will be rendered as novelties. Another example of a novelty could be a new group of customers that behave differently from others but have some similarities to other customers. The main feature of novelty objects is that they are new, in that it's impossible to have information about all possible virus infections or breakdowns in the training set. Creating such a training dataset is a complicated process and often does not make sense. However, fortunately, we can obtain a large enough dataset by focusing on the ordinary (regular) operations of the system or mechanism.

Often, the task of anomaly detection is similar to the task of classification, but there is an essential difference: class imbalances. For example, equipment failures (anomalies) are significantly rarer than having the equipment functioning normally.

We can observe anomalies in different kinds of data. In the following graph, we can see an example of anomalies in a numeric series:

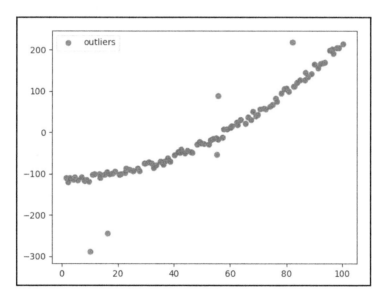

In the following diagram, we can see anomalies in graphs; these anomalies can be as edges as well as vertices (see elements marked with a lighter color):

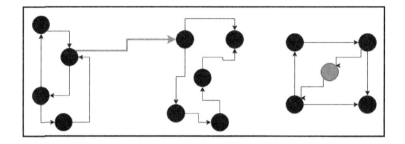

The following text shows anomalies in a sequence of characters:

AABBCCCAABBCCCAACABBBCCCAABB

The quality or performance of anomaly detection tasks can be estimated, just like classification tasks can, by using, for example, AUC-ROC.

We have discussed what anomalies are, so let's see what approaches there are to detect them.

Learning approaches for anomaly detection

In this section, we'll look at the most popular and straightforward methods we can use for anomaly detection.

Detecting anomalies with statistical tests

Statistical tests are usually used to catch extreme values for individual features. The general name for this type of test is extreme-value analysis. An example of such a test is the use of the Z-score measure:

$$Z_i = \frac{|x_i - \mu|}{\delta}$$

Here, x_i is a sample from the dataset, μ is the mean of all samples from the dataset, and δ is the standard deviation of samples in the dataset. Z-values are placed in the interval [-1, 1] and the smallest values that are close to zero are the most normal or expected ones. The following graph shows which values from some type of normally distributed data can be treated as anomalies or outliers by using the Z-score test:

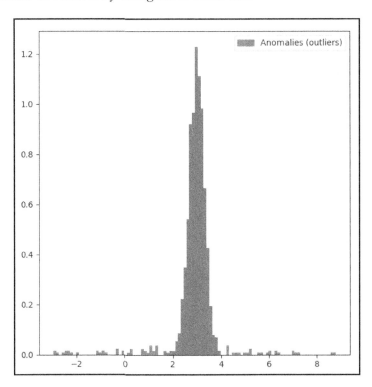

One important concept that we should mention is extreme values – the maximum and minimum values from the given dataset. It is important to understand that extreme values and anomalies are different concepts. The following is a small data sample:

```
[1, 39, 2, 1, 101, 2, 1, 100, 1, 3, 101, 1, 3, 100, 101, 100, 100]
```

We can consider the value 39 as an anomaly, but not because it is a maximal or minimal value. It is crucial to understand that an anomaly needn't be an extreme value.

Despite the fact that extreme values are not anomalies in general, in some cases, we can adapt methods of extreme-value analysis to the needs of anomaly detection. But this depends on the task at hand and should be carefully analyzed by machine learning practitioners.

Detecting anomalies with the Local Outlier Factor method

The distance measurement-based methods are widely used for solving different machine learning problems, as well as for anomaly detection. These methods assume that there is a specific metric in the object space that helps us find anomalies. The general assumption when we use distance-based methods for anomaly detection is that the anomaly only has a few neighbors, while a normal point has many. Therefore, for example, the distance to the kth neighbor can serve as a good measure of anomalies, as reflected in the **Local Outlier Factor (LOF)** method. This method is based on estimating the density of objects that have been checked for anomalies. Objects lying in the areas of lowest density are considered anomalies or outliers. The advantage of the LOF method over other methods is that it works in conjunction with the local density of objects. Thus, the LOF successfully recognizes outliers in situations where there are objects of different classes that are not necessarily anomalies in the training dataset.

For example, let's assume that there is a distance, k-distance(A), from the object $[A]$ to the kth nearest neighbor. Note that the set of nearest neighbors includes all objects at this distance. We denote the set of k nearest neighbors as $N_k(A)$. This distance is used to determine the reachability distance:

$$\text{reachability-distance}_k(A, B) = max(\text{k-distance}(B), dist(A, B))$$

If point A lies among k neighbors of point B, then reachability-distance will be equal to the k-distance of point B. Otherwise, it will be equal to the exact distance between points A and B, which is given by the *dist* function. The local reachability density of an object A is defined as follows:

$$ldr_k(A) = 1/(\frac{\sum_{B \in N_k(A)} \text{reachability-distance}_k(A, B)}{|N_k(A)|})$$

Local reachability density is the inverse of the average reachability distance of the object, A, from its neighbors. Note that this is not the average reachability distance of neighbors from A (which, by definition, should have been k-distance(A)), but is the distance at which A can be reached from its neighbors. The local reachability densities are then compared with the local reachability densities of the neighbors:

$$LOF_k(A) = (\frac{\sum_{B \in N_k(A)} ldr_k(B)}{|N_k(A)|})/ldr_k(A)$$

The provided formula gives the average local reachability density of the neighbors, divided by the local reachability density of the object itself. A value of approximately 1 means that the object can be compared with its neighbors (and therefore it is not an outlier). A value less than 1 indicates a dense area (objects have many neighbors), while values that are significantly larger than 1 indicate anomalies.

The disadvantage of this method is the fact that the resulting values are difficult to interpret. A value of 1 or less indicates that a point is purely internal, but there is no clear rule by which a point will be an outlier. In one dataset, the value 1.1 may indicate an outlier. However, in another dataset with a different set of parameters (for example, if there is data with sharp local fluctuations), the value 2 may also indicate internal objects. These differences can also occur within a single dataset due to the locality of the method.

Detecting anomalies with isolation forest

The idea of an isolation forest is based on the Monte Carlo principle: a random partitioning of the feature space is carried out so that, on average, isolated points are cut off from normal ones. The final result is averaged over several runs of the stochastic algorithm, and the result will form an isolation forest of corresponding trees. The isolation tree algorithm then builds a random binary decision tree. The root of the tree is the whole feature space. In the next node, a random feature and a random partitioning threshold are selected, and they are sampled from a uniform distribution on the range of the minimum and maximum values of the selected feature. The stopping criterion is the identical coincidence of all objects in the node, which means that the decision tree's construction has finished. The mark of the leaves is the `anomaly_score` value of the algorithm, which is the depth of the leaves in the constructed tree. The following formula shows how the anomaly score can be calculated:

$$s(x,n) = 2^{-\frac{E(h(x))}{c(n)}}$$

Here, $h(x)$ is the path length of the observation, x, $E(h(x))$ is an average of $h(x)$ from a collection of isolation trees, $c(n)$ is the average path length of the unsuccessful search in a binary search tree, and n is the number of external nodes.

We're assuming that it is common for anomalies to appear in leaves with a low depth, which is close to the root, but for regular objects, the tree will build several more levels. The number of such levels is proportional to the size of the cluster. Consequently, `anomaly_score` is proportional to the points lying in it.

This assumption means that objects from clusters of small sizes (which are potentially anomalies) will have a lower `anomaly_score` than those from clusters of regular data:

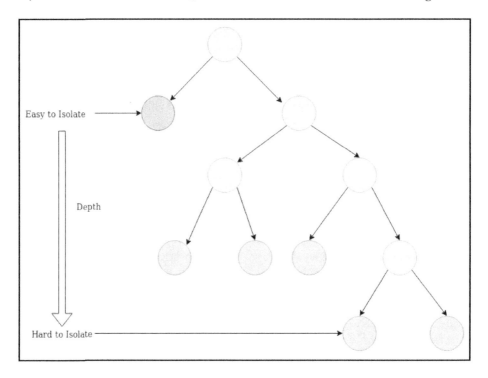

Detecting anomalies with One-Class SVM (OCSVM)

The support vector method is a binary classification method based on using a hyperplane to divide objects into classes. The dimensions of the hyperplane are always chosen so that they're less than the dimensions of the original space. In $\mathfrak{R}^3$, for example, a hyperplane is an ordinary two-dimensional plane. The distance from the hyperplane to each class should be as short as possible. The vectors that are closest to the separating hyperplane are called support vectors. In practice, cases where the data can be divided by a hyperplane – in other words, linear cases – are quite rare. In this case, all the elements of the training dataset are embedded in the higher dimension space, X, using a special mapping. In this case, the mapping is chosen so that in the new space, X, the dataset is linearly separable.

One-Class SVM (OCSVM) is an adaptation of the support vector method that focuses on anomaly detection. OCSVM differs from the standard version of SVM in a way that, the resulting optimization problem includes an improvement for determining a small percentage of predetermined anomalous values, which allows this method to be used to detect anomalies. These anomalous values lie between the starting point and the optimal separating hyperplane. All other data belonging to the same class falls on the opposite side of the optimal separating hyperplane.

There's also another type of OCSVM that uses a spherical, instead of a planar (or linear), approach. The algorithm obtains a spherical boundary, in the feature space, around the data. The volume of this hypersphere is minimized to reduce the effect of incorporating outliers in the solution.

OCSVM assigns a label, which is the distance from the test data point to the optimal hyperplane. Positive values in the OCSVM output represent normal behavior (with higher values representing greater normality), while negative values represent anomalous behavior (the lower the value, the more significant the anomaly).

Density estimation approach (multivariate Gaussian distribution) for anomaly detection

Let's assume we have some samples $x^{(i)}$ in a dataset and that they are labeled and normally distributed (Gaussian distribution). In such a case, we can use distribution properties to detect anomalies. Let's assume that the function $p(x)$ gives us the probability of a sample being normal. A high probability corresponds to a regular sample, while a low probability corresponds to an anomaly. We can, therefore, choose thresholds to distinguish between regular values and anomalies with the following **anomaly model** formula:

$$p(x_{test}) < \epsilon, \text{ flag as an outlier or an anomaly}$$
$$p(x_{text}) \geq \epsilon, \text{ flag as a normal or a non-anomalous}$$

If $[x \in \mathbb{R}]$ and x follows the Gaussian distribution with the mean, μ, and the variance, σ^2, it is denoted as follows:

$$x \sim \mathcal{N}(\mu, \sigma^2)$$

The following formula gives the probability of x in a Gaussian distribution:

$$p(x; \mu, \sigma^2) = \frac{1}{\sqrt{2\pi}\sigma} exp(-\frac{(x - \mu)^2}{2\sigma^2})$$

Here, $\mu = \frac{1}{m}\sum_{i=1}^{m} x^{(i)}$ is the mean and $\sigma^2 = \frac{1}{m}\sum_{i=1}^{m}(x^{(i)} - \mu)^2$ is the variance (σ is the standard deviation).

Next, we'll introduce an example of the general approach we follow for anomaly detection with Gaussian distribution density estimation:

1. Let's say we're given a new example, $x = \{x_1, x_2 \ldots x_n\}$.
2. Select the features, x_i, that are regular, meaning they determine anomalous behavior.
3. Fit the μ_i and σ_i^2 parameters.
4. Compute $p(x) = \prod_{j=1}^{n} p(x_j; \mu_j, \sigma_j^2)$ using an equation to calculate the probability of x in a Gaussian distribution.
5. Determine if x is an anomaly by comparing it with the threshold, ϵ; see the **anomaly model** formula.

The following graph shows an example of Gaussian distribution density estimation for normally distributed data:

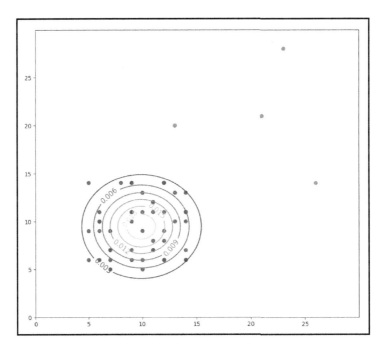

In this approach, we assume that selected features are independent, but usually, in real data, there are some correlations between them. In such a case, we should use a multivariate Gaussian distribution model instead of a univariate one.

The following formula gives the probability of x in a multivariate Gaussian distribution:

$$p(x; \mu, \Sigma) = \frac{1}{(2\pi)^{n/2} |\Sigma|^{1/2}} exp\left(-\frac{1}{2}(x - \mu)^T \Sigma^{-1}(x - \mu)\right)$$

Here, μ is the mean, Σ is the correlation matrix, and $|\Sigma|$ is the determinant of the matrix, Σ:

$$\Sigma = \frac{1}{m}\sum_{i=1}^{m}(x^{(i)} - \mu)(x^{(i)} - \mu)^T$$

The following diagram shows the difference between the univariate and the multivariate Gaussian distribution estimation models for a dataset with correlated data. Notice how distribution boundaries cover the regular data with a blue color, while the anomalies are marked with a lighter color:

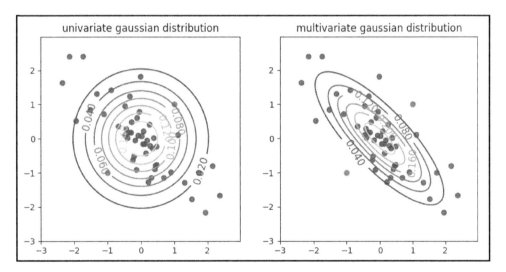

We can see that the multivariate Gaussian distribution can take into account correlations in the data and adapt its shape to them. This characteristic allows us to detect anomalies correctly for types of data whose distribution follows a Gaussian (normal) distribution shape.

In the current section, we discussed various anomaly detection approaches, and in the following sections, we will see how to use various C++ libraries to deal with the anomaly detection task.

Examples of using different C++ libraries for anomaly detection

In this section, we'll look at some examples of how to implement the algorithms we described previously for anomaly detection.

C++ implementation of the isolation forest algorithm for anomaly detection

Isolation forest algorithms can be easily implemented in pure C++ because its logic is pretty straightforward. Also, there are no implementations of this algorithm in popular C++ libraries. Let's assume that our implementation will only be used with two-dimensional data. We are going to detect anomalies in a range of samples where each sample contains the same number of features.

Because our dataset is large enough, we can define a wrapper for the actual data container. This allows us to reduce the number of copy operations we perform on the actual data:

```
using DataType = double;
template <size_t Cols>
using Sample = std::array<DataType, Cols>;
template <size_t Cols>
using Dataset = std::vector<Sample<Cols>>;
...
template <size_t Cols>
struct DatasetRange {
    DatasetRange(std::vector<size_t>&& indices, const Dataset<Cols>*
    dataset)
        : indices(std::move(indices)), dataset(dataset) {}
    size_t size() const { return indices.size(); }
    DataType at(size_t row, size_t col) const {
        return (*dataset)[indices[row]][col];
```

```
    }

    std::vector<size_t> indices;
    const Dataset<Cols>* dataset;
};
```

The `DatasetRange` type holds a reference to the `vector` of `Sample` type objects and to the container of indices that point to the samples in the dataset. These indices define the exact dataset objects that this `DatasetRange` object points to.

Next, we define the elements of the isolation tree, with the first one being the `Node` type:

```
struct Node {
    Node() {}
    Node(const Node&) = delete;
    Node& operator=(const Node&) = delete;
    Node(std::unique_ptr<Node> left,
         std::unique_ptr<Node> right,
         size_t split_col,
         DataType split_value)
        : left(std::move(left)),
          right(std::move(right)),
          split_col(split_col),
          split_value(split_value) {}
    Node(size_t size) : size(size), is_external(true) {}
    std::unique_ptr<Node> left;
    std::unique_ptr<Node> right;
    size_t split_col{0};
    DataType split_value{0};
    size_t size{0};
    bool is_external{false};
};
```

This type is a regular tree node structure. The following members are specific to the isolation tree algorithm:

- `split_col`: This is the index of the feature column where the algorithm caused a split.
- `split_value`: This is the value of the feature where the algorithm caused a split.
- `size`: This is the number of underlying items for the node.
- `is_external`: This is the flag that indicates whether the node is a leaf.

Taking the `Node` type as a basis, we can define the procedure of building an isolation tree. We aggregate this procedure with the auxiliary `IsolationTree` type. Because the current algorithm is based on random splits, the auxiliary data is the random engine object.

We only need to initialize this object once, and then it will be shared among all tree type objects. This approach allows us to make the results of the algorithm reproducible in the case of constant seeding. Furthermore, it makes debugging the randomized algorithm much simpler:

```
template <size_t Cols>
class IsolationTree {
public:
    using Data = DatasetRange<Cols>;

    IsolationTree(const IsolationTree&) = delete;
    IsolationTree& operator=(const IsolationTree&) = delete;
    IsolationTree(std::mt19937* rand_engine, Data data, size_t hlim)
        : rand_engine(rand_engine) {
        root = MakeIsolationTree(data, 0, hlim);
    }
    IsolationTree(IsolationTree&& tree) {
        rand_engine = std::move(tree.rand_engine);
        root = td::move(tree.root);
    }

    double PathLength(const Sample<Cols>& sample) {
        return PathLength(sample, root.get(), 0);
    }

private:
    std::unique_ptr<Node> MakeIsolationTree(const Data& data,
                                            size_t height,
                                            size_t hlim);
    double PathLength(const Sample<Cols>& sample,
                      const Node* node,
                      double height);

private:
    std::mt19937* rand_engine;
    std::unique_ptr<Node> root;
};
```

Next, we'll do the most critical work in the `MakeIsolationTree()` method, which is used in the constructor to initialize the root data member:

```
std::unique_ptr<Node> MakeIsolationTree(const Data& data,
                                        size_t height,
                                        size_t hlim) {
    auto len = data.size();
    if (height >= hlim || len <= 1) {
        return std::make_unique<Node>(len);
```

```
    } else {
        std::uniform_int_distribution<size_t> cols_dist(0, Cols - 1);
        auto rand_col = cols_dist(*rand_engine);
        std::unordered_set<DataType> values;
        for (size_t i = 0; i < len; ++i) {
            auto value = data.at(i, rand_col);
            values.insert(value);
        }
        auto min_max = std::minmax_element(values.begin(), values.end());
        std::uniform_real_distribution<DataType>
            value_dist(*min_max.first, *min_max.second);
        auto split_value = value_dist(*rand_engine);
        std::vector<size_t> indices_left;
        std::vector<size_t> indices_right;
        for (size_t i = 0; i < len; ++i) {
            auto value = data.at(i, rand_col);
            if (value < split_value) {
                indices_left.push_back(data.indices[i]);
            } else {
                indices_right.push_back(data.indices[i]);
            }
        }
        return std::make_unique<Node>(
            MakeIsolationTree(Data{std::move(indices_left), data.dataset},
                          height + 1, hlim),
            MakeIsolationTree(Data{std::move(indices_right),
                          data.dataset}, height + 1, hlim),
            rand_col,
            split_value);
    }
}
```

Initially, we checked the termination conditions to stop the splitting process. If we meet them, we return a new node marked as an external leaf. Otherwise, we start splitting the passed data range. For splitting, we randomly select the feature column and determine the unique values of the selected feature. Then, we randomly select a value from an interval between the **max** and the **min** values among the feature values from all the samples. After we make these random selections, we compare the values of the selected splitting feature to all the samples from the input data range and put their indices into two lists. One list is for values higher than the splitting values, while another list is for values that are lower than them. Then, we return a new tree node initialized with references to the left and right nodes, which are initialized with recursive calls to the `MakeIsolationTree()` method.

Another vital method of the `IsolationTree` type is the `PathLength()` method. We use it for anomaly score calculations. It takes the sample as an input parameter and returns the amortized path length to the corresponding tree leaf from the root node:

```
double PathLength(const Sample<Cols>& sample,
                  const Node* node,
                  double height) {
    assert(node != nullptr);
    if (node->is_external) {
        return height + CalcC(node->size);
    } else {
        auto col = node->split_col;
        if (sample[col] < node->split_value) {
            return PathLength(sample, node->left.get(), height + 1);
        } else {
            return PathLength(sample, node->right.get(), height + 1);
        }
    }
}
```

The `PathLength()` method finds the leaf node during tree traversal based on sample feature values. These values are used to select a tree traversal direction based on the current node splitting values. During each step, this method also increases the resulting height. The result of this method is a sum of the actual tree traversal height and the value returned from the call to the `CalcC()` function, which then returns the average path's length of unsuccessful searches in a binary search tree of equal height to the leaf node. The `CalcC()` function can be implemented in the following way, according to the formula from the original paper, which describes the isolation forest algorithm (you can find a reference to this in the *Further reading* section):

```
double CalcC(size_t n) {
    double c = 0;
    if (n > 1)
        c = 2 * (log(n - 1) + 0.5772156649) - (2 * (n - 1) / n);
    return c;
}
```

The final part of the algorithm's implementation is the creation of the forest. The forest is an array of trees built from a limited number of samples, randomly chosen from the original dataset. The number of samples used to build the tree is a hyperparameter of this algorithm. Furthermore, this implementation uses heuristics as the stopping criteria, in that, it is a maximum tree height `hlim` value.

Let's see how it is used in the tree building procedure. The `hlim` value is calculated only once, and the following code shows this. Moreover, it is based on the number of samples that are used to build a single tree:

```cpp
template <size_t Cols>
 class IsolationForest {
 public:
     using Data = DatasetRange<Cols>;
     IsolationForest(const IsolationForest&) = delete;
     IsolationForest& operator=(const IsolationForest&) = delete;
     IsolationForest(const Dataset<Cols>& dataset,
     size_t num_trees,
     size_t sample_size)
     : rand_engine(2325) {
         std::vector<size_t> indices(dataset.size());
         std::iota(indices.begin(), indices.end(), 0);
         size_t hlim = static_cast<size_t>(ceil(log2(sample_size)));
         for (size_t i = 0; i < num_trees; ++i) {
             std::vector<size_t> sample_indices;
             std::sample(indices.begin(), indices.end(),
             std::back_insert_iterator(sample_indices), sample_size,
             rand_engine);
             trees.emplace_back(&rand_engine,
             Data(std::move(sample_indices), &dataset), hlim);
         }
         double n = dataset.size();
         c = CalcC(n);
     }
     double AnomalyScore(const Sample<Cols>& sample) {
         double avg_path_length = 0;
         for (auto& tree : trees) {
             avg_path_length += tree.PathLength(sample);
         }
         avg_path_length /= trees.size();
         double anomaly_score = pow(2, -avg_path_length / c);
         return anomaly_score;
     }
 private:
     std::mt19937 rand_engine;
     std::vector<IsolationTree<Cols>> trees;
     double c{0};
 };
 }
```

The tree forest is built in the constructor of the `IsolationForest` type. We also calculated the value of the average path length of the unsuccessful search in a binary search tree for all of the samples in the constructor. We use this forest in the `AnomalyScore()` method for the actual process of anomaly detection. It implements the formula for the anomaly score value for a given sample. It returns a value that can be interpreted in the following way: if the returned value is close to `1`, then the sample has anomalous features, while if the value is less then `0.5`, then we can assume that the sample is a normal one.

The following code shows how we can use this algorithm. Furthermore, it uses `Dlib` primitives for the dataset's representation:

```
void IsolationForest(const Matrix& normal,
                     const Matrix& test) {
    iforest::Dataset<2> dataset;
    auto put_to_dataset = [&](const Matrix& samples) {
        for (long r = 0; r < samples.nr(); ++r) {
            auto row = dlib::rowm(samples, r);
            double x = row(0, 0);
            double y = row(0, 1);
            dataset.push_back({x, y});
        }
    };

    put_to_dataset(normal);
    put_to_dataset(test);

    iforest::IsolationForest iforest(dataset, 300, 50);

    double threshold = 0.6;  // change this value to see isolation
                             // boundary
    for (auto& s : dataset) {
        auto anomaly_score = iforest.AnomalyScore(s);
        // std::cout << anomaly_score << " " << s[0] << " " << s[1]
        // << std::endl;
        if (anomaly_score < threshold) {
            // Do something with normal
        } else {
            // Do something with anomalies
        }
    }
}
```

In the preceding example, we converted and merged the given datasets for the container that's suitable for our algorithm. Then, we initialized the object of the `IsolationForest` type, which immediately builds the isolation forest with the following hyperparameters: the number of trees is 100 and the number of samples used for one tree is 50.

Finally, we called the `AnomalyScore()` method for each sample from the dataset in order to detect anomalies with thresholds and return their values. In the following graph, we can see the result of anomaly detection after using the `Isolation Forest` algorithm. The red points are the anomalies:

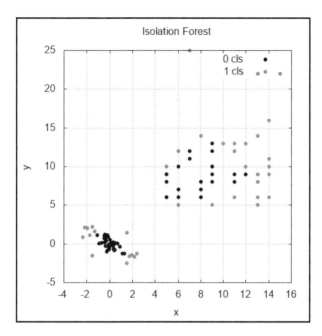

Using the Dlib library for anomaly detection

The `Dlib` library provides a couple of implemented algorithms that we can use for anomaly detection: the OCSVM model and the multivariate Gaussian model.

One-Cass SVM with Dlib

There is only one algorithm that's implemented in the `Dlib` library straight out of the box: OCSVM. There is a `svm_one_class_trainer` class in this library that can be used to train the corresponding algorithm, which should be configured with a kernel object, and the `nu` parameter, which controls the smoothness (in other words, the degree to which it controls the ratio between generalization and overfitting) of the solution.

The most widely used kernel is based on the Gaussian distribution and is known as the Radial Basis Kernel. It is implemented in the `radial_basis_kernel` class. Typically, we represent datasets in the `Dlib` library as a C++ `vector` of separate samples. So, before using this trainer object, we have to convert a matrix dataset into a vector:

```
void OneClassSvm(const Matrix& normal,
                 const Matrix& test) {
    typedef matrix<double, 0, 1> sample_type;
    typedef radial_basis_kernel<sample_type> kernel_type;
    svm_one_class_trainer<kernel_type> trainer;
    trainer.set_nu(0.5);                // control smoothness of the solution
    trainer.set_kernel(kernel_type(0.5));   // kernel bandwidth
    std::vector<sample_type> samples;
    for (long r = 0; r < normal.nr(); ++r) {
        auto row = rowm(normal, r);
        samples.push_back(row);
    }
    decision_function<kernel_type> df = trainer.train(samples);
    Clusters clusters;
    double dist_threshold = -2.0;
    auto detect = [&](auto samples) {
        for (long r = 0; r < samples.nr(); ++r) {
            auto row = dlib::rowm(samples, r);
            auto dist = df(row);
            if (p > dist_threshold) {
                // Do something with anomalies
            } else {
                // Do something with normal
            }
        }
    };
    detect(normal);
    detect(test);
}
```

The result of the training process is a decision function object of the `decision_function<kernel_type>` class that we can use for single sample classification. Objects of this type can be used as a regular function. The result of a decision function is the distance from the normal class boundary, so the most distant samples can be classified as anomalies. The following diagram shows an example of how the OCSVM algorithm from the `Dlib` library works. Note that the red dots correspond to anomalies:

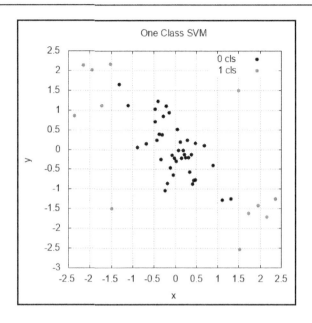

Multivariate Gaussian model with Dlib

Using the linear algebra facilities of the Dlib library (or any other library, for that matter), we can implement anomaly detection with the multivariate Gaussian distribution approach. The following example shows how to implement this approach with the Dlib linear algebra routines:

```
void multivariateGaussianDist(const Matrix& normal,
                              const Matrix& test) {
    // assume that rows are samples and columns are features
    // calculate per feature mean
    dlib::matrix<double> mu(1, normal.nc());
    dlib::set_all_elements(mu, 0);
    for (long c = 0; c < normal.nc(); ++c) {
        auto col_mean = dlib::mean(dlib::colm(normal, c));
        dlib::set_colm(mu, c) = col_mean;
    }
    // calculate covariance matrix
    dlib::matrix<double> cov(normal.nc(), normal.nc());
    dlib::set_all_elements(cov, 0);
    for (long r = 0; r < normal.nr(); ++r) {
        auto row = dlib::rowm(normal, r);
        cov += dlib::trans(row - mu) * (row - mu);
    }
    cov *= 1.0 / normal.nr();
```

```
double cov_det = dlib::det(cov); // matrix determinant
dlib::matrix<double> cov_inv = dlib::inv(cov); // inverse matrix
// define probability function
auto first_part =
1. / std::pow(2. * M_PI, normal.nc() / 2.) / std::sqrt(cov_det);
auto prob = [&](const dlib::matrix<double>& sample) {
    dlib::matrix<double> s = sample - mu;
    dlib::matrix<double> exp_val_m = s * (cov_inv * dlib::trans(s));
    double exp_val = -0.5 * exp_val_m(0, 0);
    double p = first_part * std::exp(exp_val);
    return p;
};
// change this parameter to see the decision boundary
double prob_threshold = 0.001;
auto detect = [&](auto samples) {
    for (long r = 0; r < samples.nr(); ++r) {
        auto row = dlib::rowm(samples, r);
        auto p = prob(row);
        if (p >= prob_threshold) {
            // Do something with anomalies
        } else {
            // Do something with normal
        }
    }
};
detect(normal);
detect(test);
}
```

The idea of this approach is to define a function that returns the probability of appearing, given a sample in a dataset. To implement such a function, we calculate the statistical characteristics of the training dataset. In the first step, we calculate the mean values of each feature and store them into the one-dimensional matrix. Then, we calculate the covariance matrix for the training samples using the formula for the correlation matrix that was given in the prior theoretical section named *Density estimation approach for anomaly detection*. Next, we determine the correlation matrix determinant and inverse version. We define a lambda function named prob to calculate the probability of a single sample using the formula for the probability calculation that was given in the *Density estimation approach for anomaly detection* section. We also define a probability threshold to separate anomalies.

Then, we iterate over all the examples (including the training and testing datasets) to find out how the algorithm separates regular samples from anomalies. In the following graph, we can see the result of this separation. The dots marked with a lighter color are anomalies:

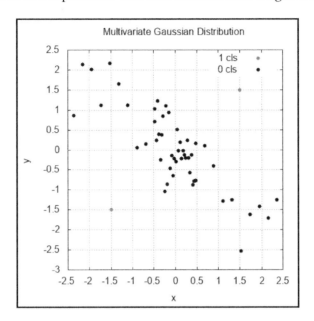

OCSVM with Shogun

Anomaly detection algorithms in the Shogun library are represented with the OCSVM algorithm. This algorithm is implemented in two classes: `CSVMLightOneClass` and `CLibSVMOneClass`. Note that they have different backends for SVM implementation: the former uses the `SVMLight` library (http://svmlight.joachims.org/), while the latter uses the `LibSVM` library (https://www.csie.ntu.edu.tw/~cjlin/libsvm/).

Let's start by looking at using the `CLibSVMOneClass` class for anomaly detection:

```
auto csv_file = some<CCSVFile>(dataset_name.string().c_str());
Matrix data;
data.load(csv_file);

Matrix train = data.submatrix(0, 50);
train = train.clone();
Matrix test = data.submatrix(50, data.num_cols);
test = test.clone();
```

```
// create a dataset
auto features = some<CDenseFeatures<DataType>>(train);
auto test_features = some<CDenseFeatures<DataType>>(test);

auto gauss_kernel = some<CGaussianKernel>(features, features, 0.5);

auto c = 0.5;
auto svm = some<CLibSVMOneClass>(c, gauss_kernel);
svm->train(features);

double dist_threshold = -3.15;

auto detect = [&](Some<CDenseFeatures<DataType>> data) {
    auto labels = svm->apply(data);
    for (int i = 0; i < labels->get_num_labels(); ++i) {
        auto dist = labels->get_value(i);
        if (dist > dist_threshold) {
            // Do something with anomalies
        } else {
            // Do something with normal
        }
    }
};

detect(features);
detect(test_features);
```

First, we loaded the dataset from the CSV file so that it's an object of the Matrix type and split it into two parts for training and testing. Then, we declared objects of the CDenseFeatures type in order to use loaded data in the Shogun algorithms. Next, we declared the kernel object of the CGaussianKernel type and used it to initialize the SVM algorithm object of the CLibSVMOneClass type. Note that the SVM object also takes a parameter that controls the smoothness of the solution. After we had the SVM object in place, we used the train() method with the training dataset to fit the algorithm to our data. Finally, we defined a distance threshold and used the apply() method on each of the datasets to detect anomalies. Notice that we used a different threshold value here than for the Dlib implementation. The following graph shows that the result of this algorithm is the same as our multivariate Gaussian distribution approach. The two samples from the dataset were detected as anomalies because they were artificially added to the dataset:

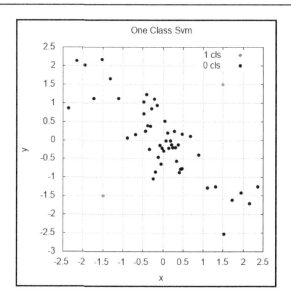

OCSVM with Shark-ML

The `Shark-ML` library also implements the OCSVM algorithm for anomaly detection. In this case, the `OneClassSvmTrainer` and the `KernelExpansion` classes implement the algorithm. The following example shows how it works:

```
UnlabeledData<RealVector> data;
importCSV(data, dataset_name);

// separate last two samples in test dataset
data.splitBatch(0, 50);
auto test_data = data.splice(1);

double gamma = 0.5;  // kernel bandwidth parameter
GaussianRbfKernel<> kernel(gamma);
KernelExpansion<RealVector> ke(&kernel);

double nu = 0.5;  // parameter of the method for controlling the
                  //smoothness of the solution

OneClassSvmTrainer<RealVector> trainer(&kernel, nu);
trainer.stoppingCondition().minAccuracy = 1e-6;
trainer.train(ke, data);

double dist_threshold = -0.2;
RealVector output;
```

```
auto detect = [&](const UnlabeledData<RealVector>& data) {
    for (size_t i = 0; i < data.numberOfElements(); ++i) {
        ke.eval(data.element(i), output);
        if (output[0] > dist_threshold) {
            // Do something with anomalies
        } else {
            // Do something with normal
        }
    }
};
detect(data);
detect(test_data);
```

First, we loaded the object of the `UnlabeledData` class from the CSV file and split it into two parts: one for training and one for testing. Then, we declared the kernel object of the `GaussianRbfKernel` type and initialized an object of the `KernelExpansion` class with it. The `KernelExpansion` class implements an affine linear kernel expansion. This can be represented with the following formula:

$$x : \mathbb{R}^d \to \mathbb{R}^d \ , \ \ x \mapsto \sum_{n=1}^{\ell} \alpha_n k(x_n, x) + b$$

Using this object's type is a requirement defined by the Shark-ML API, but we can use it for a more precise configuration of the algorithm. After we put the kernel expansion object in place, we initialized an object of the `OneClassSvmTrainer` class and configured it. We also configured the stopping criteria and the solution smoothness parameter. Then, we used the `train()` method to fit this algorithm to our training data. After training was completed, we used the `eval()` method of the `KernelExpansion` object to detect anomalies. This method returns values that we can interpret as distances from the class boundary. By doing this, we can compare them with the threshold.

Summary

In this chapter, we examined anomalies in data. We discussed several approaches to anomaly detection and looked at two kinds of anomalies: outliers and novelties. We considered the fact that anomaly detection is primarily an unsupervised learning problem, but despite this, some algorithms require labeled data, while others are semi-supervised. The reason for this is that, generally, there is a tiny number of positive examples (that is, anomalous samples) and a large number of negative examples (that is, standard samples) in anomaly detection tasks.

In other words, we usually don't have enough positive samples to train algorithms. That is why some solutions use labeled data to improve algorithm generalization and precision. On the contrary, supervised learning usually requires a large number of positive and negative examples, and their distribution needs to be balanced.

Also, notice that the task of detecting anomalies does not have a single formulation and that it is often interpreted differently, depending on the nature of the data and the goal of the concrete task. Moreover, choosing the correct anomaly detection method depends primarily on the task, data, and available a priori information. We also learned that different libraries can give slightly different results, even for the same algorithms.

In the following chapter, we will discuss the dimension reduction methods. Such methods help us to reduce the dimensionality of data with high dimensionality into a new representation of data with lower dimensionality while preserving the essential information from the original data.

Further reading

- Anomaly Detection Learning Resources: https://github.com/yzhao062/anomaly-detection-resources.
- Anomaly Detection: A Tutorial : http://webdocs.cs.ualberta.ca/~icdm2011/downloads/ICDM2011_anomaly_detection_tutorial.pdf.
- Anomaly Detection (Basics of Machine Learning Series): https://machinelearningmedium.com/2018/05/02/anomaly-detection/.
- Outlier Detection with One-Class SVMs: An Application to Melanoma Prognosis: https://www.ncbi.nlm.nih.gov/pmc/articles/PMC3041295/.
- Introduction to One-class Support Vector Machines: http://rvlasveld.github.io/blog/2013/07/12/introduction-to-one-class-support-vector-machines/.
- Isolation Forest: https://feitonyliu.files.wordpress.com/2009/07/liu-iforest.pdf.

6
Dimensionality Reduction

In this chapter, we'll go through a number of dimension reduction tasks. We'll look at the conditions in which dimension reduction is required and learn how to use dimension reduction algorithms efficiently in C++ with various libraries. Dimensionality reduction is where you transfer data that has a higher dimension into a new data representation with a lower dimension, all while preserving the most crucial information from the original data. Such a transformation can help us visualize multidimensional space, which can be useful in the data exploration stage or when identifying the most relevant features in dataset samples. Some **machine learning** (ML) techniques can perform better or faster if our data has a smaller number of features since it can consume fewer computational resources. The main purpose of this kind of transformation is to save the essential features—those features that hold the most critical information present in the original data.

The following topics will be covered in this chapter:

- An overview of dimension reduction methods
- Exploring linear methods for dimension reduction
- Exploring non-linear methods for dimension reduction
- Understanding dimension reduction algorithms with various C++ libraries

Technical requirements

The technologies you'll need for this chapter are as follows:

- The Shogun-toolbox library
- The Shark-ML library
- The Dlib library
- The plotcpp library
- A modern C++ compiler with C++17 support
- The CMake build system, version >= 3.8

The code files for this chapter can be found at the following GitHub repo: `https://github.com/PacktPublishing/Hands-On-Machine-Learning-with-CPP/tree/master/Chapter06`

An overview of dimension reduction methods

The main goal of dimension reduction methods is to make the dimension of the transformed representation correspond with the internal dimension of the data. In other words, it should be similar to the minimum number of variables necessary to express all the possible properties of the data. Reducing the dimension helps mitigate the impact of the curse of dimensionality and other undesirable properties that occur in high-dimensional spaces. As a result, reducing dimensionality can effectively solve problems regarding classification, visualization, and compressing high-dimensional data. It makes sense to apply dimensionality reduction only when particular data is redundant; otherwise, we can lose important information. In other words, if we are able to solve the problem using data of smaller dimensions with the same level of efficiency and accuracy, then some of our data is redundant. Dimensionality reduction allows us to reduce the time and computational costs of solving a problem. It also makes data and the results of data analysis easier to interpret.

It makes sense to reduce the number of features when the information that can be used to solve the problem at hand qualitatively is contained in a specific subset of features. Non-informative features are a source of additional noise and affect the accuracy of the model parameter's estimation. In addition, datasets with a large number of features can contain groups of correlated variables. The presence of such feature groups leads to the duplication of information, which may distort the model's results and affect how well it estimates the values of its parameters.

The methods surrounding dimensionality reduction are mainly unsupervised because we don't know which features or variables can be excluded from the original dataset without losing the most crucial information.

Dimensionality reduction methods can be classified into two groups: feature selection and the creation of new low-dimensional features. These methods can then be subdivided into *linear* and *non-linear* approaches, depending on the nature of the data and the mathematical apparatus being used.

Feature selection methods

Feature selection methods don't change the initial values of the variables or features; instead, they remove particular features from the source dataset that aren't relevant. Some of the feature selection methods we can use are as follows:

- **Missing value ratio:** This method is based on the idea that a feature that misses many values should be eliminated from a dataset because it doesn't contain valuable information and can distort the model's performance results. So, if we have some criteria for identifying missing values, we can calculate their ratio to typical values and set a threshold that we can use to eliminate features with a high missing value ratio.

- **Low variance filter**: This method is used to remove features with low variance because such features don't contain enough information to improve model performance. To apply this method, we need to calculate the variance for each feature, sort them in ascending order by this value, and leave only those with the highest variance values.

- **High correlation filter**: This method is based on the idea that if two features have a high correlation, then they carry similar information. Also, highly correlated features can significantly reduce the performance of some machine learning models, such as linear and logistic regression. Therefore, the primary goal of this method is to leave only the features that have a high correlation with target values and don't have much correlation between each other.

- **Random forest**: This method can be used for feature selection effectively (although it wasn't initially designed for this kind of task). After we've built the forest, we can estimate what features are most important by estimating the impurity factor in the tree's nodes. This factor shows the measure of split distinctness in the tree's nodes, and it demonstrates how well the current feature (a random tree only uses one feature in a node to split input data) splits data into two distinct buckets. Then, this estimation can be averaged across all the trees in the forest. Features that split data better than others can be selected as the most important ones.

- **Backward feature elimination and forward feature selection**: These are iterative methods that are used for feature selection. In backward feature elimination, after we've trained the model with a full feature set and estimated its performance, we remove its features one by one and train the model with a reduced feature set. Then, we compare the model's performances and decide how much performance is improved by removing feature changes – in other words, we're deciding how important each feature is. In forward feature selection, the training process goes in the opposite direction. We start with one feature and then add more of them. These methods are very computationally expensive and can only be used on small datasets.

Dimensionality reduction methods

Dimensionality reduction methods transform an original feature set into a new feature set that usually contains new features that weren't present in the initial dataset. These methods can also be divided into two subclasses—linear and non-linear. The non-linear methods are usually more computationally expensive, so if we have a prior assumption about our feature's data linearity, we can choose the more suitable class of methods at the initial stage.

The following sections will describe the various linear and non-linear methods we can use for dimension reduction.

Exploring linear methods for dimension reduction

This section describes the most popular linear methods that are used for dimension reduction.

Principal component analysis

Principal component analysis (PCA) is one of the most intuitively simple and frequently used methods for applying dimension reduction to data and projecting it onto an orthogonal subspace of features. In a very general form, it can be represented as the assumption that all our observations look like some ellipsoid in the subspace of our original space. Our new basis in this space coincides with the axes of this ellipsoid. This assumption allows us to get rid of strongly correlated features simultaneously since the basis vectors of the space we project them onto are orthogonal.

The dimension of this ellipsoid is equal to the dimension of the original space, but our assumption that the data lies in a subspace of a smaller dimension allows us to discard the other subspaces in the new projection; namely, the subspace with the least extension of the ellipsoid. We can do this greedily, choosing a new element one by one on the basis of our new subspace, and then taking the axis of the ellipsoid with maximum dispersion successively from the remaining dimensions.

To reduce the dimension of our data from n to $k, k \leq n$, we need to choose the top k axes of such an ellipsoid, sorted in descending order by dispersion along the axes. To begin with, we calculate the variances and covariances of the original features. This is done by using a covariance matrix. By the definition of covariance, for two signs, X_i and X_j, their covariance should be as follows:

$$cov(X_i, X_j) = E[(X_i - \mu_i)(X_j - \mu_j)] = E[X_i X_j] - \mu_i \mu_j$$

Here, μ_i is the mean of the ith feature.

In this case, we note that the covariance is symmetric and that the covariance of the vector itself is equal to its dispersion. Thus, the covariance matrix is a symmetric matrix where the dispersions of the corresponding features lie on the diagonal and the covariances of the corresponding pairs of features lie outside the diagonal. In the matrix view, where X is the observation matrix, our covariance matrix looks like this:

$$\Sigma = E[(\mathbf{X} - E[\mathbf{X}])(\mathbf{X} - E[\mathbf{X}])^T]$$

The covariance matrix is a generalization of variance in the case of multidimensional random variables – it also describes the shape (spread) of a random variable, as does the variance. Matrices such as linear operators have eigenvalues and eigenvectors. They are interesting because when we act on the corresponding linear space or transform it with our matrix, the eigenvectors remain in place, and they are only multiplied by the corresponding eigenvalues. This means they define a subspace that remains in place or *goes into itself* when we apply a linear operator matrix to it. Formally, an eigenvector, w_i, with an eigenvalue for a matrix is defined simply as $M w_i = \lambda_i w_i$.

The covariance matrix for our sample, x, can be represented as a product, $x^T x$. From the Rayleigh relation, it follows that the maximum variation of our dataset can be achieved along the eigenvector of this matrix, which corresponds to the maximum eigenvalue. This is also true for projections on a higher number of dimensions – the variance (covariance matrix) of the projection onto the m-dimensional space is maximum in the direction of m eigenvectors with maximum eigenvalues. Thus, the principal components that we would like to project our data for are simply the eigenvectors of the corresponding top k pieces of the eigenvalues of this matrix.

The largest vector has a direction similar to the regression line, and by projecting our sample onto it, we lose information, similar to the sum of the residual members of the regression. It is necessary to make the operation, $v^T X$ (the vector length (magnitude) should be equal to one), perform the projection. If we don't have a single vector and have a hyperplane instead, then instead of the vector, v^T, we take the matrix of basis vectors, V^T. The resulting vector (or matrix) is an array of projections of our observations; that is, we need to multiply our data matrix on the basis vectors matrix, and we get the projection of our data orthogonally. Now, if we multiply the transpose of our data matrix and the matrix of the principal component vectors, we restore the original sample in the space where we projected it onto the basis of the principal components. If the number of components was less than the dimension of the original space, we lose some information.

Singular value decomposition

Singular value decomposition (SVD) is an important method that's used to analyze data. The resulting matrix decomposition has a meaningful interpretation from a machine learning point of view. It can also be used to calculate PCA. SVD is rather slow. Therefore, when the matrices are too large, randomized algorithms are used. However, the SVD calculation is computationally more efficient than the calculation for the covariance matrix and its eigenvalues in the original PCA approach. Therefore, PCA is often implemented in terms of SVD. Let's take a look.

The essence of SVD is pure—any matrix (real or complex) is represented as a product of three matrices:

$$X = U\Sigma V^*$$

Here, $\mathbf{U}$ is a unitary matrix of order m and $\boldsymbol{\Sigma}$ is a matrix of size $m \times n$ on the main diagonal, which is where there are non-negative numbers called singular values (elements outside the main diagonal are zero—such matrices are sometimes called rectangular diagonal matrices).$\mathbf{V}^*$ is a Hermitian-conjugate $\mathbf{v}$ matrix of order n. The m columns of the matrixes $\mathbf{U}$ and n columns of the matrix $\mathbf{V}$ are called the left and right singular vectors of matrix $\mathbf{x}$, respectively. To reduce the number of dimensions, matrix $\boldsymbol{\Sigma}$ is important, the elements of which, when raised to the second power, can be interpreted as a variance that each component puts into a joint distribution, and they are in descending order:
$\sigma_1 \geq \sigma_2 \geq \cdots \geq \sigma_{noise}$. Therefore, when we choose the number of components in SVD (as in PCA), we should take the sum of their variances into account.

The relation between SVD and PCA can be described in the following way: $\mathbf{C}$ is the covariance matrix given by $\mathbf{C} = \mathbf{X}^\top \mathbf{X}/(n-1)$. It is a symmetric matrix, so it can be diagonalized: $\mathbf{C} = \mathbf{V}\mathbf{L}\mathbf{V}^\top$, where $\mathbf{V}$ is a matrix of eigenvectors (each column is an eigenvector) and $\mathbf{L}$ is a diagonal matrix of eigenvalues, λ_i, in decreasing order on the diagonal. The eigenvectors are called principal axes or principal directions of the data. Projections of the data on the principal axes are called **principal components**, also known as **principal component scores**. They are newly transformed variables. The jth principal component is given by the jth column of $\mathbf{xv}$. The coordinates of the ith data point in the new principal component's space are given by the ith row of $\mathbf{xv}$.

By performing SVD on $\mathbf{x}$, we get $\mathbf{X} = \mathbf{USV}^\top$, where $\mathbf{U}$ is a unitary matrix and $\mathbf{S}$ is the diagonal matrix of singular values, s_i. We can observe that $\mathbf{C} = \mathbf{VSU}^\top \mathbf{USV}^\top/(n-1) = \mathbf{V}\dfrac{\mathbf{S}^2}{n-1}\mathbf{V}^\top$, which means that the right singular vectors, $\mathbf{V}$, are principal directions and that singular values are related to the eigenvalues of the covariance matrix via $\lambda_i = s_i^2/(n-1)$. Principal components are given by $\mathbf{XV} = \mathbf{USV}^\top \mathbf{V} = \mathbf{US}$.

Independent component analysis

The **independent component analysis (ICA)** method was proposed as a way to solve the problem of **blind signal separation (BSS)**; that is, selecting independent signals from mixed data. Let's look at an example of the task of BSS. Suppose we have two people in the same room who are talking, generating acoustic waves. We have two microphones in different parts of the room, recording sound. The analysis system receives two signals from the two microphones, each of which is a digitized mixture of two acoustic waves – one from people speaking and one from some other noise (for example, playing music). Our goal is to select our initial signals from the incoming mixtures. Mathematically, the problem can be described as follows. We represent the incoming mixture in the form of a linear combination, where a represents the displacement coefficients and **s** represents the values of the vector of independent components:

$$x_i(t) = \sum_{j=1}^{n} a_{i,j} s_j(t), (i = 1, \ldots, m)$$

In matrix form, this can be expressed as follows:

$$\mathbf{x} = \mathbf{A}\mathbf{s}$$

Here, we have to find the following:

$$\mathbf{y} = \mathbf{A}^{-1}\mathbf{x} = \mathbf{W}\mathbf{x}.$$

In this equation, X is a matrix of input signal values, A is a matrix of displacement coefficients or mixing matrix, and s is a matrix of independent components. Thus, the problem is divided into two. The first part is to get the estimate, $\mathbf{y} = \mathbf{W}\mathbf{x}$, of the variables, $s_j(t)$, of the original independent components. The second part is to find the matrix, $\mathbf{A}$. How this method works is based on two principles:

- Independent components must be statistically independent (s matrix values). Roughly speaking, the values of one vector of an independent component do not affect the values of another component.
- Independent components must have a non-Gaussian distribution.

The theoretical basis of ICA is the central limit theorem, which states that the distribution of the sum (average or linear combination) of N independent random variables approaches Gaussian for $N \to \infty$. In particular, if x_i are random variables independent of each other, taken from an arbitrary distribution with an average, μ, and a variance of σ^2, then if we denote the mean of these variables as $\bar{x} = \frac{1}{N}\sum_{i=1}^{N} x_i$, we can say that $\frac{\bar{x}-\mu}{\sigma/\sqrt{N}}$ approaches the Gaussian with a mean of 0 and a variance of 1. To solve the BSS problem, we need to find the matrix, $\mathbf{W}$, so that $y = \mathbf{W}x = \mathbf{W}\mathbf{A}s$. Here, the $\mathbf{S}$ should be as close as possible to the original independent sources. We can consider this approach as the inverse process of the central limit theorem. All ICA methods are based on the same fundamental approach – finding a matrix, $\mathbf{W}$, that maximizes non-Gaussianity, thereby minimizing the independence of $\mathbf{S}$.

The Fast ICA algorithm aims to maximize the function, $\sum_i E\{G(y_i)\}$, where $y_i = w_i^T x$ are components of $y = \mathbf{W}x$. Therefore, we can rewrite the function's equation in the following form:

$$\sum_i E\{G(y_i)\} = \sum_i E\{G\left(w_i^T x\right)\}$$

Here, the w_i^T vector is the ith row of the matrix, $\mathbf{W}$.

The ICA algorithm performs the following steps:

1. Chooses the initial value of w.

2. Calculates $w \Rightarrow E\{xg'\left(w^T x\right)\} - E\{g'\left(w^T x\right)\}w$, where $g(z) = \frac{dG(z)}{dz}$ is the derivative of the function, $G(z)$.

3. Normalizes $w \Rightarrow \frac{w}{\|w\|}$.

4. Repeats the previous two steps until w stops changing.

To measure non-Gaussianity, Fast ICA relies on a nonquadratic nonlinear function, *G (z)*, that can take the following forms:

$$G(z) = logcosh(u), g(z) = tanh(z), g'(z) = 1 - tanh^2(z)$$
$$G(z) = -\exp^{\frac{-z^2}{2}}, g(z) = z\exp^{\frac{-z^2}{2}}, g'(z) = (1 - z^2)\exp^{\frac{-z^2}{2}}$$

Linear discriminant analysis

Linear discriminant analysis (LDA) is a type of multivariate analysis that allows us to estimate differences between two or more groups of objects at the same time. The basis of discriminant analysis is the assumption that the descriptions of the objects of each kth class are instances of a multidimensional random variable that's distributed according to the normal (Gaussian) law, $N_m(\mu_k; \Sigma_k)$, with an average, μ_k, and the following covariance matrix:

$$\mathbf{C}_k = \frac{1}{n_k - 1} \sum_{i=1}^{n_k} (\mathbf{x}_{ik} - \mu_k)^T (\mathbf{x}_{ik} - \mu_k)$$

The index, m, indicates the dimension of the feature space. Consider a simplified geometric interpretation of the LDA algorithm for the case of two classes. Let the discriminant variables, x, be the axes of the m-dimensional Euclidean space. Each object (sample) is a point of this space with coordinates representing the fixed values of each variable. If both classes differ from each other in observable variables (features), they can be represented as clusters of points in different regions of the considered space that may partially overlap. To determine the position of each class, we can calculate its centroid, which is an imaginary point whose coordinates are the average values of the variables (features) in the class. The task of discriminant analysis is to create an additional z axis that passes through a cloud of points in such a way that the projections on it provide the best separability into two classes (in other words, it maximizes the distance between classes). Its position is given by a linear discriminant function (linear discriminant, LD) with weights, β_j, that determine the contribution of each initial variable, x_j:

$$z(\mathbf{x}) = \beta_1 x_1 + \beta_2 x_2 + \cdots + \beta_m x_m$$

If we assume that the covariance matrices of the objects of classes 1 and 2 are equal, that is, $C = C_1 = C_2$, then the vector of coefficients, $\beta_1, \ldots, \beta_m$, of the linear discriminant, $z(x)$, can be calculated using the formula $\beta = C^{-1}(\mu_1 - \mu_2)$, where C^{-1} is the inverse of the covariance matrix and μ_k is the mean of the kth class. The resulting axis coincides with the equation of a line passing through the centroids of two groups of class objects. The generalized Mahalanobis distance, which is equal to the distance between them in the multidimensional feature space, is estimated as $D^2 = \beta(\mu_1 - \mu_2)$. Thus, in addition to the assumption regarding the normal (Gaussian) distribution of class data, which in practice occurs quite rarely, the LDA has a stronger assumption about the statistical equality of intragroup dispersions and correlation matrices. If there are no significant differences between them, they are combined into a calculated covariance matrix, as follows:

$$C = (C_1(n_1 - 1) + C_2(n_2 - 1)) / (n_1 + n_2 - 2)$$

This principle can be generalized to a larger number of classes. The final algorithm may look like this:

$$S_W = \sum_{i=1}^{n} \Sigma_i$$

The interclass scattering matrix is calculated like this:

$$S_B = \sum_{i=1}^{n} N_i (\mu_i - \mu)(\mu_i - \mu)^T$$

Here, $\mu = \dfrac{1}{n} \sum_{i=1}^{n} x_i$ is the mean of all objects (samples), n is the number of classes, N_i is the number of objects in the ith class, $\mu_i = \dfrac{1}{n_i} \sum \{x \,|\, x \in c_i\}$ is the intraclass' mean, $\Sigma_i = X_i C_n X_i^T$ is the scattering matrix for the ith class, and $C_n = I_n - \dfrac{1}{n} J$ is a centering matrix where J is the $n \times n$ matrix of all 1s.

Based on these matrices, the $S_W^{-1} S_B$ matrix is calculated, for which the eigenvalues and the corresponding eigenvectors are determined. In the diagonal elements of the matrix, we must select the *s* of the largest eigenvalues and transform the matrix, leaving only the corresponding *s* rows in it. The resulting matrix can be used to convert all objects into the lower-dimensional space.

This method requires labeled data, meaning it is a supervised method.

Factor analysis

Factor analysis is used to reduce the number of variables that are used to describe data and determine the relationships between them. During the analysis, variables that correlate with each other are combined into one factor. As a result, the dispersion between components is redistributed, and the structure of factors becomes more understandable. After combining the variables, the correlation of components within each factor becomes higher than their correlation with components from other factors. It is assumed that known variables depend on a smaller number of unknown variables and that we have a random error that can be expressed as follows:

$$X_{ij} = \sum_{k=1}^{K} \alpha_{i,k} W_{j,k} + \varepsilon_{ij}$$

Here, α is the load and W is the factor.

The concept of **factor load** is essential. It is used to describe the role of the factor (variable) when we wish to form a specific vector from a new basis. The essence of factor analysis is the procedure of rotating factors, that is, redistributing the dispersion according to a specific method. The purpose of rotations is to define a simple structure of factor loadings. Rotation can be orthogonal and oblique. In the first form of rotation, each successive factor is determined to maximize the variability that remains from the previous factors. Therefore, the factors are independent and uncorrelated with each other. The second type is a transformation in which factors correlate with each other. There are about 13 methods of rotation that are used in both forms. The factors that have a similar effect on the elements of the new basis are combined into one group. Then, from each group, it is recommended to leave one representative. Some algorithms, instead of choosing a representative, calculate a new factor with some heuristics that becomes central to the group.

Dimensionality reduction occurs while transitioning to a system of factors that are representatives of groups, and the other factors are discarded. There are several commonly used criteria for determining the number of factors. Some of these criteria can be used together to complement each other. An example of a criterion that's used to determine the number of factors is the Kaiser criterion or the eigenvalue criterion: only factors with eigenvalues equal to or greater than *one* are selected. This means that if a factor does not select a variance equivalent to at least one variance of one variable, then it is omitted. The general factor analysis algorithm follows these steps:

1. Calculates the correlation matrix.
2. Selects the number of factors for inclusion, for example, with the Kaiser criterion.
3. Extracts the initial set of factors. There are several different extraction methods, including maximum likelihood, principal component analysis, and principal axis extraction.
4. Rotates the factors to a final solution that is equal to the one that was obtained in the initial extraction but that has the most straightforward interpretation.

Multidimensional scaling

Multidimensional scaling (MDS) can be considered as an alternative to factor analysis when, in addition to the correlation matrices, an arbitrary type of object similarity matrix can be used as input data. MDS is not so much a formal mathematical procedure but rather a method of efficiently placing objects, thus keeping an appropriate distance between them in a new feature space. The dimension of the new space in MDS is always substantially less than the original space. The data that's used for analysis by MDS is often obtained from the matrix of pairwise comparisons of objects. The main MDS algorithm's goal is to restore the unknown dimension, p, of the analyzed feature space and assign coordinates to each object in such a way that the calculated pairwise Euclidean distances between the objects coincide as much as possible with the specified pairwise comparison matrix. We are talking about restoring the coordinates of the new reduced feature space with the accuracy of orthogonal transformation, ensuring the pairwise distances between the objects do not change.

Thus, the aim of multidimensional scaling methods can also be formulated in order to display the configuration information of the original multidimensional data that's given by the pairwise comparison matrix. This is provided as a configuration of points in the corresponding space of lower dimension.

Classical MDS assumes that the unknown coordinate matrix, X, can be expressed by eigenvalue decomposition, $B = XX'$. B can be computed from the proximity matrix D (a matrix with distances between samples) by using double centering. The general MDS algorithm follows these steps:

1. Computes the squared proximity matrix, $D^{(2)} = \left[d_{ij}^2 \right]$.

2. Applies double centering, $B = -\frac{1}{2} J D^{(2)} J$ using the centering matrix, $J = I - \frac{1}{n} \mathbf{1} \mathbf{1}'$, where n is the number of objects.

3. Determines the m largest eigenvalues, $\lambda_1, \lambda_2, \ldots, \lambda_m$, and the corresponding eigenvectors, $e_1, e_2, \ldots, e_m$, of B (where m is the number of dimensions desired for the output).

4. Computes $X = E_m \Lambda_m^{1/2}$, where E_m is the matrix of m eigenvectors and Λ_m is the diagonal matrix of m eigenvalues of B.

The disadvantage of the multidimensional scaling method is that it does not take into account the distribution of nearby points since it uses Euclidean distances in calculations. If you ever find multidimensional data lying on a curved manifold, the distance between data points can be much more than Euclidean.

Now that we've discussed the linear methods we can use for dimension reduction, let's look at what non-linear methods exist.

Exploring non-linear methods for dimension reduction

In this section, we'll discuss the widespread non-linear methods and algorithms that are used for dimension reduction.

Kernel PCA

Classic PCA is a linear projection method that works well if the data is linearly separable. However, in the case of linearly non-separable data, a non-linear approach is required. The basic idea of working with linearly inseparable data is to project it into a space with a larger number of dimensions, where it becomes linearly separable. We can choose a non-linear mapping function, ϕ, so that the sample mapping, x, can be written as $x \rightarrow \phi(x)$. This is called the **kernel function**. The term **kernel** describes a function that calculates the scalar product of mapping (in a higher-order space) samples x with ϕ, $k(x_i, x_j) = \phi(\mathbf{x_i})\phi(\mathbf{x_j})^T$. This scalar product can be interpreted as the distance measured in the new space. In other words, the ϕ function maps the original d-dimensional elements into the k-dimensional feature space of a higher dimension by creating non-linear combinations of the original objects. For example, a function that displays 2D samples, $x = \{x_1, x_2\}$, in 3D space can look like $\phi(x) \rightarrow x_1^2, x_2^2, \sqrt{2}x_1x_2$.

In a linear PCA approach, we are interested in the principal components that maximize the variance in the dataset. We can maximize variance by calculating the eigenvectors (principal components) that correspond to the largest eigenvalues based on the covariance matrix of our data and project our data onto these eigenvectors. This approach can be generalized to data that is mapped into a higher dimension space using the kernel function. But in practice, the covariance matrix in a multidimensional space is not explicitly calculated since we can use a method called the **kernel trick**. The kernel trick allows us to project data onto the principal components without explicitly calculating the projections, which is much more efficient. The general approach is as follows:

1. Compute the *kernel matrix* equal to $K_{i,j} = k(x_i, x_j)$.
2. Make it so that it has a zero mean value, $K' = K - 1_N K - K 1_N + 1_N K 1_N$, where 1_N is a matrix of N x N size with 1/N elements.
3. Calculate the eigenvalues and eigenvectors of K.
4. Sort the eigenvectors in descending order, according to their eigenvalues.
5. Take n eigenvectors that correspond to the largest eigenvalues, where n is the number of dimensions of a new feature space.

These eigenvectors are projections of our data onto the corresponding main components. The main difficulty of this process is selecting the correct kernel and configuring its hyperparameters. Two frequently used kernels are the polynomial kernel $k(x, y) = (x^T y + c)^d$ and the Gaussian (RBF) $k(x, y) = exp\left(-\gamma \|\mathbf{x} - \mathbf{y}\|_2^2\right)$ ones.

IsoMap

The IsoMap algorithm is based on the manifold projection technique. In mathematics, the manifold is a topological space (which is, in general, a set of points with their neighbors) that locally resembles the Euclidian space near each point. For example, one-dimensional manifolds include lines and circles but not figures with self-intersections. Two-dimensional manifolds are called **surfaces**; for example, they can be a sphere, a plane, or a torus, but these surfaces can't have self-intersection. For example, a circle is a one-dimensional manifold embedded into a two-dimensional space. Here, each arc of the circle locally resembles a straight line segment. A 3D curve can also be a manifold if it can be divided into straight-line segments that can be embedded in 3D space without self-intersections. A 3D shape can be a manifold if its surface can be divided into flat plane patches without self-intersections.

The basics of applying manifold projection techniques are to search for a manifold that is close to the data, project the data onto the manifold, and then unfold it. The most popular technique that's used to find the manifold is to build a graph based on information about data points. Usually, these data points are placed into the graph nodes, and the edges simulate the relationships between the data points.

The IsoMap algorithm depends on two parameters:

- The number of neighbors, k, used to search for geodetic distances
- The dimension of the final space, m

In brief, the IsoMap algorithm follows these steps:

1. First, it constructs a graph representing geodesic distances. For each point, we search the k nearest neighbors and construct a weighted, undirected graph from the distances to these nearest neighbors. The edge weight is the Euclidean distance to the neighbor.

2. Using an algorithm to find the shortest distance in the graph, for example, Dijkstra's algorithm, we need to find the shortest distance between each pair of vertices. We can consider this distance as a geodesic distance on a manifold.

3. Based on the matrix of pairwise geodesic distances we obtained in the previous step, train the MDS algorithm.

4. The MDS algorithm associates a set of points in the m-dimensional space with the initial set of distances.

Sammon mapping

Sammon mapping is one of the first non-linear dimensionality reduction algorithms. In contrast to traditional dimensionality reduction methods, such as PCA, Sammon mapping does not define a data conversion function directly. On the contrary, it only determines the measure of how well the conversion results (a specific dataset of a smaller dimension) correspond to the structure of the original dataset. In other words, it does not try to find the optimal transformation of the original data; instead, it searches for another dataset of lower dimensions with a structure that's as close to the original one as possible. The algorithm can be described as follows. Let's say we have nN-dimensional vectors, $x_i (i = 1, 2, \ldots, n)$. Here, n vectors are defined in the M-dimensional space, $(M = 2, 3)$, which is denoted by y_i. The distances between the vectors in the N-dimensional space will be denoted by $d_{ij}^* = (y_i, y_j)$ and in the M-dimensional space, $d_{ij} = (x_i, x_j)$. To determine the distance between the vectors, we can use any metric; in particular, the Euclidean distance. The goal of non-linear Sammon mapping is to search a selection of vectors, y, in order to minimize the error function, E, which is defined by the following formula:

$$E = \frac{1}{c} \sum_{i<j}^{n} \frac{\left[d_{ij}^* - d_{ij} \right]^2}{d_{ij}^*}$$

$$c = \sum_{i<j}^{n} d_{ij}^*$$

$$d_{ij} = \sqrt{\sum_{k=1}^{M} \left[y_{ik} - y_{jk} \right]^2}$$

To minimize the error function, E, Sammon used Newton's minimization method, which can be simplified as follows:

$$y_{pq}^{k+1} = y_{pq} - \eta \Delta_{pq}(k)$$

$$\Delta_{pq} = \frac{\frac{\partial E}{\partial y_{pq}}}{\frac{\partial^2 E}{\partial y_{pq}^2}}$$

Here, η is the learning rate.

Distributed stochastic neighbor embedding

The **stochastic neighbor embedding** (SNE) problem is formulated as follows: we have a dataset with points described by a multidimensional variable with a dimension of space substantially higher than three. It is necessary to obtain a new variable that exists in a two-dimensional or three-dimensional space that would maximally preserve the structure and patterns in the original data. The difference between t-SNE and the classic SNE lies in the modifications that simplify the process of finding the global minima. The main modification is replacing the normal distribution with the Student's t-distribution for low-dimensional data. SNE begins by converting the multidimensional Euclidean distance between points into conditional probabilities that reflect the similarity of points. Mathematically, it looks like this:

$$p_{j|i} = \frac{\exp\left(-||x_i - x_j||^2/2\delta_i^2\right)}{\sum_{k \neq i} \exp\left(-||x_i - x_k||^2/2\delta_i^2\right)}$$

This formula shows how close the point x_j lies to the point x_i with a Gaussian distribution around x_i, with a given deviation of δ. δ is different for each point. It is chosen so that the points in areas with higher density have less variance than others.

Let's denote two-dimensional or three-dimensional mappings of the (x_i, x_j) pair as the (y_i, y_j) pair. It is necessary to estimate the conditional probability using the same formula. The standard deviation is $\frac{1}{\sqrt{2}}$:

$$q_{j|i} = \frac{\exp\left(-\|y_i - y_j\|^2\right)}{\sum_{k \neq i} \exp\left(-\|y_i - y_k\|^2\right)}$$

If the mapping points, y_i and y_j, correctly simulate the similarity between the original points of the higher dimension, x_i and x_j, then the corresponding conditional probabilities, $p_{j|i}$ and $q_{j|i}$, will be equivalent. As an obvious assessment of the quality of how $q_{j|i}$ reflects $p_{j|i}$, divergence, or the Kullback-Leibler distance, is used. SNE minimizes the sum of such distances for all mapping points using gradient descent. The following formula determines the loss function for this method:

$$Cost = \sum_i \sum_j p_{j|i} \log\left(\frac{p_{j|i}}{q_{j|i}}\right)$$

It has the following gradient:

$$\frac{\partial Cost}{\partial y} = 2 \sum_j (p_{j|i} - q_{j|i} + p_{i|j} - q_{i|j})(y_i - y_j)$$

The authors of this problem proposed the following physical analogy for the optimization process. Let's imagine that springs connect all the mapping points. The stiffness of the spring connecting points i and j depends on the difference between the similarity of two points in a multidimensional space and two points in a mapping space. In this analogy, the gradient is the resultant force that acts on a point in the mapping space. If we let the system go, after some time, it results in balance, and this is the desired distribution. Algorithmically, it searches for balance while taking the following moments into account:

$$Y^{(t)} = Y^{(t+1)} + \eta \frac{\partial Cost}{\partial y} + \alpha(t)(Y^{(t-1)} - Y^{(t-2)})$$

Here, η is the learning rate and α is the coefficient of inertia. Classic SNE also allows us to get good results but can be associated with difficulties when optimizing the loss function and the crowding problem. t-SNE doesn't solve these problems in general, but it makes them much more manageable.

The loss function in t-SNE has two principal differences from the loss function of the classic SNE. The first one is that it has a symmetric form of similarity in a multidimensional space and a simpler gradient version. Secondly, instead of using a Gaussian distribution for points from the mapping space, the t-distribution (Student) is used.

Autoencoders

Autoencoders represent a particular class of neural networks that are configured so that the output of the autoencoder is as close as possible to the input signal. In its most straightforward representation, the autoencoder can be modeled as a multilayer perceptron in which the number of neurons in the output layer is equal to the number of inputs. The following diagram shows that by choosing an intermediate hidden layer of a smaller dimension, we compress the source data into the lower dimension. Usually, values from this intermediate layer are a result of an autoencoder:

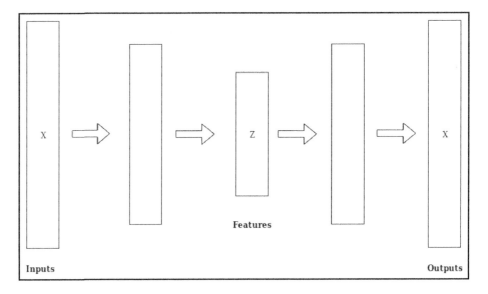

Now that we have learned about the linear and non-linear methods that can be used for dimension reduction and explored the components of each of the methods in detail, we can enhance our implementation of dimension reduction with the help of some practical examples.

Understanding dimension reduction algorithms with various C++ libraries

Let's look at how to use dimensionality reduction algorithms in practice. All of these examples use the same dataset, which contains four normally distributed 2D point sets that have been transformed with Swiss roll mapping, $f(x, y) \rightarrow x\cos(x), y, x\sin(x)$, into a 3D space. The following graph shows the result of this mapping. You can find the original dataset and mapping details at `http://people.cs.uchicago.edu/~dinoj/manifold/swissroll.html`:

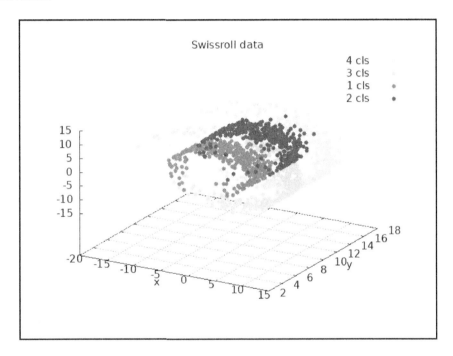

This dataset is labeled. Each of the normally distributed parts has its own labels, and we can see these labels as a certain color on the result. We use these colors to show transformation results for each of the algorithms we'll be using in the following samples. This gives us an idea of how the algorithm works. The following sections provide concrete examples of how to use the `Dlib`, `Shogun`, and `Shark-ML` libraries.

Using the Dlib library

There are three dimensionality reduction methods in the `Dlib` library – two linear ones, known as PCA and LDA, and one non-linear one, known as Sammon mapping.

PCA

PCA is one of the most popular dimensionality reduction algorithms and it has a couple of implementations in the `Dlib` library. There is the `Dlib::vector_normalizer_pca` type, for which objects can be used to perform PCA on user data. This implementation also normalizes the data. In some cases, this automatic normalization is useful because we always have to perform PCA on normalized data. An object of this type should be parameterized with the input data sample type. After we've instantiated an object of this type, we use the `train()` method to fit the model to our data. The `train()` method takes `std::vector` as samples and the `eps` value as parameters. The `eps` value controls how many dimensions should be preserved after the PCA has been transformed. This can be seen in the following code:

```
void PCAReduction(const std::vector<Matrix> &data, double target_dim) {
  Dlib::vector_normalizer_pca<Matrix> pca;
  pca.train(data, target_dim / data[0].nr());

  std::vector<Matrix> new_data;
  new_data.reserve(data.size());
  for (size_t i = 0; i < data.size(); ++i) {
    new_data.emplace_back(pca(data[i]));
  }

  for (size_t r = 0; r < new_data.size(); ++r) {
    Matrix vec = new_data[r];
    double x = vec(0, 0);
    double y = vec(1, 0);
  }
}
```

After the algorithm has been trained, we use the object to transform individual samples. Take a look at the first loop in the code and notice how the `pca([data[i]])` call performs this transformation.

The following graph shows the result of the PCA transformation:

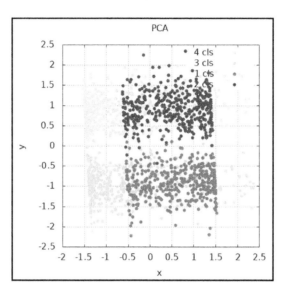

Data compression with PCA

We can use dimensionality reduction algorithms for a slightly different task – data compression with information loss. This can be easily demonstrated when applying the PCA algorithm to images. Let's implement PCA from scratch with the `Dlib` library using SVD decomposition. We can't use an existing implementation because it performs normalization in a way we can't fully control.

First, we need to load an image and transform it into matrix form:

```
void PCACompression(const std::string& image_file, long target_dim) {
    array2d<Dlib::rgb_pixel> img;
    load_image(img, image_file);

    array2d<unsigned char> img_gray;
    assign_image(img_gray, img);
    save_png(img_gray, "original.png");

    array2d<DataType> tmp;
    assign_image(tmp, img_gray);
```

```
Matrix img_mat = Dlib::mat(tmp);
img_mat /= 255.;   // scale

std::cout << "Original data size " << img_mat.size() << std::endl;
```

After we've loaded the RGB image, we convert it into grayscale and transform its values into floating points. The next step is to transform the image matrix into samples that we can use for PCA training. This can be done by splitting the image into rectangular patches that are 8 x 8 in size with the `Dlib::subm()` function and then flattening them with the `Dlib::reshape_to_column_vector()` function:

```
std::vector<Matrix> data;
int patch_size = 8;

for (long r = 0; r < img_mat.nr(); r += patch_size) {
    for (long c = 0; c < img_mat.nc(); c += patch_size) {
        auto sm = Dlib::subm(img_mat, r, c, patch_size, patch_size);
        data.emplace_back(Dlib::reshape_to_column_vector(sm));
    }
}
```

When we have our samples, we can normalize them by subtracting the mean and dividing them by their standard deviation. We can make these operations vectorized by converting our vector of samples into the matrix type. We do this with the `Dlib::mat()` function:

```
// normalize data
auto data_mat = mat(data);
Matrix m = mean(data_mat);
Matrix sd = reciprocal(sqrt(variance(data_mat)));

matrix<decltype(data_mat)::type, 0, 1,
decltype(data_mat)::mem_manager_type>
x(data_mat);
for (long r = 0; r < x.size(); ++r)
  x(r) = pointwise_multiply(x(r) - m, sd);
```

After we've prepared the data samples, we calculate the covariance matrix with the `Dlib::covariance()` function and perform SVD with the `Dlib::svd()` function. The SVD results are the eigenvalues matrix and the eigenvectors matrix. We sorted the eigenvectors according to the eigenvalues and left only a small number (in our case, 10 of them) of eigenvectors correspondent to the biggest eigenvalues. The number of eigenvectors we left is the number of dimensions in the new feature space:

```
Matrix temp, eigen, pca;
// Compute the svd of the covariance matrix
Dlib::svd(covariance(x), temp, eigen, pca);
```

```
Matrix eigenvalues = diag(eigen);

rsort_columns(pca, eigenvalues);

// leave only required number of principal components
pca = trans(colm(pca, range(0, target_dim)));
```

Our PCA transformation matrix is called pca. We used it to reduce the dimensions of each of our samples with simple matrix multiplication. Look at the following cycle and notice the pca * data[i] operation:

```
// dimensionality reduction
std::vector<Matrix> new_data;
size_t new_size = 0;
new_data.reserve(data.size());
for (size_t i = 0; i < data.size(); ++i) {
  new_data.emplace_back(pca * data[i]);
  new_size += static_cast<size_t>(new_data.back().size());
}

std::cout << "New data size " << new_size +
    static_cast<size_t>(pca.size())
<< std::endl;
```

Our data has been compressed and we can see its new size in the console output. Now, we can restore the original dimension of the data to be able to see the image. To do this, we need to use the transposed PCA matrix to multiply the reduced samples. Also, we need to denormalize the restored sample to get actual pixel values. This can be done by multiplying the standard deviation and adding the mean we got from the previous steps:

```
auto pca_matrix_t = Dlib::trans(pca);
Matrix isd = Dlib::reciprocal(sd);
for (size_t i = 0; i < new_data.size(); ++i) {
  Matrix sample = pca_matrix_t * new_data[i];
  new_data[i] = Dlib::pointwise_multiply(sample, isd) + m;
}
```

After we've restored the pixel values, we reshape them and place them in their original location in the image:

```
size_t i = 0;
for (long r = 0; r < img_mat.nr(); r += patch_size) {
  for (long c = 0; c < img_mat.nc(); c += patch_size) {
    auto sm = Dlib::reshape(new_data[i], patch_size, patch_size);
    Dlib::set_subm(img_mat, r, c, patch_size, patch_size) = sm;
    ++i;
  }
}
```

```
    }

    img_mat *= 255.0;
    assign_image(img_gray, img_mat);
    equalize_histogram(img_gray);
    save_png(img_gray, "compressed.png");
}
```

Let's look at the result of compressing a standard test image that is widely used in image processing. The following is the Lena 512 x 512 image:

Its original grayscaled size is 262,144 bytes. After we perform PCA compression with only 10 principal components, its size becomes 45,760 bytes. We can see the result in the following image:

Here, we can see that most of the essential visual information was preserved, despite the high compression rate.

LDA

The `Dlib` library also has an implementation of the linear discriminant analysis algorithm, which can be used for dimensionality reduction. It's a supervised algorithm, so it needs labeled data. This algorithm is implemented with the `Dlib::compute_lda_transform()` function, which takes four parameters. The first one is the input/output parameter – as input, it is used to pass input training data (in matrix form) and as output, it receives the LDA transformation matrix. The second parameter is the output for the mean values. The third parameter is the labels for the input data, while the fourth one is the desired number of target dimensions. The following code shows an example of how to use LDA for dimension reduction with the `Dlib` library:

```
void LDAReduction(const Matrix &data,
                  const std::vector<unsigned long> &labels,
                  unsigned long target_dim) {
  Dlib::matrix<DataType, 0, 1> mean;
  Matrix transform = data;
  Dlib::compute_lda_transform(transform, mean, labels, target_dim);

  for (long r = 0; r < data.nr(); ++r) {
    Matrix row = transform * Dlib::trans(Dlib::rowm(data, r)) - mean;
    double x = row(0, 0);
    double y = row(1, 0);
  }
}
```

To perform an actual LDA transform after the algorithm has been trained, we multiply our samples with the LDA matrix. In our case, we also transposed them. The following code shows the essential part of this example:

```
transform * Dlib::trans(Dlib::rowm(data, r))
```

The following graph shows the result of using LDA reduction on two components:

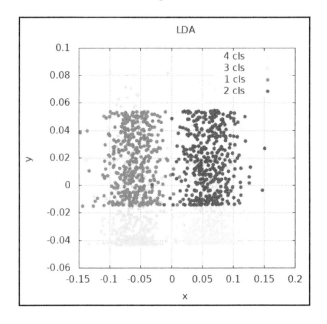

Sammon mapping

In the `Dlib` library, Sammon mapping is implemented with the `Dlib::sammon_projection` type. We need to create an instance of this type and then use it as a functional object. Functional object call arguments are the data that we need to transform and the number of dimensions of the new feature space. The input data should be in the form of the `std::vector` of the single samples of the `Dlib::matrix` type. All samples should have the same number of dimensions. The result of using this functional object is a new vector of samples with a reduced number of dimensions:

```
void SammonReduction(const std::vector<Matrix> &data, long target_dim) {
  Dlib::sammon_projection sp;
  auto new_data = sp(data, target_dim);

  for (size_t r = 0; r < new_data.size(); ++r) {
    Matrix vec = new_data[r];
    double x = vec(0, 0);
    double y = vec(1, 0);
  }
}
```

The following graph shows the result of using this dimensionality reduction algorithm:

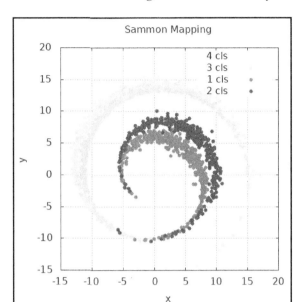

Using the Shogun library

The `Shogun` library contains numerous dimensionality reduction algorithms, both linear and non-linear ones. It uses the `Tapkee` library (`http://tapkee.lisitsyn.me/`) for backend implementation.

PCA

In the `Shogun` library, the PCA algorithm is implemented in the `CPCA` class. It has one primary configuration option – the number of target dimensions, which can be modified with the `set_target_dim()` method. After we make this configuration, we need to execute the `fit()` method for training purposes and then use the `apply_to_feature_vector()` method to transform an individual sample:

```
void PCAReduction(Some<CDenseFeatures<DataType>> features,
                  const int target_dim) {
  auto pca = some<CPCA>();
  pca->set_target_dim(target_dim);
  pca->fit(features);
```

```
auto feature_matrix = features->get_feature_matrix();
for (index_t i = 0; i < features->get_num_vectors(); ++i) {
  auto vector = feature_matrix.get_column(i);
  auto new_vector = pca->apply_to_feature_vector(vector);
}
}
```

The following graph shows the result of applying Shogun PCA implementation to our data:

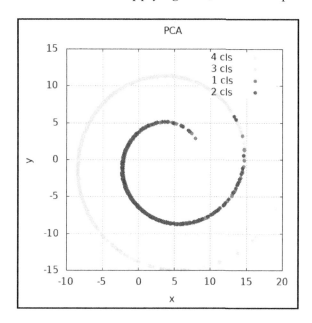

Kernel PCA

The non-linear version of PCA in the Shogun library is implemented in the CKernelPCA class. It works the same as if we were to use the linear version of the CPCA class. The main difference is that it's configured with an additional method, set_kernel(), which should be used to pass the pointer to the specific kernel object. In the following example, we're initializing the instance of the CGaussianKernel class for a kernel object:

```
void KernelPCAReduction(Some<CDenseFeatures<DataType>> features,
                        const int target_dim) {
  auto gauss_kernel = some<CGaussianKernel>(features, features, 0.5);
  auto pca = some<CKernelPCA>();
  pca->set_kernel(gauss_kernel.get());
  pca->set_target_dim(target_dim);
  pca->fit(features);
```

```
    auto feature_matrix = features->get_feature_matrix();
    for (index_t i = 0; i < features->get_num_vectors(); ++i) {
      auto vector = feature_matrix.get_column(i);
      auto new_vector = pca->apply_to_feature_vector(vector);
    }
}
```

The following graph shows the result of applying `Shogun` kernel PCA implementation to our data:

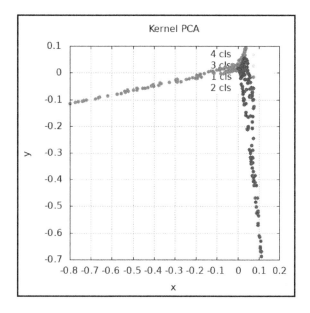

We can see that this type of kernel makes some parts of the data separated, but that other ones were reduced too much.

MDS

A multidimensional scaling algorithm is implemented in the `Shogun` library in the `MultidimensionalScaling` class. Objects of this class should be configured, along with the number of desired features, with the `set_target_dim()` method. Then, the `fit()` method should be used for training. Unlike the previous types, this class provides the `transform()` method, which transforms the whole dataset into a new number of dimensions. It returns a pointer to the `CDenseFeatures` type object:

```
void MDSReduction(Some<CDenseFeatures<DataType>> features,
                  const int target_dim) {
```

```
auto IsoMap = some<CMultidimensionalScaling>();
IsoMap->set_target_dim(target_dim);
IsoMap->fit(features);

auto new_features =
    static_cast<CDenseFeatures<DataType> *>(IsoMap->transform
    (features));

auto feature_matrix = new_features->get_feature_matrix();
for (index_t i = 0; i < new_features->get_num_vectors(); ++i) {
  auto new_vector = feature_matrix.get_column(i);
}
}
```

The following graph shows the result of applying the Shogun MDS algorithm to our data:

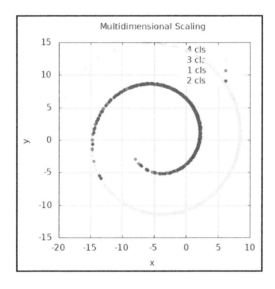

IsoMap

In the Shogun library, the IsoMap dimensionality reduction algorithm is implemented in the CIsoMap class. Objects of this class should be configured with the target number of dimensions and the number of neighbors for graph construction. The set_target_dim() and set_k() methods should be used for this. The fit() and transform() methods should be used for the training and data dimensionality reduction, respectively:

```
void IsoMapReduction(Some<CDenseFeatures<DataType>> features,
                     const int target_dim) {
    auto IsoMap = some<CIsoMap>();
```

```
IsoMap->set_target_dim(target_dim);
IsoMap->set_k(100);
IsoMap->fit(features);

auto new_features =
    static_cast<CDenseFeatures<DataType> *>(IsoMap->transform
    (features));

auto feature_matrix = new_features->get_feature_matrix();
for (index_t i = 0; i < new_features->get_num_vectors(); ++i) {
  auto new_vector = feature_matrix.get_column(i);
}
}
```

The following graph shows the result of applying the Shogun IsoMap implementation to our data:

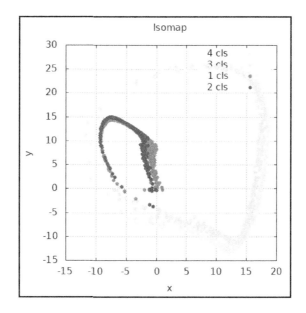

ICA

In the Shogun library, the ICA algorithm is implemented in the CFast ICA class. There is no particular configuration for the object of this class. The fit() and transform() methods should be used for training and data dimensionality reduction, respectively. After we've transformed the data, we can use some components as new features.

We can also use a reduced number of features to make low-dimensional data:

```
void ICAReduction(Some<CDenseFeatures<DataType>> features,
                  const int target_dim) {
  auto ica = some<CFast ICA>();
  ica->fit(features);

  auto new_features =
      static_cast<CDenseFeatures<DataType> *>(ica->transform(features));
  auto casted =
      CDenseFeatures<float64_t>::obtain_from_generic(new_features);

  Clusters clusters;
  auto unmixed_signal = casted->get_feature_matrix();
  for (index_t i = 0; i < new_features->get_num_vectors(); ++i) {
    auto new_vector = unmixed_signal.get_column(i);
    // choose 1 and 2 as our main components
    new_vector[1];
    new_vector[2];
  }
}
```

The following graph shows the result of applying the Shogun ICA implementation to our data. In this example, we've only used two components for the visualization:

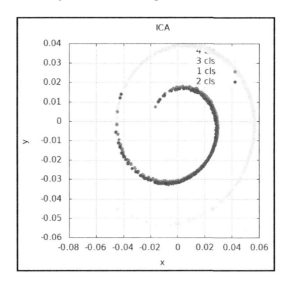

Factor analysis

In the `Shogun` library, the factor analysis algorithm is implemented in the `CFactorAnalysis` class. Objects of this class should be configured with the target number of dimensions. The `set_target_dim()` method should be used to modify the value of the target dimensions, while the `fit()` and `transform()` methods should be used for training and data dimensionality reduction, respectively:

```
void FAReduction(Some<CDenseFeatures<DataType>> features,
                 const int target_dim) {
  auto fa = some<CFactorAnalysis>();
  fa->set_target_dim(target_dim);
  fa->fit(features);

  auto new_features =
      static_cast<CDenseFeatures<DataType> *>(fa->transform(features));

  auto feature_matrix = new_features->get_feature_matrix();
  for (index_t i = 0; i < new_features->get_num_vectors(); ++i) {
    auto new_vector = feature_matrix.get_column(i);
  }
}
```

The following graph shows the result of applying `Shogun` factor analysis implementation to our data:

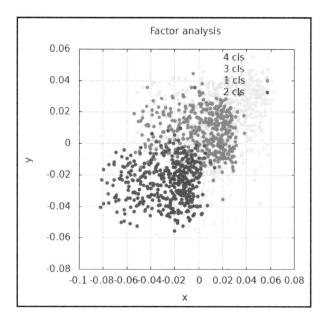

t-SNE

In the Shogun library, the t-SNE algorithm is implemented in the CTDistributedStochasticNeighborEmbedding class. Objects of this class should be configured with the target number of dimensions and the set_target_dim() method. The fit() and transform() methods should be used for training and data dimensionality reduction, respectively:

```
void TSNEReduction(Some<CDenseFeatures<DataType>> features,
                   const int target_dim) {
  auto tsne = some<CTDistributedStochasticNeighborEmbedding>();
  tsne->set_target_dim(target_dim);
  tsne->fit(features);

  auto new_features =
      static_cast<CDenseFeatures<DataType> *>(tsne->transform(features));

  auto feature_matrix = new_features->get_feature_matrix();
  for (index_t i = 0; i < new_features->get_num_vectors(); ++i) {
    auto new_vector = feature_matrix.get_column(i);
  }
}
```

The following graph shows the result of applying the Shogun t-SNE implementation to our data:

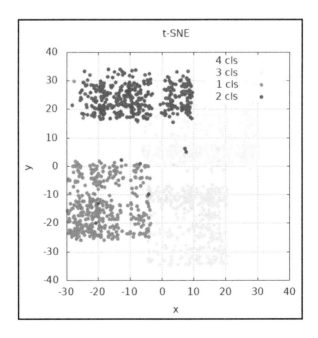

Using the Shark-ML library

The Shark-ML library contains implementations of the PCA and LDA algorithms, both of which can be used for data dimensionality reduction.

PCA

The PCA algorithms in the Shark-ML library are implemented in the PCA class. Objects of this class should be configured with the number of target dimensions. We can use the encoder() method for this. This method takes two parameters: the first one is the reference to the object of the LinearModel class, while the second one is the number of target dimensions. After the object of the LinearModel class has been configured, it can be used for data transformation regarding the functional object. Its called result is a new object of the Data<RealVector> class:

```
void PCAReduction(const UnlabeledData<RealVector> &data,
                  const UnlabeledData<RealVector>& lables,
                  size_t target_dim) {
  PCA pca(data);
  LinearModel<> encoder;
  pca.encoder(encoder, target_dim);
  auto new_data = encoder(data);

  for (size_t i = 0; i < new_data.numberOfElements(); ++i) {
    auto x = new_data.element(i)[0];
    auto y = new_data.element(i)[1];
  }
}
```

The following graph shows the result of applying the `Shark-ML` PCA implementation to our data:

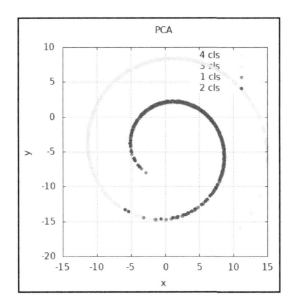

LDA

The LDA algorithms in the `Shark-ML` library are implemented in the `LDA` class. First, we have to train the algorithm with the `train()` method, which takes two parameters: the first one is a reference to the object of the `LinearClassifier` class, while the second is the dataset reference. Notice that the LDA algorithm uses objects of `LinearClassifier` because, in the `Shark-ML` library, LDA is used mostly for classification. Also, because this is a supervised algorithm, we should provide labels for the data. We can do this by initializing the `LabeledData<RealVector, unsigned int>` class object. In the following example, we can see how to combine `UnlabeledData<RealVector>` datasets with the labeled one. Note that labels should start from 0.

After the object of the `LinearClassifier` class has been trained, we can use it for data classification as the functional object. Its call result is a new labeled dataset. For dimensionality reduction, we have to use the decision function for data transformation. This function can be retrieved using the `decisionFunction()` method of the `LinearClassifier` class. The decision function object can be used to transform the input data into a new projection that can be obtained with the LDA. After we have the new labels and projected data, we can use them to obtain dimensionality reduced data. In the following example, we only used one label, which corresponds to the one dimension of the projection so that we can visualize the result. This means we're performing dimensionality reduction for the only feature (component):

```
void LDAReduction(const UnlabeledData<RealVector> &data,
                  const UnlabeledData<RealVector> &labels,
                  size_t target_dim) {
  LinearClassifier<> encoder;
  LDA lda;

  LabeledData<RealVector, unsigned int> dataset(
      labels.numberOfElements(), InputLabelPair<RealVector, unsigned int>(
                                 RealVector(data.element(0).size()), 0));

  for (size_t i = 0; i < labels.numberOfElements(); ++i) {
    // labels should start from 0
    dataset.element(i).label =
        static_cast<unsigned int>(labels.element(i)[0]) - 1;
    dataset.element(i).input = data.element(i);
  }
  lda.train(encoder, dataset);

  // project data
  auto new_labels = encoder(data);
  auto dc = encoder.decisionFunction();
  auto new_data = dc(data);

  for (size_t i = 0; i < new_data.numberOfElements(); ++i) {
    auto l = new_labels.element(i);
    auto x = new_data.element(i)[l];
    auto y = new_data.element(i)[l];
  }
}
```

The following graph shows the result of applying `Shark-ML` LDA dimensionality reduction to our data on the only feature:

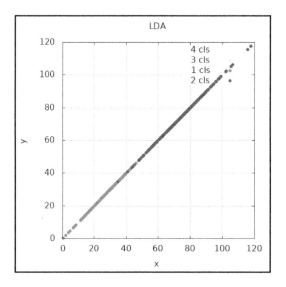

Summary

In this chapter, we learned that dimensionality reduction is the process of transferring data that has a higher dimension into a new representation of data with a lower dimension. It is used to reduce the number of correlated features in a dataset and extract the most informative features. Such a transformation can help increase the performance of other algorithms, reduce computational complexity, and make human-readable visualizations.

We learned that there are two different approaches to solve this task. One is feature selection, which doesn't create new features, while the second one is dimensionality reduction algorithms, which make new feature sets. We also learned that dimensionality reduction algorithms are linear and non-linear and that we should select either type, depending on our data. We saw that there are a lot of different algorithms with different properties and computational complexity and that it makes sense to try different ones to see which are the best solution for particular tasks. Note that different libraries have different implementations for identical algorithms, so their results can differ, even for the same data.

The area of dimensionality reduction algorithms is a field that's in continual development. There is, for example, a new algorithm called **Uniform Manifold Approximation and Projection (UMAP)** that's based on Riemannian geometry and algebraic topology. It competes with the t-SNE algorithm in terms of visualization quality but also preserves more of the original data's global structure after the transformation is complete. It is also much more computationally effective, which makes it suitable for large-scale datasets. However, at the moment, there is no C++ implementation of it.

In the next chapter, we will discuss classification tasks and how to solve them. Usually, when we have to solve a classification task, we have to divide a group of objects into several subgroups. Objects in such subgroups share some common properties that are distinct from the properties in other subgroups.

Further reading

- A survey of dimensionality reduction techniques: `https://arxiv.org/pdf/1403.2877.pdf`

- A short tutorial for dimensionality reduction: `https://www.math.uwaterloo.ca/~aghodsib/courses/f06stat890/readings/tutorial_stat890.pdf`

- Guide to 12 dimensionality reduction techniques (with Python code): `https://www.analyticsvidhya.com/blog/2018/08/dimensionality-reduction-techniques-python/`

- A geometric and intuitive explanation of the covariance matrix and its relationship with linear transformation, an essential building block for understanding and using PCA and SVD: `https://datascienceplus.com/understanding-the-covariance-matrix`

- The kernel trick: `https://dscm.quora.com/The-Kernel-Trick`

Classification

7

In machine learning, the task of classification is that of dividing a set of observations (objects) into groups called *classes*, based on an analysis of their formal description. For classification, each observation (object) is mapped to a certain group or nominal category based on a certain qualitative property. Classification is a supervised task because it requires known classes for training samples. Labeling of a training set is usually done manually, with the involvement of specialists in the given field of study. It's also notable that if classes are not initially defined, then there will be a problem with clustering. Furthermore, in the classification task, there may be more than two classes (multi-class), and each of the objects may belong to more than one class (intersecting).

In this chapter, we will discuss various approaches to solving a classification task with machine learning. We are going to look at some of the most well-known and widespread algorithms that are logistic regression, **Support Vector Machine (SVM)**, and **k-Nearest Neighbors (kNNs)**. Logistic regression is one of the most straightforward algorithms based on linear regression and a special loss function. SVM is based on a concept of support vectors that helps to build a decision boundary to separate data. This approach can be effectively used with high-dimensional data. kNN has a simple implementation algorithm that uses the idea of data compactness. Also, we will show how the multi-class classification problem can be solved with the algorithms mentioned previously. We will implement program examples to see how to use these algorithms to solve the classification task with different C++ libraries.

The following topics are covered in this chapter:

- An overview of classification methods
- Exploring various classification methods
- Examples of using C++ libraries for dealing with the classification task

Technical requirements

The required technologies and installations for this chapter include the following:

- The `Shogun toolbox` library
- The `Shark-ML` library
- The `Dlib` library
- The `plotcpp` library
- A modern C++ compiler with C++17 support
- CMake build system version >= 3.8

The code files for this chapter can be found at the following GitHub repo: `https://github.com/PacktPublishing/Hands-On-Machine-Learning-with-CPP/tree/master/Chapter07`

An overview of classification methods

The classification task is one of the basic tasks of applied statistics and machine learning, as well as **artificial intelligence** (**AI**) as a whole. This is because classification is one of the most understandable and easy-to-interpret data analysis technologies, and classification rules can be formulated in a natural language. In machine learning, a classification task is solved using supervised algorithms because the classes are defined in advance, and the objects in the training set have class labels. Analytical models that solve a classification task are called **classifiers**.

Classification is the process of moving an object to a predetermined class based on its formalized features. Each object in this problem is usually represented as a vector in N-dimensional space. Each dimension in that space is a description of one of the features of the object.

We can formulate the classification task with mathematical notation. Let X denote the set of descriptions of objects, and Y be a finite set of names or class labels. There is an unknown objective function—namely, the mapping $y^* : X \to Y$, whose values are known only on the objects of the final training sample $X^m = (x_1, y_1), \ldots, (x_m, y_m)$. So, we have to construct an $a : X \to Y$ algorithm, capable of classifying an $x \in X$ arbitrary object. In mathematical statistics, classification problems are also called discriminant analysis problems.

The classification task is applicable to many areas, including the following:

- **Trade**: The classification of customers and products allows a business to optimize marketing strategies, stimulate sales, and reduce costs.
- **Telecommunications**: The classification of subscribers allows a business to appraise customer loyalty, and therefore develop loyalty programs.
- **Medicine and health care**: Assisting the diagnosis of disease by classifying the population into risk groups.
- **Banking**: The classification of customers is used for credit-scoring procedures.

Classification can be solved by using the following methods:

- Logistic regression
- The kNN method
- SVM
- Discriminant analysis
- Decision trees
- Neural networks

We have looked into discriminant analysis in Chapter 6, *Dimensionality Reduction*, as an algorithm for dimensionality reduction, but most libraries provide an **application programming interface** (**API**) for working with the discriminant analysis algorithm as a classifier, too. We will discuss decision trees in Chapter 9, *Ensemble Learning*, focusing on algorithm ensembles. We will also discuss neural networks in the chapter that follows this: Chapter 10, *Neural Networks for Image Classification*.

Now we've discussed what the classification task is, let's look at various classification methods.

Exploring various classification methods

In this chapter, we will discuss some of the classification methods such as logistic regression, **kernel ridge regression** (**KRR**), the kNN method, and SVM approaches.

Logistic regression

Logistic regression determines the degree of dependence between the categorical dependent and one or more independent variables by using the logistic function. It aims to find the values of the coefficients for the input variables, as with linear regression. The difference, in the case of logistic regression, is that the output value is converted by using a non-linear (logistic) function. The logistic function essentially looks like a big letter S and converts any value to a number in a range from 0 to 1. This property is useful because we can apply the rule to the output of the logistic function to bind 0 and 1 to a class prediction. The following screenshot shows a logistic function graph:

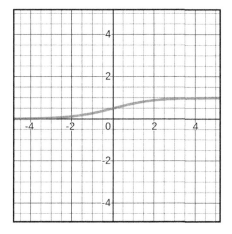

For example, if the result of the function is less than 0.5, then the output is 0. Prediction is not just a simple answer (**+1** or **-1**) either, and we can interpret it as a probability of being classified as **+1**.

In many tasks, this interpretation is an essential business requirement. For example, in the task of credit scoring, where logistic regression is traditionally used, the probability of a loan being defaulted on is a common prediction. As with the case of linear regression, logistic regression performs the task better if outliers and correlating variables are removed. The logistic regression model can be quickly trained and is well suited for binary classification problems.

The basic idea of a linear classifier is that the feature space can be divided by a hyperplane into two half-spaces, in each of which one of the two values of the target class is predicted. If we can divide a feature space without errors, then the training set is called **linearly separable**. Logistic regression is a unique type of a linear classifier, but it is able to predict the probability of p_+, attributing the example of $\overrightarrow{x_i}$ to the class **+**, as illustrated here:

$$p_+ = P\left(y_i = 1 \mid \overrightarrow{x_i}, \vec{w}\right)$$

Consider the task of binary classification, with labels of the target class denoted by **+1** (positive examples) and **-1** (negative examples). We want to predict the probability of $p_+ \in [0, 1]$; so, for now, we can build a linear forecast using the following optimization technique: $b(\vec{x}) = \vec{w}^T \vec{x} \in \mathbb{R}$. So, how do we convert the resulting value into a probability whose limits are [0, 1]? This approach requires a specific function. In the logistic regression model, the specific function $\sigma(z) = \dfrac{1}{1 + \exp^{-z}}$ is used for this.

Let's denote $P(X)$ by the probability of the occurring event X. The probability odds ratio $OR(X)$ is determined from $\dfrac{P(X)}{1 - P(X)}$. This is the ratio of the probabilities of whether the event will occur or not. We can see that the probability and the odds ratio both contain the same information. However, while $P(X)$ is in the range of 0 to 1, $OR(X)$ is in the range of 0 to ∞. If you calculate the logarithm of $OR(X)$ (known as the **logarithm of the odds**, or the **logarithm of the probability ratio**), it is easy to see that the following applies: $\log OR(X) \in \mathbb{R}$.

Using the logistic function to predict the probability of p_+, it can be obtained from the probability ratio (for the time being, let's assume we have the weights too) as follows:

$$p_+ = \frac{OR_+}{1 + OR_+} = \frac{\exp^{\vec{w}^T \vec{x}}}{1 + \exp^{\vec{w}^T \vec{x}}} = \frac{1}{1 + \exp^{-\vec{w}^T \vec{x}}} = \sigma(\vec{w}^T \vec{x})$$

So, the logistic regression predicts the probability of classifying a sample to the **+** class as a sigmoid transformation of a linear combination of the model weights vector, as well as the sample's features vector, as follows:

$$p_+(x_i) = P\left(y_i = 1 \mid \overrightarrow{x_i}, \vec{w}\right) = \sigma(\vec{w}^T \overrightarrow{x_i})$$

From the maximum likelihood principle, we can obtain an optimization problem that the logistic regression solves—namely, the minimization of the logistic loss function. For the - class, the probability is determined by a similar formula, as illustrated here:

$$p_-(\vec{x_i}) = P\left(y_i = -1 \mid \vec{x_i}, \vec{w}\right) = 1 - \sigma(\vec{w}^T \vec{x_i}) = \sigma(-\vec{w}^T \vec{x_i})$$

The expressions for both classes can be combined into one, as illustrated here:

$$P\left(y = y_i \mid \vec{x_i}, \vec{w}\right) = \sigma(y_i \vec{w}^T \vec{x_i})$$

Here, the expression $M(\vec{x_i}) = y_i \vec{w}^T \vec{x_i}$ is called the margin of classification of the $\vec{x_i}$ object. The classification margin can be understood as a model's *confidence* in the object's classification. An interpretation of this margin is as follows:

- If the margin vector's absolute value is large and is positive, the class label is set correctly, and the object is far from the separating hyperplane. Such an object is therefore classified confidently.
- If the margin is large (by modulo) but is negative, then the class label is set incorrectly. The object is far from the separating hyperplane. Such an object is most likely an anomaly.
- If the margin is small (by modulo), then the object is close to the separating hyperplane. In this case, the margin sign determines whether the object is correctly classified.

In the discrete case, the likelihood function $f(x_1, \ldots, x_n, \theta)$ can be interpreted as the probability that the sample $X_1, \ldots, X_n$ is equal to $x_1, \ldots, x_n$ in the given set of experiments. Furthermore, this probability depends on θ, as illustrated here:

$$f(\mathbf{x}, \theta) = \prod_{i=1}^{n} f_\theta(x_i) \ldots \ldots ta\, (X_n = x_n) = \mathsf{P}_\theta\,(X_1 = x_1, \ldots, X_n = x_n).$$

The maximum likelihood estimate $\hat{\theta}$ for the unknown parameter θ is called the value of θ, for which the function $f(\mathbf{X}, \theta)$ reaches its maximum (as a function of θ, with fixed $X_1, \ldots, X_n$), as illustrated here:

$$\hat{\theta} = \arg\max_\theta f(\mathbf{X}, \theta).$$

Now, we can write out the likelihood of the sample—namely, the probability of observing the given vector $\vec{y}$ in the sample X. We make one assumption—objects arise independently from a single distribution, as illustrated here:

$$P(\vec{y} \mid X, \vec{w}) = \prod_{i=1}^{\ell} P\left(y = y_i \mid \vec{x_i}, \vec{w}\right)$$

Let's take the logarithm of this expression since the sum is much easier to optimize than the product, as follows:

$$\log P(\vec{y} \mid X, \vec{w}) = \qquad \log \prod_{i=1}^{\ell} P\left(y = y_i \mid \vec{x_i}, \vec{w}\right)$$

$$= \qquad -\sum_{i=1}^{\ell} \log(1 + \exp^{-y_i \vec{w}^T \vec{x_i}})$$

In this case, the principle of maximizing the likelihood leads to a minimization of the expression, as illustrated here:

$$\mathcal{L}_{log}(X, \vec{y}, \vec{w}) = \sum_{i=1}^{\ell} \log(1 + \exp^{-y_i \vec{w}^T \vec{x_i}}).$$

This formula is a logistic loss function, summed over all objects of the training sample. Usually, it is a good idea to add some regularization to a model to deal with overfitting. L2 regularization of logistic regression is arranged in much the same way as linear regression (ridge regression). However, it is common to use the controlled variable decay parameter C that is used in SVM models, where it denotes soft margin parameter denotation. So, for logistic regression, C is equal to the inverse regularization coefficient $C = \frac{1}{\lambda}$. The relationship between C and λ would be the following: lowering C would strengthen the regularization effect. Therefore, instead of the functional $\mathcal{L}_{log}(X, \vec{y}, \vec{w})$, the following function should be minimized:

$$J(X, \vec{y}, \vec{w}) = \arg\min_{\vec{w}} \left(C \sum_{i=1}^{\ell} \log(1 + \exp^{-y_i \vec{w}^T \vec{x_i}}) + |\vec{w}|^2\right)$$

For this function minimization, we can apply different methods—for example, the method of least squares, or the **gradient descent** (**GD**) method. The vital issue with logistic regression is that it is generally a linear classifier, in order to deal with non-linear decision boundaries, which typically use polynomial features with original features as a basis for them. This approach was discussed in the earlier chapters when we discussed polynomial regression.

KRR

KRR combines linear ridge regression (linear regression and L2 norm regularization) with the kernel trick and can be used for classification problems. It learns a linear function in the higher-dimensional space produced by the chosen kernel and training data. For non-linear kernels, it learns a non-linear function in the original space.

The model learned by KRR is identical to the SVM model, but these approaches have the following differences:

- The KRR method uses squared error loss, while the SVM model uses insensitive loss or hinge loss for classification.
- In contrast to the SVM method, the KRR training can be completed in the closed-form so that it can be trained faster for medium-sized datasets.
- The learned KRR model is non-sparse and can be slower than the SVM model when it comes to prediction times.

Despite these differences, both approaches usually use L2 regularization.

SVM

The SVM method is a set of algorithms used for classification and regression analysis tasks. Considering that in an *N*-dimensional space, each object belongs to one of two classes, SVM generates an (*N-1*)-dimensional hyperplane to divide these points into two groups. It's similar to an on-paper depiction of points of two different types that can be linearly divided. Furthermore, the SVM selects the hyperplane, which is characterized by the maximum distance from the nearest group elements.

The input data can be separated using various hyperplanes. The best hyperplane is a hyperplane with the maximum resulting separation and the maximum resulting difference between the two classes.

Imagine the data points on the plane. In the following case, the separator is just a straight line:

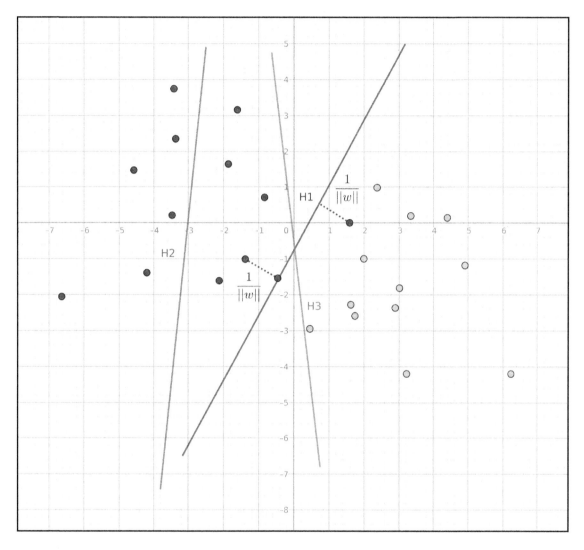

Let's draw distinct straight lines that divide the points into two sets. Then, choose a straight line as far as possible from the points, maximizing the distance from it to the nearest point on each side. If such a line exists, then it is called the maximum margin hyperplane. Intuitively, a good separation is achieved due to the hyperplane itself (which has the longest distance to the nearest point of the training sample of any class), since, in general, the bigger the distance, the smaller the classifier error.

Consider learning samples given with the set $D = \{(x_i, y_i)\}$ consisting of n objects with p parameters, where y takes the values -1 or 1, therefore defining the point's classes. Each point x is a vector of the dimension p. Our task is to find the maximum margin hyperplane that separates the observations. We can use analytic geometry to define any hyperplane as a set of points x that satisfy the condition, as illustrated here:

$$g(x) = w^t x + w_0$$

Here, $g(x) > 0 \Rightarrow x \in \text{class}[1]$ and $g(x) < 0 \Rightarrow x \in \text{class}[2]$.

Thus, the linear separating (discriminant) function is described by the equation g(x)=0. The distance from the point to the separating function g(x)=0 (the distance from the point to the plane) is equal to the following:

$$\frac{|w^t x + w_0|}{\|w\|}$$

x_i lies in the closure of the boundary that is $|w^t x_i + w_0| = 1$. The border, which is the width of the dividing strip, needs to be as large as possible. Considering that the closure of the boundary satisfies the condition $|w^t x_i + w_0| = 1$, then the distance from x_i to $g(x) = 0$ is as follows:

$$\frac{|w^t x + w_0|}{\|w\|} = \frac{1}{\|w\|}$$

Thus, the width of the dividing strip is $\frac{2}{\|w\|}$. To exclude points from the dividing strip, we can write out the following conditions:

$$\begin{cases} w^t x_i + w_0 \geq 1, & \text{if } x_i \text{ belongs to the first class,} \\ w^t x_i + w_0 \leq -1, & \text{if } x_i \text{ belongs to the second class.} \end{cases}$$

Let's also introduce the index function u_i that shows to which class x_i belongs, as follows:

$$\begin{cases} u_i = 1, & \text{if } x_i \text{ belongs to the first class,} \\ u_i = -1, & \text{if } x_i \text{ belongs to the second class.} \end{cases}$$

Thus, the task of choosing a separating function that generates a corridor of the greatest width can be written as follows:

$$J(w) = \frac{1}{2}\|w\|^2 \to \min$$

The $J(w)$ function was introduced with the assumption that $u_i\left(w^t x_i + w_0\right) \geq 1$ for all i. Since the objective function is quadratic, this problem has a unique solution.

According to the Kuhn-Tucker theorem, this condition is equivalent to the following problem:

$$L\left(\alpha\right) = \sum_{i=1}^{n} \alpha_i - \frac{1}{2}\sum_{i=1}^{n}\sum_{j=1}^{n} \alpha_i \alpha_j u_i u_j x_i^T x_j \to \max$$

This is provided that $\alpha > 0 \forall i$ and $\sum_{i=1}^{n} \alpha_i u_i = 0$, where $\alpha = \{\alpha_1, \ldots, \alpha_n\}$, are new variables. We can rewrite $L\left(\alpha\right)$ in the matrix form, as follows:

$$L\left(\alpha\right) = \sum_{i=1}^{n} \alpha_i - \frac{1}{2}\begin{bmatrix} \alpha_1 \\ \vdots \\ \alpha_n \end{bmatrix}^T H \begin{bmatrix} \alpha_1 \\ \vdots \\ \alpha_n \end{bmatrix},$$

The H coefficients of the matrix can be calculated as follows: $H_{i,j} = u_i u_j x_i^T x_j$. Quadratic programming methods can solve the task $L\left(\alpha\right) \to \max$.

After finding the optimal $\alpha = \{\alpha_1, \ldots, \alpha_n\}$ for every i, one of the two following conditions is fulfilled:

1. $\alpha_i = 0$ (i corresponds to a non-support vector.)
2. $\alpha_i \neq 0$ and $u_i\left(w^t x_i + w_0 - 1\right) = 0$ (i corresponds to a support vector.)

$$w = \sum_{i=1}^{n} \alpha_i u_i x_i$$

Then, w can be found from the relation, and the value of w_0 can be determined, considering that for any $\alpha_i > 0$ and $\alpha_i \left[u_i \left(w^t x_i + w_0 \right) - 1 \right] = 0$, as follows:

$$w_0 = \frac{1}{u_i} - w^t x_i$$

Finally, we can obtain the discriminant function, illustrated here:

$$g(x) = \left(\sum \{ \alpha_i u_i x_i \, | x_i \in S \} \right)^T x + w_0$$

Note that the summation is not carried out over all vectors, but only over the set S, which is the set of support vectors $S = \{ x_i \, | \alpha_i \neq 0 \}$.

Unfortunately, the described algorithm is realized only for linearly separable datasets, which in itself occurs rather infrequently. There are two approaches for working with linearly non-separable data.

One of them is called a soft margin, which chooses a hyperplane that divides the training sample as purely (with minimal error) as possible, while at the same time maximizing the distance to the nearest point on the training dataset. For this, we have to introduce additional variables ξ_i, which characterize the magnitude of the error on each object x_i. Furthermore, we can introduce the penalty for the total error into the goal functional, like this:

$$
\begin{cases}
\frac{1}{2} \|w\|^2 + \lambda \sum_{i=1}^{n} \xi_i \rightarrow \min, \\
u_i \left(w^t x_i + w_0 \right) \geq 1 - \xi_i, i = 1, \ldots, n, \\
\xi_i \geq 0_i, i = 1, \ldots, n,
\end{cases}
$$

Here, λ is a method tuning parameter that allows you to adjust the relationship between maximizing the width of the dividing strip and minimizing the total error. The value of the penalty ξ_i for the corresponding object x_i depends on the location of the object x_i relative to the dividing line. So, if x_i lies on the opposite side of the discriminant function, then we can assume the value of the penalty $\xi_i > 1$, if x_i lies in the dividing strip, and comes from its class. The corresponding weight is, therefore, $0 < \xi_i < 1$. In the ideal case, we assume that $\xi_i < 0$. The resulting problem can then be rewritten as follows:

$$J(w, \xi_1, \ldots, \xi_n) = \frac{1}{2}\|w\|^2 + \beta \sum_{i=1}^{n} I\left(\xi_i > 0\right) \to \min$$

Notice that elements that are not an ideal case are involved in the minimization process too, as illustrated here:

$$I\left(\xi_i > 0\right) = \begin{cases} 1, & \xi_i > 0, \\ 0, & \xi_i \leq 0, \end{cases}$$

Here, the constant β is the weight that takes into account the width of the strip. If β is small, then we can allow the algorithm to locate a relatively high number of elements in a non-ideal position (in the dividing strip). If β is vast, then we require the presence of a small number of elements in a non-ideal position (in the dividing strip). Unfortunately, the minimization problem is rather complicated due to the $I(\xi_i)$ discontinuity. Instead, we can use the minimization of the following:

$$J(w, \xi_1, \ldots, \xi_n) = \frac{1}{2}\|w\|^2 + \beta \sum_{i=1}^{n} \xi_i$$

This occurs under restrictions $\forall i$, as illustrated here:

$$\begin{cases} u_i\left(w^t x_i + w_0\right) \geq 1 - \xi_i, \\ \xi_i \geq 0. \end{cases}$$

Another idea of the SVM method in the case of the impossibility of a linear separation of classes is the transition to a space of higher dimension, in which such a separation is possible. While the original problem can be formulated in a finite-dimensional space, it often happens that the samples for discrimination are not linearly separable in this space. Therefore, it is suggested to map the original finite-dimensional space into a larger dimension space, which makes the separation much easier. To keep the computational load reasonable, the mappings used in support vector algorithms provide ease of calculating points in terms of variables in the original space, specifically in terms of the kernel function.

First, the function of the mapping $\varphi(x)$ is selected to map the data of x into a space of a higher dimension. Then, a non-linear discriminant function can be written in the form $g(x) = w^t \varphi(x) + w_0$. The idea of the method is to find the kernel function $K(x_i, x_j) = \varphi(x_i)^T \varphi(x_j)$ and maximize the objective function, as illustrated here:

$$L(\alpha) = \sum_{i=1}^{n} \alpha_i - \frac{1}{2} \sum_{i=1}^{n} \sum_{j=1}^{n} \alpha_i \alpha_j u_i u_j K(x_i, x_j) \to \max$$

Here, to minimize computations, the direct mapping of data into a space of a higher dimension is not used. Instead, an approach called the kernel trick (see Chapter 6, *Dimensionality Reduction*) is used—that is, $K(x, y)$, which is a kernel matrix.

In general, the more support vectors the method chooses, the better it generalizes. Any training example that does not constitute a support vector is correctly classified if it appears in the test set because the border between positive and negative examples is still in the same place. Therefore, the expected error rate of the support vector method is, as a rule, equal to the proportion of examples that are support vectors. As the number of measurements grows, this proportion also grows, so the method is not immune from the curse of dimensionality, but it is more resistant to it than most algorithms.
It is also worth noting that the support vector method is sensitive to noise and data standardization.

Also, the method of SVMs is not only limited to the classification task but can also be adapted for solving regression tasks too. So, you can usually use the same SVM software implementation for solving classification and regression tasks.

kNN method

The kNN is a popular classification method that is sometimes used in regression problems. It is one of the most natural approaches to classification. The essence of the method is to classify the current item by the most prevailing class of its neighbors. Formally, the basis of the method is the hypothesis of compactness: if the metric of the distance between the examples is clarified successfully, then similar examples are more likely to be in the same class. For example, if you don't know what type of product to specify in the ad for a Bluetooth headset, you can find five similar headset ads. If four of them are categorized as *Accessories* and only one as *Hardware*, common sense will tell you that your ad should probably be in the *Accessories* category.

In general, to classify an object, you must perform the following operations sequentially:

1. Calculate the distance from the object to other objects in the training dataset.
2. Select the k of training objects, with the minimal distance to the object that is classified.
3. Set the classifying object class to the class most often found among the nearest k neighbors.

If we take the number of nearest neighbors $k = 1$, then the algorithm loses the ability to generalize (that is, to produce a correct result for data not previously encountered in the algorithm), because the new item is assigned to the closest class. If we set too high a value, then the algorithm may not reveal many local features.

The function for calculating the distance must meet the following rules:

- $d(x, y) \geq 0$
- $d(x, y) = 0$ only when $x = y$
- $d(x, y) = d(y, x)$
- $d(x, z) \leq d(x, y) + d(y, z)$ in the case when points x, y, z don't lie on one straight line

In this case, x, y, z are feature vectors of compared objects. For ordered attribute values, Euclidean distance can be applied, as illustrated here:

$$D_E = \sqrt{\sum_{i}^{n} (x_i - y_i)^2}$$

In this case, n is the number of attributes.

For string variables that cannot be ordered, the difference function can be applied, which is set as follows:

$$dd\,(x,\,y) = \begin{cases} 0, & x = y \\ 1, & x \neq y \end{cases}$$

When finding the distance, the importance of the attributes is sometimes taken into account. Usually, attribute relevance can be determined subjectively by an expert or analyst, and is based on their own experience, expertise, and problem interpretation. In this case, each ith square of the difference in the sum is multiplied by the coefficient Z_j. For example, if the attribute A is three times more important than the attribute B ($Z_A = 3$, $Z_B = 1$), then the distance is calculated as follows:

$$D_E = \sqrt{3(x_A - y_A)^2 + (x_B - y_B)^2}$$

This technique is called **stretching the axes**, which reduces the classification error.

The choice of class for the object of classification can also be different, and there are two main approaches to make this choice: *unweighted voting* and *weighted voting*.

For unweighted voting, we determine how many objects have the right to vote in the classification task by specifying the k number. We identify such objects by their minimal distance to the new object. The individual distance to each object is no longer critical for voting. All have equal rights in a class definition. Each existing object votes for the class to which it belongs. We assign a class with the most votes to a new object. However, there may be a problem if several classes scored an equal number of votes. Weighted voting removes this problem.

During the weighted vote, we also take into account the distance to the new object. The smaller the distance, the more significant the contribution of the vote. The votes for the class (formula) is as follows:

$$votes\,(class) = \sum_{i=1}^{n} \frac{1}{d^2\,(X,\,Y_i)}$$

In this case, $d^2(X, Y_i)$ is the square of the distance from the known object Y_i to the new object X, while n is the number of known objects of the class for which votes are calculated. `class` is the name of the class. The new object corresponds to the class with the most votes. In this case, the probability that several classes gain the same number of votes is much lower. When $k = 1$, the new object is assigned to the class of the nearest neighbor.

A notable feature of the kNN approach is its laziness. Laziness means that the calculations begin only at the moment of the classification. When using training samples with the kNN method, we don't simply build the model, but also do sample classification simultaneously. Note that the method of nearest neighbors is a well-studied approach (in machine learning, econometrics, and statistics, only linear regression is more well known). For the method of nearest neighbors, there are quite a few crucial theorems that state that on *infinite* samples, kNN is the optimal classification method. The authors of the classic book *The Elements of Statistical Learning* consider kNN to be a theoretically ideal algorithm, the applicability of which is limited only by computational capabilities and the curse of dimensionality.

kNN is one of the simplest classification algorithms, so it is often ineffective in real-world tasks. The KNN algorithm has several disadvantages. Besides a low classification accuracy when we don't have enough samples, the kNN classifier's problem is the speed of classification: if there are N objects in the training set and the dimension of the space is K, then the number of operations for classifying a test sample can be estimated as $O(K * M * N)$. The dataset used for the algorithm must be representative. The model cannot be *separated* from the data: to classify a new example, you need to use all the examples.

The positive features include the fact that the algorithm is resistant to abnormal outliers, since the probability of such a record falling into the number of kNN is small. If this happens, then the impact on the vote (uniquely weighted) with $k > 2$ is also likely to be insignificant, and therefore, the impact on the classification result is also small. The program implementation of the algorithm is relatively simple, and the algorithm result is easily interpreted. Experts in applicable fields, therefore, understand the logic of the algorithm, based on finding similar objects. The ability to modify the algorithm by using the most appropriate combination functions and metrics allows you to adjust the algorithm for a specific task.

Multi-class classification

Most of the existing methods of multi-class classification are either based on binary classifiers or are reduced to them. The general idea of such an approach is to use a set of binary classifiers trained to separate different groups of objects from each other. With such a multi-class classification, various voting schemes for a set of binary classifiers are used.

In the **one-against-all** strategy for N classes, N classifiers are trained, each of which separates its class from all other classes. At the recognition stage, the unknown vector X is fed to all N classifiers. The membership of the vector X is determined by the classifier that gave the highest estimate. This approach can meet the problem of class imbalances when they arise. Even if the task of a multi-class classification is initially balanced (that is, it has the same number of training samples in each class), when training a binary classifier, the ratio of the number of samples in each binary problem increases with an increase in the number of classes, which therefore significantly affects tasks with a notable number of classes.

The **each-against-each** strategy allocates $\frac{N(N-1)}{2}$ classifiers. These classifiers are trained to distinguish all possible pairs of classes of each other. For the input vector, each classifier gives an estimate of $f_{ij}(X)$, reflecting membership in the classes i and j. The result is a class with a maximum sum $\sum_{i \neq j}(g(f_{ij}(X)))$, where g is a monotonically non-decreasing function—for example, identical or logistic.

The **shooting tournament** strategy also involves training $\frac{N(N-1)}{2}$ classifiers that distinguish all possible pairs of classes. Unlike the previous strategy, at the stage of classification of the vector X, we arrange a tournament between classes. We create a tournament tree, where each class has one opponent and only a winner can go to the next tournament stage. So, at each step, only the one classifier determines the vector X class, then the *winning* class is used to determine the next classifier with the next pair of classes. The process is carried out until there is only one winning class left, which should be considered the result.

Some methods can produce multi-class classification immediately, without additional configuration and combinations. The kNN algorithms or neural networks can be considered examples of such methods.

Now we have become familiar with some of the most widespread classification algorithms, let's look at how to use them in different C++ libraries.

Examples of using C++ libraries for dealing with the classification task

Let's now see how to use the methods we've described for solving a classification task on artificial datasets, which we can see in the following screenshot:

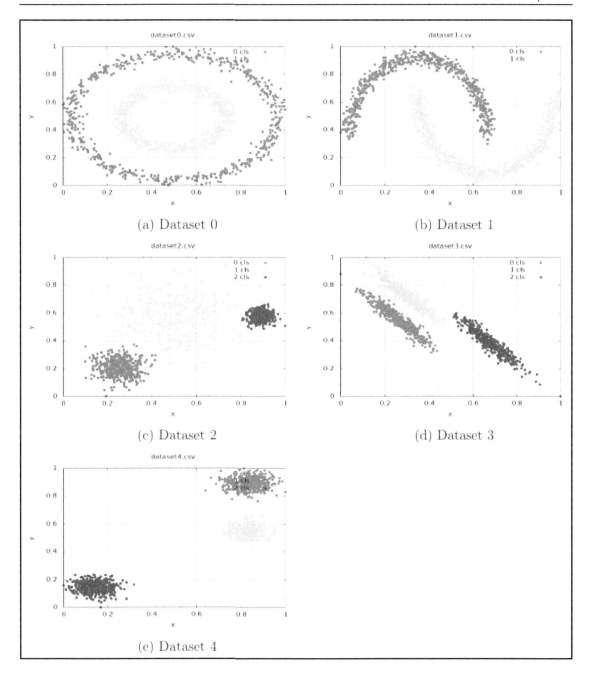

(a) Dataset 0

(b) Dataset 1

(c) Dataset 2

(d) Dataset 3

(e) Dataset 4

As we can see, these datasets contain two and three different classes of objects, so it makes sense to use methods for multi-class classification because such tasks appear more often in real life; they can be easily reduced to binary classification.

Classification is a supervised technique, so we usually have a training dataset, as well as new data for classification. To model this situation, we will use two datasets in our examples, one for training and one for testing. They come from the same distribution in one large dataset. However, the test set won't be used for training, therefore we can evaluate the accuracy metric and see how well models perform and generalize.

Using the Shogun library

In this section, we show how to use the `Shogun` library for solving the classification task. This library provides the implementation of all three main types of classification algorithms: logistic regression, kNN, and SVM.

With logistic regression

The `Shogun` library implements multi-class logistic regression in the `CMulticlassLogisticRegression` class. This class has a single configurable parameter named z, and it is a regularization coefficient. To select the best value for it, we use the grid search approach with cross-validation. The following code snippets show this approach.

Assume we have the following train and test data:

```
Some<CDenseFeatures<DataType>> features;
Some<CMulticlassLabels> labels;
Some<CDenseFeatures<DataType>> test_features;
Some<CMulticlassLabels> test_labels;
```

As we decided to use a cross-validation process, let's define the required objects as follows:

```
// search for hyper-parameters
auto root = some<CModelSelectionParameters>();
// z - regularization parameter
CModelSelectionParameters* z = new CModelSelectionParameters("m_z");
root->append_child(z);
z->build_values(0.2, 1.0, R_LINEAR, 0.1);
```

Firstly, we created a configurable parameter tree with instances of the
CModelSelectionParameters class. As we already saw in Chapter 3, *Measuring Performance and Selecting Models*, there should always be a root node and a child with exact parameter names and value ranges. Every trainable model in the Shogun library has the print_model_params() method, which prints all model parameters available for automatic configuration with the CGridSearchModelSelection class, so it's useful to check exact parameter names. The code can be seen in the following block:

```
index_t k = 3;
CStratifiedCrossValidationSplitting* splitting =
    new CStratifiedCrossValidationSplitting(labels, k);

auto eval_criterium = some<CMulticlassAccuracy>();

auto log_reg = some<CMulticlassLogisticRegression>();
auto cross = some<CCrossValidation>(log_reg, features, labels, splitting,
eval_criterium);

cross->set_num_runs(1);
```

We configured the instance of the CCrossValidation class, which took instances of a splitting strategy and an evaluation criterium object, as well as training features and labels for initialization. The splitting strategy is defined by the instance of the CStratifiedCrossValidationSplitting class and evaluation metric. We used the instance of the CMulticlassAccuracy class as an evaluation criterium, as illustrated in the following code block:

```
auto model_selection = some<CGridSearchModelSelection>(cross, root);
CParameterCombination* best_params =
wrap(model_selection->select_model(false));
best_params->apply_to_machine(log_reg);
best_params->print_tree();
```

After we configured the cross-validation objects, we used it alongside the parameters tree to initialize the instance of the CGridSearchModelSelection class, and then we used its method (namely, select_model()) to search for the best model parameters.

This method returned the instance of the CParameterCombination class, which used the apply_to_machine() method for the initialization of model parameters with this object's specific values, as illustrated in the following code block:

```
// train
log_reg->set_labels(labels);
log_reg->train(features);

// evaluate model on test data
auto new_labels = wrap(log_reg->apply_multiclass(test_features));

// estimate accuracy
auto accuracy = eval_criterium->evaluate(new_labels, test_labels);

// process results
auto feature_matrix = test_features->get_feature_matrix();
for (index_t i = 0; i < new_labels->get_num_labels(); ++i) {
    auto label_idx_pred = new_labels->get_label(i);
    auto vector = feature_matrix.get_column(i)
    ...
}
```

After we found out the best parameters, we trained our model on the full training dataset and evaluated it on the test set. The CMulticlassLogisticRegression class has a method named apply_multiclass() that we used for a model evaluation on the test data. This method returned an object of the CMulticlassLabels class. The get_label() method was then used to access labels values.

The following screenshot shows the results of applying the Shogun implementation of the logistic regression algorithm to our datasets:

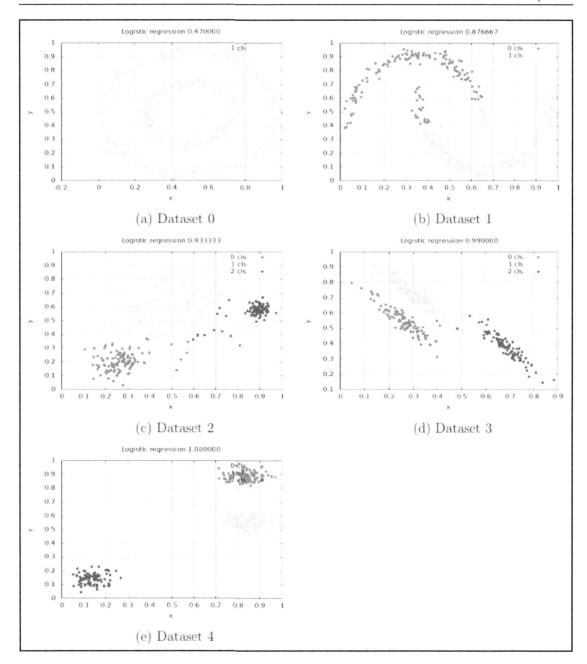

(a) Dataset 0

(b) Dataset 1

(c) Dataset 2

(d) Dataset 3

(e) Dataset 4

Notice that we have classification errors in the **Dataset 0**, **Dataset 1**, and **Dataset 2** datasets, and other datasets were classified almost correctly.

With SVMs

The `Shogun` library also has an implementation of the multi-class SVM algorithm in the `CMulticlassLibSVM` class. The instances of this class can be configured with a parameter named C, which is a measure of the allowance of misclassification with a kernel object. In the following example, we use an instance of the `CGaussianKernel` class for the kernel object. This object also has parameters for configuration, but we used only one named the `combined_kernel_weight` parameter because it gave the most reasonable configuration for our model after a series of experiments. Let's look at the code in the following block:

```
Some <CDenseFeatures<DataType>> features;
Some<CMulticlassLabels> labels;
Some<CDenseFeatures<DataType>> test_features;
Some<CMulticlassLabels> test_labels;
```

These are our train and test dataset objects' definition:

```
auto kernel = some<CGaussianKernel>(features, features, 5);
// one vs one classification
auto svm = some<CMulticlassLibSVM>();
svm->set_kernel(kernel);
```

Using these datasets, we initialized the `CMulticlassLibSVM` class object and configured its kernel, as follows:

```
// search for hyper-parameters
auto root = some<CModelSelectionParameters>();
// C - how much you want to avoid misclassifying
CModelSelectionParameters* c = new CModelSelectionParameters("C");
root->append_child(c);
c->build_values(1.0, 1000.0, R_LINEAR, 100.);

auto params_kernel = some<CModelSelectionParameters>("kernel", kernel);
root->append_child(params_kernel);

auto params_kernel_width =
some<CModelSelectionParameters>("combined_kernel_weight");
params_kernel_width->build_values(0.1, 10.0, R_LINEAR, 0.5);

params_kernel->append_child(params_kernel_width);
```

Then, we configured cross-validation parameters objects to look for the best hyperparameters combination, as follows:

```
index_t k = 3;
CStratifiedCrossValidationSplitting* splitting =
```

```
new CStratifiedCrossValidationSplitting(labels, k);

auto eval_criterium = some<CMulticlassAccuracy>();

auto cross =
some<CCrossValidation>(svm, features, labels, splitting,
                       eval_criterium);
cross->set_num_runs(1);

auto model_selection = some<CGridSearchModelSelection>(cross, root);
CParameterCombination* best_params =
wrap(model_selection->select_model(false));
best_params->apply_to_machine(svm);
best_params->print_tree();
```

Having configured the cross-validation parameters, we initialized the CCrossValidation class object and ran the grid-search process for model selection, as follows:

```
// train SVM
svm->set_labels(labels);
svm->train(features);

// evaluate model on test data
auto new_labels = wrap(svm->apply_multiclass(test_features));

// estimate accuracy
auto accuracy = eval_criterium->evaluate(new_labels, test_labels);
std::cout << "svm " << name << " accuracy = " << accuracy << std::endl;

// process results
auto feature_matrix = test_features->get_feature_matrix();
for (index_t i = 0; i < new_labels->get_num_labels(); ++i) {
auto label_idx_pred = new_labels->get_label(i);
auto vector = feature_matrix.get_column(i);
...
}
```

When the best hyperparameters were found and applied to the model, we repeated training and did the evaluation.

Notice that, with the exception of the different parameters for model configuration, the code is the same as for the previous example. We created the parameters' tree, the cross-validation object, the same evaluation metrics object, and used the grid-search approach for finding the best combination of the model parameters. Then, we trained the model and used the apply_multiclass() method for evaluation. These facts show you that the library has a unified API for different algorithms, which allows us to try different models with minimal modifications in the code.

The following screenshot shows the results of applying the `Shogun` implementation of the SVM algorithm to our datasets:

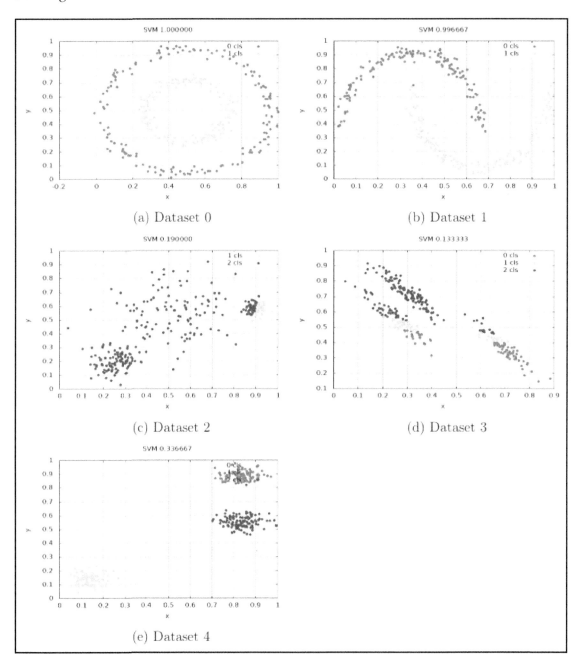

(a) Dataset 0

(b) Dataset 1

(c) Dataset 2

(d) Dataset 3

(e) Dataset 4

Notice that SVM made another classification error, and we have incorrect labels in **Dataset 2**, **Dataset 3**, and **Dataset 4**. Other datasets were classified almost correctly.

With the kNN algorithm

The Shogun library also has an implementation of the kNN algorithm, and it is placed in the CKNN class. Before using this algorithm, we have to calculate the distance between all features in the training dataset. This operation can be done, for example, with the instance of the CEuclideanDistance class (or an alternative), which implements the CDistance interface. There are many distance implementation classes in the Shogun library, such as cosine similarity, and Manhattan and Hamming distances. After we have the object containing the distances for our training set, we can initialize the object of the CKNN class, which takes the distance object, training labels, and the *k* parameter (which is the number of searched-for neighbors). This object uses the train() method to perform model training. The following code shows this approach:

```
void KNNClassification(Some<CDenseFeatures<DataType>> features,
                       Some<CMulticlassLabels> labels,
                       Some<CDenseFeatures<DataType>> test_features,
                       Some<CMulticlassLabels> test_labels) {
    int32_t k = 3;
    auto distance = some<CEuclideanDistance>(features, features);
    auto knn = some<CKNN>(k, distance, labels);
    knn->train();

    // evaluate model on test data
    auto new_labels = wrap(knn->apply_multiclass(test_features));

    // estimate accuracy
    auto eval_criterium = some<CMulticlassAccuracy>();
    auto accuracy = eval_criterium->evaluate(new_labels, test_labels);


    // process results
    auto feature_matrix = test_features->get_feature_matrix();
    for (index_t i = 0; i < new_labels->get_num_labels(); ++i) {
        auto label_idx_pred = new_labels->get_label(i);
        ...
    }
}
```

As we can see, the code is pretty simple. After the model is trained, we can use the already known apply_multiclass() method for evaluation.

The following screenshot shows the results of applying the Shogun implementation of the kNN algorithm to our datasets:

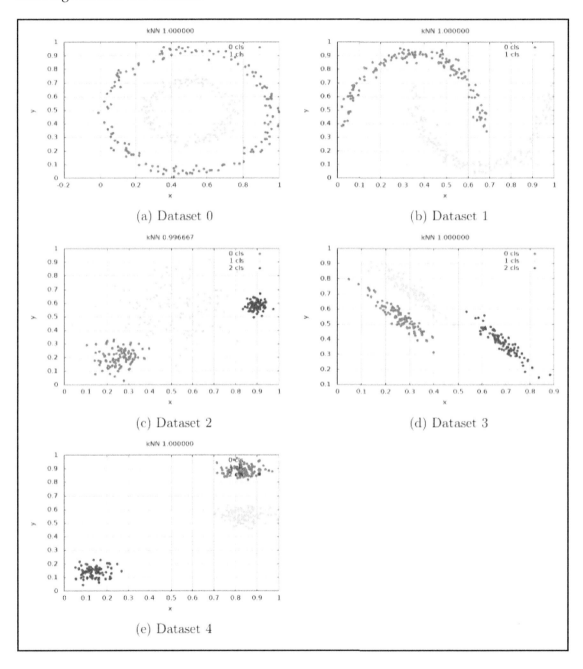

(a) Dataset 0

(b) Dataset 1

(c) Dataset 2

(d) Dataset 3

(e) Dataset 4

Notice that the kNN algorithm classified all datasets almost correctly.

Using the Dlib library

The `Dlib` library doesn't have many classification algorithms. There are two that are most applicable: *KRR* and *SVM*. These methods are implemented as binary classifiers, but for multi-class classification, this library provides the `one_vs_one_trainer` class, which implements the voting strategy. Note that this class can use classifiers of different types so that you can combine the KRR and the SVM for one classification task. We can also specify which classifiers should be used for which distinct classes.

With KRR

The following code sample shows how to use Dlib's KRR algorithm implementation for the multi-class classification:

```
void KRRClassification(const Samples& samples,
                       const Labels& labels,
                       const Samples& test_samples,
                       const Labels& test_labels) {
    using OVOtrainer = one_vs_one_trainer<any_trainer<SampleType>>;
    using KernelType = radial_basis_kernel<SampleType>;

    krr_trainer<KernelType> krr_trainer;
    krr_trainer.set_kernel(KernelType(0.1));

    OVOtrainer trainer;
    trainer.set_trainer(krr_trainer);

    one_vs_one_decision_function<OVOtrainer> df = trainer.train(samples,
                            labels);

    // process results and estimate accuracy
    DataType accuracy = 0;
    for (size_t i = 0; i != test_samples.size(); i++) {
        auto vec = test_samples[i];
        auto class_idx = static_cast<size_t>(df(vec));
        if (static_cast<size_t>(test_labels[i]) == class_idx)
            ++accuracy;
        ...
    }

    accuracy /= test_samples.size();
}
```

Firstly, we initialized the object of the `krr_trainer` class, and then we configured it with the instance of a kernel object. In this example, we used the `radial_basis_kernel` type for the kernel object, in order to deal with samples that can't be linearly separated. After we obtained the binary classifier object, we initialized the instance of the `one_vs_one_trainer` class and added this classifier to its stack with the `set_trainer()` method. Then, we used the `train()` method for training our multi-class classifier. As with most of the algorithms in the `Dlib` library, this one assumes that the training samples and labels have the `std::vector` type, whereby each element has a `matrix` type. The `train()` method returns a decision function—namely, the object that behaves as a functor, which then takes a single sample and returns a classification label for it. This decision function is an object of the `one_vs_one_decision_function` type. The following piece of code demonstrates how we can use it:

```
auto vec = test_samples[i];
auto class_idx = static_cast<size_t>(df(vec));
```

There is no explicit implementation for the accuracy metric in the `Dlib` library; so, in this example, accuracy is calculated directly as a ration of correctly classified test samples against the total number of test samples.

The following screenshot shows the results of applying the Dlib implementation of the KRR algorithm to our datasets:

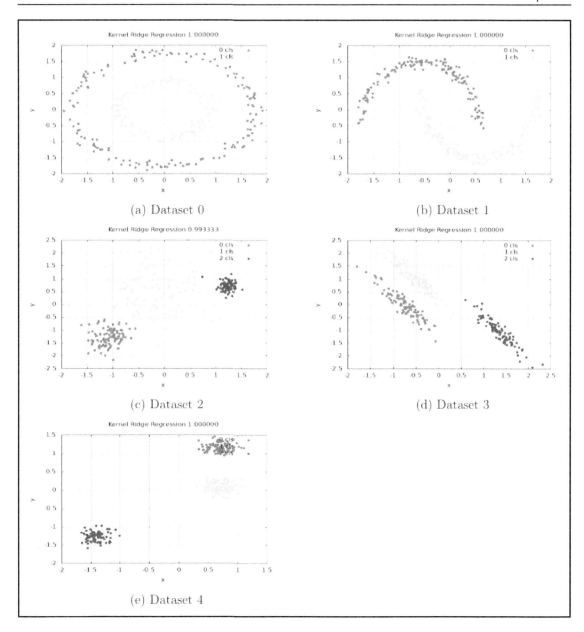

(a) Dataset 0

(b) Dataset 1

(c) Dataset 2

(d) Dataset 3

(e) Dataset 4

Notice that the KRR algorithm performed a correct classification on all datasets.

With SVM

The following code sample shows how to use `Dlib`'s SVM algorithm implementation for multi-class classification:

```
void SVMClassification(const Samples& samples,
                       const Labels& labels,
                       const Samples& test_samples,
                       const Labels& test_labels) {
    using OVOtrainer = one_vs_one_trainer<any_trainer<SampleType>>;
    using KernelType = radial_basis_kernel<SampleType>;

    svm_nu_trainer<KernelType> svm_trainer;
    svm_trainer.set_kernel(KernelType(0.1));

    OVOtrainer trainer;
    trainer.set_trainer(svm_trainer);

    one_vs_one_decision_function<OVOtrainer> df = trainer.train(samples,
                              labels);

    // process results and estimate accuracy
    DataType accuracy = 0;
    for (size_t i = 0; i != test_samples.size(); i++) {
        auto vec = test_samples[i];
        auto class_idx = static_cast<size_t>(df(vec));
        if (static_cast<size_t>(test_labels[i]) == class_idx)
            ++accuracy;
        ...
    }

    accuracy /= test_samples.size();
}
```

This sample shows that the `Dlib` library also has a unified API for using different algorithms, and the main difference from the previous example is the object of binary classifier. For the SVM classification, we used an object of the `svm_nu_trainer` type, which was also configured with the kernel object of the `radial_basis_kernel` type.

The following screenshot shows the results of applying the Dlib implementation of the KRR algorithm to our datasets:

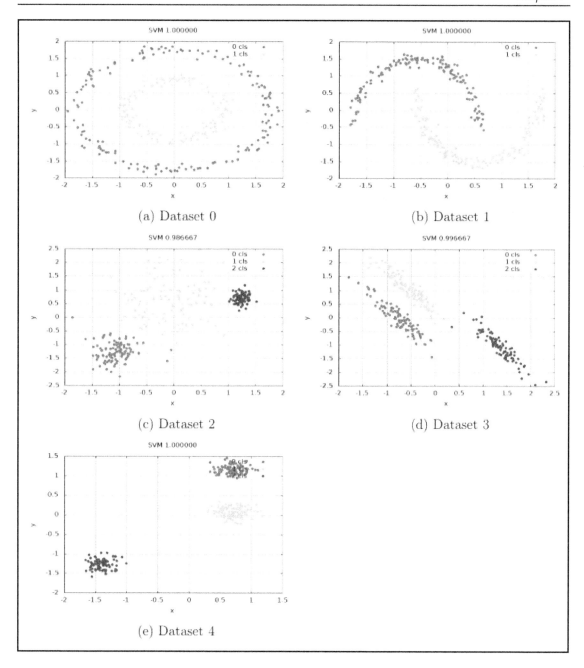

(a) Dataset 0

(b) Dataset 1

(c) Dataset 2

(d) Dataset 3

(e) Dataset 4

You can see the Dlib implementation of the SVM algorithm also did correct classification on all datasets without additional configurations. Remember that the Shogun implementation of the same algorithm made incorrect classification in some cases.

Using the Shark-ML library

The `Shark-ML` library has a more low-level approach to the multi-class classification problem. Logistic regression and SVM classifiers are implemented as binary classifiers. The user therefore has to explicitly train $\frac{N(N-1)}{2}$ classifiers and configure the object of the `OneVersusOneClassifier` class to combine them in a multi-class classifier. The kNN algorithm is a multi-class classifier by nature.

With logistic regression

The following example shows how to implement the multi-class classification with `Shark-ML` and the logistic regression algorithm. The following code snippet introduces a function declaration for this kind of task:

```
void LRClassification(const ClassificationDataset& train,
                      const ClassificationDataset& test,
                      unsigned int num_classes) {
...
}
```

The following code snippet shows how to configure an object for multi-class classification:

```
OneVersusOneClassifier<RealVector> ovo;
unsigned int pairs = num_classes * (num_classes - 1) / 2;
std::vector<LinearClassifier<RealVector> > lr(pairs);

for (std::size_t n = 0, cls1 = 1; cls1 < num_classes; cls1++) {
    using BinaryClassifierType =
        OneVersusOneClassifier<RealVector>::binary_classifier_type;
    std::vector<BinaryClassifierType*> ovo_classifiers;
    for (std::size_t cls2 = 0; cls2 < cls1; cls2++, n++) {
        // get the binary subproblem
        ClassificationDataset binary_cls_data =
            binarySubProblem(train, cls2, cls1);

        // train the binary machine
        LogisticRegression<RealVector> trainer;
        trainer.train(lr[n], binary_cls_data);
```

```
        ovo_classifiers.push_back(&lr[n]);
    }
    ovo.addClass(ovo_classifiers);
}
```

In the previous code snippet, we used the following steps, which showed us how to configure an object for multi-class classification:

1. Firstly, we defined the `ovo` object of the `OneVersusOneClassifier` class, which encapsulates the single multi-class classifier.
2. Then, we initialized all binary classifiers for the one-versus-one strategy and placed them in the `lr` container object of the `std::vector<LinearClassifier<RealVector>>` type.
3. We then trained the set of binary classifiers with the trainer object of the `LogisticRegression` type and put them into the `lr` container.
4. We then ran the training with nested cycles over all classes. Notice that the `lr` container holds the instances of classifiers, but the `ovo` object needs pointers to classifiers' instances to perform the final classification.
   The `ovo_classifiers` object contains the pointers to binary classifiers. These classifiers are configured in such a way that each of them classifies a single class (`cls1`) as positive, and all other classes are treated as negative (`cls2`).
5. We then used the `ovo_classifiers` object to populate the `ovo` object, using the `addClass` method.

Another important factor is how we separate the data needed for training a single binary classifier. The `Shark-ML` library has a particular function for this task called `binarySubProblem`, which takes the object of the `ClassificationDataset` type and splits it in a way that is suitable for binary classification, even if the original dataset is a multi-class one. The second and the third arguments of this function are the `zero` class label index and the `one` class label index respectively.

After we trained all binary classifiers and configured the OneVersusOneClassifier object, we used it for model evaluation on a test set. This object can be used as a functor to classify the set of test examples, but they need to have the UnlabeledData type. In our example, the test dataset has the ClassificationDataset type, so it is labeled. We used the inputs() method to retrieve unlabeled samples from it. The result of the classification has the Data<unsigned int> type.

The following code snippet shows how to use a trained ovo object for evaluation:

```
// estimate accuracy
ZeroOneLoss<unsigned int> loss;
Data<unsigned int> output = ovo(test.inputs());
double accuracy = 1. - loss.eval(test.labels(), output);

// process results
for (std::size_t i = 0; i != test.numberOfElements(); i++) {
    auto cluser_idx = output.element(i);
    auto element = test.inputs().element(i);
        ...
}
```

For an evaluation metric, we used the object of the ZeroOneLoss type, which returns the value opposite to the accuracy, therefore we inverted it for our purposes.

The following screenshot shows the results of applying the Shark-ML implementation of the logistic regression algorithm to our datasets:

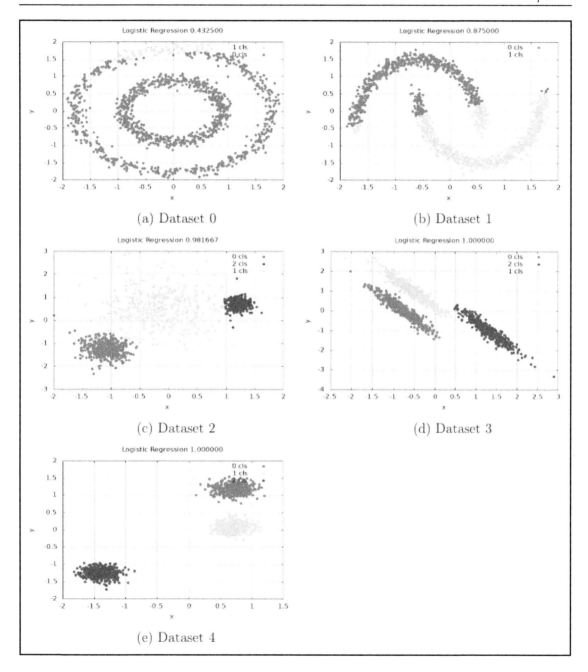

(a) Dataset 0

(b) Dataset 1

(c) Dataset 2

(d) Dataset 3

(e) Dataset 4

You can see that the multi-class logistic regression algorithm implementation performs better than its implementation in the `Shogun` library. However, it made some errors in the **Dataset 0** and **Dataset 1** datasets.

With SVM

To implement the SVM multi-class classification with the `Shark-ML` library, we should use the same approach as we used before for the logistic regression approach. The main difference is the type of binary classifiers. In this case, it is the `KernelClassifier` class, and the trainer for it is the `CSvmTrainer` class.

In the following sample, we will use two predefined parameters for the model, one being the C parameter for the SVM algorithm, and the second being the `gamma` for the kernel. The kernel object in this sample has the `GaussianRbfKernel` type, to deal with non-linearly separable data.

The following code snippet shows a function declaration with dataset objects as arguments:

```
void SVMClassification(const ClassificationDataset& train,
                       const ClassificationDataset& test,
                       unsigned int num_classes) {
    ...
}
```

Then, we define a kernel object, as follows:

```
double gamma = 0.5;
GaussianRbfKernel<> kernel(gamma);
```

The following code snippet shows how to initialize and configure a one-versus-one classifier object:

```
OneVersusOneClassifier<RealVector> ovo;
unsigned int pairs = num_classes * (num_classes - 1) / 2;
std::vector<KernelClassifier<RealVector> > svm(pairs);
for (std::size_t n = 0, cls1 = 1; cls1 < num_classes; cls1++) {
    using BinaryClassifierType =
        OneVersusOneClassifier<RealVector>::binary_classifier_type;
    std::vector<BinaryClassifierType*> ovo_classifiers;
    for (std::size_t cls2 = 0; cls2 < cls1; cls2++, n++) {
        // get the binary subproblem
        ClassificationDataset binary_cls_data =
            binarySubProblem(train, cls2, cls1);

        // train the binary machine
        double c = 10.0;
        CSvmTrainer<RealVector> trainer(&kernel, c, false);
        trainer.train(svm[n], binary_cls_data);
        ovo_classifiers.push_back(&svm[n]);
    }
    ovo.addClass(ovo_classifiers);
}
```

And after the training completion, we use the ovo object for evaluation, as follows:

```
// estimate accuracy
ZeroOneLoss<unsigned int> loss;
Data<unsigned int> output = ovo(test.inputs());
double accuracy = 1. - loss.eval(test.labels(), output);

// process results
for (std::size_t i = 0; i != test.numberOfElements(); i++) {
    auto cluser_idx = output.element(i);
    auto element = test.inputs().element(i);
    ...
}
```

The following screenshot shows the results of applying the Shark-ML implementation of the SVM algorithm to our datasets:

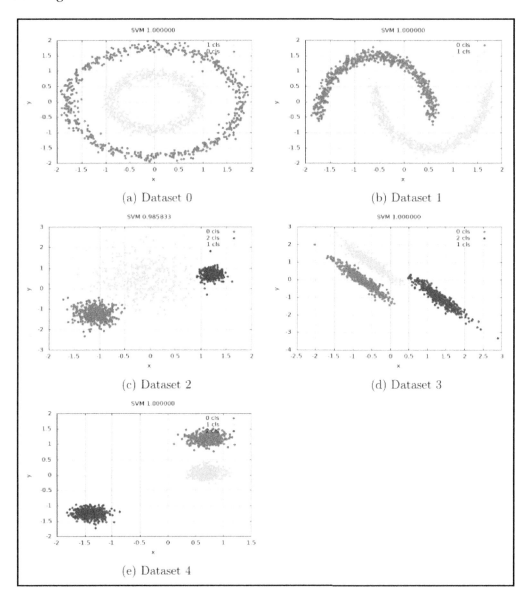

Notice that the Shark-ML SVM algorithm implementation did the correct classification on all datasets.

With the kNN algorithm

The kNN classification algorithm in the `Shark-ML` library is implemented in the `NearestNeighborModel` class. An object of this class can be initialized with different nearest neighbor algorithms. The two main types are the brute-force option and the space partitioning trees option. In this sample, we will use the `TreeNearestNeighbors` algorithm, because it has better performance for medium-sized datasets. The following code block shows the use of the kNN algorithm with the `Shark-ML` library:

```
void KNNClassification(const ClassificationDataset& train,
                       const ClassificationDataset& test,
                       unsigned int num_classes) {
    KDTree<RealVector> tree(train.inputs());
    TreeNearestNeighbors<RealVector, unsigned int> nn_alg(train, &tree);
    const unsigned int k = 5;
    NearestNeighborModel<RealVector, unsigned int> knn(&nn_alg, k);

    // estimate accuracy
    ZeroOneLoss<unsigned int> loss;
    Data<unsigned int> predictions = knn(test.inputs());
    double accuracy = 1. - loss.eval(test.labels(), predictions);

    // process results
    for (std::size_t i = 0; i != test.numberOfElements(); i++) {
        auto cluser_idx = predictions.element(i);
        auto element = test.inputs().element(i);
        ...
    }
}
```

The first step was the creation of the object of the `KDTree` type, which defined the KD-Tree space partitioning of our training samples. Then, we initialized the object of the `TreeNearestNeighbors` class, which takes the instances of previously created tree partitioning and the training dataset. We also predefined the *k* parameter of the kNN algorithm and initialized the object of the `NearestNeighborModel` class with the algorithm instance and the *k* parameter.

This model doesn't have a particular training method because the kNN algorithm uses all the data for evaluation. The building of a KD-Tree can, therefore, be interpreted as the training step in this case, because the tree doesn't change the evaluation data. So, after we initialized the object that implements the kNN algorithm, we can use it as a functor to classify the set of test samples. This API technique is the same for all classification models in the `Shark-ML` library. For the accuracy evaluation metric, we also used the object of the `ZeroOneLoss` type.

The following screenshot shows the results of applying the Shark-ML implementation of the kNN algorithm to our datasets:

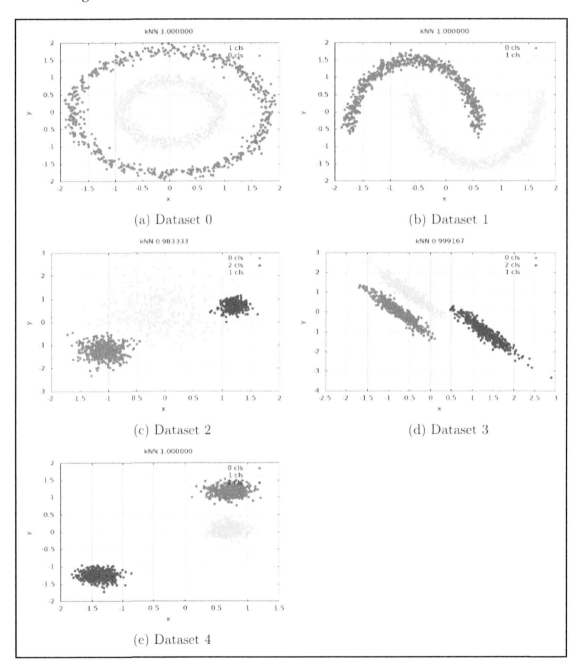

(a) Dataset 0

(b) Dataset 1

(c) Dataset 2

(d) Dataset 3

(e) Dataset 4

You can see that the Shark-ML kNN algorithm implementation also did the correct classification on all datasets, without any significant number of errors.

Summary

In this chapter, we discussed supervised machine learning approaches to solving classification tasks. These approaches use trained models to determine the class of an object according to its characteristics. We considered two methods of binary classification: logistic regression and SVMs. We looked at the approaches for the implementation of multi-class classification with the use of binary classifiers.

We also examined the nearest neighbor method, which can deal with multi-class classification without additional actions. We saw that working with non-linear data requires additional improvements in the algorithms and their tuning. Implementations of classification algorithms differ in terms of performance, as well as the amount of required memory and the amount of time required for learning. Therefore, the classification algorithm's choice should be guided by a specific task and business requirements. Furthermore, their implementations in different libraries can produce different results, even for the same algorithm. Therefore, it makes sense to have several libraries for your software.

In the next chapter, we will discuss recommender systems. We will see how they work, which algorithms exist for their implementation, and how to train and evaluate them. In the simplest sense, recommender systems are used to predict which objects (goods or services) are of interest to a user. Examples of such systems can be seen in many online stores such as Amazon or on streaming sites such as Netflix, which recommend you new content based on your previous consumption.

Further reading

- **Logistic Regression—Detailed Overview**: https://towardsdatascience.com/logistic-regression-detailed-overview-46c4da4303bc
- **Understanding Support Vector Machine (SVM) algorithm from examples (along with code)**: https://www.analyticsvidhya.com/blog/2017/09/understaing-support-vector-machine-example-code/
- **Understanding Support Vector Machines: A Primer**: https://appliedmachinelearning.blog/2017/03/09/understanding-support-vector-machines-a-primer/
- **Support Vector Machine: Kernel Trick; Mercer's Theorem**: https://towardsdatascience.com/understanding-support-vector-machine-part-2-kernel-trick-mercers-theorem-e1e6848c6c4d
- **SVMs with Kernel Trick (lecture)**: https://ocw.mit.edu/courses/sloan-school-of-management/15-097-prediction-machine-learning-and-statistics-spring-2012/lecture-notes/MIT15_097S12_lec13.pdf
- **Support Vector Machines—Kernels and the Kernel Trick**: https://cogsys.uni-bamberg.de/teaching/ss06/hs_svm/slides/SVM_Seminarbericht_Hofmann.pdf
- **A Complete Guide to K-Nearest-Neighbors with Applications in Python and R**: https://kevinzakka.github.io/2016/07/13/k-nearest-neighbor

8
Recommender Systems

Recommender systems are algorithms, programs, and services whose main task is to use data to predict which objects (goods or services) are of interest to a user. There are two main types of recommender systems: *content-based* and *collaborative filtering*. **Content-based recommender systems** are based on data collected from specific products. They recommend objects to a user that are similar to ones the user has previously acquired or shown interest in. **Collaborative filtering recommender systems** filter out objects that a user might like based on the reaction history of other similar users of these systems. They usually consider the user's previous reactions, too.

In this chapter, we'll look at the implementation of recommender system algorithms based on both content and collaborative filtering. We are going to discuss different approaches for implementing collaborative filtering algorithms, implement systems using only the linear algebra library, and see how to use the `mlpack` library to solve collaborative filtering problems. We'll use the MovieLens dataset provided by GroupLens from a research lab in the Department of Computer Science and Engineering at the University of Minnesota: `https://grouplens.org/datasets/movielens/`

The following topics will be covered in this chapter:

- An overview of recommender system algorithms
- Understanding collaborative filtering method details
- Examples of item-based collaborative filtering with C++

Technical requirements

The required technologies and installations for the chapter are as follows:

- `Eigen` library
- `Armadillo` library
- `mlpack` library
- Modern C++ compiler with C++17 support
- CMake build system version >= 3.8

The code files for this chapter can be found at the following GitHub repo: `https://github.com/PacktPublishing/Hands-On-Machine-Learning-with-CPP/tree/master/Chapter08`

An overview of recommender system algorithms

A recommender system's task is to inform a user about an object that could be the most interesting to them at a given time. Most often, such an object is a product or service, but it may be information—for example, in the form of a recommended news article.

Despite the many existing algorithms, we can divide recommender systems into several basic approaches. The most common are as follows:

- **Summary-based**: Non-personal models based on the average product rating
- **Content-based**: Models based on the intersection of product descriptions and user interests
- **Collaborative filtering**: Models based on interests of similar user groups
- **Matrix factorization**: Methods based on the preferences matrix decomposition

The basis of any recommender system is the preferences matrix. The preferences matrix has all users of the service laid on one of the axes, and recommendation objects on the other. The recommendation objects are usually called **items**. At the intersection of rows and columns (user, item), this matrix is filled with ratings—this is a known indicator of user interest in this product, expressed on a given scale (for example, from 1 to 5), as illustrated in the following table:

	item1	item 2	item3
user1	1		
user2		2	4

user3	1	1	1
user4			5
user5	3	1	
user6		4	

Users usually evaluate only a small number of the items in the catalog, and the task of the recommender system is to summarize this information and predict the attitude the user might have toward other items. In other words, you need to fill in all the blank cells in the preceding table.

People's consumption patterns are different, and new products do not have to be recommended all the time. You can show repeated items—for example, when a user has bought something they'll definitely need again. According to this principle, there are the following two groups of items:

- **Repeatable**: For example, shampoos or razors that are always needed
- **Unrepeatable**: For example, books or films that are rarely purchased repeatedly

If the product cannot be attributed to one of these groups, it makes sense to determine the group type of repetitive purchases individually (someone usually buys only a specific brand, but someone else might try everything in the catalog).

Determining what is an *interesting* product to a user is also subjective. Some users need things only from their favorite category (conservative recommendations), while someone else, on the other hand, responds more to non-standard goods (risky recommendations). For example, a video-hosting service may recommend only new series from their favorite TV series (conservative), but may periodically recommend new shows or new genres. Ideally, you should choose a strategy for displaying recommendations for each client separately, using generalized information about the client's preferences.

The essential part of datasets used to build recommendation models is user reactions to different objects or items. These reactions are typically named as user ratings of objects. We can obtain user ratings in the following two ways:

- **Explicit ratings**: The user gives their own rating for the product, leaves a review, or *likes* the page.
- **Implicit ratings**: The user clearly does not express their attitude, but an indirect conclusion can be made from their actions. For example, if they bought a product, it means they like it; if they read the description for a long time, it means there is serious interest.

Of course, explicit preferences are better. However, in practice, not all services provide an opportunity for users to express their interests clearly, and not all users have the desire to do so. Both types of assessments are most often used in tandem, and complement each other well.

It is also essential to distinguish between the terms *prediction* (prediction of the degree of interest) and the *recommendation* itself (showing the recommendation). How to show something is a separate task from the task of *what to show*. *How to show* is a task that uses the estimates obtained in the prediction step, and can be implemented in different ways.

In this section, we discussed the basics of recommender systems. In the following sections, we will look at essential building blocks of recommender systems. Let's begin by looking at the main principles of content-based filtering, user- and item-based collaborative filtering, and collaborative filtering based on matrix factorization.

Non-personalized recommendations

For non-personalized recommendations, the potential interest of the user is determined simply by the average rating of the product: *Everyone likes it—this means you will like it too*. According to this principle, most services work when the user is not authorized on the system.

Content-based recommendations

Personal recommendations use the maximum information available about the user—primarily, information on their previous purchases. Content-based filtering was one of the first approaches to this. In this approach, the product's description (content) is compared with the interests of the user, obtained from their previous assessments. The more the product meets these interests, the higher the potential interest of the user. The obvious requirement here is that all products in the catalog should have a description.

Historically, the subject of content-based recommendations was products with unstructured descriptions: films, books, or articles. Their features may be—for example—text descriptions, reviews, or casts. However, nothing prevents the use of usual numerical or categorical features.

Unstructured features are described in a text-typical way—vectors in the space of words (vector-space model). Each element of a vector is a feature that potentially characterizes the interest of the user. Similarly, an item (product) is a vector in the same space.

As users interact with the system (say, they buy films), the vector descriptions of the goods they've purchased merge (sum up and normalize) into a single vector and, thus, form the vector of a user's interests. Using this vector of interests, we can find the product, the description of which is closest to it—that is, solve the problem of finding the nearest neighbors.

When forming the vector space of a product presentation, instead of individual words, you can use shingles or n-grams (successive pairs of words, triples of words, or other numbers of words). This approach makes the model more detailed, but more data is required for training.

In different places of the description of the product, the weight of keywords may differ (for example, the description of the film may consist of a title, a brief description, and a detailed description). Product descriptions from different users can be weighed differently. For example, we can give more weight to active users who have many ratings. Similarly, you can weigh them by item. The higher the average rating of an object, the greater its weight (similar to PageRank). If the product description allows links to external sources, then you can also analyze all third-party information related to the product.

The cosine distance is often used to compare product representation vectors. This distance measures the value of proximity between two vectors.

When adding a new assessment, the vector of interests is updated incrementally (only for those elements that have changed). During the update, it makes sense to give a bit more weight to new estimates since the user's preferences may change. You'll notice that content-based filtering almost wholly repeats the query-document matching mechanism used in search engines such as Google. The only difference lies in the form of a search query—content filtering systems use a vector that describes the interests of the user, and search engines use keywords of the requested document. When search engines began to add personalization, this distinction was erased even more.

User-based collaborative filtering

This class of system began to develop in the '90s. Under this approach, recommendations are generated based on the interests of other similar users. Such recommendations are the result of the **collaboration** of many users, hence the name of the method.

The classical implementation of the algorithm is based on the principle of **k-nearest neighbors (kNN)**. For every user, we look for the k most similar to them (in terms of preferences). Then, we supplement the information about the user with known data from their neighbors. So, for example, if it is known that your neighbors are delighted with a movie, and you have not watched it for some reason, this is a great reason to recommend this movie.

The similarity is, in this case, a synonym for a *correlation* of interests and can be considered in many ways—Pearson's correlation, cosine distance, Jaccard distance, Hamming distance, and other types of distances.

The classical implementation of the algorithm has one distinct disadvantage—it is poorly applicable in practice due to the quadratic complexity of the calculations. As with any nearest neighbor method, it requires the calculation of all pairwise distances between users (and there may be millions of users). It is easy to calculate that the complexity of calculating the distance matrix is $O(n^2 m)$, where n is the number of users, and m is the number of items (goods).

This problem can be partly solved by purchasing high-performance hardware. But if you approach it wisely, then it is better to introduce some corrections into the algorithm in the following way:

- Update distances not with every purchase but with batches (for example, once a day).
- Do not recalculate the distance matrix completely, but update it incrementally.
- Choose some iterative and approximate algorithms (for example, **Alternating Least Squares (ALS)**).

Fulfill the following assumptions to make the algorithm more practical:

1. The tastes of people do not change over time (or they do change, but they are the same for everyone).
2. If people's tastes are the same, then they are the same in everything.

For example, if two clients prefer the same films, then they also like the same book. This assumption is often the case when the recommended products are homogeneous (for example, films only). If this is not the case, then a couple of clients may well have the same eating habits but their political views might be the opposite; here, the algorithm is less efficient.

The neighborhood of the user in the space of preferences (the user's neighbors), which we analyze to generate new recommendations, can be chosen in different ways. We can work with all users of the system; we can set a certain proximity threshold; we can choose several neighbors at random, or take the k most similar neighbors (this is the most popular approach). If we take too many neighbors, we get a higher chance of random noise—and vice versa. If we take too little, we get more accurate recommendations, but fewer goods can be recommended.

An interesting development in the collaborative approach is trust-based recommendations, which take into account not only the proximity of people according to their interests, but also their *social* proximity and the degree of trust between them. If, for example, we see that on Facebook, a girl occasionally visits a page that has her friend's audio recordings, then she trusts her musical taste. Therefore, when making recommendations to the girl, you can add new songs from her friend's playlist.

Item-based collaborative filtering

The item-based approach is a natural alternative to the classic user-based approach described previously, and almost repeats it, except for one thing—it applies to the transposed preference matrix, which looks for similar products instead of users.

For each client, a user-based collaborative filtering system searches a group of customers who are similar to this user in terms of previous purchases, and then the system averages their preferences. These average preferences serve as recommendations for the user. In the case of item-based collaborative filtering, the nearest neighbors are searched for on a variety of products (items)—columns of a preference matrix, and the averaging occurs precisely according to them.

Indeed, if some products are meaningfully similar to each other, then users' reactions to these products will be the same. Therefore, when we see that some products have a strong correlation between their estimates, this may indicate that these products are equivalent to each other.

The main advantage of the item-based approach over the user-based approach is lower computation complexity. When there are many users (almost always), the task of finding the nearest neighbor becomes poorly computable. For example, for 1 million users, you need to calculate and store ~500 billion distances. If the distance is encoded in 8 bytes, this is 4 **terabytes (TB)** for the distance matrix alone. If we take an item-based approach, then the computational complexity decreases from $O(N^2 n)$ to $O(n^2 N)$, and the distance matrix has a dimension no longer than 1 million per 1 million but 100 by 100 as per the number of items (goods).

Estimation of the proximity of products is much more accurate than the assessment of the proximity of users. This assumption is a direct consequence of the fact that there are usually many more users than items, and therefore the standard error in calculating the correlation of items is significantly less because we have more information to work from.

In the user-based version, the description of users usually has a very sparse distribution (there are many goods, but only a few evaluations). On the one hand, this helps to optimize the calculation—we multiply only those elements where an intersection exists. But, on the other hand, the list of items that a system can recommend to a user is minimal due to the limited number of user neighbors (users who have similar preferences). Also, user preferences may change over time, but the descriptions of the goods are much more stable.

The rest of the algorithm almost wholly repeats the user-based version: it uses the same cosine distance as the primary measure of proximity and has the same need for data normalization. Since the correlation of items is considered on a higher number of observations, it is not so critical to recalculate it after each new assessment, and this can be done periodically in a batch mode.

Let's now look at another approach to generalize user interests based on matrix factorization methods.

Factorization algorithms

It would be nice to describe the interests of the user with more extensive features—not in the format of *they love movies X, Y, and Z*, but in the format of *they love romantic comedies*. Besides the fact that it increases the generalizability of the model, it also solves the problem of having a large data dimension—after all, the interests are described not by the items vector, but by a significantly smaller preference vector.

Such approaches are also called **spectral decomposition** or **high-frequency filtering** (since we remove the noise and leave the useful signal). There are many different types of matrix decomposition in algebra, and one of the most commonly used is called **Singular Value Decomposition (SVD)**.

Initially, the SVD method was used to select pages that are similar in meaning but not in content. More recently, it has started being used in recommendations. The method is based on the decomposition of the original R rating matrix into a product of three matrices, $R = U * D * S$, where the sizes of the matrices are $(k, m) = (k, r) * (r, r) * (r, m)$ and r is the rank of the decomposition, which is the parameter characterizing the degree of detail decomposition.

Applying this decomposition to our matrix of preferences, we can get the following two matrices of factors (abbreviated descriptions):

- **U**: A compact description of user preferences.
- **S**: A compact description of the characteristics of the product.

It is important that with this approach, we do not know which particular characteristics correspond to the factors in the reduced descriptions; for us, they are encoded with some numbers. Therefore, SVD is an uninterpreted model. It is sufficient to multiply the matrix of factors to obtain an approximation of the matrix of preferences. By doing this, we get a rating for all customer-product pairs.

A typical family of such algorithms is called **non-negative matrix factorization** (NMF). As a rule, the calculation of such expansions is very computationally expensive. Therefore, in practice, they often resort to their approximate iterative variants. ALS is a popular iterative algorithm for decomposing a matrix of preferences into a product of two matrices: **user factors (U)** and **product factors (I)**. It works on the principle of minimizing the **root-mean-square error** (RMSE) on the affixed ratings. Optimization takes place alternately—first by user factors, then by product factors. Also, to avoid retraining, the regularization coefficients are added to the RMSE.

If we supplement the matrix of preferences with a new dimension containing information about the user or product, then we can work not with the matrix of preferences, but with the tensor. Thus, we use more available information and possibly get a more accurate model.

In this section, we considered different approaches to solving recommender systems tasks. Now, we are going to discuss methods for the estimation of user preferences' similarity.

Similarity or preferences correlation

We can consider the similarity or correlation of two user preferences in different ways, but in general, we need to compare two vectors. The following list shows some of the most popular vector comparison measures.

Pearson's correlation coefficient

This measure is a classic coefficient, which is quite applicable when comparing vectors. Its primary disadvantage is that when the intersection is estimated as low, then the correlation can be high by accident. To combat accidental high correlation, you can multiply by a factor of 50/min (50, rating intersection) or any other damping factor, the effect of which decreases with an increasing number of estimates. An example is shown here:

$$r = \frac{\sum_{i=1}^{n}(x_i - \bar{x})(y_i - \bar{y})}{\sqrt{\sum_{i=1}^{n}(x_i - \bar{x})^2(y_i - \bar{y})^2}}$$

Spearman's correlation

The main difference compared to Pearson's correlation is the rank factor—that is, it does not work with absolute values of ratings, but with their sequence numbers. In general, the result is very close to Pearson's correlation. An example is shown here:

$$\rho = 1 - \frac{6\sum d_i^2}{n(n^2 - 1)}$$

Cosine distance

Cosine distance is another classic measuring factor. If you look closely, the cosine of the angle between the standardized vectors is Pearson's correlation, the same formula. This distance uses cosine properties: if the two vectors are co-directed (that is, the angle between them is 0), then the cosine of the angle between them is 1. Conversely, the cosine of the angle between perpendicular vectors is 0. An example is shown here:

$$cos(\boldsymbol{x}, \boldsymbol{y}) = \frac{\boldsymbol{x} \cdot \boldsymbol{y}}{||\boldsymbol{x}|| \cdot ||\boldsymbol{y}||}$$

We discussed methods for user preferences' similarity estimation. The next important issue we will discuss is data preparation for use in recommender system algorithms.

Data scaling and standardization

All users evaluate (rate) items differently. If someone puts 5s in a row, instead of waiting for 4s from someone else, it's better to normalize the data before calculating it—that is, convert the data to a single scale, so that the algorithm can correctly compare the results with each other. Naturally, the predicted estimate then needs to be converted to the original scale by inverse transformation (and, if necessary, rounded to the nearest whole number).

There are several ways to normalize data, detailed as follows:

- **Centering (mean-centering)**: From the user's ratings, subtract their average rating. This type of normalization is only relevant for non-binary matrices.
- **Standardization (z-score)**: In addition to centering, this divides the user's rating by the standard deviation of the user. But in this case, after the inverse transformation, the rating can go beyond the scale (for example, six on a five-point scale), but such situations are quite rare and are solved simply by rounding to the nearest acceptable estimate.
- **Double standardization**: The first time normalized by user ratings; the second time, by item ratings.

The details of these normalization techniques were described in `Chapter 2`, *Data Processing*. The following section will describe a problem of recommender systems known as the **cold start problem**, which appears in the early stages of system work when the system doesn't have enough data to make predictions.

Cold start problem

A cold start is a typical situation when a sufficient amount of data has not yet been accumulated for the correct operation of the recommender system (for example, when a product is new or is just rarely bought). If the ratings of only three users estimate the average rating, such an assessment is not reliable, and users understand this. In such situations, ratings are often artificially adjusted.

The first way to do this is to show not the average value, but the smoothed average (damped mean). With a small number of ratings, the displayed rating leans more to a specific safe *average* indicator, and as soon as a sufficient number of new ratings are typed, the *averaging* adjustment stops operating.

Another approach is to calculate confidence intervals for each rating. Mathematically, the more estimates we have, the smaller the variation of the average will be and, therefore, the more confidence we have in its accuracy.

We can display, for example, the lower limit of the interval (low **confidence interval (CI)** bound) as a rating. At the same time, it is clear that such a system is quite conservative, with a tendency to underestimate ratings for new items.

Since the estimates are limited to a specific scale (for example, from 0 to 1), the usual methods for calculating the confidence interval are poorly applicable here, due to the distribution tails that go to infinity, and the symmetry of the interval itself. There is a more accurate way to calculate it—the Wilson CI.

The cold start problem is relevant for non-personalized recommendations too. The general approach here is to replace what currently cannot be calculated by different heuristics—for example, replace it with an average rating, use a simpler algorithm, or not use the product at all until the data is collected.

Another issue that should be considered when we develop a recommender system is the relevance of recommendations, which considers factors other than the user's interests—for example, it can be the freshness of a publication or a user's rating.

Relevance of recommendations

In some cases, it is also essential to consider the *freshness* of the recommendation. This consideration is especially important for articles or posts on forums. Fresh entries should often get to the top. The correction factors (damping factors) are usually used to make such updates. The following formulas are used for calculating the rating of articles on media sites.

Here is an example of a rating calculation in the *Hacker* news magazine:

$$rank = \frac{(U - D - 1)^{0.8} * P}{T^{1.8}}$$

Here, U denotes upvotes, D denotes downvotes, P denotes penalty (additional adjustment for the implementation of other business rules), and T denotes recording time.

The following equation shows a *Reddit* rating calculation:

$$rank = \log_{10}(max(1, U - D)) - \frac{|U - D| T}{const}$$

Here, U denotes the number of upvotes, D denotes the number of downvotes, and T denotes the recording time. The first term evaluates the *quality of the record,* and the second makes a correction for the time.

There is no universal formula, and each service invents the formula that best solves its problem; it can be tested only empirically.

The following section will discuss the existing approaches to testing recommender systems. This is not a straightforward task because it's usually hard to estimate the quality of a recommendation without exact target values in a training dataset.

Assessing system quality

Testing a recommender system is a complicated process that always poses many questions, mainly due to the ambiguity of the concept of *quality.*

In general, in machine learning problems, there are the following two main approaches to testing:

- Offline model testing on historical data using retro tests
- Testing the model using A/B testing (we run several options, and see which one gives the best result)

Both of the preceding approaches are actively used in the development of recommender systems. The main limitation that we have to face is that we can evaluate the accuracy of the forecast only on those products that the user has already evaluated or rated. The standard approach is cross-validation, with the **leave-one-out** and **leave-p-out** methods. Multiple repetitions of the test and averaging the results provides a more stable assessment of quality.

The *leave-one-out* approach uses the model trained on all items except one and evaluated by the user. This excluded item is used for model testing. This procedure is done for all n items, and an average is calculated among the obtained n quality estimates.

The *leave-p-out* approach is the same, but at each step, p points are excluded.

We can divide all quality metrics into the following three categories:

- **Prediction accuracy**: Estimates the accuracy of the predicted rating
- **Decision support**: Evaluates the relevance of the recommendations
- **Rank accuracy metrics**: Evaluates the quality of the ranking of recommendations issued

Unfortunately, there is no single recommended metric for all occasions, and everyone who is involved in testing a recommender system selects it to fit their goals.

In the following section, we will formalize the collaborative filtering method and show the math behind it.

Understanding collaborative filtering method details

In this section, let's formalize the recommender system problem. We have a set of users, $u \in U$, a set of items, $i \in I$ (movies, tracks, products, and so on), and a set of estimates, $(r_u i, u, i, \dots) \in D$. Each estimate is given by user u, object i, its result $r_u i$, and, possibly, some other characteristics.

We are required to predict preference as follows:

$$\hat{r}_{ui} = Predict(u, i, \dots) \approx r_{ui}$$

We are required to predict personal recommendations as follows:

$$u \mapsto (i_1, \dots, i_K) = Recommend_K(u, \dots)$$

We are required to predict similar objects as follows:

$$u \mapsto (i_1, \dots, i_M) = Similar_M(i)$$

Remember—the main idea behind collaborative filtering is that similar users usually like similar objects. Let's start with the simplest method, as follows:

- Select some conditional measures of similarity of users according to their history of $sim(u, v)$ ratings.
- Unite users into groups (clusters) so that similar users will end up in the same cluster: $u \mapsto F(u)$
- Predict the item's user rating as the cluster's average rating for this object:

$$\hat{r}_{ui} = \frac{1}{|F(u)|} \sum_{v \in F(u)} r_v i$$

This algorithm has several problems, detailed as follows:

- There is nothing to recommend to new or atypical users. For such users, there is no suitable cluster with similar users.
- It ignores the specificity of each user. In a sense, we divide all users into classes (templates).
- If no one in the cluster has rated the item, the prediction will not work.

We can improve this method and replace hard clustering with the following formula:

$$\hat{r}_{ui} = \bar{r}_u + \frac{\sum_{v \in U_i} sim(u, v)(r_{u, i - \bar{r}_v})}{\sum_{v \in U_i} sim(u, v)}$$

For an item-based version, the formula will be symmetrical, as follows:

$$\hat{r}_{ui} = \bar{r}_i + \frac{\sum_{j \in I_u} sim(i, j)(r_{u, j - \bar{r}_j})}{\sum_{j \in I_u} sim(i, j)}$$

These approaches have the following disadvantages:

- Cold start problem
- Bad predictions for new and atypical users or items
- Trivial recommendations
- Resource intensity calculations

To overcome these problems, you can use the SVD. The preference (ratings) matrix can be decomposed into the product of three matrices $A = U * \Sigma * V^T$. Let's denote the product of the first two matrices for one matrix, $R \approx U * V$, where R is the matrix of preferences, U is the matrix of parameters of users, and V is the matrix of parameters of items.

To predict the user U rating for an item, I, we take vector p_u (parameter set) for a given user and a vector for a given item, q_i. Their scalar product is the prediction we need: $\hat{r}_{ui} = \langle p_u, q_i \rangle$. Using this approach, we can identify the hidden features of items and user interests by user history. For example, it may happen that at the first coordinate of the vector, each user has a number indicating whether the user is more likely to be a boy or a girl, and the second coordinate is a number reflecting the approximate age of the user. In the item, the first coordinate shows whether it is more interesting to boys or girls, and the second one shows the age group of users this item appeals to.

However, there are also several problems. The first one is the preferences matrix R which is not entirely known to us, so we cannot merely take its SVD decomposition. Secondly, the SVD decomposition is not the only one, so even if we find at least some decomposition, it is unlikely that it is optimal for our task.

Here, we need machine learning. We cannot find the SVD decomposition of the matrix since we do not know the matrix itself. But we can take advantage of this idea and come up with a prediction model that works like SVD. Our model depends on many parameters—vectors of users and items. For the given parameters, to predict the estimate, we take the user vector, the vector of the item, and get their scalar product, $\hat{r}_{ui}(\theta) = p_u^T q_i$. But since we do not know vectors, they still need to be obtained. The idea is that we have user ratings with which we can find optimal parameters so that our model can predict these estimates as accurately as possible using the following equation: $E_{ui}(\hat{r}_{ui}(\theta) - r_{ui})^2 \rightarrow min(\theta)$. We want to find such parameters' θ so that the square error is as small as possible. We also want to make fewer mistakes in the future, but we do not know what estimates we need. Accordingly, we cannot optimize parameters' θ. We already know the ratings given by users, so we can try to choose parameters based on the estimates we already have to minimize the error. We can also add another term, the *regularizer*, shown here:

$$\sum_{(u,i)\in D} (\hat{r}_{ui}(\theta) - r_{ui})^2 + \lambda \sum_{\theta\in\Theta} \theta^2 \rightarrow min(\theta)$$

Regularization is needed to combat overfitting. To find the optimal parameters, you need to optimize the following function:

$$J(\Theta) = \sum_{(u,i)\in D} (p_u^T q_i - r_{ui})^2 + \lambda(\sum_u ||p_u||^2 + \sum_i ||q_i||^2)$$

There are many parameters: for each user, for each item, we have our vector that we want to optimize. The most well-known method for optimizing functions is **gradient descent (GD)**. Suppose we have a function of many variables, and we want to optimize it. We take an initial value, and then we look where we can move to minimize this value. The GD method is an iterative algorithm: it repeatedly takes the parameters of a certain point, looks at the gradient, and steps against its direction, as shown here:

$$\Theta_{t+1} = \Theta_t - \eta \nabla J(\Theta)$$

There are problems with this method: firstly, it works very slowly; and secondly, it finds local, rather than global, minima. The second problem is not so bad for us because in our case, the value of the function in local minima is close to the global optimum.

However, the GD method is not always necessary. For example, if we need to calculate the minimum for a parabola, there is no need to act by this method, as we know precisely where its minimum is. It turns out that the functionality that we are trying to optimize—the sum of the squares of errors plus the sum of the squares of all the parameters—is also a quadratic functional, which is very similar to a parabola. For each specific parameter, if we fix all the others, it is just a parabola. For those, we can accurately determine at least one coordinate. The ALS method is based on this assumption. We alternately accurately find minima in either one coordinate or another, as shown here:

$$\hat{p}_u(\Theta) = \arg\min_{p_u} J(\Theta) = (Q_u^T Q_u + \lambda I)^{-1} Q_u^T r_u$$
$$\hat{q}_i(\Theta) = \arg\min_{q_i} J(\Theta) = (P_i^T P_i + \lambda I)^{-1} P_u^T r_i$$

We fix all the parameters of the items, optimize the parameters of users, fix the parameters of users, and then optimize the parameters of items. We act iteratively, as shown here:

$$\forall u \in U p_u^{2t+1} = \hat{p}_u(\Theta_{2t})$$
$$\forall i \in I q_i^{2t+2} = \hat{q}_i(\Theta_{2t+1})$$

This method works reasonably quickly, and you can parallelize each step. However, there's still a problem with implicit data because we have neither full user data nor full item data. So, we can penalize the items that do not have ratings in the update rule. By doing so, we depend only on the items that have ratings from the users and do not make any assumption around the items that are not rated. Let's define a weight matrix w_{ui} as such, as follows:

$$w_{ui} = \begin{cases} 0 & \text{if } q_{ui} = 0 \\ 1 & \text{else} \end{cases}$$

The cost functions that we are trying to minimize look like the following:

$$J(x_u) = (q_u - x_u Y) W_u (q_u - x_u Y)^T + \lambda x_u x_u^T$$
$$J(y_i) = (q_i - X y_i) W_i (q_i - X y_i)^T + \lambda y_i y_i^T$$

Note that we need regularization terms to avoid overfitting the data. Solutions for factor vectors are as follows:

$$x_u = (Y W_u Y^T + \lambda I)^{-1} Y W_u q_u$$
$$y_i = (X^T W i X + \lambda I)^{-1} X^T W_i q_i$$

Here, $W_u \in \mathbb{R}^{nn}$ and $W_i \in \mathbb{R}^{mm}$ are diagonal matrices.

Another approach for dealing with implicit data is to introduce confidence levels. Let's define a set of binary observation variables, as follows:

$$p_{u,i} = \begin{cases} 1 & \text{if } q_{u,i} > 0 \\ 0 & \text{otherwise} \end{cases}$$

Now, we define confidence levels for each $p_{u,i}$. When $q_{u,i} = 0$, we have low confidence. The reason can be that the user has never been exposed to that item or it may be unavailable at the time. For example, it could be explained by the user buying a gift for someone else. Hence, we would have *low confidence*. When $q_{u,i}$ is larger, we should have much more confidence. For example, we can define confidence as follows:

$$c_{u,i} = 1 + \alpha q_{u,i}$$

Here, α is a hyperparameter, which should be tuned for a given dataset. The updated optimization function is as follows:

$$\min_{x,y} \sum_{r_{u,i} \text{ is known}} c_{u,i} (p_{u,i} - x_u^\top y_i)^2 + \lambda (\sum_u ||x_u||^2 + \sum_i ||y_i||^2)$$

C^i is a diagonal matrix with values $C^i_{u,u} = c_{u,i}$. Solutions for user and item ratings are as follows:

$$y_u = (X^\top C^i X + \lambda I)^{-1} X^\top C^i p_i$$
$$x_u = (Y^\top C^u Y + \lambda I)^{-1} Y^\top C^u p_u$$

However, it is an expensive computational problem to calculate the $X^\top C^i X$ expression. However, it can be optimized in the following way: $X^\top C^i X = X^\top X + X^\top (C^i - I) X$.

This means that $X^\top X$ can be precomputed at each of the steps, and $(C^i - I)$ has the non-zero entries only where $r_{u,i}$ was non-zero. Now that we have learned about the collaborative filtering method in detail, let's further understand it practically by considering a few examples about how to implement a collaborative filtering recommender system in the following section.

In the following sections, we will look at how to use different C++ libraries for developing recommender systems.

Examples of item-based collaborative filtering with C++

Let's look at how we can implement a collaborative filtering recommender system. As a sample dataset for this example, we use the MovieLens dataset provided by GroupLens from the research lab in the Department of Computer Science and Engineering at the University of Minnesota: `https://grouplens.org/datasets/movielens/`. They provide a full dataset with 20 million movie ratings and a smaller one for education, with 100,000 ratings. We recommend starting with the smaller one because it allows us to see results earlier and detect implementation errors faster.

This dataset consists of several files, but we are only interested in two of them: *ratings.csv* and *movies.csv*. The rating file contains lines with the following format: the user ID, the movie ID, the rating, and the timestamp. In this dataset, users made ratings on a 5-star scale, with half-star increments (0.5 stars—5.0 stars). The movie's file contains lines with the following format: the movie ID, the title, and the genre. The movie ID is the same in both files, so we can see which movies users are rating.

Using the Eigen library

For the first sample, let's see how to implement a collaborative filtering recommender system based on matrix factorization with ALS and with a pure linear algebra library as a backend. In the following sample, we're using the `Eigen` library. The steps to implement a collaborative filtering recommender system are as follows:

1. At first, we make base type definitions, as follows:

```
using DataType = float;
// using Eigen::ColMajor is Eigen restriction -  todense method
always returns
// matrices in ColMajor order
using Matrix =
Eigen::Matrix<DataType, Eigen::Dynamic, Eigen::Dynamic,
Eigen::ColMajor>;

using SparseMatrix = Eigen::SparseMatrix<DataType,
Eigen::ColMajor>;

using DiagonalMatrix =
Eigen::DiagonalMatrix<DataType, Eigen::Dynamic, Eigen::Dynamic>;
```

2. These definitions allow us to write less source code for matrices' types and to quickly change floating-point precision. Then, we define and initialize the ratings (preferences) matrix, list of movie titles, and binary rating flags matrix, as follows:

```
SparseMatrix ratings_matrix;  // user-item ratings
SparseMatrix p;               // binary variables
std::vector<std::string> movie_titles;
```

We have a particular helper function, `LoadMovies`, which loads files to the map container, as shown in the following code snippet:

```
auto movies_file = root_path / "movies.csv";
auto movies = LoadMovies(movies_file);

auto ratings_file = root_path / "ratings.csv";
auto ratings = LoadRatings(ratings_file);
```

3. After data is loaded, we initialize matrix objects with the right size, like this:

```
ratings_matrix.resize(static_cast<Eigen::Index>(ratings.size()),
                      static_cast<Eigen::Index>(movies.size()));
ratings_matrix.setZero();
p.resize(ratings_matrix.rows(), ratings_matrix.cols());
p.setZero();
movie_titles.resize(movies.size());
```

However, because we've loaded data to the map, we need to move the required rating values to the matrix object.

4. So, we initialize the movie titles list, convert user IDs to our zero-based sequential order, and initialize the binary rating matrix (this is used in the algorithm to deal with implicit data), as follows:

```
Eigen::Index user_idx = 0;
for (auto& r : ratings) {
    for (auto& m : r.second) {
        auto mi = movies.find(m.first);
        Eigen::Index movie_idx = std::distance(movies.begin(), mi);
        movie_titles[static_cast<size_t>(movie_idx)] = mi->second;
        ratings_matrix.insert(user_idx, movie_idx) =
        static_cast<DataType>(m.second);
        p.insert(user_idx, movie_idx) = 1.0;
    }
    ++user_idx;
}
ratings_matrix.makeCompressed();
```

5. After the rating matrix is initialized, we define and initialize our training variables, as follows:

```
auto m = ratings_matrix.rows();
auto n = ratings_matrix.cols();

Eigen::Index n_factors = 100;
auto y = InitializeMatrix(n, n_factors);
auto x = InitializeMatrix(m, n_factors);
```

In the preceding code snippet, the `y` matrix corresponds to user preferences, and the `x` matrix corresponds to the item parameters. Also, we defined the number of factors we were interested in after decomposition. These matrices are initialized with random values and normalized. Such an approach is used to speed up algorithm convergence, and can be seen in the following code snippet:

```
Matrix InitializeMatrix(Eigen::Index rows, Eigen::Index cols) {
    Matrix mat = Matrix::Random(rows, cols).array().abs();
    auto row_sums = mat.rowwise().sum();
    mat.array().colwise() /= row_sums.array();
    return mat;
}
```

6. Then, we define and initialize the regularization matrix and identity matrices, which are constant during all learning cycles, as follows:

```
DataType reg_lambda = 0.1f;
SparseMatrix reg = (reg_lambda * Matrix::Identity(n_factors,
n_factors)).sparseView();

// Define diagonal identity terms
SparseMatrix user_diag = -1 * Matrix::Identity(n, n).sparseView();
SparseMatrix item_diag = -1 * Matrix::Identity(m, m).sparseView();
```

7. Also, because we implement an algorithm version that can deal with implicit data, we need to convert our rating matrix to another view to decrease computational complexity. Our version of the algorithm needs user ratings in the form of $c_{u,i} = 1 + \alpha q_{u,i}$ and as diagonal matrices for every user and item so that we can make two containers with corresponding matrix objects. The code for this can be seen in the following block:

```
std::vector<DiagonalMatrix> user_weights(static_cast<size_t>(m));
std::vector<DiagonalMatrix> item_weights(static_cast<size_t>(n));
{
    Matrix weights(ratings_matrix);
    weights.array() *= alpha;
```

```
                weights.array() += 1;

                for (Eigen::Index i = 0; i < m; ++i) {
                    user_weights[static_cast<size_t>(i)] =
                        weights.row(i).asDiagonal();
                }
                for (Eigen::Index i = 0; i < n; ++i) {
                    item_weights[static_cast<size_t>(i)] =
                        weights.col(i).asDiagonal();
                }
            }
```

Now, we are ready to implement the main learning loop. As discussed, the ALS algorithm can be easily parallelized, so we use the OpenMP compiler extension to calculate user and item parameters in parallel.

Let's define the main learning cycle, which runs for a specified number of iterations, as follows:

```
    size_t n_iterations = 5;
    for (size_t k = 0; k < n_iterations; ++k) {
        auto yt = y.transpose();
        auto yty = yt * y;
        ...
        // update item parameters
        ...
        auto xt = x.transpose();
        auto xtx = xt * x;
        ...
        // update users preferences
        ...
        auto w_mse = CalculateWeightedMse(x, y, p, ratings_matrix, alpha);
    }
```

The following code shows how to update item parameters:

```
        #pragma omp parallel
        {
            Matrix diff;
            Matrix ytcuy;
            Matrix a, b, update_y;
            #pragma omp for private(diff, ytcuy, a, b, update_y)
            for (size_t i = 0; i < static_cast<size_t>(m); ++i) {
                diff = user_diag;
                diff += user_weights[i];
                ytcuy = yty + yt * diff * y;
                auto p_val = p.row(static_cast<Eigen::Index>(i)).transpose();
```

```
        a = ytcuy + reg;
        b = yt * user_weights[i] * p_val;

        update_y = a.colPivHouseholderQr().solve(b);
        x.row(static_cast<Eigen::Index>(i)) = update_y.transpose();
    }
}
```

The following code shows how to update users' preferences:

```
#pragma omp parallel
{
    Matrix diff;
    Matrix xtcux;
    Matrix a, b, update_x;
    #pragma omp for private(diff, xtcux, a, b, update_x)
    for (size_t i = 0; i < static_cast<size_t>(n); ++i) {
        diff = item_diag;
        diff += item_weights[i];
        xtcux = xtx + xt * diff * x;
        auto p_val = p.col(static_cast<Eigen::Index>(i));

        a = xtcux + reg;
        b = xt * item_weights[i] * p_val;

        update_x = a.colPivHouseholderQr().solve(b);
        y.row(static_cast<Eigen::Index>(i)) = update_x.transpose();
    }
}
```

We have two parts of the loop body that are pretty much the same because at first, we updated item parameters with frizzed user options, and then we updated user preferences with frizzed item parameters. Notice that all matrix objects were moved outside of the internal loop body to reduce memory allocations and significantly improve program performance. Also, notice that we parallelized the user and item parameters' calculations separately because one of them should always be frizzed during the calculation of the other one. To calculate exact values for user preferences and item parameters, we use this formula:

$$y_u = (X^\top X + X^\top (C^i - I)X + \lambda I)^{-1} X^\top C^i p_i$$
$$x_u = (Y^\top Y + Y^\top (C^i - I)Y + \lambda I)^{-1} Y^\top C^u p_u$$

$X^T X$ and $Y^T Y$ are precomputed at each step. Also, notice that these formulas are expressed in the form of the linear equation system, $X = AB$. We use the `colPivHouseholderQr` function from the `Eigen` library to solve it and get exact values for the user and item parameters. This linear equation system can be solved with other methods, too. The `colPivHouseholderQr` function was chosen because it shows a better ratio between computational speed and accuracy in the `Eigen` library implementation.

To estimate the progress of the learning process of our system, we can calculate the **Mean Squared Error** (**MSE**) between the original rating matrix and a predicted one. To calculate the predicted rating matrix, we define the next function, as follows:

```
Matrix RatingsPredictions(const Matrix& x, const Matrix& y) {
    return x * y.transpose();
}
```

To calculate the MSE, we can use the expression $c_{u,i}\left(p_{u,i} - x_u^\top y_i\right)^2$ from our optimization function, like this:

```
DataType CalculateWeightedMse(const Matrix& x,
                              const Matrix& y,
                              const SparseMatrix& p,
                              const SparseMatrix& ratings_matrix,
                              DataType alpha) {
    Matrix c(ratings_matrix);
    c.array() *= alpha;
    c.array() += 1.0;

    Matrix diff(p - RatingsPredictions(x, y));
    diff = diff.array().pow(2.f);

    Matrix weighted_diff = c.array() * diff.array();
    return weighted_diff.array().mean();
}
```

Please note that we have to use weights and binary ratings to get a meaningful value for the error because a similar approach was used during the learning process. Direct error calculation gives the wrong result because the predicted matrix has non-zero predictions in the place where the original rating matrix has zeros. It is essential to understand that this algorithm doesn't learn the original scale of ratings (from 0 to 5), but instead it learns prediction values in the range from 0 to 1. It follows from the function we optimize, shown here:

$$\min_{x,y} \sum_{r_{u,i}\text{is known}} c_{u,i}(p_{u,i} - x_u^\top y_i)^2 + \lambda(\sum_u ||x_u||^2 + \sum_i ||y_i||^2)$$

We can use the previously defined movies list to show movie recommendations. The following function shows user preferences and system recommendations. To identify what a user likes, we show movie titles that the user has rated with a rating value of more than 3. We show movies that the system rates as equal to or higher than a 0.8 rating coefficient to identify which movie the system recommends to the user by running the following code:

```
void PrintRecommendations(const Matrix& ratings_matrix,
                          const Matrix& ratings_matrix_pred,
                          const std::vector<std::string>& movie_titles) {
    auto n = ratings_matrix.cols();
    std::vector<std::string> liked;
    std::vector<std::string> recommended;
    for (Eigen::Index u = 0; u < 5; ++u) {
        for (Eigen::Index i = 0; i < n; ++i) {
            DataType orig_value = ratings_matrix(u, i);
            if (orig_value >= 3.f) {
                liked.push_back(movie_titles[static_cast<size_t>(i)]);
            }
            DataType pred_value = ratings_matrix_pred(u, i);
            if (pred_value >= 0.8f && orig_value < 1.f) {
                recommended.push_back(movie_titles[
                    static_cast<size_t>(i)]);
            }
        }
        std::cout << "\nUser " << u << " liked :";
        for (auto& l : liked) {
            std::cout << l << "; ";
        }
        std::cout << "\nUser " << u << " recommended :";
        for (auto& r : recommended) {
            std::cout << r << "; ";
        }
        std::cout << std::endl;
        liked.clear();
        recommended.clear();
    }
}
```

This function can be used as follows:

```
PrintRecommendations(ratings_matrix, RatingsPredictions(x, y),
movie_titles);
```

Using the mlpack library

The `mlpack` library is a general-purpose machine learning library that has a lot of different algorithms inside and command-line tools to process the data and learn these algorithms without explicit programming. As a basis, this library uses the `Armadillo` linear algebra library for math calculations. Other libraries we've used in previous chapters don't have the collaborative filtering algorithm implementations.

To load the `MovieLens` dataset, use the same loading helper function as in the previous section. After the data is loaded, convert it to a format suitable for an object of the `mlpack::cf::CFType` type. This type implements a collaborative filtering algorithm and can be configured with different types of matrix factorization approaches. The object of this type can use dense as well as sparse rating matrices. In the case of a dense matrix, it should have three rows. The first row corresponds to users, the second row corresponds to items, and the third row corresponds to the rating. This structure is called a **coordinate list format**. In the case of the sparse matrix, it should be a regular (user, item) table, as in the previous example. So, let's define the sparse matrix for ratings. It should have the `arma::SpMat<DataType>` type from the `Armadillo` library, as illustrated in the following code block:

```
arma::SpMat<DataType> ratings_matrix(ratings.size(), movies.size());
std::vector<std::string> movie_titles;
{
    // fill matrix
    movie_titles.resize(movies.size());
    size_t user_idx = 0;
    for (auto& r : ratings) {
        for (auto& m : r.second) {
            auto mi = movies.find(m.first);
            auto movie_idx = std::distance(movies.begin(), mi);
            movie_titles[static_cast<size_t>(movie_idx)] = mi->second;
            ratings_matrix(user_idx, movie_idx) =
                static_cast<DataType>(m.second);
        }
        ++user_idx;
    }
}
```

Now, we can initialize the `mlpack::cf::CFType` class object. It takes the next parameters in the constructor: the rating matrix, the matrix decomposition policy, the number of neighbors, the number of target factors, the number of iterations, and the minimum value of learning error, after which the algorithm can stop.

For this object, do the nearest neighbor search only on the *H* matrix. This means you avoid calculating the full rating matrix, using the observation that if the rating matrix is *X* = *W H*, then the following applies:

```
distance(X.col(i), X.col(j)) = distance(W H.col(i), W H.col(j))
```

This expression can be seen as the nearest neighbor search on the *H* matrix with the Mahalanobis distance, as illustrated in the following code block:

```
// factorization rank
size_t n_factors = 100;
size_t neighborhood = 50;

mlpack::cf::NMFPolicy decomposition_policy;

// stopping criterions
size_t max_iterations = 20;
double min_residue = 1e-3;

mlpack::cf::CFType cf(ratings_matrix,
                      decomposition_policy,
                      neighborhood,
                      n_factors,
                      max_iterations,
                      min_residue);
```

Notice that as a decomposition policy, the object of the `mlpack::cf::NMFPolicy` type was used. This is the non-negative matrix factorization algorithm with the ALS approach. There are several decomposition algorithms in the `mlpack` library. For example, there is a batch SVD decomposition implemented in the `mlpack::cf::BatchSVDPolicy` type. The constructor of this object also does the complete training, so after its call has finished, we can use this object to get recommendations. Recommendations can be retrieved with the `GetRecommendations` method. This method gets the number of recommendations you want to get, the output matrix for recommendations, and the list of user IDs for users you want to get recommendations from, as shown in the following code block:

```
arma::Mat<size_t> recommendations;
// Get 5 recommendations for specified users.
arma::Col<size_t> users;
users << 1 << 2 << 3;

cf.GetRecommendations(5, recommendations, users);

for (size_t u = 0; u < recommendations.n_cols; ++u) {
    std::cout << "User " << users(u) << " recommendations are: ";
    for (size_t i = 0; i < recommendations.n_rows; ++i) {
```

```
        std::cout << movie_titles[recommendations(i, u)] << ";";
    }
    std::cout << std::endl;
}
```

Notice that the `GetRecommendations` method returns the item IDs as its output. So, we can see that using this library for implementing a recommender system is much easier than writing it from scratch. Also, there are many more configuration options in the `mlpack` library for building such systems; for example, we can configure the neighbor detection policy and which distance measure to use. These configurations can significantly improve the quality of the system you build because you can make them according to your own particular task.

Summary

In this chapter, we discussed what recommender systems are and the types of these that exist today. We studied two main approaches to building recommender systems: content-based recommendations and collaborative filtering. We identified two types of collaborative filtering: user-based and item-based. We looked at the implementation of these approaches, and their pros and cons. We found out that an important issue in the implementation of recommender systems is the amount of data and the associated large computational complexity of algorithms. We considered approaches to overcome computational complexity problems, such as partial data updates and approximate iterative algorithms, such as ALS. We found out how matrix factorization can help to solve the problem with incomplete data, improve the generalizability of the model, and speed up the calculations. Also, we implemented a system of collaborative filtering based on the linear algebra library and using the `mlpack` general-purpose machine learning library.

It makes sense to look at new methods such as autoencoders, variational autoencoders, or deep collaborative approaches applied to recommender system tasks. In recent research papers, these approaches show more impressive results than classical methods such as ALS. All these new methods are non-linear models, so they can potentially beat the limited modeling capacity of linear factor models.

In the next chapter, we discuss ensemble learning techniques. The main idea of these types of techniques is to combine either different types of machine learning algorithms or use a set of the same kind of algorithms to obtain better predictive performance. Combining a number of algorithms in the one ensemble allows us to get the best characteristics of each one, to cover disadvantages in a single algorithm.

Further reading

- Collaborative Filtering for Implicit Feedback Datasets: `http://yifanhu.net/PUB/cf.pdf`
- Collaborative Filtering using Alternating Least Squares: `http://danielnee.com/2016/09/collaborative-filtering-using-alternating-least-squares/`
- ALS Implicit Collaborative Filtering: `https://medium.com/radon-dev/als-implicit-collaborative-filtering-5ed653ba39fe`
- Collaborative Filtering: `https://datasciencemadesimpler.wordpress.com/tag/alternating-least-squares/`
- The `mlpack` library official site: `https://www.mlpack.org/`
- The `Armadillo` library official site: `http://arma.sourceforge.net/`
- *Variational Autoencoders for Collaborative Filtering,* by Dawen Liang, Rahul G. Krishnan, Matthew D. Hoffman, and Tony Jebara: `https://arxiv.org/abs/1802.05814`
- *Deep Learning-Based Recommender System: A Survey and New Perspectives,* by Shuai Zhang, Lina Yao, Aixin Sun, and Yi Tay: `https://arxiv.org/abs/1707.07435`
- *Training Deep AutoEncoders for Collaborative Filtering,* by Oleksii Kuchaiev, and Boris Ginsburg: `https://arxiv.org/abs/1708.01715`

Ensemble Learning 9

Anyone who works with data analysis and machine learning will come to understand that no method is ideal or universal. This is why there are so many methods. Researchers and enthusiasts have been searching for years for a compromise between the accuracy, simplicity, and interpretability of various models. Moreover, how can we increase the accuracy of the model, preferably without changing its essence? One way to improve the accuracy of models is to create and train model ensembles—that is, sets of models used to solve the same problem. The ensemble training methodology is the training of a final set of simple classifiers, with the subsequent merging of the results of their predictions into a single forecast of the aggregated algorithm.

This chapter describes what ensemble learning is, what types of ensembles exist, and how they can help to obtain better predictive performance. In this chapter, we will also implement examples of these approaches with different C++ libraries.

The following topics will be covered in this chapter:

- An overview of ensemble learning
- Learning about decision trees and random forests
- Examples of using C++ libraries for creating ensembles

Technical requirements

The technologies and installations required in the chapter are as follows:

- The `Eigen` library
- The `Armadillo` library
- The `mlpack` library
- A modern C++ compiler with C++17 support
- CMake build system version >= 3.8

The code files for this chapter can be found at the following GitHub repo: `https://github.com/PacktPublishing/Hands-On-Machine-Learning-with-CPP/tree/master/Chapter09`

An overview of ensemble learning

The training of an ensemble of models is understood to be the procedure of training a final set of elementary algorithms, whose results are then combined to form the forecast of an aggregated classifier. The model ensemble's purpose is to improve the accuracy of the prediction of the aggregated classifier, particularly when compared with the accuracy of every single elementary classifier. It is intuitively clear that combining simple classifiers can give a more accurate result than each simple classifier separately. Despite that, simple classifiers can be sufficiently accurate on particular datasets, but at the same time, they can make mistakes on different datasets.

An example of ensembles is **Condorcet's jury theorem** (1784). A jury must come to a correct or incorrect consensus, and each juror has an independent opinion. If the probability of the correct decision of each juror is more than 0.5, then the probability of a correct decision from the jury as a whole (tending toward 1) increases with the size of the jury. If the probability of making the correct decision is less than 0.5 for each juror, then the probability of making the right decision monotonically decreases (tending toward zero) as the jury size increases.

The theorem is as follows:

- N: The number of jury members
- P: The probability of the jury member making the right decision
- μ: The probability of the entire jury making the correct decision
- **m**: The minimum majority of jury members:

$$m = \text{floor}(N/2) + 1$$

- C_N^i: The number of combinations of N by I:

$$\mu = \sum_{i=m}^{N} C_N^i p^i (1 - p)^{N-i}$$

If $p > 0.5$ then $\mu > p$

If $N \to \infty$ then $\mu \to 1$

Therefore, based on general reasoning, three reasons why ensembles of classifiers can be successful can be distinguished, as follows:

- **Statistical**: The classification algorithm can be viewed as a search procedure in the space of the H hypothesis, concerned with the distribution of data in order to find the best hypothesis. By learning from the final dataset, the algorithm can find many different hypotheses that describe the training sample equally well. By building an ensemble of models, we *average out* the error of each hypothesis and reduce the influence of instabilities and randomness in the formation of a new hypothesis.
- **Computational**: Most learning algorithms use methods for finding the extremum of a specific objective function. For example, neural networks use **gradient descent (GD)** methods to minimize prediction errors. Decision trees use greedy algorithms that minimize data entropy. These optimization algorithms can become stuck at a local extremum point, which is a problem because their goal is to find a global optimum. The ensembles of models combining the results of the prediction of simple classifiers, trained on different subsets of the source data, have a higher chance of finding a global optimum since they start a search for the optimum from different points in the initial set of hypotheses.
- **Representative**: A combined hypothesis may not be in the set of possible hypotheses for simple classifiers. Therefore, by building a combined hypothesis, we expand the set of possible hypotheses.

Condorcet's jury theorem and the reasons provided previously are not entirely suitable for real, practical situations because the algorithms are not independent (they solve one problem, they learn on one target vector, and can only use one model, or a small number of models).

Therefore, the majority of techniques in applied ensemble development are aimed at ensuring that the ensemble is diverse. This allows the errors of individual algorithms in individual objects to be compensated for by the correct operations of other algorithms. Overall, building the ensemble results in an improvement in both the quality and variety of simple algorithms.

The simplest type of ensemble is model averaging, whereby each member of the ensemble makes an equal contribution to the final forecast. The fact that each model has an equal contribution to the final ensemble's forecast is a limitation of this approach. The problem is in unbalanced contributions. Despite that, there is a requirement that all members of the ensemble have prediction skills higher than random chance.

However, it is known that some models work much better or much worse than other models. Some improvements can be made to solve this problem, using a weighted ensemble in which the contribution of each member to the final forecast is weighted by the performance of the model. When the weight of the model is a small positive value and the sum of all weights equals 1, the weights can indicate the percentage of confidence in (or expected performance from) each model.

At this time, the most common approaches to ensemble construction are as follows:

- **Bagging**: This is an ensemble of models studying in parallel on different random samples from the same training set. The final result is determined by the voting of the algorithms of the ensemble. For example, in classification, the class that is predicted by the most classifiers is chosen.
- **Boosting**: This is an ensemble of models trained sequentially, with each successive algorithm being trained on samples in which the previous algorithm made a mistake.
- **Stacking**: This is an approach whereby a training set is divided into *N* blocks, and a set of simple models is trained on *N-1* of them. An *N-th* model is then trained on the remaining block, but the outputs of the underlying algorithms (forming the so-called **meta-attribute**) are used as the target variable.
- **Random forest**: This is a set of decision trees built independently, and whose answers are averaged and decided by a majority vote.

The following sections discuss the previously described approaches in detail.

Using a bagging approach for creating ensembles

Bagging (from the bootstrap aggregation) is one of the earliest and most straightforward types of ensembles. Bagging is based on the statistical bootstrap method, which aims to obtain the most accurate sample estimates and to extend the results to the entire population. The bootstrap method is as follows.

Suppose there is an X dataset of size M. Evenly take from the dataset N objects and return each object. Before selecting the next one, we can generate N sub-datasets. This procedure means that N times, we select an arbitrary sample object (we assume that each object is *picked up* with the same probability $\frac{1}{M}$), and each time, we choose from all the original M objects.

We can imagine this as a bag from which balls are taken. The ball selected at a given step is returned to the bag following its selection, and the next choice is again made with equal probability from the same number of balls. Note that due to the ball being returned each time, there are repetitions.

Each new selection is denoted as X_1. Repeating the procedure k times, we generate k sub-datasets. Now, we have a reasonably large number of samples, and we can evaluate various statistics of the original distribution.

The main descriptive statistics are the sample mean, median, and standard deviation. Summary statistics—for example, the sample mean, median, and correlation—can vary from sample to sample. The bootstrap idea is to use sampling results as a fictitious population to determine the sample distribution of statistics. The bootstrap method analyzes a large number of phantom samples, called **bootstrap samples**. For each sample, an estimate of the target statistics is calculated, then the estimates are averaged. The bootstrap method can be viewed as a modification of the Monte Carlo method.

Suppose there is the X training dataset. With the help of bootstrap, we can generate $X_1, \ldots, X_n$ sub-datasets. Now, on each sub-dataset, we can train our $b_i(x)$ classifier. The final classifier averages these classifier responses (in the case of classification, this

$$a(x) = \frac{1}{M} \sum_{i=1}^{M} b_i(x)$$

corresponds to a vote), as follows: . The following diagram shows this scheme:

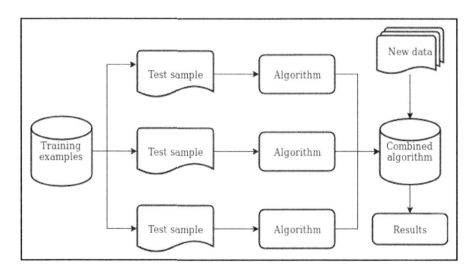

Consider the regression problem by using simple algorithms $b_1(x), \ldots, b_n(x)$. Suppose that there is a true answer function for all $y(x)$ objects, and there is also a distribution $p(x)$ on objects. In this case, we can write the error of each regression function as follows:

$$\varepsilon_i(x) = b_i(x) - y(x), i = 1, \ldots, n$$

We can also write the expectation of the **Mean Squared Error** (**MSE**) as follows:

$$E_x (b_i(x) - y(x))^2 = E_x \varepsilon_i^2(x)$$

The average error of the constructed regression functions is as follows:

$$E_1 = \frac{1}{n} E_x \sum_{i=1}^{n} \varepsilon_i^2(x)$$

Now, suppose the errors are unbiased and uncorrelated, as shown here:

$$
\begin{aligned}
E_x \varepsilon_i(x) &= 0, \\
E_x \varepsilon_i(x) \varepsilon_j(x) &= 0, i \neq j
\end{aligned}
$$

Now, we can write a new regression function that averages the responses of the functions we have constructed, as follows:

$$a(x) = \frac{1}{n} \sum_{i=1}^{n} b_i(x)$$

Let's find its **root MSE** (**RMSE**) to see an effect of averaging, as follows:

$$
\begin{aligned}
E_n &= E_x \left(a(x) - y(x) \right)^2 \\
&= E_x \left(\frac{1}{n} \sum_{i=1}^{n} b_i(x) - y(x) \right)^2 \\
&= E_x \left(\frac{1}{n} \sum_{i=1}^{n} \varepsilon_i \right)^2 \\
&= \frac{1}{n^2} E_x \left(\sum_{i=1}^{n} \varepsilon_i^2(x) + \sum_{i \neq j} \varepsilon_i(x) \varepsilon_j(x) \right) \\
&= \frac{1}{n} E_1
\end{aligned}
$$

Thus, averaging the answers allowed us to reduce the average square of the error by *n* times.

Bagging also allows us to reduce the variance of the trained algorithm and prevent overfitting. The effectiveness of bagging is based on the underlying algorithms, which are trained on various sub-datasets that are quite different, and their errors are mutually compensated during voting. Also, outlying objects may not fall into some of the training sub-datasets, which also increases the effectiveness of the bagging approach.

Bagging is useful with small datasets when the exclusion of even a small number of training objects leads to the construction of substantially different simple algorithms. In the case of large datasets, sub-datasets are usually generated that are significantly smaller than the original one.

Notice that the assumption about uncorrelated errors is rarely satisfied. If this assumption is incorrect, then the error reduction is not as significant as we might have assumed.

In practice, bagging provides a good improvement to the accuracy of results when compared to simple individual algorithms, particularly if a simple algorithm is sufficiently accurate but unstable. Improving the accuracy of the forecast occurs by reducing the spread of the error-prone forecasts of individual algorithms. The advantage of the bagging algorithm is its ease of implementation, as well as the possibility of paralleling the calculations for training each elementary algorithm on different computational nodes.

Using a gradient boosting method for creating ensembles

The main idea of boosting is that the elementary algorithms are not built independently. We build every sequential algorithm so that it corrects the mistakes of the previous ones and therefore improves the quality of the whole ensemble. The first successful version of boosting was **AdaBoost (Adaptive Boosting)**. It is now rarely used since gradient boosting has supplanted it.

Suppose that we have a set of pairs, where each pair consists of attribute x and target variable y, $\{(x_i, y_i)\}_{i=1,\dots,n}$. On this set, we restore the dependence of the form $y = f(x)$. We restore it by the approximation $\hat{f}(x)$. To select the best approximation solution, we use a specific loss function of the form $L(y, f)$, which we should optimize as follows:

$$y \approx \hat{f}(x),$$
$$\hat{f}(x) = \underset{f(x)}{\arg\min}\, L(y, f(x))$$

We also can rewrite the expression in terms of mathematical expectations, since the amount of data available for learning is limited, as follows:

$$\hat{f}(x) = \underset{f(x)}{\arg\min} \, \mathbb{E}_{x,y}[L(y, f(x))]$$

Our approximation is inaccurate. However, the idea behind boosting is that such an approximation can be improved by adding to the model with the result of another model that corrects its errors, as illustrated here:

$$\hat{f}_{m+1}(x) = \hat{f}_m(x) + h(x)$$

The following equation shows the ideal error correction model:

$$\hat{f}_{m+1}(x) = \hat{f}_m(x) + h(x) = y$$

We can rewrite this formula in the following form, which is more suitable for the corrective model:

$$h(x) = y - \hat{f}_m(x)$$

Based on the preceding assumptions listed, the goal of boosting is to approximate $h(x)$ to make its results correspond as closely as possible to the *residuals* $y - F_m(x)$. Such an operation is performed sequentially—that is, $\hat{f}_{m+1}$ improves the results of the previous $\hat{f}_m$ function.

A further generalization of this approach allows us to consider the residuals as a negative gradient of the loss function, specifically of the form $\frac{1}{2}(y - \hat{f}(x))^2$. In other words, gradient boosting is a method of GD with the loss function and its gradient replacement.

Now, knowing the expression of the loss function gradient, we can calculate its values on our data. Therefore, we can train models so that our predictions are better correlated with this gradient (with a minus sign). Therefore, we will solve the regression problem, trying to correct the predictions for these residuals. For classification, regression, and ranking, we always minimize the squared difference between the residuals and our predictions.

In the gradient boosting method, an approximation of the function of the following form is used:

$$\hat{f}(x) = \sum_{i=1}^{M} \gamma_i h_i(x) + \text{const}$$

This is the sum of $h_i(x)$ functions of the $\mathcal{H}$ class; they are collectively called **weak models** (algorithms). Such an approximation is carried out sequentially, starting from the initial approximation, which is a certain constant, as follows:

$$F_0(x) = \arg\min_{\gamma} \sum_{i=1}^{n} L(y_i, \gamma)$$

$$F_m(x) = F_{m-1}(x) + \arg\min_{h_m \in \mathcal{H}} \left[\sum_{i=1}^{n} L(y_i, F_{m-1}(x_i) + h_m(x_i)) \right]$$

Unfortunately, the choice of the h optimal function at each step for an arbitrary loss function is extremely difficult, so a more straightforward approach is used. The idea is to use the GD method, by using differentiable $h \in \mathfrak{R}$ functions, and a differentiable loss function, as illustrated here:

$$F_m(x) = F_{m-1}(x) - \gamma_m \sum_{i=1}^{n} \nabla_{F_{m-1}} L(y_i, F_{m-1}(x_i))$$

$$\gamma_m = \arg\min_{\gamma} \sum_{i=1}^{n} L(y_i, F_{m-1}(x_i) - \gamma \nabla_{F_{m-1}} L(y_i, F_{m-1}(x_i)))$$

The boosting algorithm is then formed as follows:

1. Initialize the model with constant values, like this:

$$F_0(x) = \arg\min_{\gamma} \sum_{i=1}^{n} L(y_i, \gamma)$$

2. Repeat the specified number of iterations and do the following:

- Calculate the pseudo-residuals, as follows:

$$r_{im} = -\left[\frac{\partial L(y_i, F(x_i))}{\partial F(x_i)}\right]_{F(x)=F_{m-1}(x)} \quad \text{for } i = 1, \ldots, n$$

  Here, n is the number of training samples, m is the iteration number, and L is the loss function.

- Train the elementary algorithm (regression model) $h_m(x)$ on pseudo-residuals with data of the form $\{(x_i, r_{im})\}_{i=1}^n$.
- Calculate the γ_m coefficient by solving a one-dimensional optimization problem of the form, as follows:

$$\gamma_m = \arg\min_{\gamma} \sum_{i=1}^{n} L\left(y_i, F_{m-1}(x_i) + \gamma h_m(x_i)\right)$$

- Update the model, as follows:

$$F_m(x) = F_{m-1}(x) + \gamma_m h_m(x)$$

The inputs to this algorithm are as follows:

- The $\{(x_i, y_i)\}_{i=1,\ldots,n}$ dataset
- The number of M iterations
- The $L(y, f)$ loss function with an analytically written gradient (such a form of gradient allows us to reduce the number of numerical calculations)
- The choice of the family of functions of the $h(x)$ elementary algorithms, with the procedure of their training and hyperparameters

The constant for the initial approximation, as well as the γ optimal coefficient, can be found by a binary search, or by another line search algorithm relative to the initial loss function (rather than the gradient).

Examples of loss functions for regression are as follows:

- $L(y, f) = (y - f)^2$: An L_2 loss, also called Gaussian loss. This formula is the classic conditional mean and the most common and simple option. If there are no additional information or model sustainability requirements, it should be used.
- $L(y, f) = |y - f|$: An L_1 loss, also called Laplacian loss. This formula, at first glance, is not very differentiable and determines the conditional median. The median, as we know, is more resistant to outliers. Therefore, in some problems, this loss function is preferable since it does not penalize large deviations as much as a quadratic function.
- $L(y, f) = \begin{cases} (1 - \alpha) \cdot |y - f|, & \text{if } y - f \leq 0 \\ \alpha \cdot |y - f|, & \text{if } y - f > 0 \end{cases}$: An L_q loss, also called Quantile loss. If we don't want a conditional median but do want a conditional 75 % quantile, we would use this option with $\alpha = 0.75$. This function is asymmetric and penalizes more observations that turn out to be on the side of the quantile we need.

Examples of loss functions for classification are as follows:

- $L(y, f) = log(1 + exp(-2yf))$: This is logistic loss, also known as **Bernoulli loss**. An interesting property with this loss function is that we penalize even correctly predicted class labels. By optimizing this loss function, we can continue to distance classes and improve the classifier even if all observations are correctly predicted. This function is the most standard and frequently used loss function in a binary classification task.
- $L(y, f) = exp(-yf)$: This is AdaBoost loss. It so happens that the classic AdaBoost algorithm that uses this loss function (different loss functions can also be used in the AdaBoost algorithm) is equivalent to gradient boosting. Conceptually, this loss function is very similar to logistic loss, but it has a stronger exponential penalty for classification errors and is used less frequently.

The idea of bagging is that it can be used with a gradient boosting approach too, which is known as **stochastic gradient boosting**. In this way, a new algorithm is trained on a sub-sample of the training set. This approach can help us to improve the quality of the ensemble and reduces the time it takes to build elementary algorithms (whereby each is trained on a reduced number of training samples).

Although boosting itself is an ensemble, other ensemble schemes can be applied to it—for example, by averaging several boosting methods. Even if we average boosts with the same parameters, they will differ due to the stochastic nature of the implementation. This randomness comes from the choice of random sub-datasets at each step or selecting different features when we are building decision trees (if they are chosen as elementary algorithms).

Currently, the base **gradient boosting machine (GBM)** has many extensions for different statistical tasks. These are as follows:

- GLMBoost and GAMBoost as an enhancement of the existing **generalized additive model (GAM)**
- CoxBoost for survival curves
- RankBoost and LambdaMART for ranking

Secondly, there are many implementations of the same GBM under different names and different platforms, such as these:

- Stochastic GBM
- **Gradient Boosted Decision Trees (GBDT)**
- **Gradient Boosted Regression Trees (GBRT)**
- **Multiple Additive Regression Trees (MART)**
- **Generalized Boosting Machines (GBM)**

Furthermore, boosting can be applied and used over a long period of time in the ranking tasks undertaken by search engines. The task is written based on a loss function, which is penalized for errors in the order of search results; therefore, it became convenient to insert it into a GBM.

Using a stacking approach for creating ensembles

The purpose of stacking is to use different algorithms trained on the same data as elementary models. A meta-classifier is then trained on the results of the elementary algorithms or source data, also supplemented by the results of the elementary algorithms themselves. Sometimes a meta-classifier uses the estimates of distribution parameters that it receives (for example, estimates of the probabilities of each class for classification) for its training, rather than the results of elementary algorithms.

The most straightforward stacking scheme is blending. For this scheme, we divide the training set into two parts. The first part is used to teach a set of elementary algorithms. Their results can be considered new features (meta-features). We then use them as complementary features with the second part of the dataset and train the new meta-algorithm. The problem of such a blending scheme is that neither the elementary algorithms nor the meta-algorithm use the entire set of data for training. To improve the quality of blending, you can average the results of several blends trained at different partitions in the data.

A second way to implement stacking is to use the entire training set. In some sources, this is known as *generalization*. The entire set is divided into parts (folds), then the algorithm sequentially goes through the folds, and teaches elementary algorithms on all the folds except the one randomly chosen fold. The remaining fold is used for the inference on the elementary algorithms. The output values of elementary algorithms are interpreted as the new meta-attributes (or new features) calculated from the folds. In this approach, it is also desirable to implement several different partitions into folds, and then average the corresponding meta-attributes. For a meta-algorithm, it makes sense to apply regularization or add some normal noise to the meta-attributes. The coefficient with which this addition occurs is analogous to the regularization coefficient. We can summarize that the basic idea behind the described approach is using a set of base algorithms; then, using another meta-algorithm, we combine their predictions, with the aim of reducing the generalization error.

Unlike boosting and traditional bagging, you can use algorithms of a different nature (for example, a ridge regression in combination with a random forest) in stacking. However, it is essential to remember that for different algorithms, different feature spaces are needed. For example, if categorical features are used as target variables, then the random forest algorithm can be used as-is, but for the regression algorithms, you must first run one-hot encoding.

Since meta-features are the results of already trained algorithms, they strongly correlate. This fact is *a priori* one of the disadvantages of this approach; the elementary algorithms are often under-optimized during training to combat correlation. Sometimes, to combat this drawback, the training of elementary algorithms is used not on the target feature, but on the differences between a feature and the target.

Using the random forest method for creating ensembles

Firstly, we need to introduce the decision tree algorithm, which is the basis for the random forest ensemble algorithm.

Decision tree algorithm overview

A decision tree is a supervised machine learning algorithm, based on how a human solves the task of forecasting or classification. Generally, this is a k-dimensional tree with decision rules at the nodes and a prediction of the objective function at the leaf nodes. The decision rule is a function that allows you to determine which of the child nodes should be used as a parent for the considered object. There can be different types of objects in the decision tree leaf—namely, the class label assigned to the object (in the classification tasks), the probability of the class (in the classification tasks), and the value of the objective function (in the regression task).

In practice, binary decision trees are used more often than trees with an arbitrary number of child nodes.

The algorithm for constructing a decision tree in its general form is formed as follows:

1. Firstly, check the criterion for stopping the algorithm. If this criterion is executed, select the prediction issued for the node. Otherwise, we have to split the training set into several non-intersecting smaller sets.

2. In the general case, a $Q_t(x)$ decision rule is defined at the t node, which takes into account a certain range of values. This range is divided into R_t disjoint sets of objects: $S_1, S_2, \ldots, S_{R_t}$, where R_t is the number of descendants of the node, and each S_i is a set of objects that fall into the ith descendant.

3. Divide the set in the node according to the selected rule, and repeat the algorithm recursively for each node.

Most often, the $Q_t(x)$ decision rule is simply is the feature—that is, $x^{i(t)}$. For partitioning, we can use the following rules:

- $S_t(j) = \{x \in \mathbb{X} : h_j \le xi(t) \le h_{j+1}\}$ for chosen boundary values $h_1, \ldots, h_{j+1}$
- $S_t(1) = \{x \in \mathbb{X} : \langle x, v \rangle \le 0\}$; $S_t(2) = \{x \in \mathbb{X} : \langle x, v \rangle > 0\}$, where $\langle x, v \rangle$ is a vector's scalar product. In fact, it is a corner value check
- $S_t(1) = \{x \in \mathbb{X} : \rho(x, x_0) \le h\}$; $S_t(2) = \{x \in \mathbb{X} : \rho(x, x_0) \, h\}$, where the distance ρ is defined in some metric space (for example, $\rho(x, y) = |x - y|$)
- $S_t(1) = \{x \in \mathbb{X} : xi(t) \le h\}$; $S_t(2) = \{x \in \mathbb{X} : xi(t) > h\}$, where h is a predicate

In general, you can use any decision rules, but those that are easiest to interpret are better since they are easier to configure. There is no particular point in taking something more complicated than predicates since you can create a tree with 100% accuracy on the training set, with the help of the predicates.

Usually, a set of decision rules are chosen to build a tree. To find the optimal one among them for each particular node, we need to introduce a criterion for measuring optimality. The $I(x)$ measure is introduced for this, which is used to measure how objects are scattered (regression), or how the classes are mixed (classification) in a specific t node. This measure is called the **impurity function**. It is required for finding a maximum of $\Delta I(X_t, t)$ according to all features and parameters from a set of decision rules, in order to select a decision rule. With this choice, we can generate the optimal partition for the set of objects in the current node.

Information gain $\Delta I(X_t, t)$ is how much information we can get for the selected split, and is calculated as follows:

$$\Delta I(X_t, t) = I(X_t, t) - \sum_{i=1}^{R} I(X_{t_i}, t_i) \frac{N(t_i)}{N(t)}$$

In the preceding equation, the following applies:

- R is the number of sub-nodes the current node is broken into
- t is the current node
- $t_1, \ldots, t_R$ are the descendant nodes that are obtained with the selected partition
- $N(t_i)$ is the number of objects in the training sample that fall into the child i
- $N(t)$ is the number of objects trapped in the current node
- X_{t_i} are the objects trapped in the t_i^{th} vertex

We can use the MSE or the **mean absolute error** (**MAE**) as the $I(t)$ impurity function for regression tasks. For classification tasks, we can use the following functions:

$$I(p_1 \ldots p_C) = \sum_{k \neq k'} p_k p_{k'} = \sum_i p_i (1 - p_i)$$

- Gini criterion   as the probability of misclassification, specifically if we predict classes with probabilities of their occurrence in a given node

$$I(p_1 \ldots p_C) = - \sum_i p_i \ln p_i$$

- Entropy   as a measure of the uncertainty of a random variable

- Classification error $I(p_1 \ldots p_C) = 1 - \max_i p_i$ as the error rate in the classification of the most potent class

In the functions described previously, p_i is an *a priori* probability of encountering an object of class i in a node t—that is, the number of objects in the training sample with labels of class i falling into t divided by the total number of objects in t ($p_i = \dfrac{N(t_i)}{N(t)}$).

The following rules can be applied as stopping criteria for building a decision tree:

- Limiting the maximum depth of the tree
- Limiting the minimum number of objects in the sheet
- Limiting the maximum number of leaves in a tree
- Stopping if all objects at the node belong to the same class
- Requiring that information gain is improved by at least *8* percent during splitting

There is an error-free tree for any training set, which leads to the problem of overfitting. Finding the right stopping criterion to solve this problem is challenging. One solution is **pruning**—after the whole tree is constructed, we can cut some nodes. Such an operation can be performed using a test or validation set. Pruning can reduce the complexity of the final classifier, and improve predictive accuracy by reducing overfitting.

The pruning algorithm is formed as follows:

1. We build a tree for the training set.
2. Then, we pass a validation set through the constructed tree, and consider any internal node t and its left and right sub-nodes L_t, R_t.
3. If no one object from the validation sample has reached t, then we can say that this node (and all its subtrees) is insignificant, and make t the leaf (set the predicate's value for this node equal to the set of the majority class using the training set).
4. If objects from the validation set have reached t, then we have to consider the following three values:

   - The number of classification errors from a subtree of t
   - The number of classification errors from the L_t subtree
   - The number of classification errors from the R_t subtree

If the value for the first case is zero, then we make node *t* as a leaf node with the corresponding prediction for the class. Otherwise, we choose the minimum of these values. Depending on which of them is minimal, we do the following, respectively:

- If the first is minimal, do nothing
- If the second is minimal, replace the tree from node *t* with a subtree from node L_t
- If the third is minimal, replace the tree from node *t* with a subtree from node R_t

Such a procedure regularizes the algorithm to beat overfitting and increase the ability to generalize. In the case of a *k*-dimensional tree, different approaches can be used to select the forecast in the leaf. We can take the most common class among the objects of the training that fall in this leaf for classification. Alternatively, we can calculate the average of the objective functions of these objects for regression.

We apply a decision rule to a new object starting from the tree root to predict or classify new data. Thus, it is determined which subtree the object should go into. We recursively repeat this process until we reach some leaf node, and, finally, we return the value of the leaf node we found as the result of classification or regression.

Random forest method overview

Decision trees are a suitable family of elementary algorithms for bagging since they are quite complicated and can ultimately achieve zero errors on any training set. We can use a method that uses random subspaces (such as bagging) to reduce the correlation between trees and avoid overfitting. The elementary algorithms are trained on different subsets of the feature space, which are also randomly selected. An ensemble of decision tree models using the random subspace method can be constructed using the following algorithm.

Where the number of objects for training is *N* and the number of features is *D*, proceed as follows:

1. Select L as the number of individual trees in the ensemble.
2. For each individual *l* tree, select $dl < D$ as the number of features for *l*. Typically, only one value is used for all trees.
3. For each tree, create an X_n training subset using bootstrap.

Now, build decision trees from X_n samples, as follows:

1. Select *dl*random features from the source, then the optimal division of the training set will limit its search to them.
2. According to a given criterion, we choose the best attribute and make a split in the tree according to it.
3. The tree is built until no more than n_{min} objects remain in each leaf, or until we reach a certain height of the tree, or until the training set is exhausted.

Now, to apply the ensemble model to a new object, it is necessary to combine the results of individual models by majority voting or by combining a *posteriori* probabilities. An example of a final classifier is as follows:

$$a(x) = \frac{1}{L} \sum_{i=1}^{L} l_i(x)$$

Consider the following fundamental parameters of the algorithm and their properties:

- **The number of trees**: The more trees, the better the quality, but the training time and the algorithm's workload also increase proportionally. Often, with an increasing number of trees, the quality on the training set rises (it can even go up to 100% accuracy), but the quality of the test set is asymptote (so, you can estimate the minimum required number of trees).
- **The number of features for the splitting selection**: With an increasing number of features, the forest's construction time increases too, and the trees become more uniform than before. Often, in classification problems, the number of attributes is chosen equal to $\sqrt{D}$ and $D/3$ for regression problems.
- **Maximum tree depth**: The smaller the depth, the faster the algorithm is built and will work. As the depth increases, the quality during training increases dramatically. The quality may also increase on the test set. It is recommended to use the maximum depth (except when there are too many training objects, and we obtain very deep trees, the construction of which takes considerable time). When using shallow trees, changing the parameters associated with limiting the number of objects in the leaf and for splitting does not lead to a significant effect (the leaves are already large). Using shallow trees is recommended in tasks with a large number of noisy objects (outliers).

- **The impurity function**: This is a criterion for choosing a feature (decision rule) for branching. It is usually MSE/MAE for regression problems. For classification problems, it is the Gini criterion, the entropy, or the classification error. The balance and depth of trees may vary depending on the specific impurity function we choose.

We can consider a random forest as bagging decision trees, and during these trees' training, we use features from a random subset of features for each partition. This approach is a universal algorithm since random forests exist for solving problems of classification, regression, clustering, anomaly search, and feature selection, among other tasks.

In the following section, we will see how to use different C++ libraries for developing machine learning model ensembles.

Examples of using C++ libraries for creating ensembles

The following sections will show how to use ensembles within the Shogun and Shark-ML libraries. There are out-of-the-box implementations of random forest and gradient boosting algorithms in these libraries; we will show how to use their **application programming interface (API)** to work with these algorithms. Also, we will implement a stacking ensemble technique from scratch, using primitives from the Shark-ML library.

Ensembles with Shogun

There are gradient boosting and random forest algorithm implementations in the Shogun library, and the following sections will show the specific API for using them in practice.

Using gradient boosting with Shogun

There is an implementation of the gradient boosting algorithm in the Shogun library but it is restricted, in that it only supports regression tasks. The algorithm is implemented in the CStochasticGBMachine class. The main parameters to configure objects of this class are the base ensemble algorithm model and the loss function, while other parameters include the number of iterations, the learning rate, and the fraction of training vectors to be chosen randomly at each iteration.

We will create an example using gradient boosting for cosine function approximation, assuming that we already have a training and testing dataset available (the exact implementation of a data generator can be found in the source code for this example). For this example, we will use an ensemble of decision trees. The implementation of the decision tree algorithm in the Shogun library can be found in the CCARTree class. A **classification and regression tree (CART)** is a binary decision tree that is constructed by splitting a node into two child nodes repeatedly, beginning with the root node that contains the whole dataset.

The first step is the creation and configuration of a CCARTree type object. The constructor of this object takes the vector of the feature types (nominal or continuous) and the problem type. After the object is constructed, we can configure the tree depth, which is the crucial parameter for the algorithm's performance.

Then, we have to create a loss function object. For the current task, the object of a CSquaredLoss type is a suitable choice.

With the model and the loss function object, we can then instantiate an object of the CStochasticGBMachine class. For the training, we have to use the set_labels and train methods with appropriate parameters: the object of the CRegressionLabels type and the object of the CDenseFeatures type respectively. For evaluation, the apply_regression method can be used, as illustrated in the following code block:

```
void GBMClassification(Some<CDenseFeatures<DataType>> features,
                       Some<CRegressionLabels> labels,
                       Some<CDenseFeatures<DataType>> test_features,
                       Some<CRegressionLabels> test_labels) {
    // mark feature type as continuous
    SGVector<bool> feature_type(1);
    feature_type.set_const(false);

    auto tree = some<CCARTree>(feature_type, PT_REGRESSION);
    tree->set_max_depth(3);
    auto loss = some<CSquaredLoss>();

    auto sgbm = some<CStochasticGBMachine>(tree,
                                           loss,
                                           /*iterations*/ 100,
                                           /*learning rate*/ 0.1,
                                           /*sub-set fraction*/ 1.0);
    sgbm->set_labels(labels);
    sgbm->train(features);
    // evaluate model on test data
    auto new_labels = wrap(sgbm->apply_regression(test_features));
    auto eval_criterium = some<CMeanSquaredError>();
```

```
    auto accuracy = eval_criterium->evaluate(new_labels, test_labels);
    ...
}
```

In the following diagram, we can see how gradient boosting approximates the `cosine` function in a case where we used a maximum `CART tree` depth equal to 2. Note that the generalization we achieved isn't particularly good:

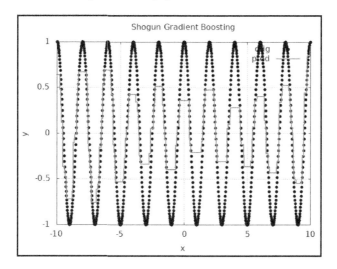

In the following diagram, we can see that the generalization significantly grew because we increased the `CART tree` depth to 3:

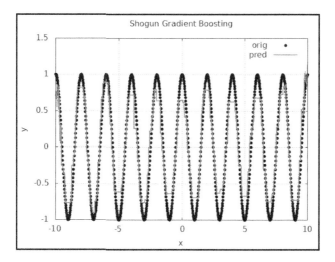

Other parameters that we can tune for this type of algorithm are the number of iterations, the learning rate, and the number of training samples used in one iteration.

Using random forest with Shogun

Another ensemble learning algorithm implemented in the Shogun library is the random forest algorithm. We'll use it for the same function approximation task. It is implemented in the CRandomForest class. To instantiate an object of this class, we have to pass two parameters to the constructor: one is the number of trees (also, it equals the number of bags the dataset should be divided to); the second is the number of attributes chosen randomly during the node splitting when the algorithm builds a tree.

The next important configuration option is the rule on how the tree results should be combined into the one final answer. The set_combination_rule method is used to configure it. In the following example, we used an object of the CMajorityVote class, which implements the majority vote scheme.

We also need to configure what type of problem we want to solve with the random forest, and we can do this with the set_machine_problem_type method of the CRandomForest class. Another required configuration is a type of feature we want to use within our problem: the nominal or continuous features. This can be done with the set_feature_types method. For the training, we will use the set_labels and the train methods with appropriate parameters, as well as an object of the CRegressionLabels type, and an object of the CDenseFeatures type. For evaluation, the apply_regression method will be used, as illustrated in the following code block:

```
void RFClassification(Some<CDenseFeatures<DataType>> features,
                      Some<CRegressionLabels> labels,
                      Some<CDenseFeatures<DataType>> test_features,
                      Some<CRegressionLabels> test_labels) {
    int32_t num_rand_feats = 1;
    int32_t num_bags = 10;
    auto rand_forest =
    shogun::some<CRandomForest>(num_rand_feats, num_bags);
    auto vote = shogun::some<CMajorityVote>();
    rand_forest->set_combination_rule(vote);
    // mark feature type as continuous
    SGVector<bool> feature_type(1);
    feature_type.set_const(false);
    rand_forest->set_feature_types(feature_type);
    rand_forest->set_labels(labels);
    rand_forest->set_machine_problem_type(PT_REGRESSION);
    rand_forest->train(features);
    // evaluate model on test data
```

```
    auto new_labels = wrap(rand_forest->apply_regression(test_features));
    auto eval_criterium = some<CMeanSquaredError>();
    auto accuracy = eval_criterium->evaluate(new_labels, test_labels);
    ...
}
```

The following diagram shows the result of applying the random forest algorithm from the `Shogun` library:

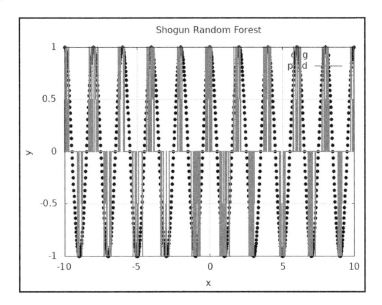

Note that this method is not very applicable to the regression task on this dataset. We can see the gradient boosting used in the previous section produced more interpretable and less error-prone output on this dataset.

Ensembles with Shark-ML

There is only one ensemble learning algorithm in the `Shark-ML` library, which is the random forest, and it can be trained only for solving classification tasks. So, for this set of samples, we will use the *Breast Cancer Wisconsin (Diagnostic)* dataset located at `https://archive.ics.uci.edu/ml/datasets/Breast+Cancer+Wisconsin+(Diagnostic)`. It is taken from *Dua, D. and Graff, C. (2019) UCI Machine Learning Repository, Irvine, CA: University of California, School of Information and Computer Science:* `http://archive.ics.uci.edu/ml`.

There are 569 instances in this dataset, and each instance has 32 attributes: the ID, the diagnosis, and 30 real-value input features. The diagnosis can have two values: **M** = malignant, and **B** = benign. Other attributes have 10 real-value features computed for each cell nucleus, as follows:

- Radius (mean distances from the center to the perimeter)
- Texture (standard deviation of grayscale values)
- Perimeter
- Area
- Smoothness (local variation in radius lengths)
- Compactness
- Concavity (severity of concave portions of the contour)
- Concave points (number of concave portions of the contour)
- Symmetry
- Fractal dimension (*coastline approximation—*1)

This dataset can be used for a binary classification task.

Using random forest with Shark-ML

The random forest algorithm in the Shark-ML library is located in the RFClassifier class, and the corresponding trainer is located in the RFTrainer class. We use the original dataset values without preprocessing for the random forest algorithm implementation. First, we configure the trainer for this type of classifier. These are the next methods for configuration:

- setNTrees: Set the number of trees.
- setMinSplit: Set the minimum number of samples that are split.
- setMaxDepth: Set the maximum depth of the tree.
- setNodeSize: Set the maximum node size when the node is considered pure.
- minImpurity: Set the minimum impurity level below which a node is considered pure.

After we configure the trainer object, we can use its `train` method for the training process. This method takes two parameters: the object of the `RFClassifier` class, which should be trained, and the `ClassificationDataset` object, which represents the dataset.

When the training is complete, we can use the classifier object as a functional object to evaluate it on other data. For example, if we have the test dataset of the type `ClassificationDataset`, we can obtain a classification in the following way: `Data<unsigned int> predictions = rf(test.inputs());`, where `rf` is the object of the `RFClassifier` class, as illustrated in the following code block:

```
void RFClassification(const ClassificationDataset& train,
                      const ClassificationDataset& test) {
  RFTrainer<unsigned int> trainer;
  trainer.setNTrees(100);
  trainer.setMinSplit(10);
  trainer.setMaxDepth(10);
  trainer.setNodeSize(5);
  trainer.minImpurity(1.e-10);
  RFClassifier<unsigned int> rf;
  trainer.train(rf, train);
  // compute errors
  ZeroOneLoss<unsigned int> loss;
  Data<unsigned int> predictions = rf(test.inputs());
  double accuracy = 1. - loss.eval(test.labels(), predictions);
  std::cout << "Random Forest accuracy = " << accuracy << std::endl;
}
```

The output of this sample on the dataset is `Random Forest accuracy = 0.971014`.

Using a stacking ensemble with Shark-ML

To show the implementation of more ensemble learning techniques, we can develop the stacking approach manually. This is not hard with the `Shark-ML` library, or indeed any other library.

First, we need to define weak (or elementary) algorithms that we are going to use for stacking. To unify access to the weak algorithms, we defined the base class, as follows:

```
struct WeakModel {
virtual ~WeakModel() {}
  virtual void Train(const ClassificationDataset& data_set) = 0;
  virtual LinearClassifier<RealVector>& GetClassifier() = 0;
};
```

We used it for creating three weak algorithms' models—the logistic regression, the **linear discriminant analysis (LDA)**, and the linear SVM models, as illustrated in the following code block:

```
struct LogisticRegressionModel : public WeakModel {
    LinearClassifier<RealVector> classifier;
    LogisticRegression<RealVector> trainer;
    void Train(const ClassificationDataset& data_set) override {
        trainer.train(classifier, data_set);
    }
    LinearClassifier<RealVector>& GetClassifier() override { return
    classifier; }
};

struct LDAModel : public WeakModel {
    LinearClassifier<RealVector> classifier;
    LDA trainer;
    void Train(const ClassificationDataset& data_set) override {
        trainer.train(classifier, data_set);
    }
    LinearClassifier<RealVector>& GetClassifier() override { return
    classifier; }
};

struct LinearSVMModel : public WeakModel {
    LinearClassifier<RealVector> classifier;
    LinearCSvmTrainer<RealVector> trainer{SVM_C, false};
    void Train(const ClassificationDataset& data_set) override {
        trainer.train(classifier, data_set);
    }
    LinearClassifier<RealVector>& GetClassifier() override { return
    classifier; }
};
```

These classes hide the usage of different types of trainer classes, but expose the standard interface for the LinearClassifier<RealVector> type through the GetClassifier() method. Furthermore, they implement the general Train method, which takes the object of the ClassificationDataset class.

One of the crucial moments for the stacking approach is combining (stacking) results of weak algorithms to one set, which is used for training or evaluating the meta-algorithm. There is the MakeMetaSet method in our implementation, which does this type of job. It takes the vector of predictions from weak algorithms, and the corresponding labels from the original dataset, and combines them into a new object of the ClassificationDataset class, as illustrated in the following code block:

```
ClassificationDataset MakeMetaSet(
                    const std::vector<Data<unsigned int>>& inputs,
                    const Data<unsigned int>& labels) {
    auto num_elements = labels.numberOfElements();
    std::vector<RealVector> vinputs(num_elements);
    std::vector<unsigned int> vlabels(num_elements);
    std::vector<RealVector::value_type> vals(inputs.size());
    for (size_t i = 0; i < num_elements; ++i) {
        for (size_t j = 0; j < inputs.size(); ++j) {
            vals[j] = inputs[j].element(i);
        }
        vinputs[i] = RealVector(vals.begin(), vals.end());
        vlabels[i] = labels.element(i);
    }
    return createLabeledDataFromRange(vinputs, vlabels);
}
```

This method creates two vectors of inputs and labels and uses the Shark-ML function createLabeledDataFromRange to create a new dataset object. Notice that new inputs are vectors of objects of the RealVector type, and these objects have a new dimension equal to 3 because there are three algorithms we used to predict meta-features. Take a look at the vals object used to combine the outputs (here, it is the inputs variable) from them. These algorithms also take the RealVector objects as input. In the original dataset, they have 30 features; however, in our implementation, they have only five after the PCA dimensionality reduction.

Because of the nature of the selected algorithms, we need to normalize our data. Let's assume we have two datasets for training and testing, as follows:

```
void StackingEnsemble(const ClassificationDataset& train,
                    const ClassificationDataset& test) {
    ...
}
```

To normalize the training dataset, we need to copy the original dataset because the `Normalizer` algorithm works in place and modifies the objects with which it works, as illustrated in the following code block:

```
ClassificationDataset train_data_set = train;
train_data_set.makeIndependent();
```

When we have a copy of the dataset, we can normalize it with the instance of the classifier object trained with the `NormalizeComponentsUnitVariance` class object. As with all algorithms in the `Shark-ML` library, we have to train the normalizer first, and only then can we apply it to the `transformInputs` function. This function transforms only input features because we don't need to normalize binary labels, and can be seen in the following code block:

```
bool removeMean = true;
Normalizer<RealVector> normalizer;
NormalizeComponentsUnitVariance<RealVector>
    normalizing_trainer(removeMean);
normalizing_trainer.train(normalizer, train_data_set.inputs());
train_data_set = transformInputs(train_data_set, normalizer);
```

To speed up and generalize the models we used, we also reduced the dimensionality of the training features with the `PCA` algorithm. Note that the `PCA` class doesn't use the `train` method, but rather has the `encoder` method for obtaining the object of the `LinearModel` class, which is then used for dimensionality reduction, as illustrated in the following code block:

```
PCA pca(train_data_set.inputs());
LinearModel<> pca_encoder;
pca.encoder(pca_encoder, 5);
train_data_set = transformInputs(train_data_set, pca_encoder);
```

Now, after preprocessing our training dataset, we can define and train the weak models that we are going to use for evaluation, as follows:

```
// weak models
std::vector<std::shared_ptr<WeakModel>> weak_models;
weak_models.push_back(std::make_shared<LogisticRegressionModel>());
weak_models.push_back(std::make_shared<LDAModel>());
weak_models.push_back(std::make_shared<LinearSVMModel>());

// train weak models for predictions
for (auto weak_model : weak_models) {
    weak_model->Train(train_data_set);
}
```

For training, the meta-algorithm needs to get the meta-features, and, according to the stacking approach, we will split our training dataset into several folds—10, in our case. We then will train several weak models separately on each of the folds. The validation aspect of the fold will be used for weak model evaluation, and its results will be added to a meta-training dataset and used for training the meta-algorithm.

There is the `createCVSameSizeBalanced` function in the `Shark-ML` library, which can be used for fold creation. It creates equal-size folds, where each consists of two parts: the training part and the validation part. We will iterate over created folds to train weak models and create meta-features. Note in the following code block that we will create new models on each iteration of the loop:

```
size_t num_partitions = 10;
ClassificationDataset meta_data_train;
auto folds = createCVSameSizeBalanced(train_data_set, num_partitions);
for (std::size_t i = 0; i != folds.size(); ++i) {
    // access the fold
    ClassificationDataset training = folds.training(i);
    ClassificationDataset validation = folds.validation(i);
    // train local weak models - new ones on each of folds
    std::vector<std::shared_ptr<WeakModel>> local_weak_models;
    local_weak_models.push_back(
        std::make_shared<LogisticRegressionModel>());
    local_weak_models.push_back(std::make_shared<LDAModel>());
    local_weak_models.push_back(std::make_shared<LinearSVMModel>());
    std::vector<Data<unsigned int>> meta_predictions;
    for (auto weak_model : local_weak_models) {
        weak_model->Train(training);
        auto predictions =
            weak_model->GetClassifier()(validation.inputs());
        meta_predictions.push_back(predictions);
    }
    // combine meta features
    meta_data_train.append(MakeMetaSet(meta_predictions,
        validation.labels()));
}
```

The `meta_data_train` object contains the meta-features and is used to train the meta-model, which is the regular linear SVM model in our case, as follows:

```
LinearClassifier<RealVector> meta_model;
LinearCSvmTrainer<RealVector> trainer(SVM_C, true);
trainer.train(meta_model, meta_data_train);
```

Having trained the ensemble, we can try it on the test dataset. Since we used data preprocessing, we should also transform our test data in the same way that we transformed our training data. This can be easily done with the `normalizer` and the `pca_encoder` objects, which are already trained and hold the required transformation options inside. Usually, such objects (as well as the model) should be stored on secondary storage. The code can be seen in the following snippet:

```
ClassificationDataset test_data_set = test;
test_data_set.makeIndependent();
test_data_set = transformInputs(test_data_set, normalizer);
test_data_set = transformInputs(test_data_set, pca_encoder);
```

The ensemble evaluation starts by predicting meta-features, using the weak models we trained before. We will make the `meta_test` dataset object in the same way as we made the training meta-dataset. We will store predictions from every weak model in the `meta_predictions` vector and will use our helper function to combine them in the object of the `ClassificationDataset` type, as follows:

```
std::vector<Data<unsigned int>> meta_predictions;
for (auto weak_model : weak_models) {
    auto predictions =
        weak_model->GetClassifier()(test_data_set.inputs());
    meta_predictions.push_back(predictions);
}
ClassificationDataset meta_test =
MakeMetaSet(meta_predictions, test_data_set.labels());
```

After we have created the meta-features, we can pass them as input to the `meta_model` object to generate the real predictions. We can also calculate the accuracy, like this:

```
Data<unsigned int> predictions = meta_model(meta_test.inputs());
ZeroOneLoss<unsigned int> loss;
double accuracy = 1. - loss.eval(meta_test.labels(), predictions);
std::cout << "Stacking ensemble accuracy = " << accuracy << std::endl;
}
```

The output of this code is `Stacking ensemble accuracy = 0.985507`. You can see that this ensemble performs better than the random forest implementation, even with default settings. In the case of some additional tuning, it could give even better results.

Summary

In this chapter, we examined various methods for constructing ensembles of machine learning algorithms. The main purposes of creating ensembles are these:

- Reducing the error of the elementary algorithms
- Expanding the set of possible hypotheses
- Increasing a probability of reaching the global optimum during optimizing

We saw that there are three main approaches for building ensembles: training elementary algorithms on various datasets and averaging the errors (bagging); consistently improving the results of the previous, weaker algorithms (boosting); and learning the meta-algorithm from the results of elementary algorithms (stacking). Note that the methods of building ensembles that we've covered, except stacking, require that the elementary algorithms belong to the same class, and this is one of the main requirements for ensembles. It is also believed that boosting gives more accurate results than bagging, but, at the same time, is more prone to overfitting. The main disadvantage of stacking is that it begins to significantly improve the results of elementary algorithms only with a relatively large number of training samples.

In the next chapter, we will discuss the fundamentals of **artificial neural networks** (**ANNs**). We'll look at the historical aspect of their creation, we will go through the basic mathematical concepts used in ANNs, we will implement a **multilayer perceptron** (**MLP**) network and a simple **convolutional neural network** (**CNN**), and we will discuss what deep learning is and why it is so trendy.

Further reading

- Ensemble methods: Bagging & Boosting: `https://medium.com/@sainikhilesh/difference-between-bagging-and-boosting-f996253acd22`
- An article explaining gradient boosting: `https://explained.ai/gradient-boosting/`
- Original article by Jerome Friedman called *Greedy Function Approximation: A Gradient Boosting Machine*: `https://statweb.stanford.edu/~jhf/ftp/trebst.pdf`
- Ensemble Learning to Improve Machine Learning Results: `https://blog.statsbot.co/ensemble-learning-d1dcd548e936`

- **Introduction to decision trees:** https://medium.com/greyatom/decision-trees-a-simple-way-to-visualize-a-decision-dc506a403aeb
- **Understanding Random Forest:** https://towardsdatascience.com/understanding-random-forest-58381e0602d2

Section 3: Advanced Examples 3

In this section, we'll describe what neural networks are and how they can be applied to solving image classification tasks. We'll also describe what recurrent neural networks are and how they assist in solving neural processing tasks such as sentiment analysis.

This section comprises the following chapters:

- Chapter 10, *Neural Networks for Image Classification*
- Chapter 11, *Sentiment Analysis with Recurrent Neural Networks*

10
Neural Networks for Image Classification

In recent years, we have seen a huge interest in neural networks, which are successfully used in various areas—business, medicine, technology, geology, physics, and so on. Neural networks have come into practice wherever it is necessary to solve problems of forecasting, classification, or control. This approach is attractive from an intuitive point of view because it is based on a simplified biological model of the human nervous system. It arose from research in the field of artificial intelligence, namely, from attempts to reproduce the ability of biological nervous systems to learn and correct mistakes by modeling the low-level structure of the brain. Neural networks are compelling modeling methods that allow us to reproduce extremely complex dependencies because they are non-linear. Neural networks also cope better with the *curse of dimensionality* than other methods that don't allow modeling dependencies for a large number of variables.

In this chapter, we'll look at the basic concepts of artificial neural networks and show you how to implement neural networks with different C++ libraries. We'll also go through the implementation of the multilayer perceptron and simple convolutional networks and find out what deep learning is and what its applications are.

The following topics will be covered in this chapter:

- An overview of neural networks
- Delving into convolutional networks
- What is deep learning?
- Examples of using C++ libraries to create neural networks
- Understanding image classification using the LeNet architecture

The code files for this chapter can be found at the following GitHub repo: `https://github.com/PacktPublishing/Hands-On-Machine-Learning-with-CPP/tree/master/Chapter10`

Technical requirements

You will need the following technical requirements to complete this chapter:

- `Dlib` library
- `Shogun` library
- `Shark-ML` library
- PyTorch library
- Modern C++ compiler with C++17 support
- CMake build system version >= 3.8

An overview of neural networks

In this section, we will discuss what artificial neural networks are and their building blocks. We will learn how artificial neurons work and how they relate to their biological analogs. We will also discuss how to train neural networks with the backpropagation method, as well as how to deal with the overfitting problem.

A neural network is a sequence of neurons interconnected by synapses. The structure of the neural network came into the world of programming directly from biology. Thanks to this structure, the computer has the ability to analyze and even remember information. In other words, neural networks are based on the human brain, which contains millions of neurons that transmit information in the form of electrical impulses.

Artificial neural networks are inspired by biology because they are composed of elements with similar functionalities to those of biological neurons. These elements can be organized in a way that corresponds to the anatomy of the brain, and they demonstrate a large number of properties that are inherent in the brain. For example, they can learn from experience, generalize previous precedents to new cases, and identify significant features from input data that contain redundant information.

Now, let's understand the process of a single neuron.

Neurons

The **biological neuron** consists of a body and processes that connect it to the outside world. The processes along which a neuron receives excitation are called **dendrites**. The process through which a neuron transmits excitation is called an **axon**. Each neuron has only one axon. Dendrites and axons have a rather complex branching structure. The junction of the axon and a dendrite is called a **synapse**. The main functionality of a neuron is to transfer excitation from dendrites to an axon. But signals that come from different dendrites can affect the signal in the axon. A neuron gives off a signal if the total excitation exceeds a certain limit value, which varies within certain limits. If the signal is not sent to the axon, the neuron does not respond to excitation. The intensity of the signal that the neuron receives (and therefore the activation possibility) strongly depends on synapse activity. A synapse is a contact for transmitting this information. Each synapse has a length, and special chemicals transmit a signal along it. This basic circuit has many simplifications and exceptions, but most neural networks model themselves on these simple properties.

The artificial neuron receives a specific set of signals as input, each of which is the output of another neuron. Each input is multiplied by the corresponding weight, which is the equivalent to its synaptic power. Then, all the products are summed up and the result of this summation is used to determine the level of neuron activation. The following diagram shows a model that demonstrates this idea:

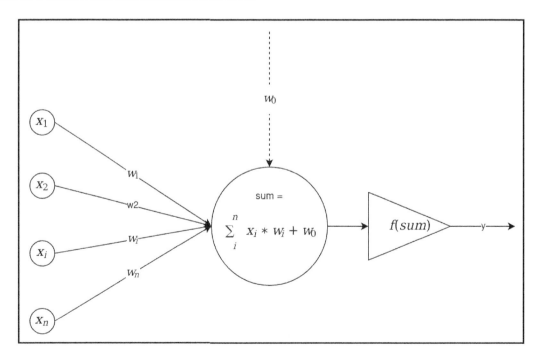

Here, a set of input signals, denoted by $x_1, x_2, \cdots, x_n$, go to an artificial neuron. These input signals correspond to the signals that arrive at the synapses of a biological neuron. Each signal is multiplied by the corresponding weight, $w_1, w_2, \cdots, w_n$, and passed to the summing block. Each weight corresponds to the strength of one biological synaptic connection. The summing block, which corresponds to the body of the biological neuron, algebraically combines the weighted inputs.

The w_0 signal, which is called bias, displays the function of the limit value, known as the shift. This signal allows us to shift the origin of the activation function, which subsequently leads to an increase in the neuron's learning speed. The bias signal is added to each neuron. It learns like all the other weights, except it connects to the signal, **+1**, instead of to the output of the previous neuron. The received signal is processed by the activation function, **f**, and gives a neural signal, **y**, as output. The activation function is a way to normalize the input data. It narrows the range of **sum** so that the values of **f (sum)** belong to a specific interval. That is, if we have a large input number, passing it through the activation function gets us output in the required range. There are many activation functions, and we'll go through them later in this chapter. To learn more about neural networks, we'll have a look at a few more of their components.

The perceptron and neural networks

The first appearance of artificial neural networks can be traced to the article *A logical calculus of the ideas immanent in nervous activity*, which was published in 1943 by *Warren McCallock* and *Walter Pitts*. They proposed an early model of an artificial neuron. *Donald Hebb*, in his 1949 book *The Organization of Behavior*, described the basic principles of neuron training. These ideas were developed several years later by the American neurophysiologist Frank Rosenblatt. Rosenblatt invented the perceptron in 1957 as a mathematical model of the human brain's information perception. The concept was first implemented on a **Mark-1 electronic machine** in 1960.

Rosenblatt posited and proved the **Perceptron Convergence Theorem** (with the help of Blok, Joseph, Kesten, and other researchers who worked with him). It showed that an elementary perceptron, trained through error correction, regardless of the initial state of the weight coefficients and the sequence stimuli, always leads to a solution in a finite amount of time. Rosenblatt also presented evidence of some related theorems, which shows what conditions should correspond to the architecture of artificial neural networks and how they're trained. Rosenblatt also showed that the architecture of the perceptron is sufficient to obtain a solution to any conceivable classification task.

This means that the perceptron is a *universal system*. Rosenblatt himself identified two fundamental limitations of three-layer perceptrons (consisting of one S-layer, one A-layer, and R-layer): they lack the ability to generalize their characteristics in the presence of new stimuli or new situations, and the fact that they can't deal with complex situations, thus dividing them into simpler tasks.

Against the backdrop of the growing popularity of neural networks in 1969, a book by Marvin Minsky and Seymour Papert was published that showed the fundamental limitations of perceptrons. They showed that perceptrons are fundamentally incapable of performing many important functions. Moreover, at that time, the theory of parallel computing was poorly developed, and the perceptron was entirely consistent with the principles of this theory. In general, Minsky showed the advantage of sequential computing over parallel computing in certain classes of problems related to invariant representation. He also demonstrated that perceptrons do not have a functional advantage over analytical methods (for example, statistical methods) when solving problems related to forecasting. Some tasks that, in principle, can be solved by a perceptron require a very long time or a large amount of memory to solve them. These discoveries led to reorienting artificial intelligence researchers to the area of symbolic computing, which is the opposite of neural networks. Also, due to the complexity of mathematically studying perceptrons and there being a lack of generally accepted terminology, various inaccuracies and misconceptions arose.

Subsequently, interest in neural networks resumed. In 1986, David I. Rumelhart, J. E. Hinton, and Ronald J. Williams rediscovered and developed the error backpropagation method, which made it possible to solve the problem of training multilayer networks effectively. This training method was developed back in 1975 by Verbos, but at that time, it did not receive enough attention. In the early 1980s, various scientists came together to study the possibilities of parallel computing and showed interest in theories of cognition based on neural networks. As a result, Hopfield developed a solid theoretical foundation for the use of artificial neural systems and used the so-called Hopfield network as an example. With the network's help, he proved that artificial neural systems could successfully solve a wide range of problems. Another factor that influenced the revival of interest in ANNs was the lack of significant success in the field of symbolic computing.

Currently, terms such as **single-layer perceptron (SLP)** (or just perceptron) and **multilayer perceptron (MLP)** are used. Usually, under the layers in the perceptron is a sequence of neurons, located at the same level and not connected. The following diagram shows this model:

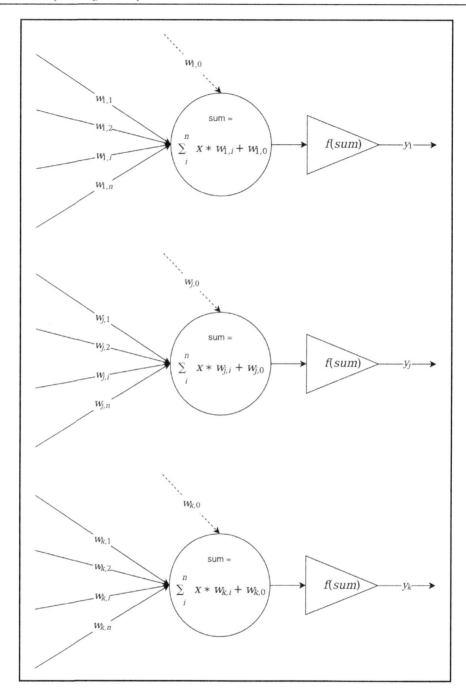

Typically, we can distinguish between the following types of neural network layers:

- **Input**: This is just the source data or signals arriving as the input of the system (model). For example, these can be individual components of a specific vector from the training set, $x = \{x_1, x_2, \ldots, x_n\}$.
- **Hidden**: This is a layer of neurons located between the input and output layers. There can be more than one hidden layer.
- **Output**: This is the last layer of neurons that aggregates the model's work, and its outputs are used as the result of the model's work.

The term single-layer perceptron is often understood as a model that consists of an input layer and an artificial neuron aggregating this input data. This term is sometimes used in conjunction with the term *Rosenblatt's perceptron*, but this is not entirely correct since Rosenblatt used a randomized procedure to set up connections between input data and neurons to transfer data to a different dimension, which made it possible to the solve problems that arose when classifying linearly non-separable data. In Rosenblatt's work, a perceptron consists of S and A neuron types, and an R adder. S neurons are the input layers, A neurons are the hidden layers, and the R neuron generates the model's result. The terminology's ambiguity arose because the weights were used only for the R neuron, while constant weights were used between the S and A neuron types. However, note that connections between these types of neurons were established according to a particular randomized procedure:

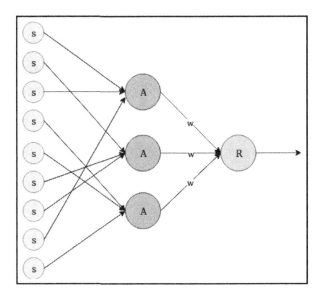

Rosenblatt perceptron

The term MLP refers to a model that consists of an input layer, a certain number of hidden neurons layers, and an output layer. This can be seen in the following diagram:

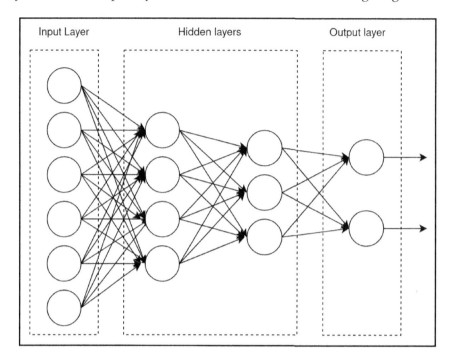

It should also be noted that the architecture of the perceptron (or neural network) includes the direction that signal propagation takes place in. In the preceding examples, all communications are directed strictly from the input neurons to the output ones – this is called a feedforward network. Other network architectures may also include feedback between neurons.

The second point that we need to pay attention to in the architecture of the perceptron is the number of connections between neurons. In the preceding diagram, we can see that each neuron in one layer connects to all the neurons in the next layer – this is called a **fully connected layer**. Such a connection is not a requirement, but we can see an example of a layer with different types of connections in the *Rosenblatt perceptron* scheme.

Now, let's learn how artificial neural networks can be trained.

Training with the backpropagation method

Let's consider the most common method that's used to train a feedforward neural network: the *error backpropagation method*. It is related to supervised methods. Therefore, it requires target values in the training examples.

The idea of the algorithm is based on the use of the output error of a neural network. At each iteration of the algorithm, there are two network passes – forward and backward. On a forward pass, an input vector is propagated from the network inputs to its outputs and forms a specific output vector corresponding to the current (actual) state of the weights. Then, the neural network error is calculated. On the backward pass, this error propagates from the network output to its inputs, and the neuron weights are corrected.

The function that's used to calculate the network error is called the *loss function*. An example of such a function is the square of the difference between the actual and target values:

$$E = \frac{1}{2}\sum_{i=1}^{k}(y_i' - y_i)^2$$

Here, k is the number of output neurons in the network, y' is the target value, and y is the actual output value. The algorithm is iterative and uses the principle of *step-by-step* training; the weights of the neurons of the network are adjusted after one training example is submitted to its input. On the backward pass, this error propagates from the network output to its inputs, and the following rule corrects the neuron's weights:

$$\Delta w_{i,j}(n) = -\eta\frac{\partial E_{av}}{\partial w_{ij}}$$
$$w_{i,j}(n) = w_{i,j}(n-1) + \Delta w_{i,j}(n)$$

Here, $w_{i,j}$ is the weight of the jth connection of the ith neuron and η is the learning rate parameter that allows us to control the value of the correction step, $\Delta w_{j,i}$. To accurately adjust to a minimum of errors, this is selected experimentally in the learning process (it varies in the range from 0 to 1). n is the number of the hierarchy of the algorithm (that is, the step number). Let's say that the output sum of the ith neuron is as follows:

$$S_i = \sum_{i=1}^{n} w_{ij}x_i$$

From this, we can show the following:

$$\frac{\partial E}{\partial w_{ij}} = \frac{\partial E}{\partial S_i} \frac{\partial S_i}{\partial w_{ij}} = x_i \frac{\partial E}{\partial S_i}$$

Here, we can see that the differential, ∂S_i, of the activation function of the neurons of the network, $f(s)$, must exist and not be equal to zero at any point; that is, the activation function must be differentiable on the entire numerical axis. Therefore, to apply the backpropagation method, sigmoidal activation functions, such as logistic or hyperbolic tangents, are often used.

In practice, training is continued not until the network is precisely tuned to the minimum of the error function, but until a sufficiently accurate approximation is achieved. This process allows us to reduce the number of learning iterations and prevent the network from overfitting.

Currently, many modifications of the backpropagation algorithm have been developed. Let's look at some of them.

Backpropagation method modes

There are three main modes of the backpropagation method:

- Stochastic
- Batch
- Mini-batch

Let's see what these modes are and how they differ from each other.

Stochastic mode

In stochastic mode, the method introduces corrections to the weight coefficients immediately after calculating the network output on one training sample.

The stochastic method is slower than the batch method. Given it does not carry out an accurate gradient descent, instead introducing some *noise* using an undeveloped gradient, it can get out of local minima and produce better results. It is also easier to apply when working with large amounts of training data.

Batch mode

For the batch mode of gradient descent, the loss function is calculated immediately for all available training samples, and then corrections of the weight coefficients of the neuron are introduced by the error backpropagation method.

The batch method is faster and more stable than stochastic mode, but it tends to stop and get stuck at local minima. Also, when it needs to train large amounts of data, it requires substantial computational resources.

Mini-batch mode

In practice, mini-batches are often used as a compromise. The weights are adjusted after processing several training samples (mini-batches). This is done less often than with stochastic descent, but more often than with batch mode.

Now that we've looked at the main backpropagation training modes, let's discuss the problems of the backpropagation method.

Backpropagation method problems

Despite the mini-batch method not being universal, it is widespread at the moment because it provides a compromise between computational scalability and learning effectiveness. It also has individual flaws. Most of its problems come from the indefinitely long learning process. In complex tasks, it may take days or even weeks to train the network. Also, while training the network, the values of the weights can become enormous due to correction. This problem can lead to the fact that all or most of the neurons begin to function at enormous values, in the region where the derivative of the loss function is very small. Since the error that's sent back during the learning process is proportional to this derivative, the learning process can practically freeze.

The gradient descent method can get stuck in a local minimum without hitting a global minimum. The error backpropagation method uses a kind of gradient descent; that is, it descends along the error surface, continuously adjusting the weights until they reach a minimum. The surface of the error of a complex network is rugged and consists of hills, valleys, folds, and ravines in a high-dimensional space. A network can fall into a local minimum when there is a much deeper minimum nearby. At the local minimum point, all directions lead up, and the network is unable to get out of it. The main difficulty in training neural networks comes down to the methods that are used to exit the local minima: each time we leave a local minimum, the next local minimum is searched by the same method, thereby backpropagating the error until it is no longer possible to find a way out of it.

A careful analysis of the proof of convergence shows that weights corrections are assumed to be infinitesimal. This assumption is not feasible in practice since it leads to an infinite learning time. The step size should be taken as the final size. If the step size is fixed and very small, then the convergence will be too slow, while if it is fixed and too large, then paralysis or permanent instability can occur. Today, many optimization methods have been developed that use a variable correction step size. They adapt the step size depending on the learning process (examples of such algorithms include Adam, Adagrad, RMSProp, Adadelta, and Nesterov Accelerated Gradient).

Notice that there is the possibility of the network overfitting. With too many neurons, the ability of the network to generalize information can be lost. The network can learn an entire set of samples provided for training, but any other images, even very similar ones, may be classified incorrectly. To prevent this problem, we need to use regularization and pay attention to this when designing our network architecture.

The backpropagation method – an example

To understand how the backpropagation method works, let's look at an example.

We'll introduce the following indexing for all expression elements: l is the index of the layer, i is the index of the neuron in the layer, and j is the index of the current element or connection (for example, weight). We use these indexes as follows:

$$q_{i,j}^l$$

This expression should be read as the jth element of the ith neuron in the lth layer.

Let's say we have a network that consists of three layers, each of which contains two neurons:

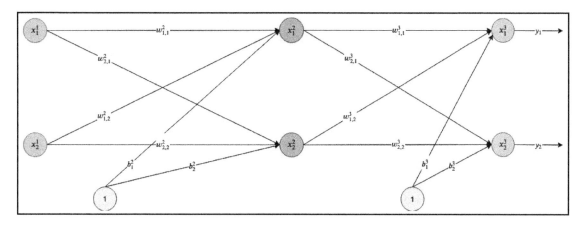

As the loss function, we choose the square of the difference between the actual and target values:

$$E = \frac{1}{2} \sum (target - output)^2$$

$$E_{total} = \frac{1}{2} \sum_{i=1}^{N^l} (y'_i - y_i)^2$$

Here, y' is the target value of the network output, y is the actual result of the output layer of the network, and N^l is the number of neurons in the output layer.

This formula calculates the output sum of the neuron, i, in the layer, l:

$$S = \sum wx + b$$

$$s_i^l = \sum_{j=1}^{K_i^l} w_{ij}^l x_{i=j}^{l-1} + b_i^l$$

Here, K_i^l is the number of inputs of a specific neuron and b_i^l is the bias value for a specific neuron.

For example, for the first neuron from the second layer, it is equal to the following:

$$s_1^2 = w_{1,1}^2 x_1^1 + w_{1,2}^2 x_2^1 + b_1^2$$

Don't forget that no weights for the first layer exist because this layer only represents the input values.

The activation function that determines the output of a neuron should be a sigmoid, as follows:

$$F(x) = \frac{1}{1 + e^{-x}}$$

Its properties, as well as other activation functions, will be discussed later in this chapter. Accordingly, the output of the i th neuron in the l th layer ($l \neq 1$) is equal to the following:

$$x_i^l = F(s_i^l)$$

Now, we implement stochastic gradient descent; that is, we correct the weights after each training example and move in a multidimensional space of weights. To get to the minimum of the error, we need to move in the direction opposite to the gradient. We have to add error correction to each weight, $w_{i,j}^l$, based on the corresponding output. The following formula shows how we calculate the error correction value, $\Delta w_{i,j}^l$, with respect to the E_{total} output:

$$\Delta w_{i,j}^l = -\eta \frac{\partial E_{total}}{\partial w_{ij}^l}$$

Now that we have the formula for the error correction value, we can write a formula for the weight update:

$$w_{ij}^l = w_{ij}^l + \Delta w_{i,j}^l$$

Here,- η is a learning rate value.

The partial derivative of the error with respect to the weights, w_{ij}^l, is calculated using the chain rule, which is applied twice. Note that w_{ij}^l only affects the error only in the sum, S_i^l:

$$E_{total} = \sum E(F(S(w)))$$

$$\frac{\partial E_{total}}{\partial w_{ij}^l} = \frac{\partial E_{total}}{\partial S_i^l} \frac{\partial S_i^l}{\partial w_{i,j}^l} = \frac{\partial E_{total}}{\partial F_i^l} \frac{\partial F_i^l}{\partial S_j^l} \frac{\partial S_j^l}{\partial w_{ij}^l}$$

We start with the output layer and derive an expression that's used to calculate the correction for the weight, $w_{1,1}^3$. To do this, we must sequentially calculate the components. Consider how the error is calculated for our network:

$$E_1 = \frac{1}{2}(y_1' - y_1)^2 = \frac{1}{2}(y_1' - F_1^3(\sum_{j=1}^{2} w_{1,j}^3 x_{i=j}^2 + b_1^2))^2$$

$$E_2 = \frac{1}{2}(y_2' - y_2)^2 = \frac{1}{2}(y_2' - F_2^3(\sum_{j=1}^{2} w_{2,j}^3 x_{i=j}^2 + b_2^2))^2$$

$$E_{total} = E_1 + E_2$$

Here, we can see that E_2 does not depend on the weight of $w_{1,1}^3$. Its partial derivative with respect to this variable is equal to 0:

$$\frac{\partial E_{total}}{\partial F_i^l} = \frac{\partial E_1}{\partial F_i^l} + \frac{\partial E_2}{\partial F_i^l} = \frac{\partial E_1}{\partial F_i^l} + 0$$

Then, the general expression changes to follow the next formula:

$$\frac{\partial E_{total}}{\partial w_{1,1}^3} = \frac{\partial E_1}{\partial F_1^3} \frac{\partial F_1^3}{\partial S_1^3} \frac{\partial S_1^3}{\partial w_{1,1}^3}$$

The first part of the expression is calculated as follows:

$$\frac{\partial E_1}{\partial F_1^3} = 2\frac{1}{2}(y_1' - y_1), \text{ where } y_1 = x_1^3$$

The sigmoid derivative is $F' = F(x)(1 - F(x))$, respectively. For the second part of the expression, we get the following:

$$\frac{\partial F_1^3}{\partial S_1^3} = y_1(1 - y_1) = x_1^3(1 - x_1^3)$$

The third part is the partial derivative of the sum, which is calculated as follows:

$$s_1^3 = w_{1,1}^3 x_1^2 + w_{1,2}^3 x_2^2 + b_1^3$$

$$\frac{\partial S_1^3}{\partial w_{1,1}^3} = 1(w_{1,1}^3)^{(1-1)} x_1^2 + 0 + 0 = x_1^2$$

Now, we can combine everything into one formula:

$$\frac{\partial E_{total}}{\partial w_{1,1}^3} = (y_1' - x_1^3) * x_1^3 (1 - x_1^3) * x_1^2$$

We can also derive a general formula in order to calculate the error correction for all the weights of the output layer:

$$\frac{\partial E_{total}}{\partial w_{i,j}^{l_{out}}} = (y_i' - x_i^{l_{out}}) x_i^{l_{out}} \left(1 - x_i^{l_{out}}\right) x_{i=j}^{l_{out}-1}$$

Here, l_{out} is the index of the output layer of the network.

Now, we can consider how the corresponding calculations are carried out for the inner (hidden) layers of the network. Let's take, for example, the weight, $w_{1,1}^2$. Here, the approach is the same, but with one significant difference – the output of the neuron of the hidden layer is passed to the input of all (or several) the neurons of the output layer, and this must be taken into account:

$$\frac{\partial E_{total}}{\partial w_{1,1}^2} = \left(\frac{\partial E_1}{\partial F_1^2} + \frac{\partial E_2}{\partial F_1^2} \right) \frac{\partial F_1^2}{\partial S_1^2} \frac{\partial S_1^2}{\partial w_{1,1}^2}$$

$$E_1 = F_1^3(S_1^3(F_1^2))$$

$$\frac{\partial E_1}{\partial F_1^2} = \frac{\partial E_1}{\partial S_1^3} \frac{\partial S_1^3}{\partial F_1^2} = \frac{\partial E_1}{\partial F_1^3} \frac{\partial F_1^3}{\partial S_1^3} \frac{\partial S_1^3}{\partial F_1^2}$$

Here, we can see that $\frac{\partial E_1}{\partial F_1^3}$ and $\frac{\partial F_1^3}{\partial S_1^3}$ have already been calculated in the previous step and that we can use their values to perform calculations:

$$F_1^2 = x_1^2$$
$$S_1^3 = w_{1,1}^3 x_1^2 + w_{1,2}^3 x_2^2 + b_1^3$$
$$\frac{\partial S_1^3}{\partial F_1^2} = \frac{\partial S_1^3}{\partial x_1^2} = w_{1,1}^3$$

By combining the obtained results, we receive the following output:

$$\frac{\partial E_1}{\partial F_1^2} = \frac{\partial E_1}{\partial F_1^3} \frac{\partial F_1^3}{\partial S_1^3} w_{1,1}^3$$

Similarly, we can calculate the second component of the sum using the values that were calculated in the previous steps – $\frac{\partial E_2}{\partial F_2^3}$ and $\frac{\partial F_2^3}{\partial S_2^3}$:

$$\frac{\partial E_2}{\partial F_1^2} = \frac{\partial E_2}{\partial F_2^3} \frac{\partial F_2^3}{\partial S_2^3} w_{2,1}^3$$

The remaining parts of the expression for weight correction, $w_{1,1}^2$, are obtained as follows, similar to how the expressions were obtained for the weights of the output layer:

$$\frac{\partial F_1^2}{\partial S_1^2} = x_1^2(1 - x_1^2)$$
$$\frac{\partial S_1^2}{\partial w_{1,1}^2} = \frac{\partial(w_{1,1}^2 x_1^1 + w_{2,1}^2 x_2^1 + b_1^2)}{\partial w_{1,1}^2} = x_1^1$$

By combining the obtained results, we obtain a general formula that we can use to calculate the magnitude of the adjustment of the weights of the hidden layers:

$$\frac{\partial E_{total}}{\partial w_{i,j}^{l_h}} = \left(\sum_{q=1}^{L_{next}} \frac{\partial E}{\partial F_q^{l_h+1}} \frac{\partial F_q^{l_h+1}}{\partial S_q^{l_h+1}} w_{q,j=i}^{l_h+1} \right) x_i^{l_h} (1 - x_i^{l_h}) x_{i=j}^{l_h-1}$$

Here, l_h is the index of the hidden layer and L_{next} is the number of neurons in the layer, l_{h+1}.

Now, we have all the necessary formulas to describe the main steps of the error backpropagation algorithm:

1. Initialize all weights, w_{ij}^l, with small random values (the initialization process will be discussed later).
2. Repeat this several times, sequentially, for all the training samples, or a mini-batch of samples:

    1. Pass a training sample (or a mini-batch of samples) to the network input and calculate and remember all the outputs of the neurons. Those calculate all the sums and values of our activation functions.
    2. Calculate the errors for all the neurons of the output layer:

    $$\delta_i^{l_{out}} = (y_i' - x_i^{l_{out}})x_i^{l_{out}}(1 - x_i^{l_{out}})$$

    3. For each neuron on all l layers, starting from the penultimate one, calculate the error:

    $$\delta_i^l = \left(\sum_{q=1}^{L_{next}} \delta_q^{l+1} w_{i=q,j=i}^{l+1}\right) x_i^l(1 - x_i^l)$$

    Here, $L_{next\ is}$ the number of neurons in the $l + 1$ layer.

    4. Update the network weights:

    $$\Delta w_{ij}^l = -\eta \delta_i^l x_i^l$$
    $$w_{ij}^l = w_{ij}^l + \Delta w_{ij}^l$$

    Here, η is the learning rate value.

There are many versions of the backpropagation algorithm that improve the stability and convergence rate of the algorithm. One of the very first proposed improvements was the use of momentum. At each step, the value Δw is memorized and at the next step, we use a linear combination of the current gradient value and the previous one:

$$\text{step n: } q_{ij}^l = \Delta w_{ij}^l$$
$$\text{step n+1: } w_{ij}^l = w_{ij}^l + \Delta w_{ij}^l + \alpha \Delta q_{ij}^l$$

α is the hyperparameter that's used for additional algorithm tuning. This algorithm is more common now than the original version because it allows us to achieve better results during training.

The next important element that's used to train the neural network is the loss function.

Loss functions

With the loss function, neural network training is reduced to the process of optimally selecting the coefficients of the matrix of weights in order to minimize the error. This function should correspond to the task, for example, categorical cross-entropy for the classification problem or the square of the difference for regression. Differentiability is also an essential property of the loss function if the backpropagation method is used to train the network. Let's look at some of the popular loss functions that are used in neural networks:

- The **mean squared error (MSE)** loss function is widely used for regression and classification tasks. Classifiers can predict continuous scores, which are intermediate results that are only converted into class labels (usually by a threshold) as the very last step of the classification process. MSE can be calculated using these continuous scores rather than the class labels. The advantage of this is that we avoid losing information due to dichotomization. The standard form of the MSE loss function is defined as follows:

$$L = \frac{1}{n} \sum_{i=1}^{n} (y_i - \hat{y}_i)^2$$

- The **mean squared logarithmic error (MSLE)** loss function is a variant of MSE and is defined as follows:

$$L = \frac{1}{n} \sum_{i=1}^{n} \left(\log(y_i + 1) - \log(\hat{y}_i + 1) \right)^2$$

By taking the log of the predictions and target values, the variance that we are measuring has changed. It is often used when we do not want to penalize considerable differences in the predicted and target values when both the predicted and actual values are big numbers. Also, MSLE penalizes underestimates more than overestimates.

- The **L2** loss function is the square of the L2 norm of the difference between the actual value and target value. It is defined as follows:

$$L = \sum_{i=1}^{n} (y_i - \hat{y}_i)^2$$

- The **mean absolute error (MAE)** loss function is used to measure how close forecasts or predictions are to the eventual outcomes:

$$L = \frac{1}{n} \sum_{i=1}^{n} |y_i - \hat{y}_i|$$

MAE requires complicated tools such as linear programming to compute the gradient. MAE is more robust to outliers than MSE since it does not make use of the square.

- The **L1** loss function is the sum of absolute errors of the difference between the actual value and target value. Similar to the relationship between MSE and L2, L1 is mathematically similar to MAE except it does not have division by *n*. It is defined as follows:

$$L = \sum_{i=1}^{n} |y_i - \hat{y}_i|$$

- The **cross-entropy** loss function is commonly used for binary classification tasks where labels are assumed to take values of 0 or 1. It is defined as follows:

$$L = -\frac{1}{n} \sum_{i=1}^{n} \left[y_i \log(\hat{y}_i) + (1 - y_i) \log(1 - \hat{y}_i) \right]$$

Cross-entropy measures the divergence between two probability distributions. If the cross-entropy is large, this means that the difference between the two distributions is significant, while if the cross-entropy is small, this means that the two distributions are similar to each other. The cross-entropy loss function has the advantage of faster convergence, and it is more likely to reach global optimization than the quadratic loss function.

- The **negative log-likelihood** loss function is used in neural networks for classification tasks. It is used when the model outputs a probability for each class rather than the class label. It is defined as follows:

$$L = \frac{1}{n} \sum_{i=1}^{n} \log(\hat{y}_i)$$

- The **cosine proximity** loss function computes the cosine proximity between the predicted value and the target value. It is defined as follows:

$$L = -\frac{\sum_{i=1}^{n} y_i \cdot \hat{y}_i}{\sqrt{\sum_{i=1}^{n} (y_i)^2} \cdot \sqrt{\sum_{i=1}^{n} (\hat{y}_i)^2}}$$

This function is the same as the cosine similarity, which is a measure of similarity between two non-zero vectors. This is expressed as the cosine of the angle between them. Unit vectors are maximally similar if they are parallel and maximally dissimilar if they are orthogonal.

- The **hinge loss** function is used for training classifiers. The hinge loss is also known as the max-margin objective and is used for *maximum-margin* classification. It uses the raw output of the classifier's decision function, not the predicted class label. It is defined as follows:

$$L = \frac{1}{n} \sum_{i=1}^{n} \max(0, 1 - y_i \cdot \hat{y}_i)$$

There are many other loss functions. Complex network architectures often use several loss functions to train different parts of a network. For example, the *Mask RCNN* architecture, which is used for predicting object classes and boundaries on images, uses different loss functions: one for regression and another for classifiers. In the next section, we will discuss the neuron's activation functions.

Activation functions

What does an artificial neuron do? Simply put, it calculates the weighted sum of inputs, adds the bias, and decides whether to exclude this value or use it further. The artificial neuron doesn't know of a threshold that can be used to figure out whether the output value switches neurons to the activated state. For this purpose, we add an activation function. It checks the value that's produced by the neuron for whether external connections should recognize that this neuron as activated or whether it can be ignored. It determines the output value of a neuron, depending on the result of a weighted sum of inputs and a threshold value.

Let's consider some examples of activation functions and their properties.

The stepwise activation function

The stepwise activation function works like this – if the sum value is higher than a particular threshold value, we consider the neuron activated. Otherwise, we say that the neuron is inactive.

A graph of this function can be seen in the following diagram:

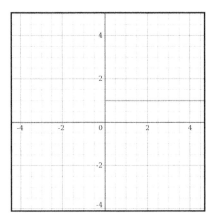

The function returns 1 (the neuron has been activated) when the argument is > 0 (the zero value is a threshold), and the function returns 0 (the neuron hasn't been activated) otherwise. This approach is easy, but it has flaws. Imagine that we are creating a binary classifier – a model that should say *yes* or *no* (activated or not). A stepwise function can do this for us—it prints 1 or 0. Now, imagine the case when more neurons are required to classify many classes: class1, class2, class3, or even more. What happens if more than one neuron is activated? All the neurons from the activation function derive 1.

In this case, questions arise about what class should ultimately be obtained for a given object. We only want one neuron to be activated, and the activation functions of other neurons should be zero (except in this case, we can be sure that the network correctly defines the class). Such a network is more challenging to train and achieve convergence. If the activation function is not binary, then the possible values are *activated at 50 %*, *activated at 20 %*, and so on. If several neurons are activated, we can find the neuron with the highest value of the activation function. Since there are intermediate values at the output of the neuron, the learning process runs smoother and faster. In the stepwise activation function, the likelihood of several fully activated neurons appearing during training decreases (although this depends on what we are training and on what data). Also, the stepwise activation function is not differentiable at point 0 and its derivative is equal to 0 at all other points. This leads to difficulties when we are using gradient descent methods for training.

The linear activation function

The linear activation function, $y = c\,x$, is a straight line and is proportional to the input (that is, the weighted sum on this neuron). Such a choice of activation function allows us to get a range of values, not just a binary answer. We can connect several neurons and if more than one neuron is activated, the decision is made based on the choice of, for example, the maximum value.

The following diagram shows what the linear activation function looks like:

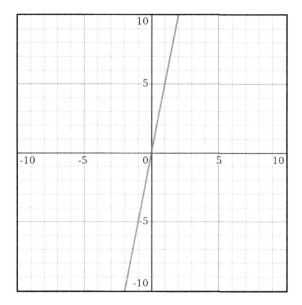

The derivative of $y = c\,x$ with respect to x is c. This conclusion means that the gradient has nothing to do with the argument of the function. The gradient is a constant vector, while the descent is made according to a constant gradient. If an erroneous prediction is made, then the backpropagation error's update changes are also constant and do not depend on the change that's made regarding the input.

There is another problem: related layers. A linear function activates each layer. The value from this function goes to the next layer as input while the second layer considers the weighted sum at its inputs and, in turn, includes neurons, depending on another linear activation function. It doesn't matter how many layers we have. If they are all linear, then the final activation function in the last layer is just a linear function of the inputs on the first layer. This means that two layers (or N layers) can be replaced with one layer. Due to this, we lose the ability to make sets of layers. The entire neural network is still similar to the one layer with a linear activation function because the linear combination of linear functions is another linear function.

The sigmoid activation function

The sigmoid activation function, $y = \dfrac{1}{1 + e^{-x}}$, is a smooth function, similar to a stepwise function:

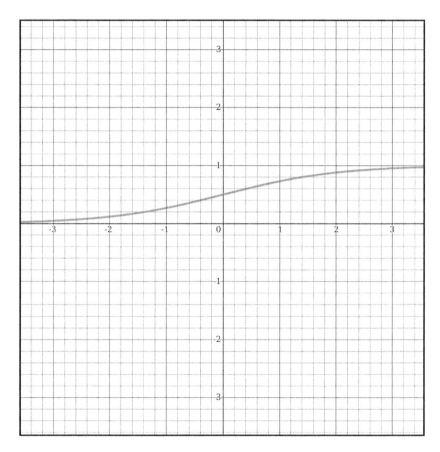

A sigmoid is a non-linear function, and a combination of sigmoids also produces a non-linear function. This allows us to combine neuron layers. A sigmoid activation function is not binary, which makes an activation with a set of values from the range [0,1], in contrast to a stepwise function. A smooth gradient also characterizes a sigmoid. In the range of values of x from -2 to 2, the values, y, change very quickly. This gradient property means that any small change in the value of x in this area entails a significant change in the value of y. This behavior of the function indicates that y tends to cling to one of the edges of the curve.

The sigmoid looks like a suitable function for classification tasks. It tries to bring the values to one of the sides of the curve (for example, to the upper edge at $x = 2$ and the lower edge at $x = -2$). This behavior allows us to find clear boundaries in the prediction.

Another advantage of a sigmoid over a linear function is as follows: In the first case, we have a fixed range of function values, **[0, 1]**, while a linear function varies within $(-\infty, \infty)$. This is advantageous because it does not lead to errors in numerical calculations when dealing with large values on the activation function.

Today, the sigmoid is one of the most widespread activation functions in neural networks. But it also has flaws that we have to take into account. When the sigmoid function approaches its maximum or minimum, the output value of y tends to weakly reflect changes in x. This means that the gradient in such areas takes small values, and the small values cause the gradient to vanish. The **vanishing gradient** problem is a situation where a gradient value becomes too small or disappears and the neural network refuses to learn further or learns very slowly.

The hyperbolic tangent

The hyperbolic tangent is another commonly used activation function. It can be represented graphically as follows:

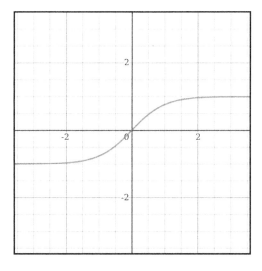

The hyperbolic tangent is very similar to the sigmoid. This is the correct sigmoid function, $y = tanh(x) = \dfrac{2}{1 + e^{-2x}} - 1$. Therefore, such a function has the same characteristics as the sigmoid we looked at earlier. Its nature is non-linear, it is well suited for a combination of layers, and the range of values of the function is $(-1, 1)$. Therefore, it makes no sense to worry about the values of the activation function leading to computational problems. However, it is worth noting that the gradient of the tangential function has higher values than that of the sigmoid (the derivative is steeper than it is for the sigmoid). Whether we choose a sigmoid or a tangent function depends on the requirements of the gradient's amplitude. As well as the sigmoid, the hyperbolic tangent has the inherent vanishing gradient problem.

The **rectified linear unit (ReLU)**, $y = max(0, x)$, returns x if x is positive, and 0 otherwise:

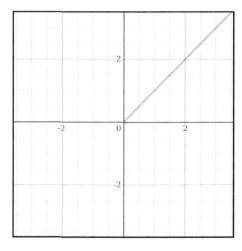

At first glance, it seems that ReLU has all the same problems as a linear function since ReLU is linear in the first quadrant. But in fact, ReLU is non-linear, and a combination of ReLU is also non-linear. A combination of ReLU can approximate any function. This property means that we can use layers and they won't degenerate into a linear combination. The range of permissible values of ReLU is $[0, \infty]$, which means that its values can be quite high, thus leading to computational problems. However, this same property removes the problem of a vanishing gradient. It is recommended to use regularization and normalize the input data to solve the problem with large function values (for example, to the range of values [0,1]).

Let's look at such a property of a neural network as the activation sparseness. Imagine a large neural network with many neurons. The use of a sigmoid or hyperbolic tangent entails the activation of all neurons. This action means that almost all activations must be processed to calculate the network output. In other words, activation is dense and costly.

Ideally, we want some neurons not to be activated, and this would make activations sparse and efficient. ReLU allows us to do this. Imagine a network with randomly initialized weights (or normalized) in which approximately 50% of activations are 0 because of the ReLU property, returning 0 for negative values of x. In such a network, fewer neurons are included (sparse activation), and the network itself becomes lightweight.

Since part of the ReLU is a horizontal line (for negative values of x), the gradient on this part is 0. This property leads to the fact that weights cannot be adjusted during training. This phenomenon is called the **Dying ReLU problem**. Because of this problem, some neurons are turned off and do not respond, making a significant part of the neural network passive. However, there are variations of ReLU that help solve this problem. For example, it makes sense to replace the horizontal part of the function (the region where $x < 0$) with the linear one using the expression $y = 0.01x$. There are other ways to avoid a zero gradient, but the main idea is to make the gradient non-zero and gradually restore it during training.

Also, ReLU is significantly less demanding on computational resources than hyperbolic tangent or sigmoid because it performs simpler mathematical operations than the aforementioned functions.

The critical properties of ReLU are its small computational complexity, nonlinearity, and unsusceptibility to the vanishing gradient problem. This makes it one of the most frequently used activation functions for creating deep neural networks.

Now that we've looked at a number of activation functions, we can highlight their main properties.

Activation function properties

The following is a list of activation function properties that are worth considering when deciding which activation function to choose:

- **Non-linearity**: If the activation function is non-linear, it can be proved that even a two-level neural network can be a universal approximator of the function.
- **Continuous differentiability**: This property is desirable for providing gradient descent optimization methods.
- **Value range**: If the set of values for the activation function is limited, gradient-based learning methods are more stable and less prone to calculation errors since there are no large values. If the range of values is infinite, training is usually more effective, but care must be taken to avoid exploding the gradient (its extremal values).

- **Monotonicity**: If the activation function is monotonic, the error surface associated with the single-level model is guaranteed to be convex. This allows us to learn more effectively.
- **Smooth functions with monotone derivatives**: It is shown that in some cases, they provide a higher degree of generality.

Now that we've discussed the main components used to train neural networks, it's time to learn how to deal with the overfitting problem, which regularly appears during the training process.

Regularization in neural networks

Overfitting is one of the problems of machine learning models and neural networks in particular. The problem is that the model only explains the samples from the training set, thus adapting to the training samples instead of learning to classify samples that were not involved in the training process (losing the ability to generalize). Usually, the primary cause of overfitting is the model's complexity (in terms of the number of parameters it has). The complexity can be too high for the training set available and, ultimately, for the problem to be solved. The task of the regularizer is to reduce the model's complexity, preserving the number of parameters. Let's consider the most common regularization methods that are used in neural networks.

Different methods for regularization

The most widespread regularization methods are L2-regularization, dropout, and batch normalization. Let's take a look:

- **L2-regularization** (weight decay) is performed by penalizing the weights with the highest values. Penalizing is performed by minimizing their L_2-norm using the λ parameter – a regularization coefficient that expresses the preference for minimizing the norm when we need to minimize losses on the training set. That is, for each weigh, w, we add the term, $\frac{\lambda}{2}||\vec{w}||^2 = \frac{\lambda}{2}\sum_{i=1}^{W} w_i^2$, to the loss function, $L(\hat{y}, y)$ (the $\frac{1}{2}$ factor is used so that the gradient of this term with respect to the w parameter is equal to λw and not $2\lambda w$ for the convenience of applying the error backpropagation method). We must select λ correctly. If the coefficient is too small, then the effect of regularization is negligible. If it is too large, the model can reset all the weights.

- **Dropout** regularization consists of changing the structure of the network. Each neuron can be excluded from a network structure with some probability, p. The exclusion of a neuron means that with any input data or parameters, it returns 0. Excluded neurons do not contribute to the learning process at any stage of the backpropagation algorithm. Therefore, the exclusion of at least one of the neurons is equal to learning a new neural network. This "thinning" network is used to train the remaining weights. A gradient step is taken, after which all ejected neurons are returned to the neural network. Thus, at each step of training, we set up one of the possible $2N$ network architectures. By architecture, we mean the structure of connections between neurons, and by N, we're denoting the total number of neurons. When we are evaluating a neural network, neurons are no longer thrown out. Each neuron output is multiplied by ($1 - p$). This means that in the neuron's output, we receive its response expectation for all $2N$ architectures. Thus, a neural network trained using dropout regularization can be considered a result of averaging responses from an ensemble of $2N$ networks.

- **Batch normalization** makes sure that the effective learning process of neural networks isn't impeded. It is possible that the input signal to be significantly distorted by the mean and variance as the signal propagates through the inner layers of a network, even if we initially normalized the signal at the network input. This phenomenon is called the internal covariance shift and is fraught with severe discrepancies between the gradients at different levels or layers. Therefore, we have to use stronger regularizers, which slows down the pace of learning.

Batch normalization offers a straightforward solution to this problem: normalize the input data in such a way as to obtain zero mean and unit variance. Normalization is performed before entering each layer. During the training process, we normalize the batch samples, and during use, we normalize the statistics obtained based on the entire training set since we cannot see the test data in advance. We calculate the mean and variance for a specific batch, $B = x_1, \ldots, x_m$, as follows:

$$\mu_\mathcal{B} = \frac{1}{m} \sum_{i=1}^{m} x_i$$

$$\sigma_\mathcal{B}^2 = \frac{1}{m} \sum_{i=1}^{m} (x_i - \mu_\mathcal{B})^2$$

Using these statistical characteristics, we transform the activation function in such a way that it has zero mean and unit variance throughout the whole batch:

$$\hat{x}_i = \frac{x_i - \mu_\mathcal{B}}{\sqrt{\sigma_\mathcal{B}^2 + \epsilon}}$$

Here, $\epsilon > 0$ is a parameter that protects us from dividing by 0 in cases where the standard deviation of the batch is very small or even equal to zero. Finally, to get the final activation function, y, we need to make sure that, during normalization, we don't lose the ability to generalize. Since we applied scaling and shifting operations to the original data, we can allow arbitrary scaling and shifting of normalized values, thereby obtaining the final activation function:

$$y_i = \gamma \hat{x}_i + \beta$$

Here, γ and β are the parameters of batch normalization that the system can be trained with (they can be optimized by the gradient descent method on the training data). This generalization also means that batch normalization can be useful when applying the input of a neural network directly.

This method, when applied to multilayer networks, almost always successfully reaches its goal – it accelerates learning. Moreover, it's an excellent regularizer, allowing us to choose the learning rate, the power of the L_2-regularizer, and the dropout. The regularization here is a consequence of the fact that the result of the network for a specific sample is no longer deterministic (it depends on the whole batch that this result was obtained from), which simplifies the generalization process.

The next important topic we'll look at is neural network initialization. This affects the convergence of the training process, training speed, and overall network performance.

Neural network initialization

The principle of choosing the initial values of weights for the layers that make up the model is very important. Setting all the weights to 0 is a severe obstacle to learning because none of the weights can be active initially. Assigning weights to the random values from the interval, [0, 1], is also usually not the best option. Actually, model performance and learning process convergence can strongly rely on correct weights initialization; however, the initial task and model complexity can also play an important role. Even if the task's solution does not assume a strong dependency on the values of the initial weights, a well-chosen method of initializing weights can significantly affect the model's ability to learn. This is because it presets the model parameters while taking the loss function into account. Let's look at two popular methods that are used to initialize weights.

Xavier initialization method

The **Xavier** initialization method is used to simplify the signal flow through the layer during both the forward pass and the backward pass of the error for the linear activation function. This method also works well for the sigmoid function, since the region where it is unsaturated also has a linear character. When calculating weights, this method relies on probability distribution (such as the uniform or the normal ones) with a variance of $\text{Var}(W) = \dfrac{2}{n_{in} + n_{out}}$, where n_{in} and n_{out} are the number of neurons in the previous and subsequent layers, respectively.

He initialization method

The **He** initialization method is a variation of the Xavier method that's more suitable for ReLU activation functions because it compensates for the fact that this function returns zero for half of the definition domain. This method of weight calculation relies on a probability distribution with the following variance:

$$\text{Var}(W) = \frac{2}{n_{in}}$$

There are also other methods of weight initialization. Which one you choose is usually determined by the problem being solved, the network topology, the activation functions being used, and the loss function. For example, for recursive networks, the orthogonal initialization method can be used. We'll provide a concrete programming example of neural network initialization in Chapter 12, *Exporting and Importing Models*.

In the previous sections, we looked at the basic components of artificial neural networks, which are common to almost all types of networks. In the next section, we will discuss the features of convolutional neural networks that are often used for image processing.

Delving into convolutional networks

The MLP is the most powerful feedforward neural network. It consists of several layers, where each neuron receives its copy of all the output from the previous layer of neurons. This model is ideal for certain types of tasks, for example, training on a limited number of more or less unstructured parameters.

Nevertheless, let's see what happens to the number of parameters (weights) in such a model when raw data is used as input. For example, the CIFAR-10 dataset contains 32 x 32 x 3 color images, and if we consider each channel of each pixel as an independent input parameter for MLP, each neuron in the first hidden layer adds about 3,000 new parameters to the model! With the increase in image size, the situation quickly gets out of hand, producing images that users can't use for real applications.

One popular solution is to lower the resolution of the images so that MLP becomes applicable. Nevertheless, when we lower the resolution, we risk losing a large amount of information. It would be great if it were possible to process the information before applying a decrease in quality so that we don't cause an explosive increase in the number of model parameters. There is a very effective way to solve this problem, which is based on the convolution operation.

Convolution operator

This approach was first used for neural networks that worked with images, but it has been successfully used to solve problems from other subject areas. Let's consider using this method for image classification.

Let's assume that the image pixels that are close to each other interact more closely when forming a feature of interest for us (the feature of an object in the image) than pixels located at a considerable distance. Also, if a small trait is considered very important in the process of image classification, it does not matter in which part of the image this trait is found.

Let's have a look at the concept of a convolution operator. We have a two-dimensional image of *I* and a small **K** matrix that has a dimension of *h x w* (the so-called convolution kernel) constructed in such a way that it graphically encodes a feature. We compute a minimized image of *I * K*, superimposing the core to the image in all possible ways and recording the sum of the elements of the original image and the kernel:

$$(I * K)_{xy} = \sum_{i=1}^{h} \sum_{j=1}^{w} K_{ij} \times I_{x+i-1,y+j-1}$$

An exact definition assumes that the kernel matrix is transposed, but for machine learning tasks, it doesn't matter whether this operation was performed or not. The convolution operator is the basis of the convolutional layer in a CNN. The layer consists of a certain number of kernels, $\vec{K}$ (with additive displacement components, $\vec{b}$, for each kernel), and calculates the convolution of the output image of the previous layer using each of the kernels, each time adding a displacement component. In the end, the activation function, σ, can be applied to the entire output image. Usually, the input stream for a convolutional layer consists of *d* channels; for example, red/green/blue for the input layer, in which case the kernels are also expanded so that they also consist of *d* channels. The following formula is obtained for one channel of the output image of the convolutional layer, where *K* is the kernel and *b* is the stride (shift) component:

$$\text{conv}(I, K)_{x,y} = \sigma\left(b + \sum_{i=1}^{h} \sum_{j=1}^{w} \sum_{k=1}^{d} K_{ijk} \times I_{x+i-1,y+j-1,k}\right)$$

The following diagram schematically depicts the preceding formula:

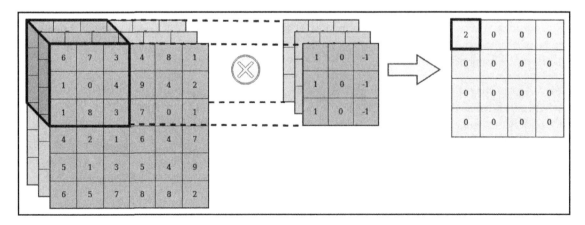

If the additive (stride) component is not equal to 1, then this can be schematically depicted as follows:

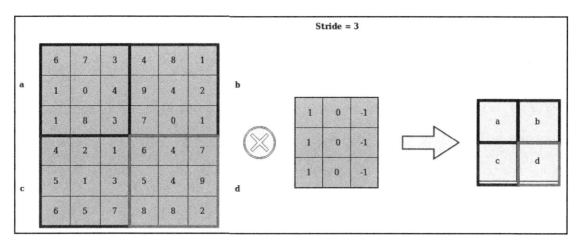

Please note that since all we are doing here is adding and scaling the input pixels, the kernels can be obtained from the existing training sample using the gradient descent method, similar to calculating weights in an MLP. An MLP could perfectly cope with the functions of the convolutional layer, but it requires a much longer training time, as well as a more significant amount of training data.

Notice that the convolution operator is not limited to two-dimensional data: most deep learning frameworks provide layers for one-dimensional or N-dimensional convolutions directly out of the box. It is also worth noting that although the convolutional layer reduces the number of parameters compared to a fully connected layer, it uses more hyperparameters—parameters that are selected before training.

In particular, the following hyperparameters are selected:

- **Depth**: How many kernels and bias coefficients will be involved in one layer.
- The **height** and **width** of each kernel.
- **Step (stride)**: How much the kernel is shifted at each step when calculating the next pixel of the resulting image. Usually, the step value that's taken is equal to 1, and the larger the value is, the smaller the size of the output image that's produced.
- **Padding**: Note that convoluting any kernel of a dimension greater than 1 x 1 reduces the size of the output image. Since it is generally desirable to keep the size of the original image, the pattern is supplemented with zeros along the edges.

One pass of the convolutional layer affects the image by reducing the length and width of a particular channel but increasing its value (depth).

Another way to reduce the image dimension and save its general properties is to downsample the image. Network layers that perform such operations are called **pooling layers**.

Pooling operation

A pooling layer receives small, separate fragments of the image and combines each fragment into one value. There are several possible methods of aggregation. The most straightforward one is to take the maximum from a set of pixels. This method is shown schematically in the following diagram:

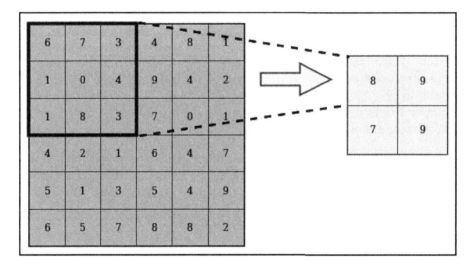

Let's consider how maximum pooling works. In the preceding diagram, we have a matrix of numbers that's 6 x 6 in size. The pooling window's size equals 3, so we can divide this matrix into the four smaller submatrices of size 3 x 3. Then, we can choose the maximum number from each submatrix and make a smaller matrix of size 2 x 2 from these numbers.

The most important characteristic of a convolutional or pooling layer is its receptive field value, which allows us to understand how much information is used for processing. Let's discuss it in detail.

Receptive field

An essential component of the convolutional neural network architecture is a reduction in the amount of data from the input to the output of the model while still increasing the channel depth. As mentioned earlier, this is usually done by choosing a convolution step (stride) or pooling layers. The receptive field determines how much of the original input from the source is processed at the output. The expansion of the receptive field allows convolutional layers to combine low-level features (lines, edges) to create higher-level features (curves, textures):

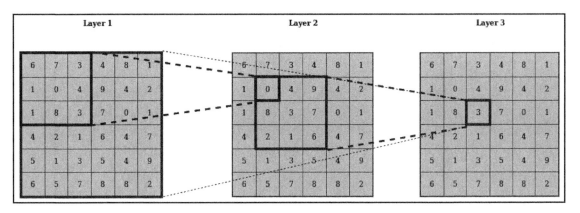

The receptive field, l_k, of layer k can be given by the following formula:

$$l_k = l_{k-1} + \left((f_k - 1) \prod_{i=1}^{k} s_i\right)$$

Here, l_{k-1} is the receptive field of the layer, k - 1, f_k is the filter size, and s_i is the stride of layer i. So, for the preceding example, the input layer has $RF = 1$, the hidden layer has $RF = 3$, and the last layer has $RF = 5$.

Now that we're acquainted with the basic concepts of convolutional neural networks, let's look at how we can combine them to create a concrete network architecture for image classification.

Convolution network architecture

The network is developed from a small number of low-level filters in the initial stages to a vast number of filters, each of which finds a specific high-level attribute. The transition from level to level provides a hierarchy of pattern recognition.

One of the first convolutional network architectures that was successfully applied to the pattern recognition task was the LeNet-5, which was developed by Yann LeCun, Leon Bottou, Yosuha Bengio, and Patrick Haffner. It was used to recognize handwritten and printed numbers in the 1990s. The following diagram shows this architecture:

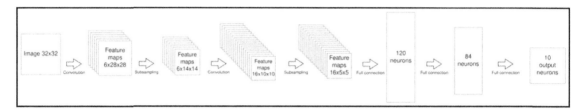

The network layers of this architecture are explained in the following table:

Number	Layer	Feature map (depth)	Size	Kernel size	Stride	Activation
Input	Image	1	32 x 32	-	-	-
1	Convolution	6	28 x 28	5 x 5	1	tanh
2	Average pool	6	14 x 14	2 x 2	2	tanh
3	Convolution	16	10 x 10	5 x 5	1	tanh
4	Average pool	16	5 x 5	2 x 2	2	tanh
5	Convolution	120	1 x 1	5 x 5	1	tanh
6	FC		84	-	-	tanh
Output	FC		10	-	-	softmax

Notice how the depth and size of the layer are changing toward the final layer. We can see that the depth was increasing and that the size became smaller. This means that toward the final layer, the number of features the network can learn increased, but their size became smaller. Such behavior is very common among different convolutional network architectures.

What is deep learning?

Most often, the term deep learning is used to describe artificial neural networks that were designed to work with large amounts of data and use complex algorithms to train the model. Algorithms for deep learning can use both supervised and unsupervised algorithms (reinforcement learning). The learning process is *deep* because, over time, the neural network covers an increasing number of levels. The deeper the network is (that is, it has more hidden layers, filters, and levels of feature abstraction it has), the higher the network's performance. On large datasets, deep learning shows better accuracy than traditional machine learning algorithms.

The real breakthrough that led to the current resurgence of interest in deep neural networks occurred in 2012, after the publication of the article *ImageNet classification with deep convolutional neural networks*, by *Alex Krizhevsky*, *Ilya Sutskever*, and *Geoff Hinton* in the *Communications of the ACM* magazine. The authors have put together many different learning acceleration techniques. These techniques include convolutional neural networks, the intelligent use of GPUs, and some innovative math tricks: optimized linear neurons (ReLU) and dropout, showing that in a few weeks they could train a complex neural network to a level that would surpass the result of traditional approaches used in computer vision.

Now, systems based on deep learning are applied in various fields and have successfully replaced the traditional approaches to machine learning. Some examples of areas where deep learning is used are as follows:

- **Speech recognition**: All major commercial speech recognition systems (such as Microsoft Cortana, Xbox, Skype Translator, Amazon Alexa, Google Now, Apple Siri, Baidu, and iFlytek) are based on deep learning.
- **Computer vision**: Today, deep learning image recognition systems are already able to give more accurate results than the human eye, for example, when analyzing medical research images (MRI, X-ray, and so on.).
- **Discovery of new drugs**: For example, the AtomNet neural network was used to predict new biomolecules and was put forward for the treatment of diseases such as the Ebola virus and multiple sclerosis.
- **Recommender systems**: Today, deep learning is used to study user preferences.
- **Bioinformatics**: It is also used to study the prediction of genetic ontologies.

Examples of using C++ libraries to create neural networks

Many machine learning libraries have an API for creating and working with neural networks. All the libraries we used in the previous chapters—Shogun, Dlib, and Shark-ML—are supported by neural networks. But there are also specialized frameworks for neural networks; for example, one popular one is the PyTorch framework. The difference between a specialized library and the common purpose libraries is that the specialized one supports more configurable options and supports different network types, layers, and loss functions. Also, specialized libraries usually have more modern instruments, and these instruments are introduced to their APIs more quickly.

In this section, we'll create a simple MLP for a regression task with the Shogun, Dlib, and Shark-ML libraries. We'll also use the PyTorch C++ API to create a more advanced network—a convolutional deep neural network with the LeNet5 architecture, which we discussed earlier in the *Convolution network architecture* section. We'll use this network for the image classification task.

Simple network example for the regression task

Let's learn how to use the Shogun, Dlib, and Shark-ML libraries to create a simple MLP for a regression task. The task is the same for all series samples—MLP should learn cosine functions at limited intervals. In this book's code samples, we can find the full program for data generation and MLP training. Here, we'll discuss the essential parts of the programs that are used for the neural network's API view. Note that the activation functions we'll be using for these samples are the Tanh and ReLU functions. We've chosen them in order to achieve better convergence for this particular task.

Dlib

The Dlib library has an API for working with neural networks. It can also be built with Nvidia CUDA support for performance optimization. Using the CUDA or the OpenCL technologies for GPUs is important if we are planning to work with a large amount of data and deep neural networks.

The approach used in the Dlib library for neural networks is the same as for other machine learning algorithms in this library. We should instantiate and configure an object of the required algorithm class and then use a particular trainer to train it on a dataset.

There is the `dnn_trainer` class for training neural networks in the `Dlib` library. Objects of this class should be initialized with an object of the concrete network and the object of the optimization algorithm. The most popular optimization algorithm is the stochastic gradient descent algorithm with momentum, which we discussed in the *Backpropagation method modes* section. This algorithm is implemented in the `sgd` class. Objects of the `sgd` class should be configured with the weight decay regularization and momentum parameter values. The `dnn_trainer` class has the following essential configuration methods: `set_learning_rate`, `set_mini_batch_size`, and `set_max_num_epochs`. These set the learning rate parameter value, the mini-batch size, and the maximum number of training epochs, respectively. Also, this trainer class supports dynamic learning rate change so that we can, for example, make a lower learning rate for later epochs. The learning rate shrink parameter can be configured with the `set_learning_rate_shrink_factor` method. But for the following example, we'll use the constant learning rate because, for this particular data, it gives better training results.

The next essential item for instantiating the trainer object is the neural network type object. The `Dlib` library uses a declarative style to define the network architecture, and for this purpose, it uses C++ templates. So, to define the neural network architecture, we should start with the network's input. In our case, this is of the `matrix<double>` type. We need to pass this as the template argument to the next layer type; in our case, this is the fully-connected layer of the `fc` type. The fully-connected layer type also takes the number of neurons as the template argument. To define the whole network, we should create the nested type definitions, until we reach the last layer and the loss function. In our case, this is the `loss_mean_squared` type, which implements the mean squared loss function, which is usually used for regression tasks.

The following code snippet shows the network definition with the `Dlib` library API:

```
using NetworkType = loss_mean_squared<fc<1,
                        htan<fc<8,
                        htan<fc<16,
                        htan<fc<32,
                        input<matrix<double>>>>>>>>>;
```

This definition can be read in the following order:

1. We started with the input layer:

```
input<matrix<double>
```

2. Then, we added the first hidden layer with 32 neurons:

```
fc<32, input<matrix<double>>
```

3. After, we added the hyperbolic tangent activation function to the first hidden layer:

```
htan<fc<32, input<matrix<double>>>
```

4. Next, we added the second hidden layer with 16 neurons and an activation function:

```
htan<fc<16, htan<fc<32, input<matrix<double>>>>>
```

5. Then, we added the third hidden layer with 8 neurons and an activation function:

```
htan<fc<8, htan<fc<16, htan<fc<32, input<matrix<double>>>>>>>
```

6. Then, we added the last output layer with 1 neuron and without an activation function:

```
fc<1, htan<fc<8, htan<fc<16, htan<fc<32,
input<matrix<double>>>>>>>>
```

7. Finally, we finished with the loss function:

```
loss_mean_squared<...>
```

The following snippet shows the complete source code example with a network definition:

```
size_t n = 10000;
...
std::vector<matrix<double>> x(n);
std::vector<float> y(n);
...
using NetworkType = loss_mean_squared<
fc<1, htan<fc<8, htan<fc<16, htan<fc<32, input<matrix<double>>>>>>>>>;
NetworkType network;
float weight_decay = 0.0001f;
float momentum = 0.5f;
sgd solver(weight_decay, momentum);
dnn_trainer<NetworkType> trainer(network, solver);
trainer.set_learning_rate(0.01);
trainer.set_learning_rate_shrink_factor(1);  // disable learning rate
changes
trainer.set_mini_batch_size(64);
trainer.set_max_num_epochs(500);
```

```
trainer.be_verbose();
trainer.train(x, y);
network.clean();

auto predictions = network(new_x);
```

Now that we've configured the trainer object, we can use the `train` method to start the actual training process. This method takes two C++ vectors as input parameters. The first one should contain training objects of the `matrix<double>` type and the second one should contain the target regression values that are `float` types. We can also call the `be_verbose` method to see the output log of the training process. After the network has been trained, we call the `clean` method to allow the network object to clear the memory from the intermediate training values and therefore reduce memory usage.

Shogun

To create the neural network with the `Shogun` library, we have to start by defining the architecture of the network. We use the `CNeuralLayers` class in the `Shogun` library to do so, which is used for aggregating the network layers. It has different methods for creating layers:

- `input`: Creates the input layer with a specified number of dimensions
- `logistic`: Creates a fully connected hidden layer with the logistic (sigmoid) activation function
- `linear`: Creates a fully connected hidden layer with the linear activation function
- `rectified_linear`: Creates a fully connected hidden layer with the ReLU activation function
- `leaky_rectified_linear`: Creates a fully connected hidden layer with the Leaky ReLU activation function
- `softmax`: Creates a fully connected hidden layer with the softmax activation function

Each of these methods returns a new object of the `CNeuralLayers` class, which contains all the previous layers with an added new one. So, to add a new layer, we can write the following code:

```
// create the initial object
auto layers = some<CNeuralLayers>();
// add the input layer
layers = wrap(layers->input(dimensions));
```

```
// add the hidden layer
layers = wrap(layers->logistic(32));
```

Each time we add a new layer, we rewrite the pointer to the CNeuralLayers type object. We have to call the done method of the CNeuralLayers class after all the layers have been added. Then, it returns an array of configured layers, which can be used to create the CNeuralNetwork type object. The CNeuralNetwork class implements functionality for network initialization and training. After we've created the CNeuralNetwork object, we have to connect all the layers by calling the quick_connect method. Then, we can initialize the weights of all the layers by calling the initialize_neural_network method. This method can take an optional parameter, sigma, which is the standard deviation of the Gaussian that's used to initialize the parameters randomly.

After we've configured the neural network, we should configure the optimization algorithm. This configuration can also be done with the CNeuralNetwork object. First, we should specify the optimization method. This class supports the gradient descent and **Broyden–Fletcher–Goldfarb–Shanno (BFGS)** algorithms. The BFGS is a second-order (based on second derivatives) iterative method for solving unconstrained, nonlinear optimization problems.

For this sample, we chose the gradient descent method by calling set_optimization method with the NNOM_GRADIENT_DESCENT enumeration value argument. Other settings are standard for the gradient descent method's configuration. The set_gd_mini_batch_size method sets the size of a mini-batch. The set_l2_coefficient method sets the value of the regularization weight decay parameter. The set_gd_learning_rate method sets the learning rate parameter. The set_gd_momentum method sets the momentum, α, parameter value. With the set_max_num_epochs method, we can set the maximum number of training epochs, and with the set_epsilon method, we can define the convergence criteria value for a loss function.

The loss function can't be explicitly configured in the Shogun library. It is automatically selected based on the type of labels specified with the set_labels method. In this example, we used the CRegressionLabels type for the labels because we are solving the regression task. Network training can be done with the {train} method, which takes an object of the CDenseFeatures type. This contains a set of all the training samples.

The source code for this example is as follows:

```
ize_t n = 10000;
...
SGMatrix<float64_t> x_values(1, static_cast<index_t>(n));
SGVector<float64_t> y_values(static_cast<index_t>(n));
...

auto x = some<CDenseFeatures<float64_t>>(x_values);
auto y = some<CRegressionLabels>(y_values);

auto dimensions = x->get_num_features();
auto layers = some<CNeuralLayers>();
layers = wrap(layers->input(dimensions));
layers = wrap(layers->rectified_linear(32));
layers = wrap(layers->rectified_linear(16));
layers = wrap(layers->rectified_linear(8));
layers = wrap(layers->linear(1));
auto all_layers = layers->done();

auto network = some<CNeuralNetwork>(all_layers);
network->quick_connect();
network->initialize_neural_network();

network->set_optimization_method(NNOM_GRADIENT_DESCENT);
network->set_gd_mini_batch_size(64);
network->set_l2_coefficient(0.0001);  // regularization
network->set_max_num_epochs(500);
network->set_epsilon(0.0);  // convergence criteria
network->set_gd_learning_rate(0.01);
network->set_gd_momentum(0.5);

network->set_labels(y);
network->train(x);
```

To see the training's progress, we can set the higher logging level for the Shogun library with the following call:

```
shogun::sg_io->set_log_evel(shogun::MSG_DEBUG);
```

This function allows us to see a lot of additional information about the overall training process, which can help us debug and find problems in the network we train.

Shark-ML

The `Shark-ML` library also has the functionality to define, train, and evaluate neural networks. This process can be divided into five parts: architecture definition, loss function definition, network initialization, optimizer configuration, and training.

Architecture definition

First, we should define all the layers and connect them in the network. The layer can be defined as an object of the `LinearModel` class, parameterized with a specific activation function type. In our case, the type of the layer is as follows:

```
using DenseLayer = LinearModel<RealVector, TanhNeuron>;
```

To instantiate objects of this type, we have to pass three arguments to the constructor: the number of inputs, the number of neurons (outputs), and the Boolean value that enables a bias if it is equal to *true*. The >> operator can be used to connect all the layers in the network:

```
auto network = layer1 >> layer2 >> layer3 >> output;
```

Loss function definition

After we've defined the network structure, we need to define the loss function for the optimization algorithm. The `ErrorFunction` class is used for this purpose. Its constructor takes four parameters:

- An object representing the training dataset
- A pointer to the object that represents the network's structure
- A pointer to the object that implements the loss function—`SquaredLoss`, in our case
- A Boolean flag telling us to use mini-batches or not

The `ErrorFunction` type object can be configured with a regularizer. For example, we can instantiate the object of the `TwoNormRegularizer` class and call the `setRegularizer` method in the `ErrorFunction` type object with two parameters: the weight decay factor value and the pointer to the regularizer object. To finish the configuration of the `ErrorFunction` type object, we need to call the `init` method.

Network initialization

The network can be randomly initialized with the `initRandomNormal` function, which takes two parameters: the pointer to the network object and the variance of normal distribution used for initialization.

Optimizer configuration

The next step is configuring an optimizer. We can use a gradient descent optimizer for our task. There is a class called `SteepestDescent` in the `Shark-ML` library for this purpose. It can be configured with the `setLearningRate` and `setMomentum` methods. After its instantiation and configuration, the `init` method should be called with an object of the `ErrorFunction` type as its parameter.

Network training

To begin training, we need to configure a dataset object first. The mini-batch size can be automatically configured when we define the dataset object. In this example, this happens when we create the `RegressionDataset` type object.

To perform one training step, we should use the `step` method of the optimizer object, but we should be aware that this method does only one pass of mini-batch training. So, to perform several epochs using the whole dataset, we have to manually calculate the number of steps.

When training is done, we have to copy the trained parameters from the optimizer object to the network object. This can be done with the `setParameterVector` method of the network object. We can use the `solution()` method to get parameters from the optimizer.

Now that we've described all the required components, let's look at the complete programming sample.

The complete programming sample

The following snippets show the complete sample source code for this example:

```
size_t n = 10000;
...
std::vector<RealVector> x_data(n);
std::vector<RealVector> y_data(n);
...
```

```
Data<RealVector> x = createDataFromRange(x_data);
Data<RealVector> y = createDataFromRange(y_data);
RegressionDataset train_data(x, y);
```

First, we defined the training dataset's `train_data` object, which was constructed from raw data arrays, that is, `x_data` and `y_data`:

```
using DenseLayer = LinearModel<RealVector, TanhNeuron>;

DenseLayer layer1(1, 32, true);
DenseLayer layer2(32, 16, true);
DenseLayer layer3(16, 8, true);

LinearModel<RealVector> output(8, 1, true);
auto network = layer1 >> layer2 >> layer3 >> output;
```

Then, we defined our neural network object, `network`, which consists of three fully connected layers:

```
SquaredLoss<> loss;
ErrorFunction<> error(train_data, &network, &loss, true);
TwoNormRegularizer<> regularizer(error.numberOfVariables());
double weight_decay = 0.0001;
error.setRegularizer(weight_decay, &regularizer);
error.init();
```

The next step was defining the loss function for the optimizer. Notice that we added a regularizer to the `error` object, which generalizes our loss function:

```
initRandomNormal(network, 0.001);
```

Then, the weights of our network were randomly initialized:

```
SteepestDescent<> optimizer;
optimizer.setMomentum(0.5);
optimizer.setLearningRate(0.01);
optimizer.init(error);
```

Then, at the training preparation step, we created the optimizer object. We also configured the momentum and learning rate parameters. We initialized this with the error object, which provides access to the loss function:

```
size_t epochs = 1000;
size_t iterations = train_data.numberOfBatches();
for (size_t epoch = 0; epoch != epochs; ++epoch) {
    double avg_loss = 0.0;
    for (size_t i = 0; i != iterations; ++i) {
        optimizer.step(error);
```

```
        if (i % 100 == 0) {
            avg_loss += optimizer.solution().value;
        }
    }
    avg_loss /= iterations;
    std::cout << "Epoch " << epoch << " | Avg. Loss " << avg_loss <<
        std::endl;
}
```

Having configured the `train_data`, `network`, and `optimizer` objects, we wrote the training cycle, which trains the network for 1,000 epochs:

```
network.setParameterVector(optimizer.solution().point);
```

After the training process was complete, we used the learned parameters (network weights) that were stored in the `optimizer` object to initialize the actual network parameters with the `setParameterVector` method.

In the next section, we will implement a more complex neural network to solve an image classification task using the `PyTorch` library.

Understanding image classification using the LeNet architecture

In this section, we'll implement a convolutional neural network for image classification. We are going to use the famous dataset of handwritten digits called the **Modified National Institute of Standards and Technology (MNIST)**, which can be found at `http://yann.lecun.com/exdb/mnist/`. The dataset is a standard that was proposed by the *US National Institute of Standards and Technology* to calibrate and compare image recognition methods using machine learning, primarily based on neural networks.

The creators of the dataset used a set of samples from the US Census Bureau, with some samples written by students of American universities added later. All the samples are normalized, anti-aliased grayscale images of 28 x 28 pixels. The MNIST database contains 60,000 images for training and 10,000 images for testing. There are four files:

- `train-images-idx3-ubyte`: Training set images
- `train-labels-idx1-ubyte`: Training set labels
- `t10k-images-idx3-ubyte`: Test set images
- `t10k-labels-idx1-ubyte`: Test set labels

The files that contain labels are in the following format:

Offset	Type	Value	Description
0	32-bit integer	0x00000801(2049)	Magic number (MSB first)
4	32-bit integer	60,000 or 10,000	Number of items
8	Unsigned char	??	Label
9	Unsigned char	??	Label
...	...	...	...

The label's values are from 0 to 9. The files that contain images are in the following format:

Offset	Type	Value	Description
0	32-bit integer	0x00000803(2051)	Magic number (MSB first)
0	32-bit integer	60,000 or 10,000	Number of images
0	32-bit integer	28	Number of rows
0	32-bit integer	28	Number of columns
0	Unsigned byte	??	Pixel
0	Unsigned byte	??	Pixel
...	...	...	...

Pixels are stored in a row-wise manner, with values in the range of [0, 255]. 0 means background (white), while 255 means foreground (black).

In this example, we are using the PyTorch deep learning framework. This framework is primarily used with the Python language. However, its core part is written in C++, and it has a well-documented and actively developed C++ client API called **LibPyTorch**. This framework is based on the linear algebra library called **ATen**, which heavily uses the Nvidia CUDA technology for performance improvement. The Python and C++ APIs are pretty much the same but have different language notations, so we can use the official Python documentation to learn how to use the framework. This documentation also contains a section stating the differences between C++ and Python APIs and specific articles about the usage of the C++ API.

The PyTorch framework is widely used for research in deep learning. As we discussed previously, the framework provides functionality for managing big datasets. It can automatically parallelize loading the data from a disk, manage pre-loaded buffers for the data to reduce memory usage, and limit expensive performance disk operations. It provides the `torch::data::Dataset` base class for the implementation of the user custom dataset. We only need to override two methods here: `get` and `size`. These methods are not virtual because we have to use the C++ template's polymorphism to inherit from this class.

Reading the training dataset

Consider the `MNISTDataset` class, which provides access to the MNIST dataset. The constructor of this class takes two parameters: one is the name of the file contains images, while the other is the name of the file that contains the labels. It loads whole files into its memory, which is not a best practice, but for this dataset, this approach works well because the dataset is small. For bigger datasets, we have to implement another scheme of reading data from the disk because usually, for real tasks, we are unable to load all the data into the computer's memory.

We use the `OpenCV` library to deal with images, so we store all the loaded images in the C++ `vector` of the `cv::Mat` type. Labels are stored in a vector of the `unsigned char` type. We write two additional helper functions to read images and labels from the disk: `ReadImages` and `ReadLabels`. The following snippet shows the header file for this class:

```
#include <torch/torch.h>
#include <opencv2/opencv.hpp>
#include <string>

class MNISTDataset : public torch::data::Dataset<MNISTDataset> {
public:
    MNISTDataset(const std::string& images_file_name,
                 const std::string& labels_file_name);
    // torch::data::Dataset implementation
    torch::data::Example<> get(size_t index) override;
    torch::optional<size_t> size() const override;
private:
    void ReadLabels(const std::string& labels_file_name);
    void ReadImages(const std::string& images_file_name);
    uint32_t rows_ = 0;
    uint32_t columns_ = 0;
    std::vector<unsigned char> labels_;
    std::vector<cv::Mat> images_;
};
```

The following snippet shows the implementation of the public interface of the class:

```
MNISTDataset::MNISTDataset(const std::string& images_file_name,
                           const std::string& labels_file_name) {
    ReadLabels(labels_file_name);
    ReadImages(images_file_name);
}
```

We can see that the constructor passed the filenames to the corresponding loader functions. The `size` method returns the number of items that were loaded from the disk into the labels container:

```
torch::optional<size_t> MNISTDataset::size() const {
  return labels_.size();
}
```

The following snippet shows the `get` method's implementation:

```
torch::data::Example<> MNISTDataset::get(size_t index) {
  return {CvImageToTensor(images_[index]),
  torch::tensor(static_cast<int64_t>(labels_[index]),
  torch::TensorOptions()
  .dtype(torch::kLong)
  .device(torch::DeviceType::CUDA))};
}
```

The `get` method returns an object of the `torch::data::Example<>` class. In general, this type holds two values: the training sample represented with the `torch::Tensor` type and the target value, which is also represented with the `torch::Tensor` type. This method retrieves an image from the corresponding container using a given subscript, converts the image into the `torch::Tensor` type with the `CvImageToTensor` function, and uses the label value converted into the `torch::Tensor` type as a target value.

There is a set of `torch::tensor` functions that are used to convert a C++ variable into the `torch::Tensor` type. They automatically deduce the variable type and create a tensor with corresponding values. In our case, we explicitly convert the label into the `int64_t` type because the loss function we'll be using later assumes that the target values have a `torch::Long` type. Also, notice that we passed `torch::TensorOptions` as a second argument to the `torch::tensor` function. We specified the torch type of the tensor values and told the system to place this tensor to the GPU memory by setting the `device` option on `torch::DeviceType::CUDA` and by using the `torch::TensorOptions` object. When we manually create the PyTorch tensors, we have to explicitly configure where to place them – in the CPU or GPU. Tensors that are placed in different types of memory can't be used together.

To convert the OpenCV image into a tensor, write the following function:

```
torch::Tensor CvImageToTensor(const cv::Mat& image) {
    assert(image.channels() == 1);
    std::vector<int64_t> dims{static_cast<int64_t>(1),
                              static_cast<int64_t>(image.rows),
                              static_cast<int64_t>(image.cols)};
    torch::Tensor tensor_image = torch::from_blob(
```

```
        image.data,
        torch::IntArrayRef(dims),
        torch::TensorOptions().dtype(torch::kFloat).requires_grad(false))
        .clone();  // clone is required to copy data from temporary object
    return tensor_image.to(torch::DeviceType::CUDA);
}
```

The most important part of this function is the call to the `torch::from_blob` function. This function constructs the tensor from values located in memory that are referenced by the pointer that's passed as a first argument. A second argument should be a C++ vector with tensor dimensions values; in our case, we specified a three-dimensional tensor with one channel and two image dimensions. The third argument is the `torch::TensorOptions` object. We specified that the data should be of the floating-point type and that it doesn't require a gradient calculation.

PyTorch uses the auto-gradient approach for model training, and it means that it doesn't construct a static network graph with pre-calculated gradient dependencies. Instead, it uses a dynamic network graph, which means that gradient flow paths for modules are connected and calculated dynamically during the backward pass of the training process. Such an architecture allows us to dynamically change the network's topology and characteristics while running the program. All the libraries we covered previously use a static network graph.

The third interesting PyTorch function that's used here is the `torch::Tensor::to` function, which allows us to move tensors from CPU memory to GPU memory and back.

Now, let's learn how to read dataset files.

Reading dataset files

We read the labels file with the `ReadLabels` function:

```
void MNISTDataset::ReadLabels(const std::string& labels_file_name) {
    std::ifstream labels_file(labels_file_name,
                              std::ios::binary | std::ios::binary);
    labels_file.exceptions(std::ifstream::failbit | std::ifstream::badbit);
    if (labels_file) {
        uint32_t magic_num = 0;
        uint32_t num_items = 0;
        if (read_header(&magic_num, labels_file) &&
            read_header(&num_items, labels_file)) {
            labels_.resize(static_cast<size_t>(num_items));
            labels_file.read(reinterpret_cast<char*>(labels_.data()),
num_items);
```

```
            }
        }
    }
```

This function opens the file in binary mode and reads the header records, the magic number, and the number of items in the file. It also reads all the items directly to the C++ vector. The most important part is to correctly read the header records. To do this, we can use the read_header function:

```
template <class T>
bool read_header(T* out, std::istream& stream) {
    auto size = static_cast<std::streamsize>(sizeof(T));
    T value;
    if (!stream.read(reinterpret_cast<char*>(&value), size)) {
        return false;
    } else {
        // flip endianness
        *out = (value << 24) | ((value << 8) & 0x00FF0000) |
        ((value >> 8) & 0X0000FF00) | (value >> 24);
        return true;
    }
}
```

This function reads the value from the input stream—in our case, the file stream—and flips the endianness. This function also assumes that header records are 32-bit integer values. In a different scenario, we would have to think of other ways to flip the endianness.

Reading the image file

Reading the images file is also pretty straightforward; we read the header records and sequentially read the images. From the header records, we get the total number of images in the file and the image size. Then, we define the OpenCV matrix object that has a corresponding size and type – the one channel image with the underlying byte CV_8UC1 type. We read images from disk in a loop directly to the OpenCV matrix object by passing a pointer, which is returned by the data object variable, to the stream read function. The size of the data we need to read is determined by calling the cv::Mat::size() function, followed by the call to the area function. Then, we use the convertTo OpenCV function to convert an image from unsigned byte type into 32-bit floating-point type. This is important so that we have enough precision while performing math operations in the network layers. We also normalize all the data so that it's in the range [0, 1] by dividing it by 255.

We resize all the images so that they're 32 x 32 in size because the LeNet5 network architecture requires us to hold the original dimensions of the convolution filters:

```cpp
void MNISTDataset::ReadImages(const std::string& images_file_name) {
    std::ifstream images_file(images_file_name,
                             std::ios::binary | std::ios::binary);
    labels_file.exceptions(std::ifstream::failbit | std::ifstream::badbit);
    if (labels_file) {
        uint32_t magic_num = 0;
        uint32_t num_items = 0;
        rows_ = 0;
        columns_ = 0;
        if (read_header(&magic_num, labels_file) &&
                read_header(&num_items, labels_file) &&
                read_header(&rows_, labels_file) &&
                read_header(&columns_, labels_file)) {
            assert(num_items == labels_.size());
            images_.resize(num_items);
            cv::Mat img(static_cast<int>(rows_),
                    static_cast<int>(columns_), CV_8UC1);
            for (uint32_t i = 0; i < num_items; ++i) {
                images_file.read(reinterpret_cast<char*>(img.data),
                        static_cast<std::streamsize>(img.size().area()));
                img.convertTo(images_[i], CV_32F);
                images_[i] /= 255;  // normalize
                cv::resize(images_[i], images_[i],
                    cv::Size(32, 32));  // Resize to 32x32 size
            }
        }
    }
}
```

Now that we've loaded the training data, we have to define our neural network.

Neural network definition

In this example, we chose the LeNet5 architecture, which was developed by Yann LeCun, Leon Bottou, Yosuha Bengio, and Patrick Haffner (http://yann.lecun.com/exdb/lenet/). The architecture's details were discussed earlier in the *Convolution network architecture* section. Here, we'll show you how to implement it with the PyTorch framework.

All the structural parts of the neural networks in the PyTorch framework should be derived from the `torch::nn::Module` class. The following snippet shows the header file of the `LeNet5` class:

```
#include <torch/torch.h>

class LeNet5Impl : public torch::nn::Module {
    public:
    LeNet5Impl();
    torch::Tensor forward(torch::Tensor x);
    private:
    torch::nn::Sequential conv_;
    torch::nn::Sequential full_;
};

TORCH_MODULE(LeNet5);
```

Notice that we defined the intermediate implementation class, which is called `LeNet5Impl`. This is because PyTorch uses a memory management model based on smart pointers, and all the modules should be wrapped in a special type. There is a special class called `torch::nn::ModuleHolder`, which is a wrapper around `std::shared_ptr`, but also defines some additional methods for managing modules. So, if we want to follow all PyTorch conventions and use our module (network) with all PyTorch's functions without any problems, our module class definition should be as follows:

```
class Name : public torch::nn::ModuleHolder<Impl> {}
```

`Impl` is the implementation of our module, which is derived from the `torch::nn::Module` class. There is a special macro that can do this definition for us automatically; it is called `TORCH_MODULE`. We need to specify the name of our module in order to use it.

The most crucial function in this definition is the `forward` function. This function, in our case, takes the network's input and passes it through all the network layers until an output value is returned from this function. If we don't implement a whole network but rather *some* custom layers or *some* structural parts of a network, this function should assume we take the values from the previous layers or other parts of the network as input. Also, if we are implementing a custom module that isn't from the PyTorch standard modules, we should define the `backward` function, which should calculate gradients for our custom operations.

The next essential thing in our module definition is the usage of the
`torch::nn::Sequential` class. This class is used to group sequential layers in the
network and automate the process of forwarding values between them. We broke our
network into two parts, one containing convolutional layers and another containing the
final fully-connected layers.

The PyTorch framework contains many functions for creating layers. For example, the
`torch::nn::Conv2d` function created the two-dimensional convolution layer. Another
way to create a layer in PyTorch is to use the `torch::nn::Functional` function to wrap
some simple function into the layer, which can then be connected with all the outputs of the
previous layer. Notice that activation functions are not part of the neurons in PyTorch and
should be connected as a separate layer. The following code snippet shows the definition of
our network components:

```
static std::vector<int64_t> k_size = {2, 2};
static std::vector<int64_t> p_size = {0, 0};

LeNet5Impl::LeNet5Impl() {
    conv_ = torch::nn::Sequential(
    torch::nn::Conv2d(torch::nn::Conv2dOptions(1, 6, 5)),
    torch::nn::Functional(torch::tanh),
    torch::nn::Functional(torch::avg_pool2d,
        /*kernel_size*/ torch::IntArrayRef(k_size),
            /*stride*/ torch::IntArrayRef(k_size),
           /*padding*/ torch::IntArrayRef(p_size),
          /*ceil_mode*/ false,
    /*count_include_pad*/ false),
    torch::nn::Conv2d(torch::nn::Conv2dOptions(6, 16, 5)),
    torch::nn::Functional(torch::tanh),
    torch::nn::Functional(torch::avg_pool2d,
        /*kernel_size*/ torch::IntArrayRef(k_size),
            /*stride*/ torch::IntArrayRef(k_size),
           /*padding*/ torch::IntArrayRef(p_size),
          /*ceil_mode*/ false,
    /*count_include_pad*/ false),
    torch::nn::Conv2d(torch::nn::Conv2dOptions(16, 120, 5)),
    torch::nn::Functional(torch::tanh));
    register_module("conv", conv_);
    full_ = torch::nn::Sequential(
    torch::nn::Linear(torch::nn::LinearOptions(120, 84)),
    torch::nn::Functional(torch::tanh),
    torch::nn::Linear(torch::nn::LinearOptions(84, 10)));
    register_module("full", full_);
}
```

Here, we initialized two `torch::nn::Sequential` modules. They take a variable number of other modules as arguments for constructors. Notice that for the initialization of the `torch::nn::Conv2d` module, we have to pass the instance of the `torch::nn::Conv2dOptions` class, which can be initialized with the number of input channels, the number of output channels, and the kernel size. We used `torch::tanh` as an activation function; notice that it is wrapped in the `torch::nn::Functional` class instance. The average pooling function is also wrapped in the `torch::nn::Functional` class instance because it is not a layer in the PyTorch C++ API; it's a function. Also, the pooling function takes several arguments, so we bound their fixed values. When a function in PyTorch requires the values of the dimensions, it assumes that we provide an instance of the `torch::IntArrayRef` type. An object of this type behaves as a wrapper for an array with dimension values. We should be careful here because such an array should exist at the same time as the wrapper lifetime; notice that `torch::nn::Functional` stores `torch::IntArrayRef` objects internally. That is why we defined `k_size` and `p_size` as static global variables.

Also, pay attention to the `register_module` function. It associates the string name with the module and registers it in the internals of the parent module. If the module is registered in such a way, we can use a string-based parameter search later (often used when we need to manually manage weights updates during training) and automatic module serialization.

The `torch::nn::Linear` module defines the fully connected layer and should be initialized with an instance of the `torch::nn::LinearOptions` type, which defines the number of inputs and the number of outputs, that is, a count of the layer's neurons. Notice that the last layer returns 10 values, not one label, despite us only having a single target label. This is the standard approach in classification tasks.

The following code shows the `forward` function's implementation, which performs model inference:

```
torch::Tensor LeNet5Impl::forward(at::Tensor x) {
    auto output = conv_->forward(x);
    output = output.view({x.size(0), -1});
    output = full_->forward(output);
    output = torch::log_softmax(output, -1);
    return output;
}
```

This function is implemented as follows:

1. We passed the input tensor (image) to the `forward` function of the sequential convolutional group.
2. Then, we flattened its output with the `view` tensor method because fully connected layers assume that the input is flat. The `view` method takes the new dimensions for the tensor and returns a tensor view without exactly copying the data; *-1* means that we don't care about the dimension's value and that it can be flattened.
3. Then, the flattened output from the convolutional group is passed to the fully connected group.
4. Finally, we applied the softmax function to the final output. We're unable to wrap `torch::log_softmax` in the `torch::nn::Functional` class instance because of multiple overrides.

The softmax function converts a vector, z, of dimension K into a vector, σ, of the same dimension, where each coordinate, σ_i, of the resulting vector is represented by a real number in the range $[0, 1]$ and the sum of the coordinates is 1.

The coordinates are calculated as follows:

$$\sigma(z)_i = \frac{e^{z_i}}{\sum_{k=1}^{K} e^{z_k}}$$

The softmax function is used in machine learning for classification problems when the number of possible classes is more than two (for two classes, a logistic function is used). The coordinates, σ_i, of the resulting vector can be interpreted as the probabilities that the object belongs to the class, i. We chose this function because its results can be directly used for the cross-entropy loss function, which measures the difference between two probability distributions. The target distribution can be directly calculated from the target label value – we create the 10 value's vector of zeros and put one in the place indexed by the label value. Now, we have all the required components to train the neural network.

Network training

First, we should create PyTorch data loader objects for the train and test datasets. The data loader object is responsible for sampling objects from the dataset and making mini-batches from them. This object can be configured as follows:

1. First, we initialize the `MNISTDataset` type objects representing our datasets.
2. Then, we use the `torch::data::make_data_loader` function to create a data loader object. This function takes the `torch::data::DataLoaderOptions` type object with configuration settings for the data loader. We set the mini-batch size equal to 256 items and set 8 parallel data loading threads. We should also configure the sampler type, but in this case, we'll leave the default one – the random sampler.

The following snippet shows how to initialize the train and test data loaders:

```
auto train_images = root_path / "train-images-idx3-ubyte";
auto train_labels = root_path / "train-labels-idx1-ubyte";
auto test_images = root_path / "t10k-images-idx3-ubyte";
auto test_labels = root_path / "t10k-labels-idx1-ubyte";

// initialize train dataset
// -------------------------------------------
MNISTDataset train_dataset(train_images.native(),
                           train_labels.native());

auto train_loader = torch::data::make_data_loader(
        train_dataset.map(torch::data::transforms::Stack<>()),
        torch::data::DataLoaderOptions().batch_size(256).workers(8));

// initialize test dataset
// -------------------------------------------
MNISTDataset test_dataset(test_images.native(),
                          test_labels.native());

auto test_loader = torch::data::make_data_loader(
        test_dataset.map(torch::data::transforms::Stack<>()),
        torch::data::DataLoaderOptions().batch_size(1024).workers(8));
```

Notice that we didn't pass our dataset objects directly to the `torch::data::make_data_loader` function, but we applied the stacking transformation mapping to it. This transformation allows us to sample mini-batches in the form of the `torch::Tensor` object. If we skip this transformation, the mini-batches will be sampled as the C++ vector of tensors. Usually, this isn't very useful because we can't apply linear algebra operations to the whole batch in a vectorized manner.

The next step to initialize the neural network object of the `LeNet5` type, which we defined previously. We'll move it to the GPU to improve training and evaluation performance:

```
LeNet5 model;
model->to(torch::DeviceType::CUDA);
```

When the model of our neural network has been initialized, we can initialize an optimizer. We chose stochastic gradient descent with momentum optimization for this. It is implemented in the `torch::optim::SGD` class. The object of this class should be initialized with model (network) parameters and the `torch::optim::SGDOptions` type object. All `torch::nn::Module` type objects have the `parameters()` method, which returns the `std::vector<Tensor>` object containing all the parameters (weights) of the network. There is also the `named_parameters` method, which returns the dictionary of named parameters. Parameter names are created with the names we used in the `register_module` function call. This method is handy if we want to filter parameters and exclude some of them from the training process.

The `torch::optim::SGDOptions` object can be configured with the values of the learning rate, the weight decay regularization factor, and the momentum value factor:

```
double learning_rate = 0.01;
double weight_decay = 0.0001;  // regularization parameter
torch::optim::SGD optimizer(model->parameters(),
                            torch::optim::SGDOptions(learning_rate)
                                .weight_decay(weight_decay)
                                .momentum(0.5));
```

Now that we have our initialized data loaders, the `network` object, and the `optimizer` object, we are ready to start the training cycle. The following snippet shows the training cycle's implementation:

```
int epochs = 100;
for (int epoch = 0; epoch < epochs; ++epoch) {
    model->train();  // switch to the training mode
    // Iterate the data loader to get batches from the dataset
    int batch_index = 0;
    for (auto& batch : (*train_loader)) {
        // Clear gradients
        optimizer.zero_grad();
        // Execute the model on the input data
        torch::Tensor prediction = model->forward(batch.data);
        // Compute a loss value to estimate error of our model
        // target should have size of [batch_size]
        torch::Tensor loss =
        torch::nll_loss(prediction, batch.target.squeeze(1));
        // Compute gradients of the loss and parameters of our model
```

```
            loss.backward();
            // Update the parameters based on the calculated gradients.
            optimizer.step();
            // Output the loss every 10 batches.
            if (++batch_index % 10 == 0) {
            std::cout << "Epoch: " << epoch << " | Batch: " << batch_index
            << " | Loss: " << loss.item<float>() << std::endl;
        }
    }
}
```

We've made a loop that repeats the training cycle for 100 epochs. At the beginning of the training cycle, we switched our network object to training mode with `model->train()`. For one epoch, we iterate over all the mini-batches provided by the data loader object:

```
for (auto& batch : (*train_loader)){
...
}
```

For every mini-batch, we did the next training steps, cleared the previous gradient values by calling the `zero_grad` method for the optimizer object, made a forward step over the network object, `model->forward(batch.data)`, and computed the loss value with the `nll_loss` function. This function computes the *negative log-likelihood* loss. It takes two parameters: the vector containing the probability that a training sample belongs to a class identified by position in the vector and the numeric class label (number). Then, we called the `backward` method of the loss tensor. It recursively computes the gradients for the overall network. Finally, we called the `step` method for the optimizer object, which updated all the parameters (weights) and their corresponding gradient values. The `step` method only updated the parameters that were used for initialization.

It's common practice to use test or validation data to check the training process after each epoch. We can do this in the following way:

```
model->eval();  // switch to the training mode
unsigned long total_correct = 0;
float avg_loss = 0.0;
for (auto& batch : (*test_loader)) {
    // Execute the model on the input data
    torch::Tensor prediction = model->forward(batch.data);
    // Compute a loss value to estimate error of our model
    torch::Tensor loss =
    torch::nll_loss(prediction, batch.target.squeeze(1));
    avg_loss += loss.sum().item<float>();
    auto pred = std::get<1>(prediction.detach_().max(1));
    total_correct += static_cast<unsigned long>(
    pred.eq(batch.target.view_as(pred)).sum().item<long>());
}
```

```
avg_loss /= test_dataset.size().value();
double accuracy = (static_cast<double>(total_correct) /
test_dataset.size().value());
std::cout << "Test Avg. Loss: " << avg_loss << " | Accuracy: " << accuracy
<< std::endl;
```

First, we switched the model to evaluation mode by calling the `eval` method. Then we iterated over all the batches from the test data loader. For each of these batches, we performed a forward pass over the network, calculating the loss value in the same way that we did for our training process. To estimate the total loss (error) value for the model, we averaged the loss values for all the batches. To get the total loss for the batch, we used `loss.sum().item<float>()`. Here, we summarized the losses for each training sample in the batch and moved it to the CPU floating-point variable with the `item<float>()` method.

Next, we calculate the accuracy value. This is the ratio between correct answers and misclassified ones. Let's go through this calculation with the following approach. First, we determine the predicted class labels by using the `max` method of the tensor object:

```
auto pred = std::get<1>(prediction.detach_().max(1));
```

The `max` method returns a tuple, where the values are the maximum value of each row of the input tensor in the given dimension and the location indices of each maximum value the method found. Then, we compare the predicted labels with the target ones and calculate the number of correct answers:

```
total_correct += static_cast<unsigned
long>(pred.eq(batch.target.view_as(pred)).sum().item<long>());
```

We used the `eq` tensor's method for our comparison. This method returns a boolean vector whose size is equal to the input vector, with values equal to 1 where the vector element components are equal and with values equal to 0 where they're not. To perform the comparison operation, we made a view for the target labels tensor with the same dimensions as the predictions tensor. The `view_as` method is used for this comparison. Then, we calculated the sum of 1s and moved the value to the CPU variable with the `item<long>()` method.

By doing this, we can see that the specialized framework has more options we can configure and is more flexible for neural network development. It has more layer types and supports dynamic network graphs. It also has a powerful specialized linear algebra library that can be used to create new layers, as well as new loss and activation functions. It has powerful abstractions that enable us to work with big training data. One more important thing to note is that it has a C++ API very similar to the Python API, so we can easily port Python programs to C++ and vice versa.

Summary

In this chapter, we looked at what artificial neural networks are, looked at their history, and examined the reasons for their appearance, rise, and fall and why they have become one of the most actively developed machine learning approaches today. We looked at the difference between biological and artificial neurons before learning the basics of the perceptron concept, which was created by Frank Rosenblatt. Then, we discussed the internal features of artificial neurons and networks, such as activation functions and their characteristics, network topology, and convolution layer concepts. We also learned how to train artificial neural networks with the error backpropagation method. We saw how to choose the right loss function for different types of tasks. Then, we discussed the regularization methods that are used to combat overfitting during training.

Finally, we implemented a simple MLP for a regression task with the Shogun, Dlib, and Shark-ML C++ machine learning libraries. Then, we implemented a more advanced convolution network for an image classification task with PyTorch, a specialized neural network framework. This showed us the benefits of specialized frameworks over general-purpose libraries.

In the next chapter, we will discuss **recurrent neural networks (RNNs)**, which are one of the most well-known and practical approaches for working with time-series data and natural language processing. The key differences from other types of neural networks are that the communication between RNN elements forms a directed sequence for processing sequential data and that the recurrent networks can use internal memory to process sequences of arbitrary lengths.

Further reading

- *Loss Functions for Deep Neural Networks in Classification*: `https://arxiv.org/pdf/1702.05659.pdf`.
- *Neural Networks and Deep Learning*, by Michael Nielsen: `http://neuralnetworksanddeeplearning.com/`.
- *Principles of Neurodynamics*, Rosenblatt, Frank (1962), Washington, DC: Spartan Books.
- *Perceptrons*, Minsky M. L. and Papert S. A. 1969. Cambridge, MA: MIT Press.
- *Neural Networks and Learning Machines*, Simon O. Haykin 2008
- *Deep Learning*, Ian Goodfellow, Yoshua Bengio, Aaron Courville 2016
- The PyTorch GitHub page: `https://github.com/pytorch/`.
- The PyTorch documentation site: `https://pytorch.org/docs/`.
- The LibPyTorch (C++) documentation site: `https://pytorch.org/cppdocs/`.

11
Sentiment Analysis with Recurrent Neural Networks

Currently, the **recurrent neural network (RNN)** is one of the most well-known and practical approaches used to construct deep neural networks. They are designed to process time-series data. Typically, data of this nature is found in the following tasks:

- Natural language text processing, such as text analysis and automatic translation
- Automatic speech recognition
- Video processing, for predicting the next frame based on previous frames, and for recognizing emotions
- Image processing, for generating image descriptions
- Time series analysis, for predicting fluctuations in exchange rates or company stock prices

In recurrent networks, communications between elements form a directed sequence. Thanks to this, it becomes possible to process a time series of events or sequential spatial chains. Unlike multilayer perceptrons, recurrent networks can use their internal memory to process sequences of arbitrary lengths. At the time of writing, many different architectural solutions for recurrent networks (from simple to complex) have been proposed. Currently, the most widespread recurrent network architectures are **long short-term memory (LSTM)** and **gated recurrent unit (GRU)**.

In this chapter, we will consider the main architectural features of recurrent networks and learn how recurrent networks are used to process natural language; describe algorithms for converting elements of a natural language into mathematical abstractions; and write a program to evaluate the emotional characteristics of the language to perform sentiment analysis on movie reviews.

Specifically, the following topics will be covered in this chapter:

- An overview of the RNN concept
- Training RNNs using the concept of backpropagation through time
- Exploring RNN architectures
- Understanding natural language processing with RNNs
- Sentiment analysis example with RNNs

Technical requirements

The following are the technical requirements for this chapter:

- PyTorch library
- Modern C++ compiler with C++17 support
- CMake build system version >= 3.8

The code files for this chapter can be found at the following GitHub repo: `https://github.com/PacktPublishing/Hands-On-Machine-Learning-with-CPP/tree/master/Chapter11/pytorch`

An overview of the RNN concept

The goal of an RNN is consistent data usage under the assumption that there is some dependency between consecutive data elements. In traditional neural networks, it is understood that all inputs and outputs are independent. But for many tasks, this independence is not suitable. If you want to predict the next word in a sentence, for example, knowing the sequence of words preceding it is the most reliable way to do so. RNNs are recurrent because they perform the same task for each element of the sequence, and the output is dependent on previous calculations.

In other words, RNNs are networks that have feedback loops and memory. RNNs use memory to take into account prior information and calculations results. The idea of a recurrent network can be represented as follows:

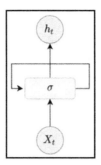

In the preceding diagram, a fragment of the neural network, σ (a layer of neurons with a sigmoidal activation function), takes the input value, x_t, and returns the value, h_t. The presence of feedback allows us to transfer information from one timestep of the network to another timestep. A recurrent network can be considered several copies of the same network, each of which transfers information to a subsequent copy. Here's what happens when we expand the feedback:

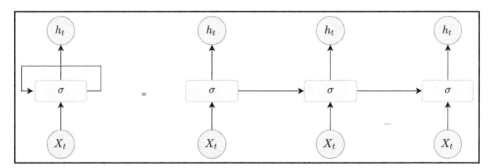

This can be represented in further detail as follows:

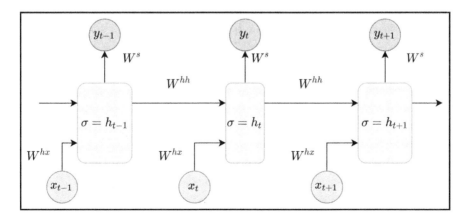

Here, we can see the input data vectors, x_{t-1}, x_t, x_{t+1}. Each vector at each step has a hidden state vector, h_{t-1}, h_t, h_{t+1}. We call this pairing a **module**. The hidden state in each RNN module is a function of the input vector and the hidden state vector from the previous step, as follows:

$$h_t = \sigma(W^{hh} h_{t-1} + W^{hx} x_t)$$

If we look at the superscript, we can see that there is a weight matrix, W^{hx}, which we multiply by the input value, and there is a recurrent weight matrix, W^{hh}, which is multiplied by a hidden state vector from the previous step. These recurrent weight matrices are the same at every step. This concept is a key component of an RNN. If you think about this carefully, this approach is significantly different from, say, traditional two-layer neural networks. In this case, we usually select a separate matrix, W, for each layer: W_1 and W_2. Here, the recurrent matrix of weights is the same for the entire network. σ denotes a neural network layer with a sigmoid as an activation function.

Furthermore, another weight matrix, W^s, is used to obtain the output values, y, of each module, which are multiplied by h:

$$y_t = softmax(W^s h_t)$$

One of the attractive ideas of RNNs is that they potentially know how to connect previous information with the task at hand. For example, in the task of video flow analysis, knowledge of the previous frame of the video can help in understanding the current frame (knowing previous object positions can help us predict their new positions). The ability of RNNs to use prior information is not absolute and usually depends on some circumstances, which we will discuss in the following sections.

Sometimes, to complete the current task, we need only recent information. Consider, for example, a language model trying to predict the next word based on the previous words. If we want to predict the last word in the phrase, *clouds are floating in the **sky***, we don't need a broader context; in this case, the last word is almost certainly *sky*. In this case, we could say that the distance between the relevant information and the subject of prediction is small, which means that RNNs can learn how to use information from the past.

But sometimes, we need more context. Suppose we want to predict the last word in the phrase, *I speak French*. Further back in the same text is the phrase, *I grew up in France*. The context, therefore, suggests that the last word should likely be the name of the country's language. However, this may have been much further back in the text – possibly on a different paragraph or page – and as that gap between the crucial context and the point of its application grows, RNNs lose their ability to bind information accurately.

In theory, RNNs should not have problems with long-term processing dependencies. A person can carefully select network parameters to solve artificial problems of this type. Unfortunately, in practice, training the RNN with these parameters seems impossible due to the vanishing gradient problem. This problem was investigated in detail by Sepp Hochreiter (1991) and Yoshua Bengio et al. (1994). They found that the lower the gradient that's used in the backpropagation algorithms, the more difficult it is for the network to update its weights and the longer the training time will be. There are different reasons why we can get low gradient values during the training process, but one of the main reasons is the network size. For RNNs, it is the most crucial parameter because it depends on the size of the input sequence we use. The longer the sequence that we use is, the bigger the network we get is. Fortunately, there are methods we can use to deal with this problem in RNNs, all of which we will discuss later in this chapter.

Training RNNs using the concept of backpropagation through time

At the time of writing, for training neural networks nearly everywhere, the error backpropagation algorithm is used. The result of performing inference on the training set of examples (in our case, the set of subsequences) is checked against the expected result (labeled data). The difference between the actual and expected values is called an error. This error is propagated to the network weights in the opposite direction. Thus, the network adapts to labeled data, and the result of this adaptation works well for the data that the network did not meet in the initial training examples (generalization hypothesis).

In the case of a recurrent network, we have several options regarding which network outputs we can consider the error. This section describes the two main approaches: the first considers the output value of the last cell, while the second considers the outputs of all the cells from the last layer. Let's have a look at these approaches one by one:

- In the first approach, we can calculate the error by comparing the output of the last cell of the subsequence with the target value for the current training sample. This approach works well for the classification task. For example, if we need to determine the sentiment of a tweet (in other words, we need to classify the polarity of a tweet; is the expressed opinion negative, positive, or neutral?). To do this, we select tweets and place them into three categories: negative, positive, and neutral. The output of the cell should be three numbers: the weights of the categories. The tweet could also be marked with three different numbers: the probabilities of the tweet belonging to the corresponding category. After calculating the error on a subset of the data, we could backpropagate it through the output and cell states.

- In the second approach, we can read the error immediately at the output of the cell's calculation for each element of the subsequence. This approach is well suited for the task of predicting the next element of a sequence from what came previously. Such an approach can be used, for example, in the problem of determining anomalies in time series data, in the task of predicting the next character in a text, or for natural language translation tasks. Error backpropagation is also possible through outputs and cell states, but in this case, we need to calculate as many errors as we have outputs. This means that we should also have target values for each sequence element we want to predict.

Unlike a regular fully connected neural network, a recurrent network is deep in the sense that the error propagates not only in the backward direction from the network outputs to its weights but also through the connections between timestep states. Therefore, the length of the input subsequence determines the network's depth. There is a variant of the method of error backpropagating called **backpropagation through time** (BPTT), which propagates the error through the state of the recurrent network.

The idea behind BPTT is quite simple – we unfold a recurrent network for a certain number of timesteps, which converts it into a usual deep neural network, which is then trained by the usual backpropagation method. Notice that this method assumes that we're using the same parameters for all timesteps. Furthermore, weight gradients are summarized with each other when the error propagates in a backward direction through the states (steps). They are duplicated during the initial configuration of the network n times, as though adding layers to a regular feedforward network. The number of steps needed to unfold the RNN corresponds to the length of the input sequence. If the input sequence is very long, then the computational cost of training the network increases.

The following diagram shows the basic principle of the BPTT approach:

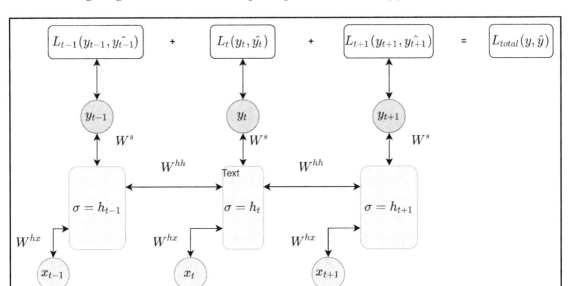

A modified version of the algorithm, called **truncated backpropagation through time (TBPTT)**, is used to reduce computational complexity. Its essence lies in the fact that we limit the number of forward propagation steps, and on the backward pass, we update the weights for a limited set of conditions. This version of the algorithm has two additional hyperparameters: *k1*, which is the number of forward pass timesteps between updates, and *k2*, which is the number of timesteps that apply BPTT. The number of times should be large enough to capture the internal structure of the problem the network learned. The error is accumulated only for *k2* states.

These training methods for RNNs are highly susceptible to the effect of bursting or vanishing gradients. Accordingly, as a result of backpropagation, the error can become very large, or conversely, fade away. These problems are associated with the great depth of the network, as well as the accumulation of errors. The specialized cells of RNNs were invented to avoid such drawbacks during training. The first such cell was the LSTM, and now there is a wide range of alternatives; one of the most popular among them is GRU. The following sections will describe different types of RNN architectures in detail.

Exploring RNN architectures

In this section, we will have a look at various kinds of RNN architectures. We will also understand how they differ from each other based on their nature and implementations.

LSTM

Long short-term memory (**LSTM**) is a special kind of RNN architecture that's capable of learning long-term dependencies. It was introduced by Sepp Hochreiter and Jürgen Schmidhuber in 1997 and was then improved on and presented in the works of many other researchers. It perfectly solves many of the various problems we've discussed, and are now widely used.

In LSTM, each cell has a memory cell and three gates (filters): an input gate, an output gate, and a forgetting gate. The purpose of these gates is to protect information. The input gate determines how much information from the previous layer should be stored in the cell. The output gate determines how much information the following layers should receive. The forget gate, no matter how strange it may seem, performs a useful function. For example, if the network studies a book and moves to a new chapter, some words from the old chapter can be safely forgotten:

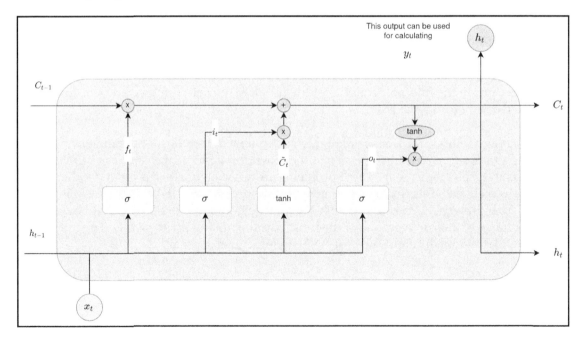

The critical component of LSTM is the cell state – a horizontal line running along the top of the circuit. The state of the cell resembles a conveyor belt. It goes directly through the whole chain, participating in only a few linear transformations. Information can easily flow through it, without being modified.

However, LSTM can remove information from the state of a cell. Structures called gates or filters govern this process. Gates or filters let you skip information based on some conditions. They consist of a sigmoidal neural network layer and pointwise multiplication operation:

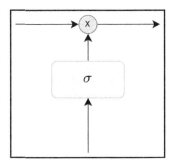

The sigmoidal layer returns numbers from zero to one, which indicates what proportion of each block of information should be skipped further along the network. A zero value, in this case, means *skip everything*, whereas one means *keep everything*.

There are three such gates in LSTM that allow you to save and control the state of a cell. The first information flow stage in the LSTM determines what information can be discarded from the state of the cell. This decision is made by the sigmoidal layer, called the **forget gate layer**. It looks at the state of the cell and returns a number from 0 to 1 for each value. 1 means *keep everything*, while 0 means *skip everything*:

$$f_t = \sigma(W_f\,[h_{t-1}, x_t] + b_f)$$

The next flow stage in the LSTM decides what new information should be stored in the cell state. This phase consists of two parts. First, a sigmoidal layer called the **input layer gate** determines which values should be updated. Then, the *tanh* layer builds a vector of new candidate values, $\tilde{C}_t$, which can be added to the state of the cell:

$$i_t = \sigma(W_i\,[h_{t-1}, x_t] + b_i)$$
$$\tilde{C}_t = tanh(W_C\,[h_{t-1}, x_t] + b_C)$$

To replace the old state of the cell with the new state, we need to multiply the old state of C_{t-1} by f_t, forgetting what we decided to forget. Then, we add $i_t\tilde{C}_t$ (the new candidate values, multiplied by how much we want to update each status value):

$$C_t = f_t C_{t-1} + i_t\tilde{C}_t$$

The output values are based on our cell state, and gate functions (filters) should be applied to them. First, we apply a sigmoidal layer named the output gate, which decides what information from the state of the cell we should output. Then, the state values of the cell pass through the *tanh* layer to get values from **-1** to **1** as the output, which is multiplied by the output values of the sigmoid layer. This allows you to output only the required information:

$$o_t = \sigma(W_o\,[h_{t-1}, x_t] + b_o)$$
$$h_t = o_t\,tanh(C_t))$$

There are many variations of LSTM based on this idea. Let's take a look at some of them now.

GRUs

The GRU is a variation of the LSTM architecture. They have one less gate (filter), and the connections are implemented differently. In this variant, the forget gate and the input gate are combined into one *update gate*. Besides this, the cell state and the latent state are combined. The resulting model is simpler than standard LSTM models, and as a result, it is gaining more popularity:

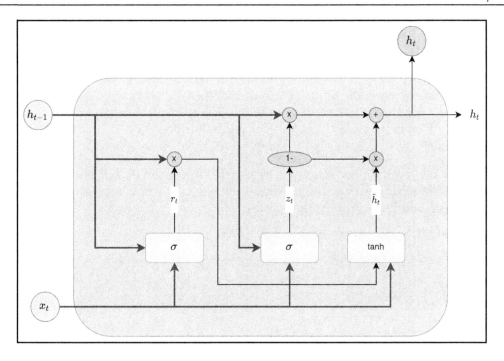

The updated gate determines how much information should remain from the last state and how much should be taken from the previous layer:

$$z_t = \sigma(W_z\,[h_{t-1}, x_t] + b_z)$$

The reset gate works like the forget gate:

$$r_t = \sigma(W_r\,[h_{t-1}, x_t] + b_r)$$

The *tanh* layer builds a vector of new candidate values, $\tilde{h}_t$, that can be added to the state of the cell. The values of the *reset gate* are applied to the values of the previous state:

$$\tilde{h}_t = tanh(W_h\,[r_t h_{t-1}, x_t] + b_h)$$

A new state is obtained based on a combination of previous state values and new candidate values. The *update gate* values control in what proportion state values should be used:

$$h_t = (1 - z_t)h_{t-1} + z_t \tilde{h}_t$$

Bidirectional RNN

Bidirectional RNNs, LSTMs, and GRUs (BiRNN, BiLSTM, and BiGRU) are not so different from their unidirectional variants. The difference is that these networks use not only data from the *past*, but also from the *future* of the series. When we work with a sequence in a recurrent network, we usually feed one element followed by the next and pass on the previous state of the network as the input. The natural direction of this process takes place from left to right.

In many cases, however, the sequence has already been given in its entirety from the very beginning. Due to this, we can pass it to the neural network from both sides with two neural networks, and then combine their result:

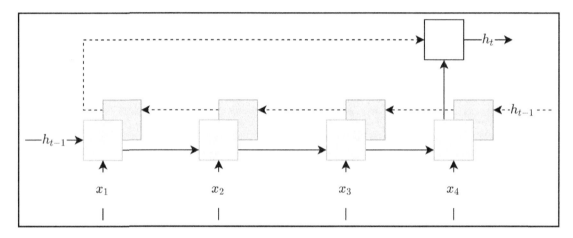

This architecture is called a bidirectional RNN. Its quality is even higher than ordinary recurrent networks because there is a broader context for each element of the sequence. There are now two contexts – one comes before, while one comes after. For many tasks, this adds quality, especially for tasks related to processing natural language.

Multilayer RNN

Multilayer RNNs (also called deep RNNs) is another concept. The idea here is that we add additional RNNs on top of the source network, where each added RNN is a different layer. The output of the hidden state of the first (or lowest) RNN is the input for the RNN of the next layer above it. The general prediction is usually calculated from the latent state of the most recent (highest current output) layer:

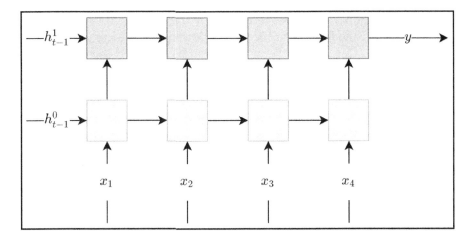

The preceding diagram shows a multilayer unidirectional RNN, where the layer number is indicated as superscript. Also, note that each layer needs its own initial hidden state, h_0^L.

Now that we've learned about the various architectures of RNN, let's take a look at another aspect of RNN in natural language processing.

Understanding natural language processing with RNNs

Natural language processing (NLP) is a subfield of computer science that studies algorithms for processing and analyzing human languages. There are a variety of algorithms and approaches for teaching computers to solve a task that assumes using human language data. Let's start with the basic principles used in this area. After all, the computer does not know how to read, so the first issue with NLP is that you have to teach a machine to work with natural language words. One idea that comes to mind is to encode words with numbers in the order they exist in the dictionary. This idea is fairly simple – numbers are endless, and you can number and renumber words with ease. But this idea has a significant drawback; the words in the dictionary are in alphabetical order, and when we add new words, we need to renumber a lot of words again. Such an approach is computationally inefficient, but even this is not an important issue. The important thing is that the spelling of the word has nothing to do with its meaning. The words *rooster*, *hen*, and *chick* have very little in common with each other alphabetically, and are far away from each other in the dictionary, even though they can determine the male, female, and young of the same bird.

Therefore, we can distinguish two types of proximity measures for words: lexical and semantic. In other words, the lexicographic (dictionary) order doesn't preserve the semantic proximity of words. For example, the word *allium* can be followed by the word *allocate* in a dictionary, but they don't have any common semantics. Another example of lexically similar words is *rain* and *pain*, but they are also usually used in different contexts. As shown in the chicken example, words that are very different lexically (*rooster* and *hen*) can have a lot of semantic similarity (they refer to birds), even if they are very distant from each in the dictionary. So, these proximity measures are independent.

To be able to represent semantic proximity, we can use embedding; that is, associating a word with a vector and displaying its meaning in the *space of meanings*. Embedding is where we map an arbitrary entity to a specific vector; for example, a node in a graph, an object in a picture, or the definition of a word.

There are many approaches to creating embedding for words. Over the next few subsections, we'll consider the two most widespread: Word2Vec and **global vectors (GloVe)**.

Word2Vec

In 2013, Tomash Mikolov proposed a new approach to word embedding, which he called Word2Vec. His approach is based on another crucial hypothesis, which in science is usually called the distributional hypothesis or locality hypothesis: *words that are similar in meaning occur in similar contexts* (Rubenstein and Goodenough, 1965). Proximity measure, in this case, is understood very broadly as the fact that only semantically similar words can be in proximity. For example, the phrase *clockwork alarm clock* is acceptable in this model, but *clockwork orange* is not. The words *clockwork* and *orange* can't be easily combined by semantics. The model proposed by Mikolov is very simple (and therefore useful)—we predict the probability of a word from its environment (context). Specifically, we learn word vectors so that the probability assigned by the model to a word is close to the probability of meeting this word in the environment (context) of the original text.

The training process is organized as follows:

1. The corpus is read, and the occurrence of each word in the corpus is calculated (that is, the number of times each word occurs in the corpus).
2. An array of words is sorted by frequency, and rare words are deleted (they are also called *hapax*).

3. The subsentence is read from the corpus, and subsampling of the most frequent words is done. A subsentence is a specific fundamental element of the corpus, usually just a sentence, but it can be a paragraph or even an entire article. Subsampling is the process of removing the most frequent words from the analysis, which speeds up the learning process of the algorithm and contributes to a significant increase in the quality of the resulting model.

4. We go through the subsentence with a window (the window size is set as a parameter). This means that we take 2k + 1 words sequentially, with the word that should be predicted in the center. The surrounding words are a context of length, k, on each side.

5. The selected words are used to train a simple feedforward neural network, usually with one hidden layer and with the hierarchical softmax and/or negative sampling activation function for the output layer. For the hidden layer, a linear activation function is used.

6. The target value for the prediction is the word in the center of the window that needs to be predicted.

7. Words during the training process are usually presented using one-hot encoding.

8. After training the network on the entire training corpus, each word in our model should be associated with a unique vector that we change in the process of training our model.

9. The size of the vector that corresponds to the word is equal to the size of the hidden layer of the learning network, while the values of the vector are the values of the outputs of the hidden layer neurons. These values can be obtained after we feed some training samples to the network input.

Although the model does not explicitly include any semantics – only the statistical properties of the corpus of texts – it turns out that the trained Word2Vec model can capture some semantic properties of words. Currently, there are various modifications of this algorithm, such as the Doc2Vec algorithm, which learns paragraph and document embeddings.

GloVe

Notice that the Word2Vec algorithm only takes the local context of words into account. It doesn't use global statistics throughout the training corpus. For example, the words *the* and *cat* will often be used together, but Word2Vec is unable to determine whether the word *the* is a standard article or whether the words *the* and *cat* have a strong implicit connection. This problem leads to the idea of using global statistics.

For example, **latent semantic analysis (LSA)** calculates the embeddings for words by factorizing the term-document matrix using singular decomposition. However, even though this method takes advantage of global information, the obtained vectors do not show the same generalization properties as those obtained using Word2Vec. For example, vectors obtained using Word2Vec have such a generalizing property that, by using arithmetic operations, you can generate the following kind of result: king - man + woman = queen.

There is also another popular algorithm called **GloVe**. GloVe aims to achieve two goals:

- Create word vectors that capture meaning in the vector space
- Take advantage of global statistics, not just use local information

Unlike Word2Vec, which is trained using a sentence's flow, GloVe is trained based on a co-occurrence matrix and trains word vectors so that their difference predicts co-occurrence ratios.

First, we need to build a co-occurrence matrix. It is possible to calculate the co-occurrence matrix using a fixed-size window to make GloVe also take into account the local context. For example, the sentence *The cat sat on the mat*, with a window size of 2, can be converted into the following co-occurrence matrix:

the	cat	sat	on	mat
the	2	1	1	1
cat	1	1	1	0
sat	2	1	1	0
on	1	1	1	1
mat	1	0	1	1

Notice that the matrix is symmetrical because when the word *cat* appears in the context of the word *sat*, the opposite happens too.

To connect the vectors with the statistics we calculated previously, we can formulate the following principle: the coincidental relationship between two words, in terms of context, are closely related to their meaning. For example, consider the words *ice* and *steam*. Ice and steam differ in their state but are similar in that they are forms of water. Therefore, we can expect that water-related words (such as *moisture* and *wet*) will be displayed equally in the context of the words *ice* and *steam*. In contrast, words such as *cold* and *solid* are likely to appear next to the word *ice*, but not the word *steam*.

Let's denote the co-occurrence matrix as X. In this case X_{ij} refers to the elements i and j, in X, which is equal to the number of times the word j appears in the context of the word i. We can also define $X_i = \sum_l X_{il}$ as the total number of words that appeared in the context of the word i.

Next, we need to generate an expression to estimate co-occurrence ratios using word vectors. To do this, we start with the following relationship:

$$F(w_i, w_j, \tilde{w}_k) \approx \frac{P_{ij}}{P_{jk}}$$

Here, P_{ij} denotes the probability of the appearance of the word j in the context of the word i, which can be expressed as follows:

$$P_{ij} = \frac{\text{number of times j appeared in context of i}}{\text{number of words that appeared in context of i}} = \frac{X_{ij}}{X_i}$$

F is an unknown function, which takes embeddings for the words i, k, and j. Note that there are two kinds of embedding: input for context and output for the target word (expressed as w and $\tilde{w}$, respectively). These two kinds of embeddings are a minor detail, but nonetheless important to remember.

Now, the question is, *how do we generate the function, F?* As you may recall, one of the goals of GloVe was to create vectors with values that have a good generalizing ability, which can be expressed using simple arithmetic operations (such as addition and subtraction). We must choose F so that the vectors that we get when using this function match this property.

Since we want the use of arithmetic operations between vectors to be meaningful, we have to make the input for the function, F, the result of an arithmetic operation between vectors. The easiest way to do this is to apply F to the difference between the vectors we are comparing, as follows:

$$F(w_i - w_j, \tilde{w}_k) \approx \frac{P_{ij}}{P_{jk}}$$

To specify a linear relationship between $w_i - w_j$ and $\tilde{w}_k$, we use the dot-product operation:

$$F(\text{dot}(w_i - w_j, \tilde{w}_k)) \approx \frac{P_{ij}}{P_{jk}}$$

Now, to simplify the expression and evaluate the function, F, we use the following approach.

First, we can take the logarithm of the probabilities ratio to convert the ratio into the difference between the probabilities. Then, we can express the fact that some words are more common than others by adding an offset term for each word.

Given these considerations, we obtain the following equation:

$$\text{dot}(w_i - w_j, \tilde{w}_k) + b_i - b_j = \log(P_{ik}) - \log(Pjk)$$

We can convert this equation into an equation for a single record from the co-occurrence matrix:

$$\text{dot}(w_i, \tilde{w}_k) + b_i = \log(P_{ik}) = \log(X_{ik}) - \log(X_i)$$

By doing this, we transform the last term of the equation on the right-hand side into the bias term. By adding the output bias for symmetry, we get the following formula:

$$\text{dot}(w_i, \tilde{w}_k) + b_i + \tilde{b}_k = \log(X_{ik})$$

This formula is the central GloVe equation. But there is one problem with this equation: it equally evaluates all co-occurrences of words. However, in reality, not all co-occurrences have the same quality of information. Co-occurrences that are rare tend to be noisy and unreliable, so we want stronger weights to be attached to more frequent co-occurrences. On the other hand, we do not want frequent co-occurrences to dominate the loss function entirely, so we do not want the estimates to be solely dependent on frequency.

As a result of experimentation, Jeffrey Pennington, Richard Socher, and Christopher D. Manning, the authors of the original article, *GloVe: Global Vectors for Word Representation*, found that the following weight function works well:

$$\text{weight}(x) = \min(1, (x/x_{max})^{\frac{3}{4}})$$

Using this function, we can transform the loss function into the following form:

$$J = \sum_{ij} \text{weight}(X_{ij})(\text{dot}(w_i, \tilde{w}_j) + b_i + \tilde{b}_k - \log(X_{ij}))^2)$$

Now, the task of finding embedding vectors is reduced to minimizing this loss function. This operation can be accomplished, for example, using the stochastic gradient descent approach.

In the next section, we will develop a sentiment analysis model with the `PyTorch` library using the RNN principles we learned about in the previous sections.

Sentiment analysis example with an RNN

In this section, we are going to build a machine learning model that can detect review sentiment (detect whether a review is positive or negative) using PyTorch. As a training set, we are going to use the Large Movie Review Dataset, which contains a set of 25,000 movie reviews for training and 25,000 for testing, both of which are highly polarized.

First, we have to develop parser and data loader classes to move the dataset to memory in a format suitable for use with PyTorch.

Let's start with the parser. The dataset we have is organized as follows: there are two folders for the train and test sets, and each of these folders contains two child folders named `pos` and `neg`, which is where the positive review files and negative review files are placed. Each file in the dataset contains exactly one review, and its sentiment is determined by the folder it's placed in. In the following code sample, we will define the interface for the reader class:

```
class ImdbReader {
    public:
    ImdbReader(const std::string& root_path);
    size_t GetPosSize() const;
    size_t GetNegSize() const;
    size_t GetMaxSize() const;
    using Review = std::vector<std::string>;
    const Review& GetPos(size_t index) const;
    const Review& GetNeg(size_t index) const;
    private:
    using Reviews = std::vector<Review>;
    void ReadDirectory(const std::string& path, Reviews& reviews);
    private:
    Reviews pos_samples_;
    Reviews neg_samples_;
    size_t max_size_{0};
};
```

We defined the `Review` type as a vector of strings. There are also two more vectors, `pos_samples_` and `neg_samples_`, which contain the reviews that were read from the corresponding folders.

We will assume that the object of this class should be initialized with the path to the root folder where one of the datasets is placed (the training set or testing set). We can initialize this in the following way:

```cpp
int main(int argc, char** argv) {
    if (argc > 0) {
        auto root_path = fs::path(argv[1]);
        . . .
        ImdbReader train_reader(root_path / "train");
        ImdbReader test_reader(root_path / "test");
    }
    . . .
}
```

The most important parts of this class are the constructor and the `ReadDirectory` methods. The constructor is the main point wherein we fill the containers, `pos_samples_` and `neg_samples_`, with actual reviews from the `pos` and `neg` folders:

```cpp
namespace fs = std::filesystem;
. . .
ImdbReader::ImdbReader(const std::string& root_path) {
    auto root = fs::path(root_path);
    auto neg_path = root / "neg";
    auto pos_path = root / "pos";
    if (fs::exists(neg_path) && fs::exists(pos_path)) {
        auto neg = std::async(std::launch::async,
        [&]() { ReadDirectory(neg_path, neg_samples_); });
        auto pos = std::async(std::launch::async,
        [&]() { ReadDirectory(pos_path, pos_samples_); });
        neg.get();
        pos.get();
    } else {
        throw std::invalid_argument("ImdbReader incorrect path");
    }
}
```

The `ReadDirectory` method implements the logic for iterating files in the given directory. It also reads them, tokenizes lines, and fills the dataset container, which is then passed as a function parameter. The following code shows the `ReadDirectory` method's implementation:

```
void ImdbReader::ReadDirectory(const std::string& path, Reviews& reviews) {
    std::regex re("[^a-zA-Z0-9]");
    std::sregex_token_iterator end;
    for (auto& entry : fs::directory_iterator(path)) {
        if (entry.is_regular_file()) {
            std::ifstream file(entry.path());
            if (file) {
                std::string text;
                {
                    std::stringstream buffer;
                    buffer << file.rdbuf();
                    text = buffer.str();
                }
                std::sregex_token_iterator token(text.begin(), text.end(),
                                                 re, -1);
                Review words;
                for (; token != end; ++token) {
                    if (token->length() > 1) {  // don't use one letter
                                                // words
                        words.push_back(*token);
                    }
                }
                max_size_ = std::max(max_size_, words.size());
                reviews.push_back(std::move(words));
            }
        }
    }
}
```

We used the standard library directory iterator class, `fs::directory_iterator`, to get every file in the folder. The object of this class returns the object of the `fs::directory_entry` class, and this object can be used to determine whether this is a regular file with the `is_regular_file` method. We got the file path of this entry with the `path` method.

We read the whole file to one string object using the `rdbuf` method of the `std::ifstream` type object. Then, we tokenized (split the distinct words) this string with the use of a regular expression. The `std::sregex_token_iterator` class in the C++ standard library can be used precisely for this purpose. The object of this class was initialized with the iterator range of the target text string we need to split, the regular expression object, and the index of the sub-match that the object will search. We defined the `re` object (which matched everything that was not the alpha-numeric character) with regular expressions. As a sub-match index, we used *-1* because *0* represents the entire match and *-1* represents the characters between matches. Iterating through the tokens, we selected words with a length greater than one in order to reduce computational complexity and eliminate meaningless characters. All the relevant tokens were placed in the `Review` container type, which represents a single review. This review was also placed in the top-level container, which is passed as a function argument. Notice that we used the `std::move` function to move containers in order to eliminate a heavy copy operation.

After we've read the train and test datasets, we need to build a word vocabulary where each string representing a word matches a unique index. We are going to use such a vocabulary to convert string-based reviews into integer-based representations that can be used with linear algebra abstractions. We can build such a vocabulary from the whole set of words that appeared in the reviews, but this would produce a huge corpus; in practice, many words are used very rarely, so they produce unnecessary noise. To avoid these issues, we can only use a certain number of the most frequently used words. To select such words, we need to calculate the frequencies of all the words in the reviews. We can do this by using the hash map object:

```
using WordsFrequencies = std::unordered_map<std::string, size_t>;
```

We can calculate frequencies by accumulating the number of times words appear in the second member of the pair from the map. This is done by iterating through all of the words in the reviews:

```
void GetWordsFrequencies(const ImdbReader& reader,
                         WordsFrequencies& frequencies) {
    for (size_t i = 0; i < reader.GetPosSize(); ++i) {
        const ImdbReader::Review& review = reader.GetPos(i);
        for (auto& word : review) {
            frequencies[word] += 1;
        }
    }
    for (size_t i = 0; i < reader.GetNegSize(); ++i) {
        const ImdbReader::Review& review = reader.GetNeg(i);
        for (auto& word : review) {
            frequencies[word] += 1;
        }
```

```
        }
    }
```

This function is used in the following way:

```
WordsFrequencies words_frequencies;
GetWordsFrequencies(train_reader, words_frequencies);
GetWordsFrequencies(test_reader, words_frequencies);
```

After we have calculated the number of occurrences of each word in the datasets, we can select a specific number of the most frequently used ones. Let's set the size of the vocabulary to 25,000 words:

```
int64_t vocab_size = 25000;
```

To select the top 25,000 most frequent words, we have to sort all the words by their frequency. To perform this operation, we need to use a container other than a hash map (because it is an unordered container). Therefore, we will use the C++ vector class. It should be parameterized with a pair type containing the frequency value and the iterator to the original item. This iterator should point to the element in the hash map. Such an approach will allow us to reduce copying operations. Then, we can use the standard sorting algorithm with a custom comparison function. This concept is fully implemented in the SelectTopFrequencies function:

```
void SelectTopFrequencies(WordsFrequencies& vocab, int64_t new_size) {
    using FreqItem = std::pair<size_t, WordsFrequencies::iterator>;
    std::vector<FreqItem> freq_items;
    freq_items.reserve(vocab.size());
    auto i = vocab.begin();
    auto e = vocab.end();
    for (; i != e; ++i) {
        freq_items.push_back({i->second, i});
    }
    std::sort(
        freq_items.begin(), freq_items.end(),
        [](const FreqItem& a, const FreqItem& b)
        { return a.first < b.first; });
    std::reverse(freq_items.begin(), freq_items.end());
    freq_items.resize(static_cast<size_t>(new_size));
    WordsFrequencies new_vocab;
    for (auto& item : freq_items) {
        new_vocab.insert({item.second->first, item.first});
    }
    vocab = new_vocab;
}
```

The standard library's `sort` function assumes that a passed comparison function returns true if the first argument is less than the second. So, after sorting, we reversed the result in order to move the most frequent words to the beginning of the container. Then, we simply resized the `freq_items` container to the desired length. The last step in this function was creating the new `WordsFrequencies` type object from the items representing the most frequently used words. Also, we replaced the content of the original `vocab` object with the `new_vocab` object content. The following code shows how to use this function:

```
SelectTopFrequencies(words_frequencies, vocab_size);
```

Before we assign indices to the words, we have to decide how we are going to generate embeddings for them. This is an important issue because the indices we assign will be used to access the word embeddings. In this example, we used the pre-trained GloVe word embeddings. We can find different variants on the original article's site: `https://nlp.stanford.edu/projects/glove/`.

Word vectors learned from the Wikipedia 2014 materials and Gigaword 5 text corpora, which contain 6 billion tokens and 100-dimensional vectors, was chosen for this example. As in the previous case, we need to create a parser for the downloaded embeddings. The downloaded embeddings file contains one key-value pair per line, where the key is the word and the value is the 100-dimensional vector. All the items in the line are separated by spaces, so the format look likes this: word $x_0 x_1 x_2 ... x99$.

The following code defines the `class` interface for the GloVe embedding's parser:

```
class GloveDict {
  public:
    GloveDict(const std::string& file_name, int64_t vec_size);
    torch::Tensor Get(const std::string& key) const;
    torch::Tensor GetUnknown() const;
  private:
    torch::Tensor unknown_;
    std::unordered_map<std::string, torch::Tensor> dict_;
};
```

The `GloveDict` class constructor takes the filename and the size of the embedding vector. There are two methods being used here. The `Get` method returns the `torch::Tensor` type object for the embedding that corresponds to the input word. The second method, `GetUnknown`, returns the tensor representing the embedding for the words that don't exist in the embeddings list. In our case, this is the zero tensor.

The main work is done by the constructor of the class, where we read a file with GloVe vectors, parse it, and initialize the `dict_` map object with words in the keys role and embed tensors as values:

```
GloveDict::GloveDict(const std::string& file_name, int64_t vec_size) {
    std::ifstream file;
    file.exceptions(std::ifstream::badbit);
    file.open(file_name);
    if (file) {
        auto sizes = {static_cast<long>(vec_size)};
        std::string line;
        std::vector<float> vec(static_cast<size_t>(vec_size));
        unknown_ = torch::zeros(sizes, torch::dtype(torch::kFloat));
        std::string key;
        std::string token;
        while (std::getline(file, line)) {
            if (!line.empty()) {
                std::stringstream line_stream(line);
                size_t num = 0;
                while (std::getline(line_stream, token, ' ')) {
                    if (num == 0) {
                        key = token;
                    } else {
                        vec[num - 1] = std::stof(token);
                    }
                    ++num;
                }
                assert(num == (static_cast<size_t>(vec_size) + 1));
                torch::Tensor tvec = torch::from_blob(
                    vec.data(), sizes,
                    torch::TensorOptions().dtype(torch::kFloat));
                dict_[key] = tvec.clone();
            }
        }
    }
}
```

In this method, we read a file line by line with the `std::getline` function from the standard library. We defined one object of the `std::vector<float>` type to hold the embedding vector values, and we initialized the `unknown_` tensor for unknown words with zeros using the `torch::zeros` function from the `PyTorch` library. To split the line in the tokens, we also used the `std::getline` function. This is because it has a second parameter that can be used to specify the delimiter. By default, the delimiter is a newline character, but we specified the space character as the delimiter. We used the first token as a keyword. Regarding the other tokens from each file line, we put them into the vector of floating-point numbers. When we parsed a whole line, we constructed the `torch::Tensor` object with the `torch::from_blob` method, which wraps existing data without copying it to the tensor object with specified options. Finally, we put the key-value pair on the map; the key is the word and the value is the tensor object. Notice that we used the `clone` method to copy exact data to a new object stored in the map. The `vec` object is used to reuse memory while parsing the vectors. The `std::stof` function from the standard library is used to convert a string into a floating-point number.

Now, we have everything we need to create a vocabulary class that can associate a word with a unique index, and the index with a vector embedding. The following snippet shows its definition:

```
class Vocabulary {
    public:
    Vocabulary(const WordsFrequencies& words_frequencies,
            const GloveDict& glove_dict);
    int64_t GetIndex(const std::string& word) const;
    int64_t GetPaddingIndex() const;
    torch::Tensor GetEmbeddings() const;
    int64_t GetEmbeddingsCount() const;
    private:
    std::unordered_map<std::string, size_t> words_to_index_map_;
    std::vector<torch::Tensor> embeddings_;
    size_t unk_index_;
    size_t pad_index_;
};
```

The object of the `Vocabulary` class should be initialized with the instances of the `WordsFrequencies` and `GloveDict` classes; it implements the next vital methods. `GetIndex` returns the index for the input word, while `GetEmbeddings` returns a tensor containing all embeddings (in rows) in the same order as the word indices. The `GetPaddingIndex` method returns the index of the embedding, which can be used for padding (it is a zero tensor in reality). The `GetEmbeddingsCount` method returns the total count of the embeddings.

Notice that this number can be different from the total number of the words in our dictionary because some words can be missed in the GloVe embeddings. Such missed words should be associated with the unknown index and zero-valued embedding.

The following code shows how the constructor is implemented:

```
Vocabulary::Vocabulary(const WordsFrequencies& words_frequencies,
const GloveDict& glove_dict) {
    words_to_index_map_.reserve(words_frequencies.size());
    embeddings_.reserve(words_frequencies.size());
    unk_index_ = 0;
    pad_index_ = unk_index_ + 1;
    embeddings_.push_back(glove_dict.GetUnknown());  // unknown
    embeddings_.push_back(glove_dict.GetUnknown());  // padding
    size_t index = pad_index_ + 1;
    for (auto& wf : words_frequencies) {
        auto embedding = glove_dict.Get(wf.first);
        if (embedding.size(0) != 0) {
            embeddings_.push_back(embedding);
            words_to_index_map_.insert({wf.first, index});
            ++index;
        } else {
            words_to_index_map_.insert({wf.first, unk_index_});
        }
    }
}
```

In this method, we populated the `words_to_index_map_` and `embeddings_` containers. First, we inserted two zero-valued tensors into the `embeddings_` container: one for the GloVe unknown word and another for padding values:

```
embeddings_.push_back(glove_dict.GetUnknown());  // unknown
embeddings_.push_back(glove_dict.GetUnknown());  // padding
```

We use padding values to create a batch of reviews for training because almost all review texts have different lengths. Then, we iterated over the `words_frequencies` object, which was passed as a parameter, and used the `glove_dict` object to search the embedding vector for the word from the dictionary. If the word is found in the `glove_dict` object, then we populate the `embeddings_` object with the tensor and the `words_to_index_map_` object with the word as a key and the index as a value. If a word is not found in the `glove_dict` object, then we populate only the `words_to_index_map_` object, with the word as a key and `unk_index_` as a value. Notice how the `index` value is initialized and incremented; it starts with 2 because the 0 index is occupied for unknown embedding and the 1 index is occupied for padding value embedding:

```
unk_index_ = 0;
pad_index_ = unk_index_ + 1;
...
size_t index = pad_index_ + 1;
```

Notice that we only increased the index after we inserted a new embedding tensor into the `embeddings_` object. In the opposite case, when an embedding for the word was not found, the word was associated with the unknown value index. The next important method in the `Vocabulary` class in the `GetEmbeddings` method, which makes a single tensor from a vector of embedding tensors. The following code shows its implementation:

```
at::Tensor Vocabulary::GetEmbeddings() const {
    at::Tensor weights = torch::stack(embeddings_);
    return weights;
}
```

Here, we used the `torch::stack` function, which concatenates tensors from the given container along a new dimension (by default, this function adds a dimension with index 0).

Other `Vocabulary` class methods return corresponding values:

- `GetIndex`: Returns the index of a given word in the vocabulary
- `GetPaddingIndex`: Returns the index of padding values in the vocabulary
- `GetEmbeddings`: Returns all embeddings as one tensor object
- `GetEmbeddingsCount`: Returns the number of embeddings in the vocabulary

Now, we have all the necessary classes for dataset class implementation. Such classes can be used for the PyTorch data loader's initialization. However, before we develop it, we should discuss how our model should process training batches. We already mentioned that review texts are of different lengths, so it is impossible to combine several of them into one rectangular tensor (remember that words are represented with numeric indices). To solve this problem, we need to make them all the same length. This operation can be done by determining the most extended text in the dataset with the `GetMaxSize` method of `ImdbReader` and allocating the tensor with this size as one of the dimensions. The shorter text is padded with zero values. We already defined the method to get the padding index in the `Vocabulary` class.

However, such an approach also leads to numerous unnecessary calculations and adds noise to our training data, which can make our model less precise. Fortunately, because this is a common problem, there is a solution. The `PyTorch` library has an LSTM module implementation, which can effectively work with padded batches by ignoring the padding values. To use such functionality, we need to add information regarding the length of each text (sequence) in the batch.

So, our dataset class should return a pair of training tensors: one representing the encoded text and another containing its length. Also, we need to develop a custom function to convert the vector of tensors in a batch into one single tensor. This function is required if we want to make PyTorch compatible with custom training data.

Let's define the `ImdbSample` type for a custom training data sample. We will use this with the `torch::data::Dataset` type:

```
using ImdbData = std::pair<torch::Tensor, torch::Tensor>;
using ImdbSample = torch::data::Example<ImdbData, torch::Tensor>;
```

`ImdbData` represents the training data and has two tensors for test sequence and length. `ImdbSample` represents the whole sample with a target value. A tensor contains a 1 or 0 for positive or negative sentiment, respectively.

The following code snippet shows the `ImdbDataset` class' declaration:

```
class ImdbDataset : public torch::data::Dataset<ImdbDataset, ImdbSample> {
    public:
        ImdbDataset(ImdbReader* reader,
                    Vocabulary* vocabulary,
                    torch::DeviceType device);
        // torch::data::Dataset implementation
        ImdbSample get(size_t index) override;
        torch::optional<size_t> size() const override;
    private:
```

```
        torch::DeviceType device_{torch::DeviceType::CPU};
        ImdbReader* reader_{nullptr};
        Vocabulary* vocabulary_{nullptr};
};
```

We inherited our dataset class from the `torch::data::Dataset` class so that we can use it for data loader initialization. The PyTorch data loader object is responsible for sampling random training objects and making batches from them. The objects of our `ImdbDataset` class should be initialized with the `ImdbReader` and `Vocabulary` class instances. We also added the `device` parameter of `torch::DeviceType` into the constructor to tell the object where to place the training object in CPU or GPU memory. In the constructor, we store the pointers to input objects and the device type. We overrode two methods from the `torch::data::Dataset` class: the `get` and `size` methods.

The following code shows how we implemented the `size` method:

```
torch::optional<size_t> ImdbDataset::size() const {
    return reader_->GetPosSize() + reader_->GetNegSize();
}
```

The `size` method returns the number of reviews in the `ImdbReader` object. The `get` method has a more complicated implementation than the previous one, as shown in the following code:

```
ImdbSample ImdbDataset::get(size_t index) {
    torch::Tensor target;
    const ImdbReader::Review* review{nullptr};
    if (index < reader_->GetPosSize()) {
        review = &reader_->GetPos(index);
        target = torch::tensor(1.f,
            torch::dtype(torch::kFloat).device(
                device_).requires_grad(false));
    } else {
        review = &reader_->GetNeg(index - reader_->GetPosSize());
        target = torch::tensor(0.f,
            torch::dtype(torch::kFloat).device(
                device_).requires_grad(false));
    }
```

First, we got the review text and sentiment value from the given index (the function argument value). In the `size` method, we returned the total number of positive and negative reviews, so if the input index is greater than the number of positive reviews, then this index points to a negative one. Then, we subtracted the number of positive reviews from it.

After we got the correct index, we also got the corresponding text review and assigned its address to the `review` pointer and initialized the `target` tensor. The `torch::tensor` function was used to initialize the target tensor. This function takes an arbitrary numeric value and tensor options such as a type and a device. Notice that we set the `requires_grad` option to false because we don't need to calculate the gradient for this variable. The following code shows the continuation of the `get` method's implementation:

```
// encode text
std::vector<int64_t> indices(reader_->GetMaxSize());
size_t i = 0;
for (auto& w : (*review)) {
    indices[i] = vocabulary_->GetIndex(w);
    ++i;
}
```

Here, we encoded the review text from string words to their indices. We defined the `indices` vector of integer values in order to store the encoding of the maximum possible length. Then, we filled it in the cycle by applying the `GetIndex` method of the vocabulary object to each of the words. Notice that we used the `i` variable to count the number of words we encode. The use of this variable was required because other positions in the sequence will be padded with a particular padding index.

The following code shows how we add the padding indices to the sequence:

```
// pad text to same size
for (; i < indices.size(); ++i) {
    indices[i] = vocabulary_->GetPaddingIndex();
}
```

When we've initialized all the data we need for one training sample, we have to convert it into a `torch::Tensor` object. For this purpose, we can use already known functions, namely `torch::from_blob` and `torch::tensor`. The `torch::from_blob` function takes the pointer for raw numeric data, the dimensions container, and tensor options. The following code shows how we used these functions to create the final tensor object at the end of the `get` method's implementation:

```
auto data = torch::from_blob(indices.data(),
                   {static_cast<int64_t>(reader_->GetMaxSize())},
                   torch::dtype(torch::kLong).requires_grad(false));
```

```
          auto data_len = torch::tensor(static_cast<int64_t>(review->size()),
                          torch::dtype(torch::kLong).requires_grad(false));

     return {{data.clone().to(device_), data_len.clone()},
        target.squeeze()};
}
```

Notice that the `data` object containing the text sequence was moved to the specific device with the `to` method, but `data_len` was left in the default (CPU) device because this is a requirement of the PyTorch LSTM implementation API. Also, look at the use of the `squeeze` method – this method removes all tensor dimensions equal to 1, so in our case, we used it to make a single value tensor (not a rectangular one).

The following code shows how to use the classes we defined previously to initialize data loaders for the training and test datasets:

```
torch::DeviceType device = torch::cuda::is_available()
                              ? torch::DeviceType::CUDA
                              : torch::DeviceType::CPU;
...
// create datasets
ImdbDataset train_dataset(&train_reader, &vocab, device);
ImdbDataset test_dataset(&test_reader, &vocab, device);

// init data loaders
size_t batch_size = 32;
auto train_loader = torch::data::make_data_loader(train_dataset,
    torch::data::DataLoaderOptions().batch_size(batch_size).workers(4));

auto test_loader = torch::data::make_data_loader(test_dataset,
    torch::data::DataLoaderOptions().batch_size(batch_size).workers(4));
```

Before we move on, we need to define one more helper function, which converts the batch vector of tensors into one tensor. This conversion is needed to vectorize the calculation for better utilization of hardware resources, in order to improve performance. Notice that when we initialized the data loaders with the `make_data_loader` function, we didn't use the mapping and transform methods for datasets objects as in the previous example. This was done because, by default, PyTorch can't automatically transform arbitrary types (in our case, the `ImdbData` pair type) into tensors. The following code shows the beginning of the `MakeBatchTensors` function's implementation:

```
std::tuple<torch::Tensor, torch::Tensor, torch::Tensor>
MakeBatchTensors(const std::vector<ImdbSample>& batch) {
    // prepare batch data
    std::vector<torch::Tensor> text_data;
    std::vector<torch::Tensor> text_lengths;
```

```
std::vector<torch::Tensor> label_data;
for (auto& item : batch) {
    text_data.push_back(item.data.first);
    text_lengths.push_back(item.data.second);
    label_data.push_back(item.target);
}
```

First, we split a single vector of the `ImdbSample` objects into three: `text_data`, which contains all texts; `text_lengths`, which contains the corresponding lengths; and `label_data`, which contains the target value. Then, we need to sort them in decreasing order of text length. This order is a requirement of the `pack_padded_sequence` function, which we will use in our model to transform padded sequences into packed ones to improve performance. We can't simultaneously sort three containers in C++, so we have to use a custom approach based on a defined permutation. The following code shows how we applied this approach while continuing to implement the method:

```
std::vector<std::size_t> permutation(text_lengths.size());
std::iota(permutation.begin(), permutation.end(), 0);
std::sort(permutation.begin(), permutation.end(),
            [&](std::size_t i, std::size_t j) {
                return text_lengths[i].item().toLong() <
                text_lengths[j].item().toLong();
            });
std::reverse(permutation.begin(), permutation.end());
```

Here, we defined the `permutation` vector of indices with a number of items equal to the batch size. Then, we filled it consistently with numbers starting from *0*, and sorted it with the standard `std::sort` algorithm function, but with a custom comparison functor, which compares the lengths of sequences with correspondent indices. Notice that to get the raw value from the `torch::Tensor` type object, the `item()` and `toLong()` methods were used. Also, because we needed the decreasing order of items, we used the `std::reverse` algorithm. The following code shows how we used the `permutation` object to sort three containers in the same way:

```
auto appy_permutation = [&permutation](
const std::vector<torch::Tensor>& vec) {
    std::vector<torch::Tensor> sorted_vec(vec.size());
    std::transform(permutation.begin(), permutation.end(),
                    sorted_vec.begin(),
        [&](std::size_t i) { return vec[i]; });
    return sorted_vec;
};
text_data = appy_permutation(text_data);
text_lengths = appy_permutation(text_lengths);
label_data = appy_permutation(label_data);
```

To perform the sorting operation, we defined a lambda function that changes the order of the container's items by the given vector of indices. This was the `appy_permutation` lambda. This function created a new intermediate vector of the same size as the one we want to reorder and filled it with the `std::transform` algorithm with a custom functor, which returns the item from the original container but with the index taken from the permutation object.

When all the batch vectors have been sorted in the required order, we can use the `torch::stack` function to concatenate each of them into the single tensor with an additional dimension. The following code snippet shows how we used this function to create the final tensor objects. This is the final part of the `MakeBatchTensors` method's implementation:

```
    torch::Tensor texts = torch::stack(text_data);
    torch::Tensor lengths = torch::stack(text_lengths);
    torch::Tensor labels = torch::stack(label_data);
    return {texts, lengths, labels};
}
```

At this point, we have written all the code required to parse and prepare the training data. Now, we can create classes for our RNN model. We are going to base our model on the LSTM architecture. There is a module called `torch::nn::LSTM` in the PyTorch C++ API for this purpose. The problem is that this module can't work with packed sequences. There is a standalone function called `torch::lstm` that can do this, so we need to create our custom module to combine the `torch::nn::LSTM` module and the `torch::lstm` function so that we can work with packed sequences. Such an approach causes our RNN to only process the non-padded elements of our sequence.

The following code shows the `PackedLSTMImpl` class' declaration and the `PackedLSTM` module's definition:

```
    class PackedLSTMImpl : public torch::nn::Module {
        public:
        explicit PackedLSTMImpl(const torch::nn::LSTMOptions& options);
        std::vector<torch::Tensor> flat_weights() const;
        torch::nn::RNNOutput forward(const torch::Tensor& input,
                                     const torch::Tensor& lengths,
                                     torch::Tensor state = {});
        const torch::nn::LSTMOptions& options() const;
        private:
        torch::nn::LSTM rnn_ = nullptr;
    };

    TORCH_MODULE(PackedLSTM);
```

The `PackedLSTM` module definition uses the `PackedLSTMImpl` class as the module function's implementation. Also, notice that the `PackedLSTM` module definition differs from the `torch::nn::LSTM` module in that the `forward` function takes the additional parameter, `lengths`. The implementation of this module is based on the code of the `torch::nn::LSTM` module from the `PyTorch` library. The `flat_weights` and `forward` functions were mostly copied from the `PyTorch` library's source code. We overrode the `flat_weights` function because it is hidden in the base class, and we can access it from the `torch::nn::LSTM` module.

The following code shows the `PackedLSTMImpl` class constructor's implementation:

```
PackedLSTMImpl::PackedLSTMImpl(const torch::nn::LSTMOptions& options) {
    rnn_ = torch::nn::LSTM(options);
    register_module("rnn", rnn_);
}
```

In the constructor, we created and registered the `torch::nn::LSTM` module object. Notice that we used an instance of the `torch::nn::LSTM` module to access the properly initialized weights for the LSTM's implementation.

The following code shows the `flat_weights` method's implementation:

```
std::vector<torch::Tensor> PackedLSTMImpl::flat_weights() const {
    std::vector<torch::Tensor> flat;
    const auto num_directions = rnn_->options.bidirectional_ ? 2 : 1;
    for (int64_t layer = 0; layer < rnn_->options.layers_; layer++) {
        for (auto direction = 0; direction < num_directions; direction++)
{
            const auto layer_idx =
            static_cast<size_t>((layer * num_directions) + direction);
            flat.push_back(rnn_->w_ih[layer_idx]);
            flat.push_back(rnn_->w_hh[layer_idx]);
            if (rnn_->options.with_bias_) {
                flat.push_back(rnn_->b_ih[layer_idx]);
                flat.push_back(rnn_->b_hh[layer_idx]);
            }
        }
    }
    return flat;
}
```

In the `flat_weights` method, we organized all the weights into a flat vector in the order $(w_i h, w_h h, b_i h, b_h h)$, repeated for each layer, and next to each other. This is a copy of the same method from the `torch::nn::LSTM` module.

The following code shows the `forward` method's implementation:

```
torch::nn::RNNOutput PackedLSTMImpl::forward(const torch::Tensor& input,
                                             const at::Tensor& lengths,
                                             torch::Tensor state) {
    if (!state.defined()) {
        const auto max_batch_size = lengths[0].item().toLong();
        const auto num_directions = rnn_->options.bidirectional_ ? 2 : 1;
        state = torch::zeros({2, rnn_->options.layers_ * num_directions,
                              max_batch_size, rnn_->options.hidden_size_},
                             input.options());
    }
    torch::Tensor output, hidden_state, cell_state;
    std::tie(output, hidden_state, cell_state) = torch::lstm(
            input, lengths, {state[0], state[1]}, flat_weights(),
            rnn_->options.with_bias_, rnn_->options.layers_,
            rnn_->options.dropout_, rnn_->is_training(),
            rnn_->options.bidirectional_);
    return {output, torch::stack({hidden_state, cell_state})};
}
```

The `forward` method is also a copy of the same method from the `torch::nn::LSTM` module, but it used a different overload of the `torch::lstm` function. We can see that the main logic in the `forward` method is to initialize the cell state if it is not defined and call the `torch::lstm` function. Notice that all the methods in this class consider the `options.bidirectional_` flag in order to configure the dimensions of the weights and state tensors. Also, notice that the module's state is a combined tensor from two tensors: the hidden state and the cell state.

The following code shows how we can define our RNN model with the `SentimentRNN` class:

```
class SentimentRNNImpl : public torch::nn::Module {
  public:
    SentimentRNNImpl(int64_t vocab_size,
                     int64_t embedding_dim,
                     int64_t hidden_dim,
                     int64_t output_dim,
                     int64_t n_layers,
                     bool bidirectional,
                     double dropout,
                     int64_t pad_idx);
    void SetPretrainedEmbeddings(const torch::Tensor& weights);
    torch::Tensor forward(const torch::Tensor& text,
                          const at::Tensor& length);
  private:
    int64_t pad_idx_{-1};
```

```
      torch::autograd::Variable embeddings_weights_;
      PackedLSTM rnn_ = nullptr;
      torch::nn::Linear fc_ = nullptr;
      torch::nn::Dropout dropout_ = nullptr;
};

TORCH_MODULE(SentimentRNN);
```

Our model can be configured so that it's multilayer and bidirectional. These properties can significantly improve model performance for the sentiment analysis task.

Notice that we defined the `embeddings_weights_` class member, which is of the `torch::autograd::Variable` type. This was done because we used the `torch::embedding` function to convert the input batch sequence's items into embeddings automatically. We can use the `torch::nn:Embeding` module for this purpose, but the C++ API can't use pre-trained values. This is why we used the `torch::embedding` function directly. We also used the `torch::autograd::Variable` type instead of a simple tensor because we need to calculate the gradient for our module during the training process.

The following code shows the `SentimentRNNImpl` class constructor's implementation:

```
SentimentRNNImpl::SentimentRNNImpl(int64_t vocab_size,
                                   int64_t embedding_dim,
                                   int64_t hidden_dim,
                                   int64_t output_dim,
                                   int64_t n_layers,
                                   bool bidirectional,
                                   double dropout,
                                   int64_t pad_idx)
    : pad_idx_(pad_idx) {
  embeddings_weights_ = register_parameter(
      "embeddings_weights", torch::empty({vocab_size, embedding_dim}));
  rnn_ = PackedLSTM(torch::nn::LSTMOptions(embedding_dim, hidden_dim)
                                    .layers(n_layers)
                                    .bidirectional(bidirectional)
                                    .dropout(dropout));
  register_module("rnn", rnn_);
  fc_ = torch::nn::Linear(torch::nn::LinearOptions(hidden_dim * 2,
                          output_dim));
  register_module("fc", fc_);
  dropout_ = torch::nn::Dropout(torch::nn::DropoutOptions(dropout));
  register_module("dropout", dropout_);
}
```

In the constructor of our module, we initialized the base blocks of our network. We used the `register_parameter` method of the `torch::nn::Module` class to create the `embeddings_weights_` object, which is filled with the empty tensor. Registration makes automatically calculating the gradient possible. Notice that the one dimension of the `embeddings_weights_` object is equal to the vocabulary length, while the other one is equal to the length of the embedding vector (100, in our case). The `rnn_` object is initialized with the `torch::nn::LSTMOptions` type object. We defined the length of the embedding, the number of hidden dimensions (number of hidden neurons in the LSTM module layers), the number of RNN layers, the flag that tells us whether the RNN is bidirectional or not, and specified the regularization parameter (the dropout factor value).

The `fc_` object is our output layer with just a fully connected layer and a linear activation function. It is configured to take the `hidden_dim * 2` number of input items, which means that we are going to pass the hidden states from the last two modules of our RNN into it. The `fc_` object returns only one value; we didn't use the sigmoid activation function for it because, as stated in the PyTorch documentation, it makes sense to use a special loss function called `binary_cross_entropy_with_logits`, which includes the sigmoid and is more stable than using a plain sigmoid followed by binary cross-entropy loss. We also initialized and registered the `dropout_` object, which is used for additional regularization; the `torch::nn::DropoutOptions` object only takes a dropout factor value as its setting.

The following code snippet shows the `forward` method's implementation:

```
torch::Tensor SentimentRNNImpl::forward(const at::Tensor& text,
                                        const at::Tensor& length) {
    auto embedded =
        dropout_(torch::embedding(embeddings_weights_, text, pad_idx_));
    torch::Tensor packed_text, packed_length;
    std::tie(packed_text, packed_length) = torch::_pack_padded_sequence(
                embedded, length.squeeze(1), /*batch_first*/ false);

    auto rnn_out = rnn_->forward(packed_text, packed_length);

    auto hidden_state = rnn_out.state.narrow(0, 0, 1);
    hidden_state.squeeze_(0);  // remove 0 dimension equals to 1 after
                               // narrowing
    // take last hidden layers state
    auto last_index = rnn_->options().layers() - 2;
    hidden_state =
        at::cat({hidden_state.narrow(0, last_index, 1).squeeze(0),
                hidden_state.narrow(0, last_index + 1, 1).squeeze(0)},
                /*dim*/ 1);

    auto hidden = dropout_(hidden_state);
```

```
    return fc_(hidden);
}
```

The implementation of the `forward` method takes two tensors as input parameters. One is the text sequences, which are `[sequence length x batch size]` in size, while the other is text lengths, which are `[batch size x 1]` in size. First, we applied the `torch::embedding` function to our text sequences. This function converts indexed sequences into ones with embedding values (this is just a table lookup operation). It also takes `embeddings_weights_` as a parameter. `embeddings_weights_` is the tensor that contains our pre-trained embeddings. The `pad_idx_` parameter tells us what index points to the padding value embedding. The result of calling this function is `[sequence length x batch size x 100]`. We also applied the dropout module to the embedded sequences to perform regularization.

Then, we converted the padded embedded sequences into packed ones with the `torch::_pack_padded_sequence` function. This function takes the padded sequences with their lengths (which should be one-dimensional tensors) and returns a pair of new tensors with different sizes, which also represent packed sequences and packed lengths, correspondingly. We used packed sequences to improve the performance of the model.

After, we passed the packed sequences and their lengths into the `PackedLSTM` module's forward function. This module processed the input sequences with the RNN and returned an object of the `torch::nn::RNNOutput` type with two members: `output` and `state`. The `state` member is in the following format: `{hidden_state, cell_state}`.

We used the values of the hidden state as input for the fully connected layer. To get the hidden state values, we extracted them from the combined state, which was done with the `narrow` method of a tensor object. This method returns the narrowed version of the original tensor. The first argument is the dimension index that narrowing should be performed along, while the next two arguments are the start position and the length. The returned tensor and input tensor share the same underlying storage.

The hidden state has the following shape: `{num layers * num directions x batch size x hid dim}`. The number of directions is 2 in the case of a bidirectional RNN. RNN layers are ordered as follows: `[forward_layer_0, backward_layer_0, forward_layer_1, backward_layer 1, ..., forward_layer_n, backward_layer n]`.

The following code shows how to get the hidden states for the last (top) layers:

```
auto last_index = rnn_->options().layers() - 2;
hidden_state =
        at::cat({hidden_state.narrow(0, last_index, 1).squeeze(0),
                hidden_state.narrow(0, last_index + 1, 1).squeeze(0)},
                /*dim*/ 1);
```

Here, we got the top two hidden layer states from the first dimension. Then, we concatenated them with the `torch::cat` function before passing them to the linear layer (after applying dropout). The `torch::cat` function combines tensors along an existing dimension. Note that the tensors should be the same shape, contrary to the `torch::stack` function (which adds a new dimension when it combines tensors). Performing these narrowing operations left the original dimensions. Due to this, we used the `squeeze` function to remove them.

The last step of the `forward` function was applying the dropout and passing the results to the fully connected layer. The following snippet shows how this was done:

```
auto hidden = dropout_(hidden_state);
return fc_(hidden);
```

The following code shows how we can initialize the model:

```
int64_t hidden_dim = 256;
int64_t output_dim = 1;
int64_t n_layers = 2;
bool bidirectional = true;
double dropout = 0.5;
int64_t pad_idx = vocab.GetPaddingIndex();

SentimentRNN model(vocab.GetEmbeddingsCount(),
                embedding_dim,
                hidden_dim,
                output_dim,
                n_layers,
                bidirectional,
                dropout,
                pad_idx);
```

We configured it to be multilayer and bidirectional with 256 hidden neurons. The next important step in the model configuration process is initializing the pre-trained embeddings. The following snippet shows how to use the `SetPretrainedEmbeddings` method to do so:

```
model->SetPretrainedEmbeddings(vocab.GetEmbeddings());
```

The `SetPretrainedEmbeddings` method is implemented in the following way:

```
void SentimentRNNImpl::SetPretrainedEmbeddings(const at::Tensor& weights)
{
    torch::NoGradGuard guard;
    embeddings_weights_.copy_(weights);
}
```

With the instance of the `torch::NoGradGuard` type, we put the `PyTorch` library into special mode, which allowed us to update the internal structure of the modules without influencing the gradient calculations. We used the tensor's `copy_` method to copy the data one by one.

When the model has been initialized and configured, we can begin training. The necessary part of the training process is an optimizer object. In this example, we will use the Adam optimization algorithm. The name Adam is derived from the adaptive moment estimation. This algorithm usually results in a better and faster convergence in comparison with pure stochastic gradient descent. The following code shows how to define an instance of the `torch::optim::Adam` class:

```
double learning_rate = 0.01;
torch::optim::Adam optimizer(model->parameters(),
                             torch::optim::AdamOptions(learning_rate));
```

As with all optimizer objects in the `PyTorch` library, it should be initialized with the list of parameters for optimization. We passed all the parameters (weights) from our model, `model->parameters()`.

Now, we can move the model to a computational device such as a GPU:

```
model->to(device);
```

Then, we can start training the model. Training will be performed for `100` epochs over all the samples in the training dataset. After each epoch, we will run the test model's evaluation to check that there is no overfitting. The following code shows how to define such a training process:

```
int epochs = 100;
for (int epoch = 0; epoch < epochs; ++epoch) {
    TrainModel(epoch, model, optimizer, *train_loader);
    TestModel(epoch, model, *test_loader);
}
```

The `TrainModel` function will be implemented in a standardized way for training neural networks with PyTorch. Its declaration is shown in the following code:

```
void TrainModel(int epoch,
                SentimentRNN& model,
                torch::optim::Optimizer& optimizer,
                torch::data::StatelessDataLoader<ImdbDataset,
                torch::data::samplers::RandomSampler>& train_loader);
```

Before we start training iterations, we have to switch the model into training mode. It is essential to do this because some modules behave differently in evaluation mode versus training mode. For example, the dropout is not applied in evaluation mode and only results in an average correction. The following code shows how to enable training mode for the model:

```
model->train();  // switch to the training mode
```

The following snippet shows the beginning of the `TrainModel` function's implementation:

```
double epoch_loss = 0;
double epoch_acc = 0;
int batch_index = 0;
for (auto& batch : train_loader) {
    ...
}
```

Here, we defined two variables to calculate the average loss value and accuracy per epoch. The iteration that we performed over all the batches from the `train_loader` object was used to train the model.

The following series of code snippets shows the implementation of a training cycle's iteration:

1. First, we clear the previous gradients from the optimizer:

   ```
   optimizer.zero_grad();
   ```

2. Then, we convert the batch data into distinct tensors:

   ```
   torch::Tensor texts, lengths, labels;
    std::tie(texts, lengths, labels) = MakeBatchTensors(batch);
   ```

3. Now that we have the sample texts and lengths, we can perform the forward pass of the model:

   ```
   torch::Tensor prediction = model->forward(texts.t(), lengths);
   prediction.squeeze_(1);
   ```

Notice that we used the transposed text sequence tensor because the LSTM module requires input data in the `[seq_len, batch_size, features]` format. Here, `seq_len` is the number of items (words) in a sequence, `batch_size` is the size of the current batch, and `features` is the number of elements in one item (it's not an embedding dimension).

4. Now that we have the predictions from our model, we use the `squeeze_` function to remove any unnecessary dimensions so that the model's compatible with the loss function. Notice that the `squeeze_` function has an underscore, which means that the function is evaluated in place, without any additional memory being allocated.

5. Then, we compute a loss value to estimate the error of our model:

```
torch::Tensor loss = torch::binary_cross_entropy_with_logits(
                        prediction, labels, {}, {},
Reduction::Mean);
```

Here, we used the `torch::binary_cross_entropy_with_logits` function, which measures the binary cross-entropy between the `prediction` logits and the target `labels`. This function already includes a sigmoid calculation. This is why our model returns the output from the linear full connection layer. We also specified the reduction type in order to apply to the loss output. Losses from each sample in the batch are summed and divided by the number of elements in the batch.

6. Then, we compute the gradients for our model and update its parameters with these gradients:

```
loss.backward();
optimizer.step();
```

7. One of the final steps of the training function is to accumulate the loss and the accuracy values for averaging:

```
auto loss_value = static_cast<double>(loss.item<float>());
auto acc_value = static_cast<double>(BinaryAccuracy(prediction,
labels));

epoch_loss += loss_value;
epoch_acc += acc_value;
```

Here, we used the custom `BinaryAccuracy` function for the accuracy calculation. The following code shows its implementation:

```
float BinaryAccuracy(const torch::Tensor& preds,
                     const torch::Tensor& target) {
    auto rounded_preds = torch::round(torch::sigmoid(preds));
    auto correct =  torch::eq(rounded_preds,
                     target).to(torch::dtype(torch::kFloat));
    auto acc = correct.sum() / correct.size(0);
    return acc.item<float>();
}
```

In this function, we applied `torch::sigmoid` to the predictions of our model. This operation converts the logits values into values we can interpret as a label (1 or 0), but because these values are floating points, we applied the `torch::round` function to them. The `torch::round` function rounds the input values to the closest integer. Then, we compared the predicted labels with the target values using the `torch::eq` function. This operation gave us an initialized tensor, with 1 where labels matched and with 0 otherwise. We calculated the ratio between the number of all labels in the batch and the number of correct predictions as an accuracy value.

The following snippet shows the end of the training function's implementation:

```
std::cout << "Epoch: "   << epoch
          << " | Loss: " << (epoch_loss / (batch_index - 1))
          << " | Acc: "  << (epoch_acc / (batch_index - 1))
          << std::endl;
```

Here, we printed the average values for the loss and accuracy. Notice that we divided the accumulated values by the number of batches.

The following code shows the `TestModel` function's implementation, which looks pretty similar to the `TrainModel` function:

```
void TestModel(int epoch, SentimentRNN& model,
               torch::data::StatelessDataLoader<ImdbDataset,
               torch::data::samplers::RandomSampler>& test_loader) {
    torch::NoGradGuard guard;
    double epoch_loss = 0;
    double epoch_acc = 0;
    model->eval();  // switch to the evaluation mode
    // Iterate the data loader to get batches from the dataset
    int batch_index = 0;
    for (auto& batch : test_loader) {
        // prepare batch data
        torch::Tensor texts, lengths, labels;
```

```
std::tie(texts, lengths, labels) = MakeBatchTensors(batch);
// Forward pass the model on the input data
torch::Tensor prediction = model->forward(texts.t(), lengths);
prediction.squeeze_(1);
// Compute a loss value to estimate error of our model
torch::Tensor loss = torch::binary_cross_entropy_with_logits(
                                    prediction, labels, {},
                                    {}, Reduction::Mean);

    auto loss_value = static_cast<double>(loss.item<float>());
    auto acc_value = static_cast<double>(BinaryAccuracy(prediction,
                                    labels));
    epoch_loss += loss_value;
    epoch_acc += acc_value;
    ++batch_index;
  }
  std::cout << "Epoch: " << epoch
  << " | Test Loss: " << (epoch_loss / (batch_index - 1))
  << " | Test Acc: " << (epoch_acc / (batch_index - 1)) << std::endl;
}
```

The main differences regarding this function are that we used the `test_loader` objects for data, switched the model to the evaluation state with the `model->eval()` call, and we didn't use any optimization operations.

This RNN architecture, with the settings we used, results in 85% accuracy in the sentiment analysis of movie reviews.

Summary

In this chapter, we learned the basic principles of RNNs. This type of neural network is commonly used in sequence analysis. The main differences between the feedforward neural network types are the existence of a recurrent link; the fact it is shared across timestep's weights; its ability to save some internal state in memory; and the fact it has a forward and backward data flow (bidirectional networks).

We became familiar with different types of RNNs and saw that the simplest one has problems with vanishing and exploding gradients, while the more advanced architectures can successfully deal with these problems. We learned the basics of the LSTM architecture, which is based on the hidden state, cell state, and three types of gates (filters), which control what information to use from the previous timestep, what information to forget, and what portion of information to pass to the next timestep.

Then, we looked at the GRU, which is simpler than LSTM and has only one hidden state and two gates. We also looked at the bidirectional RNN architecture and saw how it can be used to process input sequences backward. However, we saw that this type of architecture makes the network twice as large sometimes. We also learned how to use multiple layers in an RNN to process the hidden state from the bottom layers in upper levels, and that such an approach can significantly improve network performance.

Next, we learned that we need a modified backpropagation algorithm called BPTT to train RNNs. This algorithm assumes that the RNN is unfolded to the feedforward network with a number of layers equal to the timesteps (sequence length). Also, BPTT shares the same weights for all layers, and the gradient is accumulated before the weights are updated. Then, we talked about the computational complexity of this algorithm and that the TBPTT algorithm's modification is more suitable in practice. The TBPTT algorithm uses a limited number of timesteps for unfolding and a backward pass.

Another theme we discussed was connected to natural language processing. This theme is word embedding. An embedding, in general, is a numerical vector associated with other type items (such as words), but the algebraic properties of this vector should reflect some innate nature of the original item. Embeddings are used to convert non-numeric concepts into numeric ones so that we can work with them. We looked at the Word2Vec algorithm for creating word embeddings based on local statistics, as well as the GloVe algorithm, which is based mostly on global statistics.

Finally, in the last part of this chapter, we developed an application so that we could perform a sentiment analysis of movie reviews. We implemented a bidirectional multilayered LSTM network with the PyTorch framework. We also made helper classes so that we could read the training and test datasets and pre-trained GloVe embeddings. Then, we implemented the full training and testing cycle and applied the optimization technique with packed sequences, which improved the model's computational complexity and made it ignore the noise (zero noise) from padded sequences.

In the next chapter, we will discuss how to save and load model parameters. We will also look at the different APIs that exist in ML libraries for this purpose. Saving and loading model parameters can be quite an important part of the training process because it allows us to stop and restore training at an arbitrary moment. Also, saved model parameters can be used for evaluation purposes after the model has been trained.

Further reading

- PyTorch documentation: `https://pytorch.org/cppdocs/`
- Andrew L. Maas, Raymond E. Daly, Peter T. Pham, Dan Huang, Andrew Y. Ng, and Christopher Potts. (2011). *Learning Word Vectors for Sentiment Analysis*. The 49th Annual Meeting of the Association for Computational Linguistics (ACL 2011): `http://ai.stanford.edu/~amaas/data/sentiment`
- A simplified description of *GloVe: Global Vectors for Word Representation* algorithm: `http://mlexplained.com/2018/04/29/paper-dissected-glove-global-vectors-for-word-representation-explained/`
- *GloVe: Global Vectors for Word Representation*, Jeffrey Pennington, Richard Socher, Christopher D. Manning: `https://nlp.stanford.edu/projects/glove/`
- *Math theory behind Neural Networks*, Ian Goodfellow, Yoshua Bengio, Aaron Courville 2016, Deep Learning.
- Word embeddings: how to transform text into numbers: `https://monkeylearn.com/blog/word-embeddings-transform-text-numbers`
- A detailed LSTM architecture description: `http://colah.github.io/posts/2015-08-Understanding-LSTMs`
- *Learning Long-Term Dependencies with Gradient Descent is Difficult* by Yoshua Bengio et al. (1994): `http://www.iro.umontreal.ca/~lisa/pointeurs/ieeetrnn94.pdf`
- *On the difficulty of training recurrent neural networks* by Razvan Pascanu et al. (2013): `http://proceedings.mlr.press/v28/pascanu13.pdf`
- *Contextual Correlates of Synonymy* Communications of the ACM, 627-633. Rubenstein, H. and Goodenough, J.B. (1965).
- *Efficient Estimation of Word Representations in Vector Space*, Mikolov, Tomas; et al. (2013): `https://arxiv.org/abs/1301.3781`
- *Distributed Representations of Sentences and Documents*, Quoc Le, Tomas Mikolov: `https://arxiv.org/pdf/1405.4053v2.pdf`

Section 4: Production and Deployment Challenges

The crucial feature of C++ is the ability of the program to be compiled and run on a variety of hardware platforms. You can train your complex machine learning model on the fastest GPU in the data center, and deploy it to tiny mobile devices with limited resources. This chapter will show you how to use the C++ APIs of the TensorFlow and Caffe2 libraries to build programs that use machine learning models for Android devices and in the cloud.

This section comprises the following chapters:

- Chapter 12, *Exporting and Importing Models*
- Chapter 13, *Deploying Models on Mobile and Cloud Platforms*

Exporting and Importing Models 12

In this chapter, we will discuss how to save and load model parameters during and after training. This is quite an important issue since real model training can take a very long time (from days to weeks), and we want to be able to save intermediate results and then load them for use in evaluation mode in production.

Such regular save operations can be beneficial in the case of a random application crash. Another substantial feature of any **machine learning** (**ML**) framework is its ability to export the model architecture, which allows us to share models between frameworks and makes model deployment easier. The main topic of this chapter is to show how to export and import model parameters such as weights and bias values with different C++ libraries. The second part of this chapter is all about the **Open Neural Network Exchange** (**ONNX**) format, which is currently gaining popularity among different ML frameworks and can be used to share trained models. This format is suitable for sharing model architectures as well as model parameters.

The following topics will be covered in this chapter:

- ML model serialization APIs in C++ libraries
- Delving into ONNX format

Technical requirements

The following are the technical requirements for this chapter:

- `Dlib` library
- `Shark-ML` library
- `Shogun` library
- `PyTorch` library
- A modern C++ compiler with C++17 support
- CMake build system version >= 3.8

The code files for this chapter can be found at the following GitHub repo: `https://github.com/PacktPublishing/Hands-On-Machine-Learning-with-CPP/tree/master/Chapter12`

ML model serialization APIs in C++ libraries

In this section, we will discuss the ML model sharing APIs in the `Dlib`, `Shogun`, `Shark-ML`, and `PyTorch` libraries. There are three main types of sharing ML models among the different C++ libraries:

- Share model parameters (weights)
- Share the entire model's architecture
- Share both the model architecture and its trained parameters

In the following sections, we will look at what API is available in each library and emphasize what type of sharing it supports.

Model serialization with Dlib

The `Dlib` library uses the serialization API for `decision_function` and neural network type objects. Let's learn how to use it by implementing a real example.

First, we define the types for the neural network, regression kernel, and training sample:

```
using namespace dlib;

using NetworkType = loss_mean_squared<fc<1, input<matrix<double>>>>;
using SampleType = matrix<double, 1, 1>;
using KernelType = linear_kernel<SampleType>;
```

Then, we generate the training data with the following code:

```
size_t n = 1000;
std::vector<matrix<double>> x(n);
std::vector<float> y(n);

std::random_device rd;
std::mt19937 re(rd());
std::uniform_real_distribution<float> dist(-1.5, 1.5);

// generate data
for (size_t i = 0; i < n; ++i) {
    x[i](0, 0) = i;
```

```
    y[i] = func(i) + dist(re);
}
```

x represents the predictor variable, while y is the target variable. The target variable, y, is salted with uniform random noise to simulate real data. These variables have a linear dependency, which is defined with the following function:

```
double func(double x) {
    return 4. + 0.3 * x;
}
```

After we have generated the data, we normalize it using the `vector_normalizer` type object. Objects of this type can be reused after training to normalize data with the learned mean and standard deviation. The following snippets show how it's implemented:

```
vector_normalizer<matrix<double>> normalizer_x;
normalizer_x.train(x);

for (size_t i = 0; i < x.size(); ++i) {
    x[i] = normalizer_x(x[i]);
}
```

Finally, we train the `decision_function` object for kernel ridge regression with the `krr_trainer` type object:

```
void TrainAndSaveKRR(const std::vector<matrix<double>>& x,
                     const std::vector<float>& y) {
    krr_trainer<KernelType> trainer;
    trainer.set_kernel(KernelType());
    decision_function<KernelType> df = trainer.train(x, y);
    serialize("dlib-krr.dat") << df;
}
```

 Note that we initialized the trainer object with the instance of the `KernelType` object.

Now that we have the trained `decision_function` object, we can serialize it into a file with a stream object that's returned by the `serialize` function:

```
serialize("dlib-krr.dat") << df;
```

This function takes the name of the file for storage and returns an output stream object. We used the << operator to put the learned weights of the regression model into the file. This serialization approach only saves model parameters.

The same approach can be used to serialize almost all ML models in the `Dlib` library. The following code shows how to use it to serialize the parameters of a neural network:

```
void TrainAndSaveNetwork(const std::vector<matrix<double>>& x,
const std::vector<float>& y) {
    NetworkType network;
    sgd solver;
    dnn_trainer<NetworkType> trainer(network, solver);
    trainer.set_learning_rate(0.0001);
    trainer.set_mini_batch_size(50);
    trainer.set_max_num_epochs(300);
    trainer.be_verbose();
    trainer.train(x, y);
    network.clean();
    serialize("dlib-net.dat") << network;
    net_to_xml(network, "net.xml");
}
```

For neural networks, there is also the `net_to_xml` function, which saves the model structure, but there is no function to load this saved structure into our program. It is the user's responsibility to implement a loading function. The `net_to_xml` function exists if we wish to share the model between frameworks as it is written in the `Dlib` documentation.

To check that parameter serialization works as expected, we generate new test data to evaluate a loaded model on them:

```
std::cout << "Target values \n";
std::vector<matrix<double>> new_x(5);
for (size_t i = 0; i < 5; ++i) {
    new_x[i].set_size(1, 1);
    new_x[i](0, 0) = i;
    new_x[i] = normalizer_x(new_x[i]);
    std::cout << func(i) << std::endl;
}
```

Note that we reused the normalizer object. In general, its parameters should be serialized and loaded too because during evaluation we need to transform new data into the same statistical characteristics that we used for the training data.

To load a serialized object in the `Dlib` library, we can use the `deserialize` function. This function takes the filename and returns the input stream object:

```
void LoadAndPredictKRR(const std::vector<matrix<double>>& x) {
    decision_function<KernelType> df;
    deserialize("dlib-krr.dat") >> df;
    // Predict
    std::cout << "KRR predictions \n";
```

```
        for (auto& v : x) {
            auto p = df(v);
            std::cout << static_cast<double>(p) << std::endl;
        }
    }
```

As we discussed previously, serialization in the `Dlib` library only stores model parameters. So, to load them, we need to use the model object with the same properties that it had before serialization was performed. For a regression model, this means that we should instantiate a decision function object with the same kernel type. For a neural network model, this means that we should instantiate a network object of the same type that we used for serialization:

```
    void LoadAndPredictNetwork(const std::vector<matrix<double>>& x) {
        NetworkType network;
        deserialize("dlib-net.dat") >> network;
        // Predict
        auto predictions = network(x);
        std::cout << "Net predictions \n";
        for (auto p : predictions) {
            std::cout << static_cast<double>(p) << std::endl;
        }
    }
```

In this section, we saw that the `Dlib` serialization API allows us to save and load ML model parameters but has limited options to serialize and load model architectures. In the next section, we will look at the `Shogun` library model's serialization API.

Model serialization with Shogun

The `Shogun` library can save model parameters in different file formats such as ASCII, JSON, XML, and HDF5. This library can't load model architectures from a file and is only able to save and load the weights of the exact model. But there is an exception for neural networks: the `Shogun` library can load a network structure from a JSON file. An example of this functionality is shown in the following example.

As in the previous example, we start by generating the training data:

```
    const int32_t n = 1000;
    SGMatrix<float64_t> x_values(1, n);
    SGVector<float64_t> y_values(n);

    std::random_device rd;
    std::mt19937 re(rd());
```

```
std::uniform_real_distribution<double> dist(-1.5, 1.5);

// generate data
for (int32_t i = 0; i < n; ++i) {
    x_values.set_element(i, 0, i);
    auto y_val = func(i) + dist(re);
    y_values.set_element(y_val, i);
}

auto x = some<CDenseFeatures<float64_t>>(x_values);
auto y = some<CRegressionLabels>(y_values);

// rescale
auto x_scaler = some<CRescaleFeatures>();
x_scaler->fit(x);
x_scaler->transform(x, true);
```

We filled the x object of the CDenseFeatures type with the predictor variable values and the y object of the CRegressionLabels type with the target variable values. The linear dependence is the same as what we used in the previous example. We also rescaled the x values with the object of the CRescaleFeatures type.

To show how the serialization API in the Shogun library works, we will use the CLinearRidgeRegression and CNeuralNetwork models.

The following code sample shows how to train and serialize the CLinearRidgeRegression model:

```
void TrainAndSaveLRR(Some<CDenseFeatures<float64_t>> x,
                     Some<CRegressionLabels> y) {
    float64_t tau_regularization = 0.0001;
    auto model =
    some<CLinearRidgeRegression>(tau_regularization, nullptr, nullptr);
    model->set_labels(y);
    if (!model->train(x)) {
        std::cerr << "training failed\n";
    }
    auto file = some<CSerializableHdf5File>("shogun-lr.dat", 'w');
    if (!model->save_serializable(file)) {
        std::cerr << "Failed to save the model\n";
    }
}
```

Here, we saved the model parameters in the HDF5 file format with an object of the `CSerializableHdf5File` type. For other file formats, we can find the corresponding types in the library. All serializable models in the `Shogun` library have the `save_serializable` and `load_serializable` functions for saving and loading model parameters, respectively. These functions take a serialization file object. In this case, this object was of the `CSerializableHdf5File` type.

The following code shows how to train and save the parameters of a neural network object:

```
void TrainAndSaveNET(Some<CDenseFeatures<float64_t>> x,
                     Some<CRegressionLabels> y) {
    auto dimensions = x->get_num_features();
    auto layers = some<CNeuralLayers>();
    layers = wrap(layers->input(dimensions));
    layers = wrap(layers->linear(1));
    auto all_layers = layers->done();
    auto network = some<CNeuralNetwork>(all_layers);
    // configure network parameters
    ...

    network->set_labels(y);
    if (network->train(x)) {
        auto file = some<CSerializableHdf5File>("shogun-net.dat", 'w');
        if (!network->save_serializable(file)) {
            std::cerr << "Failed to save the model\n";
        }
    } else {
        std::cerr << "Failed to train the network\n";
    }
}
```

Here, we can see that neural network serialization is similar to serializing the linear regression model.

To test our serialized model, we will generate a new set of test data. The following code shows how we do this:

```
SGMatrix<float64_t> new_x_values(1, 5);
std::cout << "Target values : \n";
for (index_t i = 0; i < 5; ++i) {
    new_x_values.set_element(static_cast<double>(i), 0, i);
    std::cout << func(i) << std::endl;
}

auto new_x = some<CDenseFeatures<float64_t>>(new_x_values);
x_scaler->transform(new_x, true);
```

Notice that we reused the `x_scaler` object. But as we mentioned previously, it should be serialized and loaded too if we plan to stop and relaunch our application after training.

The following code shows the deserialization process:

```
void LoadAndPredictLRR(Some<CDenseFeatures<float64_t>> x) {
    auto file = some<CSerializableHdf5File>("shogun-lr.dat", 'r');
    auto model = some<CLinearRidgeRegression>();
    if (model->load_serializable(file)) {
        auto y_predict = model->apply_regression(x);
        std::cout << "LR predicted values: \n" << y_predict->to_string() <<
            << std::endl;
    }
}
...
LoadAndPredictLRR(new_x);
```

Here, the new `CLinearRidgeRegression` object was created and the `load_serializable` method was used to load its parameter.

As we mentioned previously, there is a particular function that's used to load a neural network structure from JSON files or strings. The problem is that we can't export this structure as a file with the library API, so we should make it by ourselves or write our custom exporter. However, this functionality allows us to define neural network architectures without programming in a declarative style. This can be useful for experiments because we don't need to recompile a whole application. It also allows us to deploy a new architecture to production without program updates, but note that we need to take care of preserving the input and output network tensor dimensions.

To load the neural network from the JSON-formatted string in the `Shogun` library, we can use an object of the `CNeuralNetworkFileReader` type. The following code shows how to use it:

```
Some<CNeuralNetwork> NETFromJson() {
    CNeuralNetworkFileReader reader;
    const char* net_str =
    "{"
        "\"optimization_method\": \"NNOM_GRADIENT_DESCENT\","
        "\"max_num_epochs\": 1000,"
        "\"gd_mini_batch_size\": 0,"
        "\"gd_learning_rate\": 0.01,"
        "\"gd_momentum\": 0.9,"
        "\"layers\":"
        "{"
            "\"input1\":"
            "{"
```

```
                    "\"type\": \"NeuralInputLayer\","
                    "\"num_neurons\": 1,"
                    "\"start_index\": 0"
                    "},"
                "\"linear1\":"
                "{"
                    "\"type\": \"NeuralLinearLayer\","
                    "\"num_neurons\": 1,"
                    "\"inputs\": [\"input1\"]"
                    "}"
                "}"
        "}";
    auto network = wrap(reader.read_string(net_str));
    return network;
}
```

Here, we defined the neural network architecture with a JSON string. This is the same neural network architecture that we used for training. Then, the `read_string` method of the `CNeuralNetworkFileReader` object was used to load and create an object of the `CNeuralNetwork` type.

The following code shows how to use the `NETFromJson` function to create a network object from the JSON string and initialize it with the serialized parameters:

```
void LoadAndPredictNET(Some<CDenseFeatures<float64_t>> x) {
    auto file = some<CSerializableHdf5File>("shogun-net.dat", 'r');
    auto network = NETFromJson();
    if (network->load_serializable(file)) {
        auto new_x = some<CDenseFeatures<float64_t>>(x);
        auto y_predict = network->apply_regression(new_x);
        std::cout << "Network predicted values: \n"
        << y_predict->to_string() << std::endl;
    }
}
```

The newly created neural network object is of the `CNeuralNetwork` type. We used the `load_serializable` method of the new neural network object to load the previously serialized parameters. It's essential to preserve the same architecture of ML model objects that are used for serialization and deserialization as a different architecture can lead to runtime errors when deserialization is performed.

In this section, we looked at how to use the `Shogun` library API for serialization. This library doesn't provide any functions that can be used to export ML model architectures, but it can load them from a JSON string. ML model parameters can be serialized into various file formats. In the next section, we will delve into the `Shark-ML` library's serialization API.

Model serialization with Shark-ML

The `Shark-ML` library has a unified API for serializing models of all kinds. Every model has the `write` and `read` methods for saving and loading model parameters, respectively. These methods take an instance of the `boost::archive` object as an input parameter.

Let's look at an example of model parameter serialization with the `Shark-ML` library. First, we generate training data for the linear regression model, as we did in the previous examples:

```
std::vector<RealVector> x_data(n);
std::vector<RealVector> y_data(n);

std::random_device rd;
std::mt19937 re(rd());
std::uniform_real_distribution<double> dist(-1.5, 1.5);

RealVector x_v(1);
RealVector y_v(1);
for (size_t i = 0; i < n; ++i) {
    x_v(0) = i;
    x_data[i] = x_v;
    y_v(0) = func(i) + dist(re);   // add noise
    y_data[i] = y_v;
}

Data<RealVector> x = createDataFromRange(x_data);
Data<RealVector> y = createDataFromRange(y_data);
RegressionDataset data(x, y);
```

Here, we created two vectors, `x_data` and `y_data`, which contain predictor and target value objects of the `RealVector` type. Then, we made the `x` and the `y` objects of the `Data` type and placed them into the `data` object of the `RegressionDataset` type.

The following code shows how to train a linear model object with the dataset object we initialized previously:

```
LinearModel<> model;
LinearRegression trainer;
trainer.train(model, data);
```

Here, we trained the `LinearModel` object with the trainer of the `LinearRegression` type.

Now that we've trained the model, we can save its parameters in a file using the `boost::archive::polymorphic_binary_oarchive` object. The following code shows how to do this:

```
std::ofstream ofs("shark-linear.dat");
boost::archive::polymorphic_binary_oarchive oa(ofs);
model.write(oa);
```

The archive object, `oa`, was initialized with the `ofs` object of the `std::ofstream` type. The output stream type was chosen because we needed to save the model parameters.

The following code shows how to load saved model parameters:

```
std::ifstream ifs("shark-linear.dat");
boost::archive::polymorphic_binary_iarchive ia(ifs);
LinearModel<> model;
model.read(ia);
```

We loaded the model parameters with the `read` method, which took the `boost::archive::polymorphic_binary_iarchive` object, which was initialized with the `std::ifstream` object. Notice that we created a new `LinearModel` object.

Instead of using binary serialization, the `Shark-ML` library allows us to use the `boost::archive::polymorphic_text_oarchive` and `boost::archive::polymorphic_text_iarchive` types to serialize to an ASCII text file.

The following code shows how to generate new test values so that we can check the model:

```
std::vector<RealVector> new_x_data;
for (size_t i = 0; i < 5; ++i) {
    new_x_data.push_back({static_cast<double>(i)});
    std::cout << func(i) << std::endl;
}
```

The following code shows how to use the model for prediction purposes:

```
auto prediction = model(createDataFromRange(new_x_data));
std::cout << "Predictions: \n" << prediction << std::endl;
```

The prediction was made with a call to the model's object functional operator.

In this section, we saw that the `Shark-ML` library has an API that we can use to save and load parameters but that it lacks the functions to save and load ML model architectures.

In the next section, we will look at the `PyTorch` library's serialization API.

Model serialization with PyTorch

In this section, we will discuss two approaches to network parameter serialization that are available in the `PyTorch` C++ library. The first is using the `torch::save` function, while the second is using an object of the `torch::serialize::OutputArchive` type for writing parameters into it.

Let's prepare the neural network for further use.

Neural network initialization

Let's start by generating the training data. The following code shows how we can do this:

```cpp
torch::DeviceType device = torch::cuda::is_available()
                              ? torch::DeviceType::CUDA
                              : torch::DeviceType::CPU;

std::random_device rd;
std::mt19937 re(rd());
std::uniform_real_distribution<float> dist(-0.1f, 0.1f);

// generate data
size_t n = 1000;
torch::Tensor x;
torch::Tensor y;
{
    std::vector<float> values(n);
    std::iota(values.begin(), values.end(), 0);
    std::shuffle(values.begin(), values.end(), re);
    std::vector<torch::Tensor> x_vec(n);
    std::vector<torch::Tensor> y_vec(n);
    for (size_t i = 0; i < n; ++i) {
        x_vec[i] = torch::tensor(
        values[i],
        torch::dtype(torch::kFloat).device(device).requires_grad(false));
        y_vec[i] = torch::tensor(
        (func(values[i]) + dist(re)),
        torch::dtype(torch::kFloat).device(device).requires_grad(false));
    }
```

```
        x = torch::stack(x_vec);
        y = torch::stack(y_vec);
    }

    // normalize data
    auto x_mean = torch::mean(x, /*dim*/ 0);
    auto x_std = torch::std(x, /*dim*/ 0);
    x = (x - x_mean) / x_std;
```

Usually, we want to utilize as many hardware resources as possible. So, first, we checked whether a GPU with CUDA technology was available in the system with the `torch::cuda::is_available()` call. Then, we generated 1,000 predictor variable values and shuffled them. For each value, we calculated the target value with the linear function we used in the previous examples. All the values were moved into the `torch::Tensor` objects with `torch::tensor` function calls. Notice that we used a previously detected device for tensor creation. After we moved all the values to tensors, we used the `torch::stack` function to concatenate the predictor and target values in two distinct single tensors. This was required to perform data normalization with the `PyTorch` linear algebra routines. Then, we used the `torch::mean` and `torch::std` functions to calculate the mean and standard deviation of predictor values and normalized them.

In the following code, we're defining the `NetImpl` class, which implements our neural network:

```
class NetImpl : public torch::nn::Module {
  public:
    NetImpl() {
        l1_ = torch::nn::Linear(torch::nn::LinearOptions(1,
                                    8).with_bias(true));
        register_module("l1", l1_);
        l2_ = torch::nn::Linear(torch::nn::LinearOptions(8,
                                    4).with_bias(true));
        register_module("l2", l2_);
        l3_ = torch::nn::Linear(torch::nn::LinearOptions(4,
                                    1).with_bias(true));
        register_module("l3", l3_);
        // initialize weights
        for (auto m : modules(false)) {
            if (m->name().find("Linear") != std::string::npos) {
                for (auto& p : m->named_parameters()) {
                    if (p.key().find("weight") != std::string::npos) {
                        torch::nn::init::normal_(p.value(), 0, 0.01);
                    }
                    if (p.key().find("bias") != std::string::npos) {
                        torch::nn::init::zeros_(p.value());
                    }
```

```
                    }
                }
            }
        }
    torch::Tensor forward(torch::Tensor x) {
        auto y = l1_(x);
        y = l2_(y);
        y = l3_(y);
        return y;
    }
  private:
    torch::nn::Linear l1_{nullptr};
    torch::nn::Linear l2_{nullptr};
    torch::nn::Linear l3_{nullptr};
}
TORCH_MODULE(Net);
```

Here, we defined our neural network model as a network with three fully connected neuron layers with a linear activation function. Each layer is of the `torch::nn::Linear` type. In the constructor of our model, we initialized all the network parameters with small random values. We did this by iterating over all the network modules (see the `modules` method call) and applying the `torch::nn::init::normal_` function to the parameters that were returned by the `named_parameters()` module's method. Biases were initialized to zeros with the `torch::nn::init::zeros_` function. The `named_parameters()` method returned objects consisting of a string name and a tensor value, so for initialization, we used its `value` method.

Now, we can train the model with our generated training data. The following code shows how to train our model:

```
Net model;
model->to(device);

// initialize optimizer ----------------------------------------------
double learning_rate = 0.01;
torch::optim::Adam optimizer(
        model->parameters(),
        torch::optim::AdamOptions(learning_rate).weight_decay(0.00001));

// training
int64_t batch_size = 10;
int64_t batches_num = static_cast<int64_t>(n) / batch_size;
int epochs = 10;
for (int epoch = 0; epoch < epochs; ++epoch) {
    // train the model ------------------------------------------------
    model->train();  // switch to the training mode
```

```
    // Iterate the data
    double epoch_loss = 0;
    for (int64_t batch_index = 0; batch_index < batches_num;
++batch_index) {
        auto batch_x = x.narrow(0, batch_index * batch_size, batch_size);
        auto batch_y = y.narrow(0, batch_index * batch_size, batch_size);
        // Clear gradients
        optimizer.zero_grad();
        // Execute the model on the input data
        torch::Tensor prediction = model->forward(batch_x);
        torch::Tensor loss = torch::mse_loss(prediction, batch_y);
        // Compute gradients of the loss and parameters of our model
        loss.backward();
        // Update the parameters based on the calculated gradients.
        optimizer.step();
    }
}
```

To utilize all our hardware resources, we moved the model to the selected computational device. Then, we initialized an optimizer. In our case, the optimizer used the Adam algorithm. Afterwards, we ran a standard training loop over the epochs, where for each epoch, we took the training batch, cleared the optimizer's gradients, performed a forward pass, computed the loss, performed a backward pass, and updated the model weights with the optimizer step.

To select a batch of training data from the dataset, we used the tensor's `narrow` method, which returned a new tensor with a reduced dimension. This function takes a new number of dimensions as the first parameter, the start position as the second parameter, and the number of elements to remain as the third parameter.

As we mentioned previously there are two approaches we can use to serialize model parameters in `PyTorch` in the C++ API (the Python API provides even more reach). Let's look at them.

Using the torch::save and torch::load functions

The first approach we can use to save model parameters is using the `torch::save` function, which recursively saves parameters from the passed module:

```
torch::save(model, "pytorch_net.pt");
```

To use it correctly with our custom modules, we need to register all the submodules in the parent one with the `register_module` module's method.

To load the saved parameters, we can use the `torch::load` function:

```
Net model_loaded;
torch::load(model_loaded, "pytorch_net.pt");
```

The function fills the passed module parameters with the values that are read from a file.

Using PyTorch archive objects

The second approach is to use an object of the `torch::serialize::OutputArchive` type and write the parameters we want to save into it. The following code shows how to implement the `SaveWeights` method for our model. This method writes all the parameters and buffers that exist in our module to the `archive` object, and then it uses the `save_to` method to write them in a file:

```
void NetImpl::SaveWeights(const std::string& file_name) {
    torch::serialize::OutputArchive archive;
    auto parameters = named_parameters(true /*recurse*/);
    auto buffers = named_buffers(true /*recurse*/);
    for (const auto& param : parameters) {
        if (param.value().defined()) {
            archive.write(param.key(), param.value());
        }
    }
    for (const auto& buffer : buffers) {
        if (buffer.value().defined()) {
            archive.write(buffer.key(), buffer.value(), /*is_buffer*/
true);
        }
    }
    archive.save_to(file_name);
}
```

It is important to save buffers tensors too. Buffers can be retrieved from a module with the `named_buffers` module's method. These objects represent the intermediate values that are used to evaluate different modules. For example, we can be running mean and standard deviation values for the batch normalization module. We need them to continue being trained if we used serialization to save the intermediate steps and if our training process was stopped for some reason.

To load parameters that have been saved this way, we can use the
`torch::serialize::InputArchive` object. The following code shows how to implement
the `LoadWeights` method for our model:

```
void NetImpl::LoadWeights(const std::string& file_name) {
    torch::serialize::InputArchive archive;
    archive.load_from(file_name);
    torch::NoGradGuard no_grad;
    auto parameters = named_parameters(true /*recurse*/);
    auto buffers = named_buffers(true /*recurse*/);
    for (auto& param : parameters) {
        archive.read(param.key(), param.value());
    }
    for (auto& buffer : buffers) {
        archive.read(buffer.key(), buffer.value(), /*is_buffer*/ true);
    }
}
```

This method uses the `load_from` method of the `archive` object to load parameters from
the file. Then, we took the parameters and buffers from our module with
the `named_parameters` and `named_buffers` methods and incrementally filled in their
values with the `read` method of the `archive` object. Notice that we used an instance of the
`torch::NoGradGuard` class to tell the `PyTorch` library that we don't perform any model
calculation and graph-related operations. It's essential to do this because the `PyTorch`
construct calculation graph and any unrelated operations can lead to errors.

Now, we can use the new instance of our `model_loaded` model with load parameters to
evaluate the model on some test data. Note that we need to switch the model to the
evaluation model with the `eval` method. Generated test data values should also be
converted into tensor objects with the `torch::tensor` function and moved to the same
computational device that our model uses. The following code shows how we can
implement this:

```
model_loaded->to(device);
model_loaded->eval();
std::cout << "Test:\n";
for (int i = 0; i < 5; ++i) {
    auto x_val = static_cast<float>(i) + 0.1f;
    auto tx = torch::tensor(x_val,
torch::dtype(torch::kFloat).device(device));
    tx = (tx - x_mean) / x_std;
    auto ty = torch::tensor(func(x_val),
torch::dtype(torch::kFloat).device(device));
    torch::Tensor prediction = model_loaded->forward(tx);
    std::cout << "Target:" << ty << std::endl;
```

```
            std::cout << "Prediction:" << prediction << std::endl;
    }
```

In this section, we looked at two types of serialization in the `PyTorch` library. The first approach was using the `torch::save` and `torch::load` functions, which easily save and load all the model parameters, respectively. The second approach was using objects of the `torch::serialize::InputArchive` and `torch::serialize::OutputArchive` types so that we can select what parameters we want to save and load.

In the next section, we will discuss the ONNX file format, which allows us to share our ML model architecture and model parameters among different frameworks.

Delving into ONNX format

ONNX format is a special file format used to share neural network architectures and parameters between different frameworks. It is based on the Google Protobuf format and library. The reason why this format exists is to test and run the same neural network model in different environments and on different devices. Usually, researchers use a programming framework that they know how to use in order to develop a model, and then run this model in a different environment for production purposes or if they want to share their model with other researchers or developers. This format is supported by all leading frameworks, such as `PyTorch`, `TensorFlow`, `MXNet`, and others. But now, there is a lack of support for this format from the C++ API of these frameworks and at the time of writing, they only have a Python interface for dealing with ONNX format. Some time ago, Facebook developed the Caffe2 neural network framework in order to run models on different platforms with the best performance. This framework also had a C++ API, and it was able to load and run models saved in ONNX format. Now, this framework has been merged with `PyTorch`. There is a plan to remove the Caffe2 API and replace it with a new combined API in `PyTorch`. But at the time of writing, the Caffe2 C++ API is still available as part of the `PyTorch` 1.2 (`libtorch`) library.

Usually, we, as developers, don't need to know how ONNX format works internally because we are only interested in files where the model is saved. Internally, ONNX format is a Protobuf formatted file. The following code shows the first part of the ONNX file, which describes how to use the ResNet neural network architecture for image classification:

```
ir_version: 3
graph {
    node {
        input: "data"
        input: "resnetv24_batchnorm0_gamma"
        input: "resnetv24_batchnorm0_beta"
```

```
        input: "resnetv24_batchnorm0_running_mean"
        input: "resnetv24_batchnorm0_running_var"
        output: "resnetv24_batchnorm0_fwd"
        name: "resnetv24_batchnorm0_fwd"
        op_type: "BatchNormalization"
        attribute {
            name: "epsilon"
            f: 1e-05
            type: FLOAT
        }
        attribute {
            name: "momentum"
            f: 0.9
            type: FLOAT
        }
        attribute {
            name: "spatial"
            i: 1
            type: INT
        }
    }
    node {
        input: "resnetv24_batchnorm0_fwd"
        input: "resnetv24_conv0_weight"
        output: "resnetv24_conv0_fwd"
        name: "resnetv24_conv0_fwd"
        op_type: "Conv"
        attribute {
            name: "dilations"
            ints: 1
            ints: 1
            type: INTS
        }
        attribute {
            name: "group"
            i: 1
            type: INT
        }
        attribute {
            name: "kernel_shape"
            ints: 7
            ints: 7
            type: INTS
        }
        attribute {
            name: "pads"
            ints: 3
            ints: 3
```

```
                    ints: 3
                    ints: 3
                    type: INTS
            }
            attribute {
                    name: "strides"
                    ints: 2
                    ints: 2
                    type: INTS
            }
        }
        ...
    }
```

Usually, ONNX files come in binary format to reduce file size and increase loading speed.

Now, let's learn how to use the Caffe2 C++ API to load and run ONNX models. Unfortunately, there is only one available C++ library API that can be used to run models saved in ONNX format. This because Caffe2 can automatically convert them into its internal representation. Other libraries do such conversion in their Python modules. The ONNX community provides pre-trained models for the most popular neural network architectures in the publicly available Model Zoo (https://github.com/onnx/models). There are a lot of ready to use models that can be used to solve different ML tasks. For example, we can take the ResNet-50 model for image classification tasks (https://github. com/onnx/models/tree/master/vision/classification/resnet). For this model, we have to download the corresponding synset file with image class descriptions to be able to return classification results in a human-readable manner. The link to the file is https://github. com/onnx/models/blob/master/vision/classification/synset.txt.

To be able to use the Caffe2 C++ API, we have to use the following headers:

```
#include <caffe2/core/init.h>
#include <caffe2/onnx/backend.h>
#include <caffe2/utils/proto_utils.h>
```

However, we still need to link our program to the libtorch.so library.

First, we need to initialize the Caffe2 library:

```
caffe2::GlobalInit(&argc, &argv);
```

Then, we need to load the Protobuf model representation. This can be done with an instance of the `onnx_torch::ModelProto` class. To use an object of this class to load the model, we need to use the `ParseFromIstream` method, which takes the `std::istream` object as an input parameter. The following code shows how to use an object of the `onnx_torch::ModelProto` class:

```
onnx_torch::ModelProto model_proto;
{
    std::ifstream file(argv[1], std::ios_base::binary);
    if (!file) {
        std::cerr << "File " << argv[1] << "can't be opened\n";
        return 1;
    }
    if (!model_proto.ParseFromIstream(&file)) {
        std::cerr << "Failed to parse onnx model\n";
        return 1;
    }
}
```

The `caffe2::onnx::Caffe2Backend` class should be used to convert the Protobuf ONNX model into an internal representation of Caffe2. This class contains the `Prepare` method, which takes the Protobuf formatted string, along with the model's description, a string containing the name of the computational device, and some additional settings (typically, these settings can be empty). The following code shows how to use the `SerializeToString` method of the `onnx_torch::ModelProto` class to make the model's string representation before we prepare the model:

```
std::string model_str;
if (model_proto.SerializeToString(&model_str)) {
    caffe2::onnx::Caffe2Backend onnx_backend;
    std::vector<caffe2::onnx::Caffe2Ops> ops;
    auto model = onnx_backend.Prepare(model_str, "CPU", ops);
    if (model != nullptr) {
        ...
    }
}
```

Now that we've prepared the model for evaluation, we have to prepare input and output data containers. In our case, the input is a tensor of size `1 x 3 x 224 x 224`, which represents the RGB image for classification. But the Caffe2 ONNX model takes a vector of `caffe2::TensorCPU` objects as input, so we need to move our image to the `inputs` vector. Caffe2 tensor objects are not copyable, but they can be moved. The `outputs` vector should be empty.

The following snippet shows how to prepare the input and output data for the model:

```
caffe2::TensorCPU image = ReadImageTensor(argv[2], 224, 224);

std::vector<caffe2::TensorCPU> inputs;
inputs.push_back(std::move(image));

std::vector<caffe2::TensorCPU> outputs(1);
```

The model is an object of the `Caffe2BackendRep` class, which uses the `Run` method for evaluation. We can use it in the following way:

```
model->Run(inputs, &outputs);
```

The output of this model is image scores (probabilities) for each of the 1,000 classes of the ImageNet dataset, which was used to train the model. The following code shows how to decode the model's output:

```
std::map<size_t, std::string> classes = ReadClasses(argv[3]);
for (auto& output : outputs) {
    const auto& probabilities = output.data<float>();
    std::vector<std::pair<float, int>> pairs;  // prob : class index
    for (auto i = 0; i < output.size(); i++) {
        if (probabilities[i] > 0.01f) {
            pairs.push_back(
            std::make_pair(probabilities[i], i + 1));  // 0 - background
        }
    }
    std::sort(pairs.begin(), pairs.end());
    std::reverse(pairs.begin(), pairs.end());
    pairs.resize(std::min(5UL, pairs.size()));
    for (auto& p : pairs) {
        std::cout << "Class " << p.second << " Label "
        << classes[static_cast<size_t>(p.second)] << " Prob "
        << p.first << std::endl;
    }
}
```

Here, we iterated over each output tensor from the `outputs` vector. In our case, there is only one item, but if we were to use several input images in the `inputs` vector, we would have several results. Then, we placed the score values and class indices in the vector of corresponding pairs. This vector was sorted by score, in descending order. Then, we printed five classes with the maximum score.

To access the elements of the `caffe2::TensorCPU` object, we used the `data<float>()` method, which returns the pointer to the `const` row-ordered floating-point values of the tensor. In this example, the output tensor had a dimension of `1x1000`, so we accessed its values just like we did in the linear array.

To correctly finish the program, we have to shut down the Google `protobuf` library, which we used to load the required ONNX files:

```
google::protobuf::ShutdownProtobufLibrary();
```

In this section, we looked at an example of how to deal with ONNX format in the `PyTorch` and Caffe2 libraries, but we still need to learn how load input images into Caffe2 tensor objects, which we use for the model's input.

Loading images into Caffe2 tensors

Let's learn how to load an image into the Caffe2 tensor object and modify it according to the model's input requirements. The model expects the input images to be normalized and three-channel RGB images whose shapes are (N x 3 x H x W), where N is the batch size and H and W are expected to be at least 224 pixels wide. Normalization assumes that the images are loaded into a range of `[0, 1]` and then normalized using means equal to `[0.485, 0.456, 0.406]` and standard deviations equal to `[0.229, 0.224, 0.225]`.

Let's assume that we have the following function definition for image loading:

```
caffe2::TensorCPU ReadImageTensor(const std::string& file_name,
                                  int width,
                                  int height) {
    ...
}
```

Let's write its implementation. For image loading, we will use the OpenCV library:

```
// load image
auto image = cv::imread(file_name, cv::IMREAD_COLOR);

if (!image.cols || !image.rows) {
    return {};
}

if (image.cols != width || image.rows != height) {
    // scale image to fit
    cv::Size scaled(std::max(height * image.cols / image.rows, width),
    std::max(height, width * image.rows / image.cols));
```

```
    cv::resize(image, image, scaled);

  // crop image to fit
    cv::Rect crop((image.cols - width) / 2, (image.rows - height) / 2,
width,
    height);
    image = image(crop);
}
```

Here, we read the image from a file with the `cv::imread` function. If the image dimensions are not equal to specified ones, we need to resize the image with the `cv::resize` function and crop the image if the image dimensions exceed the specified ones.

Then, we convert the image into the floating-point type and RGB format:

```
image.convertTo(image, CV_32FC3);
cv::cvtColor(image, image, cv::COLOR_BGR2RGB);
```

After formatting is complete, we can split the image into three separate channels with red, green, and blue colors. We should also normalize the color values. The following code shows how to do this:

```
std::vector<cv::Mat> channels(3);
cv::split(image, channels);

std::vector<double> mean = {0.485, 0.456, 0.406};
std::vector<double> stddev = {0.229, 0.224, 0.225};

size_t i = 0;
for (auto& c : channels) {
   c = ((c / 255) - mean[i]) / stddev[i];
   ++i;
}
```

Each channel was subtracted by the corresponding mean and divided by the corresponding standard deviation for the normalization process.

Then, we should concatenate the channels:

```
cv::vconcat(channels[0], channels[1], image);
cv::vconcat(image, channels[2], image);
assert(image.isContinuous());
```

The normalized channels were concatenated into one contiguous image with the `cv::vconcat` function.

The following code shows how to initialize the Caffe2 tensor with the image data:

```
std::vector<int64_t> dims = {1, 3, height, width};

caffe2::TensorCPU tensor(dims, caffe2::DeviceType::CPU);
std::copy_n(reinterpret_cast<float*>(image.data),
            image.size().area(),
            tensor.mutable_data<float>());

return tensor;
```

Here, the image data was copied into the `caffe2::TensorCPU` object, which was initialized with the specified dimensions. The computational device was equal to `caffe2::DeviceType::CPU`. This tensor object was created with the floating-point underlying type by default, so we used the `mutable_data<float>()` member function to access the internal storage of the tensor. The OpenCV image data was accessed with the `cv::Mat::data` type member. We cast the image data into the floating-point type because this member variable is of the `unsigned char *` type. The pixel's data was copied with the standard `std::copy_n` function. Finally, in the last snippet of code, we returned the tensor object.

Another important function that was used in the ONNX format example was a function that can read class definitions from a synset file. We will take a look at this in the next section.

Reading the class definition file

We used the `ReadClasses` function in this example to load the map of objects. Here, the key was an image class index and the value was a textual class description. This function is trivial and reads the synset file line by line. In such a file, each line contains a number and a class description string, separated with the space character. The following code shows its definition:

```
using Classes = std::map<size_t, std::string>;
Classes ReadClasses(const std::string& file_name) {
  Classes classes;
  std::ifstream file(file_name);
  if (file) {
    std::string line;
    std::string id;
    std::string label;
    std::string token;
    size_t idx = 1;
    while (std::getline(file, line)) {
```

```
            std::stringstream line_stream(line);
            size_t i = 0;
            while (std::getline(line_stream, token, ' ')) {
                switch (i) {
                  case 0:
                    id = token;
                    break;
                  case 1:
                    label = token;
                    break;
                }
                token.clear();
                ++i;
            }
            classes.insert({idx, label});
            ++idx;
        }
    }
    return classes;
}
```

Notice that we used the `std::getline` function in the internal `while` loop to tokenize a single line string. We did this by specifying the third parameter that defines the delimiter character value.

Summary

In this chapter, we learned how to save and load model parameters in different ML frameworks. We saw that all the frameworks we used in the `Shogun`, `Shark-ML`, `Dlib`, and `PyTorch` libraries have an API for model parameter serialization. Usually, these are quite simple functions that work with model objects and some input and output streams. Also, we discussed another type of serialization API that can be used to save and load the overall model architecture. At the time of writing, the frameworks we used don't fully support such functionality. The `Shogun toolkit` can load neural network architectures from the JSON descriptions, but can't export them. The `Dlib` library can export neural networks in XML format but can't load them. The `PyTorch` C++ API lacks a model architecture that supports exporting, but it can load and evaluate model architectures that have been exported from the Python API with its TorchScript functionality. However, the `PyTorch` library does provide access to the Caffe2 library API, which allows us to load and evaluate models saved in ONNX format from C++.

We briefly looked at ONNX format and realized that it is quite a popular format for sharing models among different ML frameworks. It supports almost all operations and objects that are used to serialize complex neural network models effectively. At the time of writing, it is supported by all popular ML frameworks, such as `TensorFlow`, `PyTorch`, `MXNet`, and others. Also, Microsoft provides the ONNX runtime implementation, which allows us to run the ONNX model's inference without us having to depend on any other frameworks.

And at the end of this chapter, we developed a C++ application that can be used to run the inference of the ResNet-50 model, which was trained with the MXNet framework and exported in ONNX format. This application was made with the Caffe2 C++ API in order to load the model and evaluate it on the loaded image for classification.

In the next chapter, we will discuss how to deploy ML models developed with C++ libraries to mobile devices and server instances.

Further reading

- Shark-ML documentation: `http://www.shark-ml.org/sphinx_pages/build/html/rest_sources/tutorials/tutorials.html`
- Dlib documentation: `http://dlib.net/`
- Shogun toolkit documentation: `https://www.shogun-toolbox.org/`
- PyTorch C++ API: `https://pytorch.org/cppdocs/`
- ONNX official page: `https://onnx.ai/`
- ONNX Model Zoo: `https://github.com/onnx/models`
- ONNX ResNet models for image classification: `https://github.com/onnx/models/tree/master/vision/classification/resnet`
- Caffe2 tutorials: `https://github.com/leonardvandriel/caffe2_cpp_tutorial/`

13
Deploying Models on Mobile and Cloud Platforms

In this chapter, we'll discuss deploying machine learning models on mobile devices running on both the Android operating system and the **Google Cloud Platform** (GCP).

Using C++ on mobile devices allows us to make programs faster and more compact. We can utilize as many computational resources as possible because modern compilers can optimize the program concerning the target CPU architecture. C++ doesn't use an additional garbage collector for memory management, which can have a significant impact on program performance. Program size can be reduced because C++ doesn't use an additional VM and is compiled directly to machine code. These facts make C++ the right choice for mobile devices with a limited amount of resources and can be used to solve heavy computational tasks.

Using C++ to implement machine learning models that are used for the cloud can provide other benefits. As we mentioned previously, you can increase application performance by compiling a program for your specific architecture; usually, this plays a significant role in the data preprocessing step. The starting time is also much shorter for a native application than for interpretable programs. This fact can make your application more responsive if you're using cloud machines that are only launched by client requests. These types of machines are used for reducing the cloud service's cost.

The following topics will be covered in this chapter:

- Image classification on Android mobile
- Machine learning in the cloud – using Google Compute Engine

Technical requirements

The following are the technical requirements for this chapter:

- Android Studio, Android SDK, Android NDK
- A Google account
- GCP SDK
- PyTorch library
- `cpp-httplib` library
- A modern C++ compiler with C++17 support
- CMake build system version >= 3.8

The code files for this chapter can be found at the following GitHub repo: `https://github.com/PacktPublishing/Hands-On-Machine-Learning-with-CPP/tree/master/Chapter13`

Image classification on Android mobile

There are two popular approaches regarding how to deploy a machine learning model to a mobile device with Android. We can either use the PyTorch framework, which now incorporates Caffe2, or we can use the TensorFlow Lite framework. We'll use the PyTorch framework in this chapter since we have discussed it in the previous chapters.

The mobile version of the PyTorch framework

There is no available binary distribution of PyTorch for mobile devices, so we need to build it from source code. We can do this in the same way as we compile its regular version but with additional CMake parameters to enable mobile mode. You also have to install the Android **Native Development Kit** (**NDK**), which includes an appropriate version of the C/C++ compiler and the Android native libraries that are required to build the application. The following code snippet shows how to use the command-line environment to check out PyTorch and build its Android mobile version:

```
cd /home/[USER]
git clone https://github.com/pytorch/pytorch.git
cd pytorch/
git checkout v1.2.0
git submodule update --init
export ANDROID_NDK=/home/[USER]/Android/Sdk/ndk/20.0.5594570
export ANDROID_ABI='armeabi-v7a'

/home/[USER]/pytorch/scripts/build_android.sh \
```

```
-DBUILD_CAFFE2_MOBILE=OFF \
-DBUILD_SHARED_LIBS=ON \
-DCMAKE_PREFIX_PATH=$(python -c 'from distutils.sysconfig import
get_python_lib; print(get_python_lib())') \
-DPYTHON_EXECUTABLE=$(python -c 'import sys; print(sys.executable)') \
```

Here, we assumed that `/home/[USER]` is the user's home directory. The main requirement when it comes to building the mobile version of PyTorch is to declare the `ANDROID_NDK` environmental variable, which should point to the Android NDK installation directory. The simplest way to install Android development tools is to download the Android Studio IDE and use the SDK Manager tool from that. You can find the SDK Manager under the **Tools** | **SDK Manager** menu. You can use this manager to install appropriate Android SDK versions. You can install the corresponding NDKs by using the **SDK Tools** tab in the manager's window. You can also use this tab to install the CMake utility. The `ANDROID_ABI` environment variable can be used to specify the ARM CPU architecture's compatibility for the compiler to generate architecture-specific code. In this example, we used the `armeabi-v7a` architecture.

We used the `build_android.sh` script from the PyTorch source code distribution to build mobile PyTorch binaries. This script uses the CMake command internally, which is why it takes CMake parameter definitions as arguments. Notice that we passed the `BUILD_CAFFE2_MOBILE=OFF` parameter to disable building the mobile version of Caffe2, which is hard to use in the current version because the library is deprecated. The second important parameter we used was `BUILD_SHARED_LIBS=ON`, which enabled us to build shared libraries. We did this because the static versions of the mobile PyTorch 1.2 libraries can't be used now because of broken initialization functions. The other parameters that were configured were the Python installation paths for intermediate build code generation.

Now that we have the mobile PyTorch libraries, that is, `libc10.so` and `libtorch.so`, we can start developing the application. We are going to build a simple image classification application based on the ResNet-18 neural network architecture. This architecture has the smallest number of parameters within the ResNet networks family, so we can use it on devices with a low amount of memory.

Using TorchScript for a model snapshot

In this section, we will discuss how to get the model snapshot file so that we can use it in our mobile application. In the previous chapters, we discussed how to save and load model parameters and how to use ONNX format to share models between frameworks. When we use the PyTorch framework, there is another method we can use to share models between the Python API and C++ API called TorchScript.

This method uses real-time model tracing to get a special type of model definition that can be executed by the PyTorch engine, regardless of API. For PyTorch 1.2, only the Python API can create such definitions, but we can use the C++ API to load the model and execute it. Also, the mobile version of the PyTorch framework still doesn't allow us to program neural networks with a full-featured C++ API; only the ATen library is available.

So, in this example, we are going to use the TorchScript model to perform image classification. To get this model, we need to use the Python API to load the pre-trained model, trace it, and save the model snapshot. The following code shows how to do this with Python:

```python
import torch
import urllib
from PIL import Image
from torchvision import transforms

# Download pretrained model
model = torch.hub.load('pytorch/vision', 'resnet18', pretrained=True)
model.eval()

# Download an example image from the pytorch website
url, filename = ("https://github.com/pytorch/hub/raw/master/dog.jpg",
"dog.jpg")

try:
    urllib.URLopener().retrieve(url, filename)
except:
    urllib.request.urlretrieve(url, filename)

# sample execution
input_image = Image.open(filename)
preprocess = transforms.Compose([
    transforms.Resize(256),
    transforms.CenterCrop(224),
    transforms.ToTensor(),
    transforms.Normalize(mean=[0.485, 0.456, 0.406], std=[0.229, 0.224,
    0.225]),
])
input_tensor = preprocess(input_image)

# create a mini-batch as expected by the model
input_batch = input_tensor.unsqueeze(0)

traced_script_module = torch.jit.trace(model, input_batch)

traced_script_module.save("model.pt")
```

In this programming sample, we performed the following steps:

1. We downloaded a pre-trained model with the `torch.hub.load()` function.
2. Then, we downloaded an input image with the `urllib` module.
3. With the input image acquired, we used the `PIL` library to resize and normalize it.
4. Using the `unsqueeze()` function, we added a batch size dimension to the input tensor.
5. Then, we used the `torch.jit.trace()` function to run the loaded model and trace it into a script.
6. Finally, we simply saved the `script` module into a file with the `save()` method.

Now that we have saved the script module, we can start creating an Android application that will use it for image classification.

The Android Studio project

In this section, we will use the Android Studio IDE to create our mobile application. We can use a default **Native C++** wizard in the Android Studio IDE to create an application stub. Android Studio will create a specific project structure; the following sample shows the most valuable parts of it:

```
app
  |
  src
    |
   main
      cpp
        |
       CMakeLists.txt
       native-lib.cpp
      java
        |
       com
         |
        example
            |
           Camera2
               |
              MainActivity.java
     res
       |
      layout
```

```
              |
             activity_main.xml
          values
              |
             colors.xml
             strings.xml
             styles.xml
          . . .
      build.gradle
      . . .
  build.gradle
  local.properties
  . . .
```

The `cpp` folder contains the C++ part of the whole project. In this project, the Android Studio IDE created the C++ part as a native shared library project that had been configured with the CMake build generation system. The `java` folder contains the Java part of the project. In our case, it is a single file that defines the main activity—the object that's used as a connection between the UI elements and event handlers. The `res` folder contains project resources, such as UI elements and strings definitions.

We also need to create the `jniLibs` folder, under the `main` folder, with the following structure:

```
app
  |
  src
   |
   main
    |
    . . .
   jniLibs
      |
     armeabi-v7a
          |
         libc10.so
         libtorch.so
     x86
      |
     . . .
```

Android Studio requires us to place additional native libraries in such folders to correctly package them into the final application. It also allows the JNI system to be able to find these libraries. Notice that we placed PyTorch libraries in the `armeabi-v7a` folder because they have only been compiled for this CPU architecture. If you have libraries for other architectures, you have to create folders with corresponding names.

The IDE uses the Gradle build system for project configuration, so there are two files named `build.gradle`, which contains the main settings, and `local.properties`, which contains user-defined values.

Now, we can adapt the default UI for our purposes. We'll learn how to do this in the next section.

The UI and Java part of the project

Our application will have the following user interface:

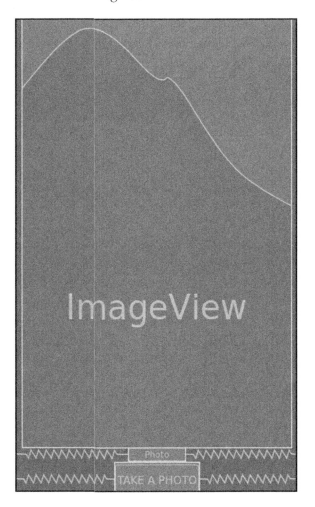

It has a button that we can use to launch a native camera application to take a photo, a text view to show image classification descriptions, and an image view to show the photo. We should define these UI elements in the `activity_main.xml` file of the project. The following snippet shows this file:

```xml
<?xml version="1.0" encoding="utf-8"?>
<RelativeLayout xmlns:android="http://schemas.android.com/apk/res/android"
    android:layout_width="match_parent"
    android:layout_height="match_parent"
    android:paddingLeft="10dp"
    android:paddingRight="10dp">
<TextView
    android:text="@string/btn_name"
    android:textStyle="bold"
    android:id="@+id/textViewClass"
    android:layout_width="wrap_content"
    android:layout_height="wrap_content"
    android:layout_centerHorizontal="true"
    android:layout_above="@+id/btnTakePicture"/>
<Button
    android:id="@+id/btnTakePicture"
    android:layout_width="wrap_content"
    android:layout_height="wrap_content"
    android:text="@string/btn_name"
    android:textStyle="bold"
    android:layout_centerHorizontal="true"
    android:layout_alignParentBottom="true" />
<ImageView
    android:layout_width="fill_parent"
    android:layout_height="fill_parent"
    android:id="@+id/capturedImage"
    android:layout_above="@+id/textViewClass"
    android:contentDescription="@string/img_desc"/>
</RelativeLayout>
```

We should also define the text captions for the UI elements in the `strings.xml` file, which you can find in the `res` folder. The following snippet shows an interesting part of this file:

```xml
<resources>
    <string name="app_name">Camera2</string>
    <string name="btn_name">Take a photo</string>
    <string name="img_desc">Photo</string>
</resources>
```

Now that the UI elements have been defined, we can connect them to event handlers in the `MainActivity` class to make our application respond to users' actions. The following code sample shows how we can modify the `MainActivity` class so that it suits our needs:

```
public class MainActivity extends AppCompatActivity {
    private ImageView imgCapture;
    private static final int Image_Capture_Code = 1;
    ...
    @Override
    protected void onCreate(Bundle savedInstanceState) {
        super.onCreate(savedInstanceState);
        initClassifier(getAssets());
        setContentView(R.layout.activity_main);
        imgCapture = findViewById(R.id.capturedImage);
        Button btnCapture = findViewById(R.id.btnTakePicture);
        btnCapture.setOnClickListener(new View.OnClickListener() {
            @Override
            public void onClick(View v) {
                Intent cInt = new Intent(MediaStore.ACTION_IMAGE_CAPTURE);
                startActivityForResult(cInt, Image_Capture_Code);
            }
        });
    }
    ...
}
```

Here, we added a reference to the `ImageView` element and the `imgCapture` member value to the `MainActivity` class. We also defined the `Image_Capture_Code` value in order to identify the activity event that corresponds to the user's request for image classification.

We made connections between the UI elements and their event handlers in the `onCreate()` method of the `MainActivity` class. In this method, we defined the UI element's layout by calling the `setContentView()` method and passing the identifier of our `Main Activity` XML definition to it. Then, we saved the reference to the `ImageView` element and the `imgCapture` variable. The `findViewById()` method was used to get the UI element's object reference from the Activity layout. In the same way, we took the reference to the button element. With the `setOnClickListener()` method of the button element, we defined the event handler for the button click event. This event handler is the `OnClickListener` class instance where we overrode the `onClick()` method. We asked the Android system to capture a photo with the default camera application by instantiating the `Intent` class object with the `MediaStore.ACTION_IMAGE_CAPTURE` parameter in the `onClick()` method.

We identified the image that was captured with our previously defined
`Image_Capture_Code` code and passed it into the `startActivityForResult()` method
with the intent class object, `cInt`. The `startActivityForResult()` method launches the
image capturing software and then passes the result to the `onActivityResult` event
handler of our Activity object. The following code shows its implementation:

```
@Override
protected void onActivityResult(int requestCode, int resultCode,
    Intent data) {
    if (requestCode == Image_Capture_Code) {
        if (resultCode == RESULT_OK) {
            Bitmap bp = (Bitmap) Objects.requireNonNull(
                            data.getExtras()).get("data");
            if (bp != null) {
                Bitmap argb_bp = bp.copy(Bitmap.Config.ARGB_8888,
                                    true);
                if (argb_bp != null) {
                    float ratio_w = (float) bp.getWidth() / (float)
                                    bp.getHeight();
                    float ratio_h = (float) bp.getHeight() / (float)
                                    bp.getWidth();
                    int width = 224;
                    int height = 224;
                    int new_width = Math.max((int) (height * ratio_w),
                                            width);
                    int new_height = Math.max(height, (int) (width *
                                            ratio_h));
                    Bitmap resized_bitmap =
                            Bitmap.createScaledBitmap(argb_bp,
                            new_width, new_height, false);
                    Bitmap cropped_bitmap =
                            Bitmap.createBitmap(resized_bitmap, 0, 0,
                            width, height);
                    int[] pixels = new int[width * height];
                    cropped_bitmap.getPixels(pixels, 0, width, 0, 0,
                                            width, height);
                    String class_name = classifyBitmap(pixels, width,
                                            height);
                    imgCapture.setImageBitmap(cropped_bitmap);
                    TextView class_view =
                                findViewById(R.id.textViewClass);
                    class_view.setText(class_name);
                }
            }
        } else if (resultCode == RESULT_CANCELED) {
            Toast.makeText(this, "Cancelled",
                        Toast.LENGTH_LONG).show();
```

```
                    }
                }
            }
```

The `onActivityResult()` method processes the application's results. `Activity` called this method when the user created a photo after they pressed the button on the main application view. In the first lines of this method, we checked that we had the `Image_Capture_Code` code, which identifies that `Intent` contains a bitmap. We also checked whether there were any errors by comparing `resultCode` with the predefined `RESULT_OK` value. Then, we got a `Bitmap` object from the `Intent` data object by accessing the `data` field of the `Bundle` object that was returned by the `getExtras` method. If the `Bitmap` object isn't null, we convert it into ARGB format with the `copy()` method of the `Bitmap` object; the `Bitmap.Config.ARGB_8888` parameter specifies the desired format. The acquired `Bitmap` object was scaled and cropped to `224x224`, as required by the ResNet architecture. The `Bitmap` class from the Android framework already has a method named `createScaledBitmap` for bitmap scaling. We also used the `createBitmap()` method to crop the original image because the `createScaledBitmap()` method created a new bitmap from the captured image but with new dimensions passed as parameters. We performed image resizing, which preserves the original width to height ratio because one of the dimensions can be larger than `224`; that is why we used cropping to make the final image.

The `Bitmap getPixels()` method was used to get raw color values from the `Bitmap` object. This method filled the array with the color values of the `Int` type. Each of the 4 bytes in this array represents one color component, the highest byte is the `Alpha` value, while the lowest one represents the `Blue` value. The method filled the color values in the row-major format. Then, the pixels values were passed to the native library for classification; see the `classifyBitmap()` method call for more details. When the native library finished performing classification, we displayed the cropped image that was used for classification by passing it into the `ImageView` object with the `setImageBitmap()` method call. We also displayed the classification text in the `TextField` object by calling the `setText` method.

There are two methods, `classifyBitmap` and `initClassifier`, which are JNI calls to the native library functions that are implemented with C++. To connect the native library with the Java code, we use the **Java Native Interface** (**JNI**). This is a standard mechanism that's used for calling C/C++ functions from Java. First, we have to load the native library with the `system.LoadLibrary` call. Then, we have to define the methods that are implemented in the native library by declaring them as `public native`. The following snippet shows how to define these methods in Java:

```
public class MainActivity extends AppCompatActivity {
```

```
...
static {
    System.loadLibrary("native-lib");
}
public native String classifyBitmap(int[] pixels, int width, int height);
public native void initClassifier(AssetManager assetManager);
...
}
```

Notice that we called the `initClassifier()` method in the `onCreate()` method and passed it into the `AssetManager` object, which was returned by the `getAssets Activity()` method. The `AssetManager` manager object allows us to read assets, such as data files that were packaged into the Android APK application bundle. To add assets to the Android application, you have to create the `assets` folder in the `main` folder of the project and place the required file there. For this example, we used the `model.pt` and `synset.txt` files as application assets. The `model.pt` file is the TorchScript model snapshot, which we use for classification. The `synset.txt` file, on the other hand, contains the ordered list of classification descriptions; their order is the same as the order that was used for the class indices for model training. You can download the file from `https://github.com/onnx/models/blob/master/vision/classification/synset.txt`.

In the next section, we will discuss the C++ part of the project.

The C++ native part of the project

We perform the main classification task in the native C++ library. The Android Studio IDE has already created the `native-lib.cpp` file for us, so we just have to modify it. The following code snippet shows what header files we should include in order to work with the JNI, PyTorch, and Android asset libraries:

```
#include <jni.h>
#include <string>
#include <iostream>

#include <torch/script.h>
#include <caffe2/serialize/read_adapter_interface.h>

#include <android/asset_manager_jni.h>
#include <android/asset_manager.h>
```

If you want to use the Android logging system to output some messages to the IDE's `logcat`, you can define the following macro, which uses the `__android_log_print()` function:

```
#include <android/log.h>

#define  LOGD(...)  __android_log_print(ANDROID_LOG_DEBUG, "CAMERA_TAG",
__VA_ARGS__)
```

The first native function we used in the Java code was the `initClassifier()` function. To implement it in the C++ code and make it visible in the Java code, we have to follow JNI rules to make the function declaration correct. The name of the function should include the full Java package name, including namespaces, and our first two required parameters should be of the `JNIEnv*` and `jobject` types. The following code shows how to define this function:

```
extern "C" JNIEXPORT void JNICALL
Java_com_example_camera2_MainActivity_initClassifier(
                  JNIEnv *env, jobject /*self*/, jobject j_asset_manager)
{
    AAssetManager *asset_manager = AAssetManager_fromJava(env,
j_asset_manager);
    if (asset_manager != nullptr) {
        LOGD("initClassifier start OK");
        auto model = ReadAsset(asset_manager, "model.pt");
        if (!model.empty()) {
            g_image_classifier.InitModel(model);
        }
        auto synset = ReadAsset(asset_manager, "synset.txt");
        if (!synset.empty()) {
            VectorStreamBuf<char> stream_buf(synset);
            std::istream is(&stream_buf);
            g_image_classifier.InitSynset(is);
        }
        LOGD("initClassifier finish OK");
    }
}
```

The `initClassifier()` function initializes the `g_image_classifier` global object, which is of the `ImageClassifier` type. We use this object to perform image classification in our application. There are two main entities that we initialized to make this object work as expected. The first one was model initialization from the snapshot, while the second was class descriptions, which we loaded from the synset file. As we saw previously, the synset and model snapshot files were attached to our application as assets, so to access them, we used the reference (or the pointer) to the application's `AssetManager` object. We passed the Java reference to the `AssetManager` object as the function's parameter when we called this function from the Java code. In the C/C++ code, we used the `AAssetManager_fromJava()` function to convert the Java reference into a C++ pointer. Then, we used the `ReadAsset()` function to read assets from the application bundle as `std::vector<char>` objects. Our `ImageClassifier` class has the `InitModel()` and `InitSynset()` methods to read the corresponding entities.

The following code shows the `ReadAsset()` function's implementation:

```
std::vector<char> ReadAsset(AAssetManager *asset_manager, const std::string
&name) {
    std::vector<char> buf;
    AAsset *asset = AAssetManager_open(asset_manager, name.c_str(),
    AASSET_MODE_UNKNOWN);
    if (asset != nullptr) {
        LOGD("Open asset %s OK", name.c_str());
        off_t buf_size = AAsset_getLength(asset);
        buf.resize(buf_size + 1, 0);
        auto num_read = AAsset_read(asset, buf.data(), buf_size);
        LOGD("Read asset %s OK", name.c_str());
        if (num_read == 0)
            buf.clear();
        AAsset_close(asset);
        LOGD("Close asset %s OK", name.c_str());
    }
    return buf;
}
```

There are four Android framework functions that we used to read an asset from the application bundle. The `AAssetManager_open()` function opened the asset and returned the not null pointer to the `AAsset` object. This function assumes that the path to the asset is in the file path format and that the root of this path is the `assets` folder. After we opened the asset, we used the `AAsset_getLength()` function to get the file size and allocated the memory for `std::vector<char>` with the `std::vector::resize()` method. Then, we used the `AAsset_read()` function to read the whole file to the `buf` object.

This function does the following:

- Takes the pointer to the asset object to read from
- The `void*` pointer to the memory buffer to read in
- Measures the size of the bytes to read.

So, as you can see, the assets API is pretty much the same as the standard C library API for file operations. When we'd finished working with the asset object, we used `AAsset_close()` to notify the system that we don't need access to this asset anymore. If your assets are in `.zip` archive format, you should check the number of bytes returned by the `AAsset_read()` function because the Android framework reads archives chunk by chunk.

You may have noticed that we used the `VectorStreamBuf` adapter to pass data to the `ImageClassifier::InitSynset()` method. This method takes an object of the `std::istream` type. To convert `std::vector<char>` into the `std::istream` type object, we developed the following adapter class:

```
template<typename CharT, typename TraitsT = std::char_traits<CharT> >
struct VectorStreamBuf : public std::basic_streambuf<CharT, TraitsT> {
    explicit VectorStreamBuf(std::vector<CharT> &vec) {
        this->setg(vec.data(), vec.data(), vec.data() + vec.size());
    }
};
```

The following code shows the `ImageClassifier` class' declaration:

```
class ImageClassifier {
  public:
    using Classes = std::map<size_t, std::string>;
    ImageClassifier() = default;
    void InitSynset(std::istream &stream);
    void InitModel(const std::vector<char> &buf);
    std::string Classify(const at::Tensor &image);
  private:
    Classes classes_;
    torch::jit::script::Module model_;
};
```

We declared the global object of this class in the following way at the beginning of the `native-lib.cpp` file:

```
ImageClassifier g_image_classifier;
```

The following code shows the `InitSynset()` method's implementation:

```
void ImageClassifier::InitSynset(std::istream &stream) {
    LOGD("Init synset start OK");
    classes_.clear();
    if (stream) {
        std::string line;
        std::string id;
        std::string label;
        std::string token;
        size_t idx = 1;
        while (std::getline(stream, line)) {
            auto pos = line.find_first_of(" ");
            id = line.substr(0, pos);
            label = line.substr(pos + 1);
            classes_.insert({idx, label});
            ++idx;
        }
    }
    LOGD("Init synset finish OK");
}
```

The lines in the synset file are in the following format:

```
[ID] space character [Description text]
```

So, we read this file line by line and split each line at the position of the first space character. The first part of each line is the class identifier, while the second one is the class description. All the classes in this file are ordered, so the line number is the class number that's used for training the model. Therefore, to match the model's evaluation result with the correct class description, we created the dictionary (map) object, where `key` is the line number and `value` is the class description. The `InitSynset()` function takes `std::istream` as a parameter because we're going to be using the same code for other samples, where we read the synset file with the standard C++ Streams API.

The following code shows the `ImageClassifier::InitModel()` method's implementation:

```
void ImageClassifier::InitModel(const std::vector<char> &buf) {
    model_ = torch::jit::load(std::make_unique<ModelReader>(buf),
    at::kCPU);
}
```

Here, we simply used a single function call to load the TorchScript model snapshot. The `torch::jit::load()` function did all the hard work for us; it loaded the model and initialized it with weights, which were also saved in the snapshot file. The main difficulty with this function is reading the model snapshot from the memory buffer, as in our case. The `torch::jit::load()` function doesn't work with standard C++ streams and types; instead, it accepts a pointer to an object of the `caffe2::serialize::ReadAdapterInterface` class. The following code shows how to make the concrete implementation of the `caffe2::serialize::ReadAdapterInterface` class, which wraps the `std::vector<char>` object:

```
class ModelReader : public caffe2::serialize::ReadAdapterInterface {
    public:
    explicit ModelReader(const std::vector<char> &buf) : buf_(&buf) {}
    ~ModelReader() override {};
    virtual size_t size() const override {
        return buf_->size();
    }
    virtual size_t read(uint64_t pos, void *buf, size_t n,
                        const char *what)
    const override {
        std::copy_n(buf_->begin() + pos, n, reinterpret_cast<char *>(buf));
        return n;
    }
    private:
    const std::vector<char> *buf_;
};
```

The `ModelReader` class overrides two methods, `size()` and `read()`, from the `caffe2::serialize::ReadAdapterInterface` base class. Their implementations are pretty obvious: the `size()` method returns the size of the underlying vector object, while the `read()` method copies the *n* bytes (chars) from the vector to the destination buffer with the standard algorithm function, that is, `std::copy_n`.

The primary purpose of the `ImageClassifier` class is to perform image classification. The following code shows the implementation of the target method of this class, that is, `Classify()`:

```
std::string ImageClassifier::Classify(const at::Tensor &image) {
    std::vector<torch::jit::IValue> inputs;
    inputs.emplace_back(image);
    at::Tensor output = model_.forward(inputs).toTensor();
    LOGD("Output size %d %d %d", static_cast<int>(output.ndimension()),
        static_cast<int>(output.size(0)),
        static_cast<int>(output.size(1)));
    auto max_result = output.squeeze().max(0);
```

```
        auto max_index = std::get<1>(max_result).item<int64_t>();
        auto max_value = std::get<0>(max_result).item<float>();
        max_index += 1;
        return std::to_string(max_index) + " - " + std::to_string(max_value) +
            " - " + classes_[static_cast<size_t>(max_index)];
    }
```

This function takes the `at::Tensor` object, which contains the image data, as an input parameter. We used the `forward()` method of the `torch::jit::script::Module` class to evaluate the model on the input image. Notice that the `forward()` method takes a vector of `torch::jit::IValue` objects. There is an implicit cast from the `at::Tensor` type to the `torch::jit::IValue` type, which means we can use the ATen library's tensor objects transparently. The output of the model is a `1x1000` dimensional tensor, where each value is the class score. To determine the most probable class for the given image, we looked for the column with the maximum value with the `at::Tensor::max()` method. The preceding `squeeze()` method removed the first dimension and made the tensor one-dimensional. The `at::Tensor::max()` method returns a pair of values; the first is the actual maximum value, while the second is its index. We incremented the index of the class we got because we have the same increment in the `InitSynset()` function. Then, we used this index to find the class description in the `classes_` map, which we found in the `InitSynset()` method and called from the `initClassifier()` function.

The last JNI function we need to implement is `classifyBitmap()`. The following code shows how we declare it:

```
    extern "C" JNIEXPORT jstring JNICALL
    Java_com_example_camera2_MainActivity_classifyBitmap(
    JNIEnv *env, jobject /*self*/, jintArray pixels, jint width, jint height) {
    ...
    }
```

This function takes three parameters: the `pixels` object and its width and height dimensions. The `pixels` object is a reference to the Java `int[]` array type, so we have to convert it into a C/C++ array to be able to process it. The following code shows how we can extract separate colors and put them into distinct buffers:

```
    jboolean is_copy = 0;
    jint *pixels_buf = env->GetIntArrayElements(pixels, &is_copy);

    auto channel_size = static_cast<size_t>(width * height);
    using ChannelData = std::vector<float>;
    size_t channels_num = 3; // RGB image
    std::vector<ChannelData> image_data(channels_num);
    for (size_t i = 0; i < channels_num; ++i) {
        image_data[i].resize(channel_size);
```

```
    }

    // split original image
    for (int y = 0; y < height; ++y) {
        for (int x = 0; x < width; ++x) {
            auto pos = x + y * width;
            auto pixel_color = static_cast<uint32_t>(pixels_buf[pos]);
                            // ARGB format
            uint32_t mask{0x000000FF};
            for (size_t i = 0; i < channels_num; ++i) {
                uint32_t shift = i * 8;
                uint32_t channel_value = (pixel_color >> shift) & mask;
                image_data[channels_num - (i + 1)][pos] =
                                    static_cast<float>(channel_value);
            }
        }
    }

    env->ReleaseIntArrayElements(pixels, pixels_buf, 0);
```

JNIEnv's `GetIntArrayElements()` method returned the pointer to the `jint` array's elements, where the `jint` type is actually the regular C/C++ `int` type. With the pointer to the image's pixels data at hand, we processed it. We separated each color value into components because we needed to normalize each color channel separately.

We defined the `image_data` object of the `std::vector<ChannelData>` type to hold the color channel's data. Each channel object is of the `ChannelData` type, which is `std::vector<float>` underneath. The channel data was filled in by iterating over the image pixels row by row and splitting each pixel color into components. We got each color component by shifting the color value, which is of the `int` type, to the right by 8 bits three times. We didn't need the alpha color component; that is why we only performed the shift three times. After shifting, we extracted the exact component value by applying the AND operator with the `0x000000FF` mask value. We also cast the color values to the floating-point type because we need values in the `[0,1]` range for later and we need to normalize them. After we'd finished working with the pixel values, we released the data pointer with the `ReleaseIntArrayElements()` method of the `JNIEnv` object.

Now that we've extracted the color channels from the pixel data, we have to create tensor objects from them. Using tensor objects allows us to perform vectorized calculations that are more computationally effective. The following code snippet shows how to create `at::Tensor` objects from floating-point vectors:

```
std::vector<int64_t> channel_dims = {height, width};

std::vector<at::Tensor> channel_tensor;
at::TensorOptions options(at::kFloat);
options = options.device(at::kCPU).requires_grad(false);

for (size_t i = 0; i < channels_num; ++i) {
    channel_tensor.emplace_back(
        torch::from_blob(image_data[i].data(),
                         at::IntArrayRef(channel_dims),
                         options).clone());
}
```

Notice that we specified the `at::kFloat` type in `at::TensorOptions` to make it compatible with our floating-point channel's vectors. We also used the `torch::from_blob()` function to make a tensor object from the raw array data; we used this function in previous chapters. Simply put, we initialized the `channel_tensor` vector, which contains three tensors with values for each color channel.

The ResNet model we're using requires that we normalize the input image; that is, we should subtract a distinct predefined mean value from each channel and divide it with a distinct predefined standard deviation value. The following code shows how we can normalize the color channels in the `channel_tensor` container:

```
std::vector<float> mean{0.485f, 0.456f, 0.406f};
std::vector<float> stddev{0.229f, 0.224f, 0.225f};

for (size_t i = 0; i < channels_num; ++i) {
    channel_tensor[i] = ((channel_tensor[i] / 255.0f) - mean[i]) /
stddev[i];
}
```

After we've normalized each channel, we have to make a tensor from them to satisfy the ResNet model's requirements. The following code shows how to use the `stack()` function to combine channels:

```
auto image_tensor = at::stack(channel_tensor);
image_tensor = image_tensor.unsqueeze(0);
```

The `stack()` function also adds a new dimension to the new tensor. This new tensor's dimensions become `3 x height x width`.

Another of the model's requirements is that it needs a batch size dimension for the input image tensor. We used the tensor's `unsqueeze()` method to add a new dimension to the tensor so that its dimensions became `1 x 3 x height x width`.

The following code shows the final part of the `classifyBitmap()` function:

```
std::string result = g_image_classifier.Classify(image_tensor);

return env->NewStringUTF(result.c_str());
```

Here, we called the `Classify()` method of the global `g_image_classifier` object to evaluate the loaded model on the prepared tensor, which contains the captured image. Then, we converted the obtained classification string into a Java `String` object by calling the `NewStringUTF()` method of the `JNIEnv` type object. As we mentioned previously, the Java part of the application will show this string to the user in the `onActivityResult()` method.

In this section, we looked at the implementation of image classification applications for the Android system. We learned how to export a pre-trained model from a Python program as a PyTorch script file. Then, we delved into developing a mobile application with Android Studio IDE and the mobile version of the PyTorch C++ library.

In the next section, we will discuss and deploy an application for image classification to the Google Compute Engine platform.

Machine learning in the cloud – using Google Compute Engine

Usually, after implementing an application in a development environment, we need to deploy it to a production environment on the customer's side or to a could service platform. Services have become very popular because you can configure the computational environments for your customer's needs with an excellent balance ratio between cost, scalability, and performance. Also, the use of such services eliminates the need for your customers to maintain the hardware devices they're using.

So, let's learn how to deploy a simple image classification application to the Google Compute Engine platform. Initially, we need to develop and test such an application in a development environment. We are going to make an HTTP service that responds to `POST` requests with image data encoded in multipart format. Let's start by implementing the server.

The server

The core of our application is the server. Let's assume that we've already implemented image classification in the same way we did in the previous section, that is, by using a model saved as a TorchScript snapshot and loaded into the `torch::jit::script::Module` object. We encapsulated this functionality in the following class:

```
class Network {
  public:
    Network(const std::string& snapshot_path,
            const std::string& synset_path,
            torch::DeviceType device_type);
    std::string Classify(const at::Tensor& image);
  private:
    torch::DeviceType device_type_;
    Classes classes_;
    torch::jit::script::Module model_;
};
```

The following code shows an implementation of the main routine of our application:

```
#include <torch/script.h>
#include "network.h"
#include "third-party/httplib/httplib.h"
#include "utils.h"

int main(int argc, char** argv) {
    try {
        std::string snapshoot_path;
        std::string synset_path;
        std::string www_path;
        std::string host = "localhost";
        int port = 8080;
        if (argc >= 4) {
            snapshoot_path = argv[1];
            synset_path = argv[2];
            www_path = argv[3];
            if (argc >= 5)
                host = argv[4];
            if (argc >= 6)
                port = std::stoi(argv[5]);
            torch::DeviceType device_type = torch::cuda::is_available()
                                                                     ?
torch::DeviceType::CUDA
                                                                     :
torch::DeviceType::CPU;
```

```
                Network network(snapshoot_path, synset_path, device_type);
                ...
                // HTTP service implementation
                ...
        } else {
            std::cout << "usage: " << argv[0]
            << " <model snapshoot path> <synset file path>
                <www dir=../../client> "
            "[host=localhost] [port=8080]\n";
        }
    } catch (const std::exception& err) {
        std::cerr << err.what();
    } catch (...) {
        std::cerr << "Unhandled exception";
    }
    return 1;
}
```

Here, we read the parameters required by our application upon startup. There are three required parameters: the path to the model snapshot file, the path to the synset file, and the path to the directory where we place our HTML client application files. There are also two optional parameters: the server host IP address and the server network port.

After we've read the program parameters, we can initialize the `Network` type object with a specified model snapshot and synset files. We also dynamically determined whether there is a CUDA device available on the machine where we start the server. We did this with the `torch::cuda::is_available()` function.

If a CUDA device is available, we can move our model to this device to increase computational performance. The following code shows how we can load a model into the specified device:

```
model_ = torch::jit::load(snapshot_path, device_type);
```

The `torch::jit::load()` function accepts the device type as its second parameter and automatically moves the model to the specified device.

There is a lightweight C++ single-file header-only cross-platform HTTP/HTTPS library available named `cpp-httplib`. We can use it to implement our server. The following code shows how we used the `httplib::Server` type to instantiate the `server` object so that it can handle HTTP requests:

```
httplib::Server server;
```

The `httplib::Server` class also implements a simple static file server. The following code snippet shows how to set up the directory for loading static pages:

```
server.set_base_dir(www_path.c_str());
```

The path that's passed into the `set_base_dir()` method should point to the directory we use to store the HTML pages for our service. To be able to see what's going on in the server when it's launched, we can configure the logging function. The following code shows how to print minimal request information when the server accepts the incoming message:

```
server.set_logger([](const auto& req, const auto& /*res*/) {
    std::cout << req.method << "\n" << req.path << std::endl;
});
```

It is also able to handle HTTP errors when our server works. The following snippet shows how to fill the response object with error status information:

```
server.set_error_handler([](const auto& /*req*/, auto& res) {
    std::stringstream buf;
    buf << "<p>Error Status: <span style='color:red;'>";
    buf << res.status;
    buf << "</span></p>";
    res.set_content(buf.str(), "text/html");
});
```

The server sends this response object to the client in the case of an error.

Now, we have to configure the handler for our server object so that it can handle POST requests. There is a POST method in the `httplib::Server` class that we can use for this purpose. This method takes the name of the request's pattern and the handler object.

The special URL pattern should be used by the client application to perform a request; for example, the address can look like `http://localhost:8080/imgclassify`, where `imgclassify` is the pattern. We can have different handlers for different requests. The handler can be any callable object that accepts two arguments: the first should be of the `const Request` type, while the second should be of the `Response&` type. The following code shows our implementation of the image classification request:

```
server.Post("/imgclassify", [&](const auto& req, auto& res) {
    std::string response_string;
    for (auto& file : req.files) {
        auto body = req.body.substr(file.second.offset,
                                    file.second.length);
        try {
            auto img = ReadMemoryImageTensor(body, 224, 224);
            response_string += "; " + network.Classify(img);
```

```
        } catch (...) {
            response_string += "; Classification failed";
        }
    }
    res.set_content(response_string.c_str(), "text/html");
});
```

In this handler, we iterated over all the files in the input request. For each file, we performed the following steps:

1. Extracted the bytes representing the image
2. Decoded the bytes into the image object
3. Converted the image object into a tensor
4. Classified the image

The `Request` type object has a `files` member, which can be used to iterate the information chunks about files that are sent with a given request. Each chunk is of the `MultipartFile` type and contains information about the filename, the type, the starting position in the whole message body, and the length. The body of the `Request` object is a `std::string` object, so we used the `substr()` method to extract the particular file data by specifying the start position and the length of the file. We used the `ReadMemoryImageTensor()` function to decode the file data into an image. This function also scaled and normalized the image to satisfy the ResNet model's requirements. The result of calling this function was a PyTorch tensor object. Then, we used the `Network` object to classify the image tensor with the ResNet model that was loaded from the snapshot. Moreover, the `Classify()` method returned a string containing the classification information we got from our classifier. This string was used to fill the response object.

We can use the `listen()` method of the `httplib::Server` type object to enable it to accept incoming connections and processing messages. The following code shows how to do this:

```
if(!server.listen(host.c_str(), port)) {
    std::cerr << "Failed to start server\n";
}
```

The `listen()` method automatically binds the server socket to the given IP address and the port number.

In this section, we looked at the main implementation stages for the server part of our service. In the next section, we'll look at the implementation of the client.

The client

The client part of our server can be implemented in different languages and with different technologies that support the HTTP protocol. The most straightforward implementation of the client application can be written with HTML and Javascript. We can use such a client with any modern browser.

There will be two files in our client application. The first one will be the index.html file, which should contain the definition of a simple web page with a form for uploading files. The following code shows how we can write this file:

```html
<html lang="en">
    <head>
        <title>Upload Files</title>
    </head>
    <body>
        <form method="post" enctype="multipart/form-data">
            <input type="file" name="files[]" multiple>
            <input type="submit" value="Upload File" name="submit">
        </form>
        <script src="upload.js"></script>
    </body>
</html>
```

The form is a standard HTML element with two fields inside it. The first field is a standard input element for file selection, while the second is a standard input element for form data submission.

The second file is a JavaScript implementation of the HTML form event handler. The following snippet represents the upload.js file's implementation:

```javascript
const url = 'http://localhost:8080/imgclassify';
const form = document.querySelector('form');

form.addEventListener('submit', e => {
    e.preventDefault();
    const files = document.querySelector('[type=file]').files;
    const formData = new FormData();
    for (let i = 0; i < files.length; i++) {
        let file = files[i];
        formData.append('files[]', file);
    }
    fetch(url, {
        method: 'POST',
        body: formData
    }).then(response => {
```

```
        console.log(response);
        if (response.ok) {
            let text = response.text();
            text.then(data=>{
                alert(data)});
        } else {
            alert("Error :" + response.status);
        }
    });
});
```

In this implementation, we got the form element object from the HTML document with the `document.querySelector('form').files` call. Then, we added an event listener for the `submit` event using the `addEventListener()` method. The `submit` event occurs when a user presses the submit button. Regarding the event listener's implementation, we did the following:

1. First, we got the list of files our user selected for submission with the following code:

   ```
   document.querySelector('[type=file]').files
   ```

2. Then, we created the `FormData` object.
3. Next, we populated the form data object with `files` data by sequentially calling the `append()` method by passing the `file` object to it.
4. Finally, we used the `formData` object to send a request to the server using the `fetch()` method.

We defined the target server request URL in the `url` string object at the beginning of the file. You should change the IP address in this URL to the external address of your server.

The `fetch()` method returned the `promise` object, which belongs to the asynchronous API, so we used the `then()` method to define the code that will run after the client receives a response. In the response handler, we checked the error status with the `ok` field of the response object. In the case of an error, we show the alert message with an error status code. In the case of a successful response, we gather the text data from the response object. Note that this operation is performed asynchronously. When the text data is ready, our handler will show it in the alert window.

Now that we have the server and client parts of our service, we recommend that you test them in your local development environment. After doing this, we can compile the server part and start it locally. Here, the path to the folder that contains the client source code should be passed as a command-line parameter. Then, we can test our service by opening the `http://localhost:8080` URL in a browser.

Now, we'll learn how to deploy this service to the server.

Service deployment

Now that we've implemented and tested our server application in our local development environment, we are ready to deploy it to the cloud. We need to have a Google account and be registered in the GCP to be able to continue. It is enough to have a free subscription to GCP to perform the following steps and try our server application in the Google Compute Engine:

1. Log into your Google account and go to GCP: `https://console.cloud.google.com`.
2. On the main page, open the **Go to Compute Engine** link or use the **Navigation Menu** and select the **Compute Engine** link.
3. On the **Compute Engine** page, select the **VM Instances** option.
4. Click the **Create instance** link at the top of the page and create a VM instance with the following characteristics:

   ```
   Name: classify-server
   Zone: choose appropriate to you, us-central1-a
   Generation: first
   Machine-type: n1-standard-1
   CPU platform: automatic
   Boot disk: New 10 GB standard persistent disk
   Image: Debian GNU/Linux 9 (stretch)
   Identity and API access: Compute Engine default service account
   Access scopes: Allow default access
   Firewall: Allow HTTP traffic
   ```

   We can also add a GPU to our VM instance configuration. Be aware that a GPU can significantly raise the cost of the service, so think carefully about whether using a GPU is right for you. Usually, for machine learning inference tasks, having multi-core CPUs is more than enough. In other cases, if we plan to use GCP to train machine learning algorithms, its powerful GPUs can significantly reduce training time.

5. On the **VM instances** page, select the VM instance that we created. Start it by clicking the **Start** button at the top of the page.

6. To be able to work with GCP effectively, we need to install the GCP SDK. The SDK can help us share files from our local system to the remote VM instance machine without a browser. Before installing the GCP SDK, please make sure that your system has Python 2 installed with a release number of Python 2.7.9 or higher. The GCP SDK can be downloaded from `https://cloud.google.com/sdk/docs/`. The SDK is an archive file. We can extract the contents of the file into any location on our filesystem. Then, we can run the **gcloud** application from the `[bin]` folder with the `init` parameter to initialize the SDK. This should look similar to `./google-cloud-sdk/bin/gcloud init`. This utility should ask us to log into our Google account to continue. The following snippet shows the possible command-line session:

```
Would you like to log in (Y/n)?  y
Your browser has been opened to visit:
https://accounts.google.com/o/oauth2/auth?...
```

After authorization, we can select the project for the current work session. The GCP initialized the project when we initially created the VM instance, so if we take a look at the top of the **Compute Engine** page, we should see a tab called `My First Project`. The following snippet shows the possible command-line session:

```
Pick cloud project to use:
[1] hardy-aleph-253219
[2] Create a new project
Please enter numeric choice or text value (must exactly match list
item):  1
```

Now, we can select default choices for the other questions to finish the GCP SDK's initialization.

7. We can use the GCP SDK to copy the server application's source code to the running instance. To copy a folder from our local machine to the remote one, we can use the following command:

```
gcloud compute scp --recurse [LOCAL_PATH]
[INSTANCE_NAME]:~/[DEST_PATH]
```

Here, `LOCAL_PATH` is the path to some folder on our local machine, `INSTANCE_NAME` is the name of the target VM instance, and `DEST_PATH` is the name of the folder in the home directory of our user on the remote machine. We should verify that we're using the same username on the local machine and the remote machine because the gcloud utility always places files in the home directory with the username that's being used on the local machine.

8. On the **VM instances** page, we have to identify the VM instance that we started previously and where we copied the source files. Then, we should find the column named `Connect`, select **SSH**, and choose the **Open in browser window** option. This action opens a new browser window with an interactive command-line session connected to your remote machine. We can also use the GCP SDK to configure the SSH session with standard utilities.

9. In the command-line window, we can use the following commands to configure the development environment that's required for us to build our server application on the remote machine:

```
sudo apt-get install git
sudo apt-get install cmake
sudo apt-get install g++
sudo apt-get install libopencv-dev
sudo apt-get install libprotobuf-dev
sudo apt-get install unzip
sudo apt-get install python-pip
sudo apt-get install libopenblas-dev
sudo apt-get install pybind11-dev
pip install pyyaml
pip install typing
```

10. Now that we've configured the development environment, we can continue working with the source code and build the required third-party libraries. We have two such dependencies: the `cpp-httplib` library and the PyTorch framework. The `cpp-httplib` library is a single-file header-only library, so it is enough to clone it to our source code tree. The following snippet shows the commands you'll need to use to do this:

```
cd ~/[DEST_PATH]/server
git clone https://github.com/yhirose/cpp-httplib third-
party/httplib
```

11. There are two ways to get the PyTorch framework's dependency. If your environment has a GPU with CUDA support, you can download the pre-compiled binaries from the official site. The following snippet shows how to do this:

```
cd third-party
wget --no-check-certificate
https://download.pytorch.org/libtorch/cu100/libtorch-shared-with-de
ps-1.2.0.zip
unzip libtorch-shared-with-deps-1.2.0.zip
cd ..
```

12. The second way is to build PyTorch from certain sources. This is the only option you have if your environment doesn't have a GPU because the official binaries require working CUDA support. However, if your goal is to perform inference only, you won't need this because, in many cases, a modern CPU can fully satisfy your needs. Also, when you build PyTorch from sources, you can include the FBGEMM library in your build. It is a low-precision, high-performance matrix-matrix multiplication and convolution library for server-side inference that was developed by Facebook engineers. Now, you can use FBGEMM as a backend of the Caffe2 and PyTorch quantized operators for *x86* machines by using the USE_FBGEMM CMake option during a build. The following snippet shows how to clone, build, and install the PyTorch C++ library from sources:

```
cd third-party
git clone https://github.com/pytorch/pytorch.git
cd pytorch/
git checkout v1.2.0
git submodule update --init --recursive
mkdir build
cd build
cmake .. -DCMAKE_INSTALL_PREFIX=~/dev/server/third-party/libtorch -
DUSE_CUDA=OFF -DUSE_CUDNN=OFF -DUSE_OPENMP=ON -DBUILD_TORCH=ON -
DUSE_FBGEMM=ON -DBUILD_PYTHON=OFF
cmake --build . --target install -- -j8
```

Notice that we have to recursively initialize the PyTorch git submodules because many of them also contain many dependencies as submodules.

13. Now that we've configured the development environment and gathered all the dependencies, we can build our server application on the removed VM. To do this, use the following commands:

```
cd ~/[DEST_PATH]/server
mkdir build
cd build
cmake .. -DCMAKE_PREFIX_PATH=~/dev/server/third-party/libtorch
cmake --build . --target all
```

14. To run the server application, we need two more files: the model snapshot file and the synset file, which contains class descriptions. We can copy them from the local development environment to the remote machine with the following commands while using the GCP SDK:

```
gcloud compute scp [LOCAL_PATH]/model.pt
[INSTANCE_NAME]:~/[DEST_PATH]/model
gcloud compute scp [LOCAL_PATH]/synset.txt
[INSTANCE_NAME]:~/[DEST_PATH]/model
```

If you only need to copy a couple of files, you can use a web-based SSH connection window. There is a menu for copying files from the local machine.

15. Before we can start our application, we need to configure the GCP Firewall to allow incoming connections to the server program we want to launch. On the **GCP Console** page, go to the **Navigation Menu** and open the **VPC network** link. On the **VPC network** page, open the **Firewall rules** link. Then, on the **Firewall rules** page, click the **Create a firewall rule** button to create a new firewall rule. We can find this button at the top of the page. For a new firewall rule, we have to enter the following information:

```
Name: classify-server
Target tags: http-server
Actions on match: allow
Source IP ranges: 0.0.0.0/0
Protocol and ports: tcp:8080
```

Then, we need to click on the **Create** button to finish the rule creation process.

16. We also need to remember the IP addresses that have been assigned to the VM instance we are using. There are two IP addresses: one that's internal and one that's external. We can find them on the **VM Instance** page when we're looking at a particular VM instance record. The internal IP address is statically assigned, and we can even see it for stopped instances. The external IP address is dynamically assigned when you start the instance.

17. To start our server application, we can use the following command:

```
cd ~/[DEST_PATH]/server/build
./classify-server ~/[DEST_PATH]/model/model.pt
~/[DEST_PATH]/model/synset.txt ~/[DEST_PATH]/client/ [internal ip]
8080
```

[internal ip] is the IP address we examined in *step 16*. The number 8080 means that the application has been configured to listen for incoming messages on port 8080. We also have to carefully check the paths to the model snapshot file, the synset file, and the path to the directory where we placed our static client files.

18. To make our HTML client work, we have to update the upload.js file. At the beginning of the file, there's a definition for the url string. It will be in the following form:

```
const url = 'http://localhost:8080/imgclassify';
```

Change the localhost address to the external IP address that we examined in *step 16*. By doing this, we can access our service by using the following URL in any browser:

```
http://[external ip]:8080
```

The client's page should look as follows:

You would see the following response message if you submit the Newfoundland dog image:

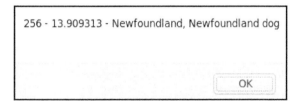

This page shows that our model assigned a value of **13.909313** to the **256** class, which is **Newfoundland dog**. This score was the highest among our classes.

Summary

In this chapter, we discussed how to deploy machine learning models, especially neural networks, to mobile and cloud platforms. We examined that, on these platforms, we usually need a customized build of the machine learning framework that we used in our project. Mobile platforms use different CPUs, and sometimes, they have specialized neural network accelerator devices, so you need to compile your application and machine learning framework in regards to these architectures. The architectures that are used for cloud machines differ from development environments, and you often use them for two different purposes. The first case is to use powerful machine configuration with GPUs to accelerate the machine learning training process, so you need to build your application while taking the use of one or multiple GPUs into account. The other case is using a cloud machine for inference only. In this case, you typically don't need a GPU at all because a modern CPU can satisfy your performance requirements.

In this chapter, we developed an image classification application for the Android platform. We learned how to connect the Java module with the native C++ library through JNI. Then, we examined how to build the PyTorch C++ library for Android using the NDK and saw what limitations there are to using the mobile version.

Finally, we implemented and deployed the HTTP image classification service for the Google Compute Engine platform. We learned how to create and configure VM instances, as well as how to configure the environment on a particular VM instance machine so that we could build our application and its third-party dependencies. We saw that different configurations for VM instances might require different runtime binaries for machine learning frameworks, so we built the PyTorch C++ library for the selected configuration. This custom build allowed us to utilize the maximum performance of the CPU-only machine. We also implemented a simple HTML client for our service for testing purposes.

Further reading

- PyTorch C++ API: `https://pytorch.org/cppdocs/`
- Transferring files to instances (GCP): `https://cloud.google.com/compute/docs/instances/transfer-files`
- Google Cloud SDK documentation: `https://cloud.google.com/sdk/docs/`
- Build a Mobile App Using Compute Engine and REST: `https://cloud.google.com/solutions/mobile/mobile-compute-engine-rest`
- Documentation for app developers: `https://developer.android.com/docs`
- Android NDK: `https://developer.android.com/ndk`
- Android NDK: Using C/C++ Native Libraries to Write Android Apps: `https://expertise.jetruby.com/android-ndk-using-c-c-native-libraries-to-write-android-apps-21550cdd86a`

Other Books You May Enjoy

If you enjoyed this book, you may be interested in these other books by Packt:

The C++ Workshop
Dale Green, Kurt Guntheroth, Et al

ISBN: 978-1-83921-374-8

- Get to grips with fundamental concepts and conventions of C++ 11
- Learn about best practices for clean code and how to avoid common pitfalls
- Reuse and reduce common code using the C++ standard library
- Debug and compile logical errors and handle exceptions in your programs
- Keep your development process bug-free with C++ unit testing

Expert C++

Vardan Grigoryan, Shunguang Wu

ISBN: 978-1-83855-265-7

- Understand memory management and low-level programming in C++ to write secure and stable applications
- Discover the latest C++20 features such as modules, concepts, ranges, and coroutines
- Understand debugging and testing techniques and reduce issues in your programs
- Design and implement GUI applications using Qt5
- Use multithreading and concurrency to make your programs run faster
- Develop high-end games by using the object-oriented capabilities of C++
- Explore AI and machine learning concepts with C++

Leave a review - let other readers know what you think

Please share your thoughts on this book with others by leaving a review on the site that you bought it from. If you purchased the book from Amazon, please leave us an honest review on this book's Amazon page. This is vital so that other potential readers can see and use your unbiased opinion to make purchasing decisions, we can understand what our customers think about our products, and our authors can see your feedback on the title that they have worked with Packt to create. It will only take a few minutes of your time but is valuable to other potential customers, our authors, and Packt. Thank you!

Index

meta-attribute 290
ML model serialization APIs, with PyTorch C++
    library
  neural network initialization 448, 449, 450, 451
  PyTorch archive objects, using 452, 453, 454
  torch functions, using 451
ML model serialization APIs
  using, in C++ libraries 438
  using, with Dlib library 438, 439, 440, 441
  using, with PyTorch C++ library 448
  using, with SharkML library 446, 447
  using, with Shogun library 441, 442, 443, 444,
    445
ML models
  performance metrics 78
MLP, creating for regression task
  C++ libraries, used 360
  Dlib library, used 360, 362, 363
  SharkML library, used 366
  Shogun library, used 363, 364, 365
mlpack library
  used, for implementing collaborative filtering
    282, 284
model parameter estimation 17, 18
model selection, with grid search technique
  about 94
  cross-validation technique 95
  DLib example 100, 102
  grid search approach 96
  SharkML example 99, 100
  Shogun example 97, 98, 99
model selection
  grid search technique 94
Model Zoo
  URL 456
model-based clustering algorithms 117
Modified National Institute of Standards and
    Technology (MNIST)
  URL 369
multi-class classification 229
multidimensional scaling (MDS) 183, 184
multilayer perceptron (MLP) 325
multilayer RNN 398, 399
Multiple Additive Regression Trees (MART) 298
multiple linear regression 34

multivariable linear regression 34
Multivariate Gaussian model
  using, with Dlib library 163, 164

N

Native Development Kit (NDK) 466
natural language processing (NLP)
  with RNN 399, 400
negative log-likelihood loss function 341
neural network initialization
  about 352
  He initialization method 352, 353
  Xavier initialization method 352
neural network layers, types
  hidden 327
  input 327
  output 327
Newman modularity-based graph clustering
    algorithm
  implementing, with Dlib library 135, 137
non-linear methods, for dimension reduction
  about 184
  autoencoders 190
  distributed stochastic neighbor embedding 188,
    189, 190
  ISOMAP algorithm 186
  kernel PCA 185
  sammon mapping 187
non-negative matrix factorization (NMF) 265
non-parametric 16
non-personalized recommendations 260
normalization, type
  centering (mean-centering) 267
  double standardization 267
  standardization (z-score) 267
normalized cuts problem task 114
novelty detection 144

O

one-against-all strategy 230
One-Class SVM (OCSVM)
  about 151
  implementing, with Dlib library 161, 162
  implementing, with SharkML library 167, 168
  implementing, with Shogun library 165, 166

Printed in Great Britain
by Amazon

26175266R00295